RELIGION IN THE KITCHEN

NORTH AMERICAN RELIGIONS

Series Editors: Tracy Fessenden (Religious Studies, Arizona State University), Laura Levitt (Religious Studies, Temple University), and David Harrington Watt (History, Temple University)

In recent years a cadre of industrious, imaginative, and theoretically sophisticated scholars of religion have focused their attention on North America. As a result, the field is far more subtle, expansive, and interdisciplinary than it was just two decades ago. The North American Religions series builds on this transformative momentum. Books in the series move among the discourses of ethnography, cultural analysis, and historical study to shed new light on a wide range of religious experiences, practices, and institutions. They explore topics such as lived religion, popular religious movements, religion and social power, religion and cultural reproduction, and the relationship between secular and religious institutions and practices. The series focuses primarily, but not exclusively, on religion in the United States in the twentieth and twenty-first centuries.

BOOKS IN THE SERIES:

Ava Chamberlain, *The Notorious Elizabeth Tuttle: Marriage, Murder, and Madness in the Family of Jonathan Edwards*

Terry Rey and Alex Stepick, *Crossing the Water and Keeping the Faith: Haitian Religion in Miami*

Jodi Eichler-Levine, *Suffer the Little Children: Uses of the Past in Jewish and African American Children's Literature*

Isaac Weiner, *Religion Out Loud: Religious Sound, Public Space, and American Pluralism*

Hillary Kaell, *Walking Where Jesus Walked: American Christian Holy Land Pilgrimage*

Brett Hendrickson, *Border Medicine: A Transcultural History of Mexican American Curanderismo*

Annie Blazer, *Playing for God: Sports Ministry, Gender, and Embodied Worship in Evangelical America*

Elizabeth Pérez, *Religion in the Kitchen: Cooking, Talking, and the Making of Black Atlantic Traditions*

# Religion in the Kitchen

*Cooking, Talking, and the Making of*
*Black Atlantic Traditions*

Elizabeth Pérez

NEW YORK UNIVERSITY PRESS
*New York and London*

NEW YORK UNIVERSITY PRESS
New York and London
www.nyupress.org

© 2016 by New York University
All rights reserved

ISBN: 978-1-4798-6161-3
ISBN: 978-1-4798-3955-1

For Library of Congress Cataloging-in-Publication data, please contact the Library of Congress.

10 9 8 7 6 5 4 3 2 1

Also available as an ebook

*For my parents, Bernardo (1939–2006) and Ivonne Pérez*
*por lo mucho que siempre se dedicaron*

# CONTENTS

## ILLUSTRATIONS

The illustrations appear as a group following page 140.

## ACKNOWLEDGMENTS

None of this would have been possible without the hospitality and generous collaboration of many. Foremost among them, Ashabi Mosley deserves acknowledgment for her kindness, grace, and forbearance. I have been blessed with the assistance of Fadesiye, Mr. Mosley, Alimayu Harris, Arlene Stevens, Omisade, Miguel "Willie" Ramos, and Yomí Yomí. My love and gratitude also go out to Abirola; Damon Baggs; Mike Banish; Pedro Bonetti; Mike Cassidy; Glenda Kposivi Clark; Lucy Diaz; Kysha Egungbemi; Shukrani Gray; Mobosade and Shashu Harris; Markeya Howard; Ilé Afolabi; Kalimah Johnson; Salim Kenyatta; Chinaka Kizart; James Kubie; Gwen Luster; Marianne; Mayodumi; Alexandra Moffett-Bateau; Oba, Nosa, and Oyeyei; Okandinije; Olubi; Oshunleye, Nailah, and Jaylen; Keisha Price; Maddy Ramos; Toya, Maria, Jalyn, and Will Sevier; Jeanette and "Poppy" Shorter; Deidra Somerville and the boys; Cory Stephenson; Shanita Tyler; Kylah Williams; and Vicky Zuñiga-Winkler. María-Pimpa Junqueira and Alina Barranco, *Ibae*. Those left unnamed are not forgotten.

I am indebted to Bruce Lincoln and Stephan Palmié at the University of Chicago for their mentorship and critical insight. The late Martin Riesebrodt contributed analytical rigor and organizational acuity; I remain most appreciative for his patience. I enjoyed the administrative support of Teresa Hord Owens and Sandy Norbeck, as well as Wendy Doniger's constant encouragement. Andrew Apter, Robin Derby, and Dwight N. Hopkins inspired me to keep moving forward. Stuart Michaels, Deborah Nelson, and Gina Olson were instrumental in ensuring that my time at the Center for Gender Studies (now the Center for the Study of Gender and Sexuality) was intellectually rewarding.

I am humbled to recall the thoughtfulness of Alan Hodder at Hampshire College; Roger R. Jackson, Michael McNally, Louis Newman, Anne Patrick, Lori Pearson, Asuka Sango, and Shana Sippy at Carleton College; and Loïc Wacquant at the University of California, Berkeley. At

Dartmouth College, I have benefited from the guidance of Susan Ackerman, Ehud Benor, Rebecca Biron, Randall Balmer, Nancy Frankenberry, and Adrian Randolph, and from the collegiality of Christopher MacEvitt, Ronald Green, Susannah Heschel, Reiko Ohnuma, Catharine Randall, and A. Kevin Reinhart. I am honored to have had Stefania Capone, Yvonne Daniel, Robert M. Baum, Reena N. Goldthree, Deborah K. King, and Gil Raz read an earlier version of the manuscript in its entirety as part of a Leslie Center for the Humanities Manuscript Review. Their invaluable suggestions for revision, along with those of Colleen Glenney Boggs, transformed this book. The help of Meredyth Morley and Marcia Welsh was indispensable.

Without Jennifer Hammer's persistent herculean efforts to bring this volume to press, the manuscript would still be in search of a hope and a home. She and Janna R. White gave it much-needed direction and editorial aid. I am also grateful to Constance Grady, Dorothea S. Halliday, Rosalie Morales Kearns, and the editors of the North American Religions series, Tracy Fessenden, Laura Levitt, and David Harrington Watt. My anonymous reviewers improved the book immeasurably with their detailed reports, and the exceptional staff of New York University Press shepherded it through the publication process. Any errors are mine alone.

An extraordinary group of confidants lent me their shoulders, ears, and books: Sandra Abdelmalak, Monica Coleman, Rosana Cruz, Laura Desmond, Yasser Elhariry, Martín Espada, Holly Fogleboch, Stephanie Frank, Alysia Garrison, Rory Johnson, Marta Nelson, Bernardo Pérez, Julie Püttgen, Andy Rotman, Cristal and Eli Sabbagh, Gregory Spinner, Jon Varese, Natalie Washington-Weik, John "Thabiti" Willis, and my fellow travelers in the History of Religions.

I would like to recognize the members of institutional bodies whose faith in this project took it through data collection and write-up. Funding was provided by the University of Chicago Martin Marty Center and the Center for the Study of Race, Politics, and Culture; the Ford Foundation; the University of Chicago Office of Multicultural Student Affairs; the University of Chicago Center for the Study of Gender and Sexuality; the University of California President's Postdoctoral Fellowship Program; and Walter and Constance Burke Research Initiation Awards for Junior Faculty at Dartmouth College.

Brief portions of chapter 1 first appeared in "Working Roots and Conjuring Traditions: Relocating 'Cults and Sects' in African American Religious History," in *Esotericism, Gnosticism, and Mysticism in African American Religious Experience*, ed. Stephen C. Finley and Margarita Guillory (Leiden: Brill, 2015), 40–61. Passages from chapter 2 are borrowed from "Crystallizing Subjectivities in the African Diaspora: Sugar, Honey, and the Gods of Afro-Cuban Santería," in *Religion, Food, and Eating in North America*, ed. Benjamin Zeller et al. (New York: Columbia University Press, 2014), 175–94; and "Cooking for the Gods: Sensuous Ethnography, Sensory Knowledge, and the Kitchen in Lucumí Tradition," *Religion* 41, no. 4 (2011): 665–83. Chapter 3 is a much expanded and revised version of "Cooking for the Gods." Chapter 5 contains reworked and updated material previously published in "Willful Spirits and Weakened Flesh: Historicizing the Initiation Narrative in Afro-Cuban Religions," *Journal of Africana Religions* 1, no. 2 (2013): 151–93. I am grateful to the editors and reviewers involved in the production of these publications for their emboldening and constructive feedback.

My son Raphael has sweetened my life and William Elison has sustained it—not least by doing the cooking. For waulking the tweed of this book with me, I give deepest thanks.

# Introduction

Tropical aromas waft to the entrance of the house, enveloping visitors as they brush the snow from their shoulders. Men, women, and children have braved this winter night to honor the god of the ocean's depths with an array of culinary delights. Aglow with purpose, the head cook accepts compliments on her bronze blazer and dress. Clad in white from sneakers to head-kerchiefs, her teenage assistants dash from the shrine room to the basement, site of the ritual about to take place. At the kitchen table, a young priest waits. He adjusts his chunky-knit cap, takes a sip of espresso, and plays a melody on his laptop. Unadorned but for a kiss of coral lipstick, his mentor raises her voice in song. The space between her two front teeth is a West African mark of beauty, called *eji* in the Yorùbá language. Earthenware plates crowd the kitchen counter: corn on the cob; red snapper fried whole, then drizzled with mouth-wateringly tart parsley sauce; balls of yam flour, sour as buttermilk and the same shade of pale; beans savory with hambone stock—twenty-one dishes in all. At a lull in the song, a cook at the stove suddenly turns and stage-whispers a rap verse, all the more comical for being so dramatic. Other women scour pots, scrub bowls, and fold spoonfuls of steaming grits into banana leaves. They are ready to work, and be worked by their religion.

In Caribbean and Latin American religions of African origin, the gods feel. They crave the sight of symbols and gestures; the sounds of oracles and instruments; the scent of breath and cigar smoke. They also want food. Their hunger for it dictates the ceremonial calendar in houses of worship, the division of labor within religious families, and the allocation of monetary funds and other resources. While major rituals such as initiations require banquets for the gods and communal meals for practitioners, even most smaller ceremonies call for an offering of some refreshment for the spirits. Priestly elders and novices alike render service to them by anticipating their culinary desires, differentiating between the dietary preferences of distinct entities and training others to do so. Among those responsible for feeding the deities and ancestors in Haitian Vodou, Brazilian Candomblé, and Cuban Lucumí—among other traditions that crystallized during the transatlantic slave trade— recipes circulate through printed manuals, handwritten notebooks, and word of mouth.

Practitioners talk while they cook. They chat around kitchen tables; over charcoal grills, wood fires, and gas stoves; on temple floors; in bungalow basements and the courtyards of tenements and compounds. They not only speak in divination verses, myths, and proverbs, they use their own words to enact their worlds. Practitioners define their traditions as moral-ethical communities through the informal genres of communication that accompany food preparation.[1] In common acts of religious self-definition, practitioners share the stories of their lives, and tell how they came to serve the gods. They do so with such regularity, in fact, that the swapping of these anecdotes should be regarded as a ritual in its own right. Nourishment of the deities stimulates discussion about practitioners' nurturance by them, often unfolding at the far threshold of sacred spaces. Transcribed into oral histories by generations of researchers, they are now critical to the scholarship on West and Central African traditions in the Americas.

This book focuses on domestic labor in the kitchen of one house of worship, and the conversations that arise in the context of fixing sacred food. It considers the flavor of everyday religious experience in a Black Atlantic tradition. Practitioners conversant with the gods' tastes already know that they respond to requests only if and when their hungers are satisfied. Accordingly, this book investigates food preparation for the relationships it structures and the types of bodies—both divine and human—that it produces. It reconceptualizes the role of race, gender, and sexuality in the way that people become subjects of a particular religion. It reveals that the seemingly trivial kinds of activities involved in ceremonial cooking turn out to be emotionally and somatically intricate sites in which individuals are socialized.[2]

The gods' hunger is no more a metaphor than their reality, and practitioners conceptualize divine sense perception with special reference to oral consumption. Yet cooking for the deities remains inadequately appreciated as a ceremonial endeavor rife with cosmological significance, inviolable taboos, and reckoning of sacred time.[3] Despite a few exceptions, scholarly neglect of religious food preparation may be traced back to an ingrained suspicion of gastronomic pleasure and shallow estimation of day-to-day cookery in the Western philosophical tradition. Classical Enlightenment texts vigorously reinforced the negative connotations attached in Christian moral thought to appetite and other sensations. Casting the tongue as an organ of indulgence rather than discernment, influential treatises, commentaries, and lectures put taste at the bottom of the sensory hierarchy. They excluded gustatory events from the ranks of experiences able to deliver a morally valuable encounter with beauty, deeming the judgments of the palate too fickle and instantaneous to qualify as universal.[4]

This attitude relied in part on the relationship seen to obtain between food, women from the European "laboring classes," and enslaved Africans whose prowess was counted on to turn raw ingredients into edible fare.[5] Not coincidentally, the same texts laid the foundation for modern definitions of religion, and dismissed people of African descent as having none. They depicted both continental Africans and Black folk in the Americas as prisoners of primitive instincts and passions, trifling in sentiment as well as intellect, with neither culture nor past. It is no wonder, then, that many scholarly attempts to confer validity on maligned Caribbean and Latin American traditions have proceeded by accentuating their similarities with those esteemed as "world religions"—most typically, monotheisms endowed with imposing edifices, universalizing scriptures, and literate male clerics, among other criteria for legitimacy.[6] A number of Black Atlantic religions diverge strikingly from Eurocentric classificatory schemes not only in valorizing spirit possession and sacrifice, but also in prizing food preparation.[7] It should not come as any shock, then, that explaining the culinary ingenuity involved in feeding the gods and the moral-ethical imperative to do so has historically received much lower priority than tackling the bleakest of stereotypes.

The gods have been obliged to adhere to the same politics of respectability that have constrained people of African descent throughout the

Americas.[8] Since the late nineteenth century, when social scientists "discovered" African-derived traditions in the New World, Black Atlantic spirits have had to uphold bourgeois standards of propriety, decorum, and restraint in order to count as religious, rather than as criminal remnants of fetishism or idolatry. Their travails have resembled those of Black men and women compelled to surpass their white detractors in education, refinement, and Christian piety in order to achieve some measure of professional advancement and legal protection. Even as people of African descent have aspired to middle-class ideals of masculine industry and feminine virtue in a strategic bid for the rights of citizenship, the gods of various Caribbean and Latin American traditions have had to verify the authenticity of their Africanity, investment in cultural and political resistance, and usefulness for a range of nationalist movements.[9] These deities have been policed by states no less than by ideologues and elites, leading their worshippers to partner repeatedly with scholars in hopes of securing accurate, or at least advantageous, representation.[10]

To be accepted as rational actors and rehabilitate their gods, practitioners of Black Atlantic traditions have highlighted certain areas of salient religious concern: theologies, cosmologies, genealogies, and mythologies. Scholars, in their turn, have illuminated the *logos* of these traditions, elucidating beliefs and observances correlated with reason, logic, terrestrial order, and heavenly law, particularly as laid down by men. Although this approach has endorsed a culturally specific construal of religion as an issue of personal faith and private conscience—heart and mind rather than body and community, creed as opposed to ritual—it has corrected some long-standing misconceptions about Black Atlantic religions.[11] It has also allowed for the study of them to reach an extraordinarily high level of theoretical and analytical complexity. On the other hand, an emphasis on elevated modes of religious conduct and discourse has overshadowed the less lofty aspects of religious experience. Fleeting, humble acts such as those involved in food preparation may not be enshrined within the "world religions" paradigm, yet they have historically determined the texture and density of practitioners' everyday lives.

Similarly, casual conversation—the lifeblood of social relations—has not tended to figure prominently in the analysis of religious utterances. Light banter and storytelling pale in grandeur when set against prayers, songs, oracular signs, folklore, and spirit possession trance speech, especially as recorded in Black Atlantic sacred registers: Vodou's *langaj*, Santería's Lucumí, and Candomblé Ketu's Nagô, to name a few.[12] The assumption that everyday verbal interaction lacks meaning and purpose runs deep. Idioms in American English commonly allude to talk as "hot air": long-winded, breezy, empty, frivolous, small, loose, and cheap. To be "all talk" is to be without action; fast-talk, big-talk, sweet-talk, and double-talk skirt the truth.[13] Consonant expressions in other lexicons invite gendered comparisons between the vapor of womanish words and the substance of manly deeds. Ritual "speech acts" have usually escaped consignment to the first half of the dichotomy only by dint of their performative power, association with learned men, and amenability to analysis as symbolic of national struggles over sovereignty and identity.[14]

While everyday talking and cooking have occupied analogous positions on the periphery of religious scholarship, the literature on Black Atlantic traditions abounds with allusions to the importance of making food for gods and ancestors, for instance, in Belizean and Honduran Garifuna; Afro-Surinamese Creole Winti; Grenadian Shango; and Big Drum dance in Carriacou, Trinidad, Tobago, and elsewhere. Trinidadian Spiritual Baptists hold Kabala banquets; Guyanese Comfa practitioners put on English and Chinese Dinners; Jamaican Kumina and Revival Zion both have "tables."[15] Unfortunately, references to food preparation itself seldom go beyond the cursory. It may be extrapolated from recent studies concerning the geography of women's domestic "kitchenspaces" that religious cooking furnishes participants with occasions to enforce and oppose norms for gendered conduct, as well as to collaborate on the creation of collective memory.[16] Trailblazing ethnographies of lived religion in sites that are not avowedly "sacred," including airports and nail salons, point toward the ways that religions can be rethought to prioritize what practitioners actually spend much of their time doing—whether or not it has appeared sufficiently religious to outsiders—and what they say when they talk about it.[17] Black Atlantic traditions also foster modes of speech and action uniquely rooted in the enterprise of feeding the spirits, requiring research embedded in mundane arrangements of ritual behavior within specific houses of worship.

This is easier said than done. Only after prolonged scrutiny do the little things—the micropractices—that simultaneously feed the gods and foster fellow feeling between practitioners come into sharp focus.[18] The word "feeling" is key here, because religious micropractices mobilize emotions ranging from delight to disgust as a means of cultivating highly valued states and sensibilities. Practitioners gradually learn to master these micropractices through intensely sensory apprenticeships to authoritative members of their communities. Micropractices habituate or "season" them into the social relations and signifying systems of Black Atlantic religions bit by bit, plate by plate, as they serve not only their divine patrons but also their human elders. Over time, micropractices instill a palpable sense of the spirits' reality—including the unapologetic urgency of their desires—while inculcating obedience to the religious leadership of a tradition. Since micropractices inhere in the everyday routines of local institutions, they can become difficult, if not impossible, to discern as anything other than unremarkable background noise, or grunt work incidental to more serious ritual business taking place elsewhere.

## Cooking the Book

Although there are several Afro-Cuban religious formations, this book concentrates on Lucumí, popularly called Santería. During the colonial period, sugarcane cultivation called for the unprecedented movement of accumulated capital and unfree labor from Europe, Africa, and Asia to the Americas. Most enslaved peoples from West and Central Africa disembarked in Cuba between 1764 and 1868; during the middle third of the nineteenth century, many hailed from linguistically related semi-autonomous groups—Egba, Ife, Ijebu, Ileṣa, and Oyo, among others—later to be called Yorùbá. Referred to as "Lucumí" in Cuba, these men and women carried with them the memory of festivals and calendrical rites; verses of different oracular forms; rituals of spirit possession and rites of passage; sacred drums and vestments; the account of a universal creator's origin from a primordial energy termed aché; and a category of divine patrons called òrìṣà (orisha). Distinguished by preferences in food, dress, emblems, environment, and spheres of influence, orishas possess distinct characteristics and personae.[19] Lucumí, the religion, emerged in Havana, as devotees of the orishas began to pass on their beliefs and practices through initiation not only to others of African descent, but to anyone willing to assume its rigors.

Some worshippers observed correspondences between orishas and Roman Catholic saints, and—entirely in line with African interpretive precedents—went on to adopt appealing Christian representational modes and iconographic objects (such as chromolithographs and statues) to venerate them. For this reason, by the middle of the twentieth century, devotion to the orishas would be termed Santería—saint worship—by its detractors and Lucumí, Lukumí, or *regla de ocha*, "the rule of the orishas," by adherents.[20] The orishas are treated as embodied in material objects, such as stones and shells maintained on altars in vessels, mainly porcelain tureens and lidded bowls. Practitioners receive personalized versions of these and other consecrated items in a series of ceremonies that culminate in priestly ordination. Since the late nineteenth century, their communities have been organized into house-temples or *ilé*. Ilé means "house" in Yorùbá, and refers to both physical structure and an extended kinship unit in the context of religious practice. As in the case of "church," ilé denotes both a religious fellowship and architectural edifice, and ilés have mostly been located in private homes where leaders live with their relatives.

It was in the community called Ilé Laroye (pronounced "la-RO-yeh"), led for over almost thirty years by the Lucumí diviner and praise-singer Ashabi Mosley, that I became acquainted with everyday religious experience in a Black Atlantic house of worship.[21] I first entered Ashabi's home on a day of feasting, during a party celebrating the fifteenth anniversary of her initiation. She had been initiated in 1986 as a child of Elegguá, deity of communications, master of crossroads, and messenger of the gods. That day in her bungalow on the South Side of Chicago, my eyes returned repeatedly to the greenery of her "birthday" altar, a tropical forest in miniature sprouting from a corner of her living room. I watched intently as visitors unfurled a woven mat before the altar, then saluted the orishas within it with rattles and the ringing of bells—some lying flat on their stomachs, others propped up on their elbows and hips. What met my ears as the sounds of Afro-Cuban religion were the syllables of Yorùbá terms overheard between snatches of English and Spanish. If I went in the kitchen, it was to ask for a cup of water, but I did not think to linger.

Ashabi was, and remains, a medium in the tradition of Puerto Rican Espiritismo, and had been inducted into the Kongo-inspired Afro-

Cuban religion of Palo Monte Mayombe.[22] She had traveled to Nigeria and Cuba to enlarge her understanding of Black Atlantic religions and strengthen the transnational linkages that had enabled her admission into them.[23] She directed a satellite community of practitioners in St. Louis and regularly hosted priests from New York City and the Detroit area assisting in initiations and other rituals, as she did theirs. Like Ashabi, most members of Ilé Laroye were African American, born and raised in the United States, becoming practitioners of Afro-Cuban religions as adults. Ashabi's relationships with them were ordered less in a sprawling network—the dominant contemporary social and technological metaphor for "making connections"—than in an ornate fretwork cut into durable shapes by religious kinship ties and ownership of specialized ritual knowledge.[24] Inside her home, she carved out the time to venerate orishas as well as other spirits, deftly alternating between the ritual protocols observed for each set of beings, and drilling her protégés in their service.

With my Cuban American upbringing, I might have expected that studying patterns of religious experience would entail more than gazing at shrines. To the contents of the standard ethnographic toolkit—notepad, pencil, voice recorder—I added a knife and sponge.[25] In Ilé Laroye, practitioners' wordcraft testified to the vital presence of the gods in their everyday lives. Their fingers, with no little eloquence, precisely described the movements needed to turn the flesh and bone of sacrifice into sacred meals. Watching the process was instructive; to attempt to replicate it, serrated blade in hand, was to be schooled both in the requirements for mastery and in the importance of food preparation as ritual performance. After years of kitchen chores and so-called chitchat, I came to question their relegation to the footnotes of publications on Afro-Diasporic traditions. To insert these activities in the body of a text is to invite a reconsideration not merely of their existence at the edges of "lived religion," but of religious embodiment itself.

This book is meant to extend just such an invitation. It argues that cooking and talking are at the very quick of Black Atlantic religions. It asserts that to feed the gods and speak of them is to make them real to others, and to keep their namesake traditions alive. It shows that tasks like butchering, although manual, are far from menial, and "idle chatter" does a surprising amount of heavy lifting in Afro-Diasporic houses of worship. My thesis is that such material and discursive acts get under the skin of practitioners, equipping them with the repertoire of skills, dispositions, and habits necessary for religious norms to be internalized, then reproduced. To substantiate my more provocative claims for the visceral effects of domestic labor and conversational interaction, I rely on several years of "observant participation" in Ilé Laroye. I marshal evidence from both the ethnographic and archival record to establish that, although I reached my conclusions through engagement with one tradition, the models sketched in this case study are relevant across analogous religious formations.

This book centers on two commonplace yet transformative kinds of kitchen work and talk: preparation of food for the gods and narration of stories about ritual experience. These undertakings are best described as "micropractices": routine and intimate sequences of operations that can be broken down into more minute units of activity. Micropractices accumulate and leave residues of experience in the larger processes fundamental to the preservation of social institutions.[26] Despite their modest scale and narrow limits, micropractices sustain religious formations by naturalizing the conventions that govern particular communities. In Black Atlantic religions, micropractices are carried out at the fringes and in the gaps of ceremonies such as divination sessions, rites of consecration, and drum feasts. Although inconsequential to outsiders, micropractices like plucking chickens and trading anecdotes organize space, time, and intensities of affect for participants.[27] They also progressively implicate their performers in the material and conceptual worlds of religious authorities.[28] I demonstrate that the transformation of individuals into the subjects of Black Atlantic traditions does not result in, but follows from, their enactment of micropractices at the spatial and temporal interstices of better-known rituals.[29]

This book maintains that to understand Black Atlantic religions, one must grasp not only their ethics and aesthetics but also their synaesthetics—the somatic and emotional dimensions of practitioners' everyday experience.[30] This is not to deny the artistry involved in cooking and talking; in fact, it is crucial for my project to yoke the aesthetic and ethical to the multisensory. In so doing, I build on contemporary scholarship exploring the sacred arts of Vodou, Candomblé, and Lucumí, including their signature styles of beadwork, altar display, sculpture, textile design, and manufacture of devotional objects, such as divination implements. Afro-Diasporic culinary techniques betoken creative genius, as diverse efforts to document them so richly attest.[31] Yet sacred cuisine continues to escape contemplation as an art form, due in part to the difficulty of cataloguing and assessing preparation methods; distinguishing the tolerable execution of dishes from the virtuosic; putting their sacrificial components in perspective; and exhibiting perishable artifacts without destroying them. In addition, the composite, transitory, and interactive nature of food preparation makes cooking more closely akin to multimedia installation than to the plastic arts.

The very physicality of food preparation has militated against its sustained examination. Its dependence on muscle memory and the "secondary" or "animal" senses of touch, smell, and taste complicate any analysis predicated on the preeminence of visual and sonic phenomena. Over the last two decades, scholars engaged in the academic study of religion have increasingly come to regard the human body as a malleable multisensory interface continually reconfigured through ritual practice. Researchers in the sociology and history of religions have profited immensely within their own disciplines from anthropological and neuroscientific studies of emotion, synchronized ritual movement, and the enlacement of sensorimotor and conceptual repertoires with material objects.[32] Such developments may be viewed as a product of the "sensory turn" in the social sciences that succeeded the "literary turn" of the mid-1970s to early 1990s. However, the matter of sacred food preparation calls for an especially acute sensitivity to the most fugitive and contingent aspects of religious experience.

By insisting on the significance of heretofore undertheorized micropractices, this book ventures into lines of inquiry that have opened up in the anthropology and history of religions regarding the stylized expression of sentiment, corporeal regimes, affective registers, and the culturally specific configuration of sensory faculties and apprehensive modalities called the sensorium.[33] It is intended to supplement, rather than supplant, projects tracking the transnational social and cultural networks that link religious practitioners to their communities.[34] It benefits from work with compatible premises and complementary approaches to cooking and talking, as well as from projects exploring other aspects of Black Atlantic religions, such as the "religious cosmopolitanisms" engendered by televisual recording of rituals.[35] Such studies exemplify the insights to be reaped from attention to the substance of everyday religious life, down to the observable goose bumps raised on practitioners' arms when viewing video footage of ceremonies. They also stand as a necessary corrective to more linear and logocentric accounts of Afro-Diasporic traditions that have attained nearly canonical status.[36] Although this book surveys domestic labor and conversational interaction in just one Lucumí house of worship, it answers the need to look beyond valorized genres of ritual action to see the centrality of micropractices in fashioning sacred selves, spaces, and societies.

The principal objective of this book is to help reorient the study of Black Atlantic religions toward an interrogation of religious micropractices. It proposes that micropractices hold the chief ingredients for the survival of Black Atlantic religions because they develop the faculties, sentiments, and expertise indispensable for their viability and spread. To hazard this conjecture is to imply a degree of cultural continuity between diverse traditions that may seem dubious at best, bearing in mind the deliberate construction of them as discrete "religions" by both practitioners and researchers.[37] I share the hermeneutic of suspicion that should accompany efforts to evaluate apparent similarities between temporally and spatially remote phenomena. However, to arrive at a more complete account of religious life in the African Diaspora, we need to navigate between the extremes of cultural particularism and the generalizing comparativism once associated with the history of religions.[38] I thus conclude this book by bringing my argument to bear on religion as a social formation, and suggest that every religion depends on a "secret recipe" of micropractices responsible for its perpetuation.

What we stand to gain from an investigation of cooking and talking in a Black Atlantic religion is more than the satisfaction of curiosity about underestimated forms of embodied perception. It has the potential to provide a more accurate understanding of women and gay men—particularly those deemed effeminate—as social actors within Afro-Diasporic houses of worship.[39] As the literary scholar Meredith Gadsby writes, "Black feminist theorists such as Barbara Smith have already reclaimed the kitchen as a space of women's power and creativity."[40] To shed light on both the gendered and racialized landscape of everyday religious experience, this book locates the kitchen on the

"Diasporic horizon" of Lucumí.[41] This is the field of possibilities for action envisioned as practitioners clock the distance of current ritual protocols from those of the remembered Afro-Cuban past, and yearn for a collective future in greater alignment with the dictates of tradition. While cooking, practitioners speculate on the legitimacy of the sacred world their aesthetic decisions have created, in effect setting the limits of ethical practice.[42] The role played by women and homosexual men in demarcating these boundaries has yet to be fully realized. In order to understand their place at the table, we need to get in the kitchen.

## Utensils: Research Methods

And I'll have you know I'm fed up with both the young lady
and her "qualities." Studying me as if I were a play or a blueprint, how I walk, talk, think, act, sleep. . . . As it happens,
there are particular aspects of my life to which I would like
to maintain sole and exclusive rights and privileges.
—*All about Eve*

It is in poor taste for a guest to bemoan the richness of the dinner set before her. Yet that was the temptation, after almost two years of dissertation research had yielded a record as lavish as a banquet: fieldnotes, headnotes, videocassettes, compact discs, photographs, and quotations jotted on everything from coffee filters to cereal boxes. In the early 2000s, there were only fifteen or so houses of worship in Chicagoland for practitioners of Afro-Cuban religions.[43] Yet on any given Saturday, there were any number of Afro-Cuban drumming rituals being performed within the city limits: a *tambor* for the orishas, during which a set of consecrated bàtá drums would be played; a *cajón pa' muertos* for the ancestors; a raucous "Congo party" for the spirits of Palo Monte Mayombe; and so on. Large numbers of Puerto Ricans came to the Midwest in search of manufacturing jobs in the 1950s, and the concentration of Boricuas in Chicago made Puerto Rican Spiritism, or Espiritismo, a feature of many communities.[44] The religious supply stores called *botánicas*, owned by Latino/a Lucumí initiates, dotted the North Side of the city. West Indians, along with Central and South Americans, were a vital and visible presence in houses of ocha.[45]

I was fortunate to have received my introduction to Ashabi at an op-portune moment from the scholar and senior priest Miguel "Willie" Ramos, after having attended the 2001 exhibit co-curated by him, "At the Crossroads: Afro-Cuban Orisha Arts in Miami," at the Historical Museum of Southern Florida. I began jotting journal entries based on trips to the ilé in 2003, and continued to add the odd line to my field-notes well into 2007, but my IRB-approved research period lasted for twenty months, from 2005 to 2006. After an initial set of discussions with Ashabi and her son Fadesiye over the possibility of conducting re-search on Ilé Laroye in 2004, in person and through e-mail messages, I brought the matter to the elders in an ilé meeting. After I obtained their informed consent for the project, my observant participation largely en-tailed assisting in the portions of ceremonies I had permission to join in as an *aleyo*, or uninitiated person. I was one of the assistants coordinated into shifts for one rite of passage called a *pinaldo*, five initiations (two of these with "twins," or two novices) in Chicago, and one initiation in Miami, as the guest of an affiliated house of worship. I served as "scribe" for over a dozen Spiritist ceremonies called *misas blancas*.[46]

I largely rejected formal discussions in favor of more sustained inter-action, chiefly in the kitchen, and in "go-alongs," during which I accom-panied practitioners on outings of both a secular and religious nature.[47] Whether on ordinary trips to the grocery store, or to the park ("forest"), river, or dumpster to dispose of religious offerings, I tried to flow with others in ever-fluctuating streams of activity that brought me closer to their "environmental perception[s], spatial practices, biographies, social architecture and social realms."[48] Upholstered in warm acoustics, the inside of automobiles proved to be the most confessional of fieldwork sites, yet my interlocutors took the driver's seat on our excursions and in all our verbal exchanges. During such outings, I recorded portions of one-on-one conversations that approached life history interviews in my fieldnotes, as interlocutors related details of their upbringing, edu-cational experiences, professional preparation and aspirations, family lives, and religious practices.

I pursued Ashabi in particular to such an extent that I sometimes expected her to utter the words of the epigraph above, drawn from one of her favorite films, although any one of my interlocutors would have been justified in expressing the same sentiment. Nevertheless, I attempted to proceed ethnographically in such a way as to allow ethical relationships to unfold.[49] During the research itself I focused less on overcoming limitations to identifying with others than on entering into multivocal dialogues. However much I may have wanted to put myself in others' shoes, I knew that I was stuck not only with my own clumsy feet, but also with my walk, so to speak, shaped in relation to my cultural center of gravity and sociopolitical location. It was not an option to borrow another's stance to position myself or to employ it as a data-gathering instrument. Yet the approach to fieldwork I took demanded that I "see it feelingly"—to quote the blind Gloucester's description of how he manages to grasp the world.[50] It called for a comparably "sensuous ethnography" to illuminate the instability, dynamism, and non-linearity of embodied perception and behavior as thrown into relief by religious practices, especially those seldom acknowledged as such.[51]

Although I conducted my research in Ilé Laroye—whether in Ashabi's home, or in its temporary relocation to other spaces—the kitchen became the micro-site of my ethnography. In kitchens, I worked, doing whatever I was asked. I worked under a group of ten initiated elders, ranging in age from early twenties to mid-sixties, and with another fifteen uninitiated people.[52] I collected much of my information through engagement in ritual labor highly attentive to "delicate distinctions upon which depended the differentiation between fit and unfit foods . . . and between permitted and forbidden activities."[53] Since the kitchen frequently served as a holding cell for the conveyance of exceptionally potent sacred matter from the living room to the back porch, problems of purity, danger, and contamination seldom left my mind. Such concerns were brought home in close quarters and potentially compromising situations, as when I once drew near to, and almost grazed, an unassuming white soup tureen containing the consecrated objects of the orisha Obatalá placed on the kitchen table. My presence at the ilé late in the evening, often after midnight, only increased the chances that an accident would occur, and that I would see or touch what I, as an uninitiated person, should not. What I learned of ritual prohibitions sometimes came at the cost of almost unwittingly transgressing them.

The circumstances of data collection were structured according to the Lucumí economy of secrecy and power. I had to read between the lines while communicating with my interlocutors not only to do the research, but simply in order to stay out of the way. My uninitiated status prevented me from receiving completely candid answers—or at least uncensored ones—when I posed questions both thorny and banal. Coping with a similar set of methodological issues, the ethnographer and historian of religions Paul Christopher Johnson found that even if the religious knowledge called "secrets" in Afro-Brazilian religions may circulate among scholars, the transmission of the same information from person to person acts to reinforce the hierarchy between initiates and non-initiates, as well as to accentuate gradations of status among initiates with differing levels of seniority.[54] Part of my work entailed becoming comfortable with circumlocution and the fact that acknowledging ignorance—knowing that one does not know—is a precondition for knowledge.

Elders regarded kitchen work as a prelude to eventual initiation. This is part of my argument. I did feel a heady sense of being "way beyond seduction" by the community, pulled into what Luce Giard has called "Kitchen Women Nation": that space in which the feminine—yet not entirely female—labor of cooking creates bonds of belonging.[55] When my mentor Arlene praised my habit of organizing quartered poultry on a cutting board as if depicted in an anatomical diagram, she beamed with pride that was of a piece with her hope that I would someday assume the mantle of the ritual cook, or *alashé*.[56] I had become a presence, and no longer what she once described, in comparing my investigations to those of a shadowy detective, as a "partially invisible sleuth."[57] Partly by virtue of the "mimetic empathy" induced by research, I did inhabit the subject-position of servant to the orishas.[58] On the other hand, in a range of academic disciplines, "narratives of conversion are used as a practice of representing/constituting 'discoveries' in texts that claim to proffer new kinds of knowledge."[59] As a historian of religions, I am doubly at risk of describing my "find"—should it be so judged—according to this template, an irony always pulsing beneath the surface of what follows.[60]

The figure of the white male anthropologist has become a much-burlesqued commonplace: fountain pen in hand, camera dangling from sunburned throat. The writings of Black womanist and feminist ethnographers of color suggest other ways of problematizing the status of the researcher in the field. To import an image from provocative recent ethnographies of Black and Dominican beauty shops, I would nuance the cultural dimensions of embodiment in my research by evoking the historically African American definition of "kitchen": "The patch of hair at the nape of the neck" that "most transgressively resists processing, straightening, and conditioning."[61] It was often in the architectural kitchen of Ashabi's home that members of the community made the sacred necklaces called *elekes*, their arched fingers stringing hundreds of beads onto nylon cords in the chromatic and numerical patterns appropriate to each orisha. Curls sometimes became snagged between the tight strands of these necklaces, causing discomfort and, when forcefully dislodged, pain. It is possible to see elekes as shaping practitioners' sensorimotor repertoires and affective responses, training them gradually to accept *mazos*, the much heftier, more elaborate necklaces donned ceremonially at the start of the ordination ritual and during other pivotal moments in initiates' lives.

Both types of kitchen await more careful and culturally sensitive theorization as sacred spaces than I am able to offer here. By invoking the double meaning of "kitchen," I am interested in situating myself within the specific research environment to be encountered in the following pages, particularly with regard to race/ethnicity, gender, and class. The enskilled bodies of scholars are among those that most urgently need fleshing out, and not merely in textual reflections on past projects, but in the midst of social scientific praxis. Due to my coloring and features, I was frequently perceived as racially white and correctly seen to have "skin privilege" outside Ilé Laroye, a matter of life and death in the twenty-first-century United States.[62] My Cuban parentage and fluency in Spanish afforded me further privileges in the form of access to both Hispanophone Lucumí elders and writing on the tradition. I was not just working in the kitchen of Ashabi's home; I was, at times, a pain in the neck. What a scholar takes away from research is often predicated on what interlocutors make of her body, and the tall demands her very presence makes on their persons.[63]

My interlocutors peppered interviews with stories of film footage illicitly obtained, conversations misquoted, sacrifices sensationalized in print. I have struggled to ensure that my narrative decisions were motivated neither by nostalgia for the empathetic solidarity of fieldwork nor by the "fable of rapport" that in ethnography "permits the writer to function in his subsequent analyses as an omnipresent, knowledgeable exegete and spokesman."[64] Through fieldnotes and ethnographic vignettes designed to be thick—both "contextualized" and, in the sense sometimes heard on the South Side of Chicago, "voluptuous" or "zaftig"—I give passing glimpses into the lives of distinct individuals. Their biographical trajectories may seem elliptical, but they reveal the play of larger sociocultural and historical forces.[65] While I present certain social patterns as representative, descriptions of the recent past gesture toward the particularity of experience as it exists beyond—and flagrantly in excess of—the ethnographic present.

## Place Setting

The remaining chapters are arranged as follows. Chapter 1 locates Ilé Laroye within the historical context of Chicago's South Side and treats the everyday conversion of architectural spaces in Ilé Laroye. I introduce Ashabi Mosley herself and the changes wrought in her domestic environment according to the requirements of her religious office. Chapter 1 then unfolds into a brief history of the Lucumí house-temple before turning to Ashabi's home in particular. Attention to the aesthetics of interior décor and spatial organization leads to the analysis of Ilé Laroye's institutional structure and religious ethos. Finally, I consider ritual time in the ilé during the course of my research and the ilé's ceremonial calendar, as its members honored multiple traditions—Lucumí, Palo Monte, and Espiritismo—under one roof.

Chapter 2 enters into the kitchen of the ilé and the way that members' relationships with the orishas are shaped by the act of consumption. I open with the construction of divine hunger and its satisfaction as organizing an awareness of the orishas' personhood and subjectivity. I pivot off the foundational characterization of Lucumí cooking by the larger-than-life twentieth-century historian and self-taught ethnologist Fernando Ortiz to examine the space of Ashabi's kitchen as a matrix of tradition—with reference to both African roots and routes to Cuba—as well as innovation in pedagogical method. I review some of the dishes served to the orishas on ritual occasions within the ilé and the care taken to prepare them. Then, with an eye toward the use of food as media for the absorption and dissemination of divine energy, I elaborate on the idea that eating makes for kinship.

Chapter 3 takes on ritual performances that are a sine qua non of Lucumí ceremonial and community life: the preparation of food for the orishas in the wake of sacrifice. After rituals of initiation and consecration, slain animals—mostly birds and goats—must be dressed, cleaned, and roasted in a highly systematized manner to be turned into meals for the gods. I document the cumulative impact of elders' "scaffolding" as they instructed their juniors to anticipate the orishas' gustatory desires. I argue that the kitchen of the ilé was a veritable laboratory of embodied cognition, wherein the mastery of technique went hand in hand with the recalibration of emotions, reflexes, and affective responses, such as disgust. I show that cooking to the elders' exacting specifications fostered a sense of camaraderie among the uninitiated that bolstered preexisting sentiments of affinity and led to firmer affiliation with the ilé.

In Chapter 4 I address issues of race, sexuality, and the gendered division of labor that obtains in the Lucumí kitchen, as well as in other spaces of food preparation in Black Atlantic religions. Even scholarship anchored in feminist and queer theory has been prone to misrepresent the roles played by women and gay, nonbinary, and genderqueer men in houses of worship, for the religious undertakings usually privileged—including drumming, sacrifice, and Ifá divination—tend to exclude them. I therefore turn to the much larger literature in Afro-Brazilian religions on cooking, gay men, and transgender/transsexual female practitioners as a partial corrective. Even in this broadened context, however, much of gay, nonbinary, and genderqueer men's ritual labor apart from spirit possession has hitherto gone unremarked. This chapter therefore renders explicit the extent and nature of their engagement with the primary modalities of everyday praxis that convert homes into houses of worship throughout the African Diaspora.

Of the micropractices discussed in this book, part 3 reckons with those of the least magnitude and greatest prevalence. Chapter 5 details the ubiquity of incapacitating illness, injury, and adversity in everyday talk as the impetus for priestly service to the orishas. I make the case that narratives of initiation, frequently recounted around a kitchen table, teach interlocutors the appropriate manner of verbalizing, and therefore comprehending, the relationship between human beings and the spirits. I observe that they belong to a distinct speech genre that has given full-throated voice to practitioners' distress, delivered an endorsement of religious norms, and constructed the feeling of affliction as an urgent summons to the priesthood. I attribute the persuasive force of conversational micropractices to interlocutors' absorbing enactment and emplotment of their recollections. For instance, practitioners often employed discursive modes rooted in Black talk, most notably "testifying"—the bearing of witness to common experience—when ascribing sickness to their lack of attention to the spirits.[66]

Chapter 6 zooms in on the quips and asides of my interlocutors as they reflected on rites of passage. Most of the statements transcribed in this chapter were made in the kitchen, and the historical marginality of that space mirrors the peripheral position of such utterances in the study of Afro-Cuban religions. I expand on them in order to devise a genealogical account of the practitioner "life cycle" according to my interlocutors' interpretations of ritual efficacy, rather than the theological concepts purportedly encoded in ceremonies or the African origins of the same. I chart practitioners' movement through bodily terrain suddenly made strange by new proscriptions and prescriptions in order to underscore the role of feeling—including physical pain—in navigating communal experience. I aim to convey the progressive, reciprocal transformation of corporeal and spatiotemporal spaces in religious practice. Religious subjectivity and the reality of the orishas are bound together in a process of coproduction, as individuals come to acquire and display proficiency in the Lucumí spirit idiom.

The brief glossary is meant to assist with unfamiliar terminology, but there is no lengthy synopsis of Lucumí's historical genesis, its West and Central African influences, central concepts, and ceremonies in a separate chapter, along with a table of correspondences between Roman Catholic saints and orishas as a shortcut to exposition. More thorough accounts than I deliver here may be found elsewhere.[67] I address the religious life of Ilé Laroye in the ethnography itself, rather than abstract its salient features into an "ideal type," leaving criteria for legitimacy unproblematized. I am wary of perpetuating a fundamentally theological discourse of orthodox Lucumí practice, held up as such by virtue of an adherence to reconstructed Yorùbá precedents. My interlocutors sometimes criticized the innovations of communities or individuals as spurious "inventions," but this is not my prerogative.

As will emerge in due course, many of the ilé's members shared family histories of migration to Chicago from the rural South and encounters with such church movements as Black Spiritualism. A handful of excellent studies have established motives for religious disaffiliation and commitment among African Americans involved in orisha worship; this book concerns the mechanisms that transformed their religious subjectivity. Since religious identities are ineluctably intertwined with local configurations of race/ethnicity, gender/sexuality, and class, my argument incorporates Black feminist and womanist thought regarding the intersectionality of these axes of oppression. Some religious micropractices can be plotted along these axes; for example, I contend that my main interlocutors came to inhabit a spirit idiom articulated in a distinctively African American vernacular. Yet I insist that practitioners' religious trajectories cannot be reduced to either their social positions or their cultural locations.

## Consumer Advisory: A Note on Transcription

The argument that I am making comes shrink-wrapped in academic prose that has little in common with the expansive linguistic rhythms in which my research was conducted. I have tried to preserve the prosodic features of my interlocutors' speech without reinforcing stereotypes of African American Vernacular English as a socially stigmatized dialect. It is a task made difficult by the frequent use of the rhetorical genre called *prosopopoeia*, or speech-in-character, to introduce another person or a fictitious character in a dialogue.[68] Most often this fictional character was a version of the speaker herself, whose advent would be announced by an interruption of her conventional diction with elements of "street" phonology, morphosyntactical features, and lexemes—including malapropisms, copula and auxiliary deletion, double negatives, multiple negation, and subject-verb nonagreement. By engaging in these linguistic practices to impersonate "ghetto" folk, my interlocutors constructed comic foils for themselves while expressing a more sober critique of ghettoization as a form of social violence.

Language is never not political. In the Afro-Atlantic world, attitudes toward everyday speech are both gendered and racialized; national and regional "grammars of racism" have undergirded associations of Black talk with not just linguistic but also moral and mental incompetence.[69] The caricature of Black speech in an array of minstrelsy genres throughout the Americas has undoubtedly factored into the tendency to treat informal dialogues—particularly in local vernaculars—as superficial and bereft of gravitas.[70] The academic bias in favor of more formulaic and solemn liturgical language can be connected to anti-Black stereotypes as well as the abiding interest in locating material evidence of African customs and processes in the New World so as to refute the image of Africa as a "land without history." Ironically, the emphasis placed on "survivals," cultural continuities, and authentic African origins has tended to bolster the equation of religion with Eurocentric notions of the same.[71] The resulting inattention to ordinary modes of religious communication has mirrored the scholarly avoidance of activities that seem monotonous, squalid, or simply irreligious when compared against an implicit Christian prototype.

Speech as an index of racial, gendered, and class difference reaches an apotheosis of sorts in Afro-Cuban spirit possession, when orishas converse in a combination of the esoteric, Yorùbá-based liturgical language called Lucumí and the sociolect Bozal, while the spirits of the dead speak almost exclusively in the latter. In my research, however, the conversational "I" was seldom to be understood as "a secure index of the self within language."[72] "I" was, instead, an edifice erected at a particular moment, toward specific ends, in relation to an immediate interlocutor as well as with reference to more distant audience. As the comedian Dave Chappelle has stated, "Every Black American is bilingual. We speak street vernacular, and we speak job interview."[73] Members of Ilé Laroye switched between class-marked racialized speech registers in order to get their meanings across, often in descents into bathos that left no doubt as to either the thrust of particular remarks or the fact that speakers were uncontrovertibly talented in self-expression.[74] The quotations extracted from my fieldnotes for the purpose of analysis come from neither plays nor blueprints, but from streams of conversation that deviated far away from me, laden with relations of power only dimly intimated in my vignettes. I may have the last say here, yet I write as if no word is final, counting myself among those who speak with borrowed tongues.

PART I

Ordinary Home Cooking

1

# Space, Time, and Ache

When I open the front door, I am always greeted by at least a dozen eyes. They are not human but cowrie-shell, belonging to the Yorùbá god Elegguá, the guardian of portals, crossroads, and destiny itself. Small round mounds of cement, the Elegguás are ritual objects believed to embody one of the preeminent Lucumí gods. The cowries are usually embedded three at a time to create the eyes and mouths of uncannily watchful faces; on one Elegguá, the grooves on the shells form tiny eyelashes, on another, laugh lines, as if the god were smiling at the rainbow-colored toys and cellophane-wrapped candies arrayed around the clay plate where he rests. Studded with beads, blades, rooster spurs, feathers, brain coral, or none of the above, the sculptures are thought to possess specific personalities. Although invariably vigilant, an Elegguá may be perceived as a toddler or a gramps-aged grouch, as parrot-garrulous or as mutely enigmatic as a silent film star.[1] Elegguá is the first god received ceremonially by Lucumí practitioners, and his presence—along with the metal implements of his companions, Ogún, Ochosi, and Ósun, collectively termed Warriors—indicates to those familiar with the religion that a home is under his aegis.[2]

The Elegguás with whom I am most intimately acquainted have been located a stone's throw from a massive Baptist church, a nail salon, a donut shop, and a liquor store—which is to say, they could have been almost anywhere on Chicago's South Side—at the home of Ashabi Mosley. Beyond the threshold, Ashabi's own Elegguá, as her patron deity, normally sat ensconced within his own separate altar, draped in his favorite colors—scarlet and ebony—and sporting a diadem that bore more than passing resemblance to the royal crown of the Netherlands.[3] This altar occasionally merged with another built for Yemayá, orisha of maternity, the domestic sphere, and the seven seas, to whom Ashabi's son Fadesiye has been initiated since the age of thirteen. Together Ashabi and her son have acted as the leaders, or "godparents," of a predominantly African American, working-class Lucumí community called Ilé Laroye.[4] Laroye is one of Eleggua's praise names, and Ashabi's home has been viewed as his abode, as much as that of her and Fadesiye's protégées, or "godchildren."

Staggered throughout the three levels of Ashabi's two-story bungalow were objects seen to contain or represent not only Eleggua and Yemayá, but also numerous other Lucumí gods. In addition, images of deities from other traditions were abundantly in evidence. A table above the row of Eleguás at the door displayed a drawing, as well as a print, of the obstacle-removing, sweets-eating god Ganesh, as if he were Eleggua's Hindu cousin. On an adjacent wall hung a round plaque depicting the Mesoamerican sun god Tonatiuh, tongue protruding, the disc strongly reminiscent of divining boards used by the Lucumí order of male priests called babaláwos. Standing in the front window was a two-and-a-half-foot ceramic statue of Shou-Hsing, the balding and bearded Chinese god of longevity, holding the mythical peach of immortality. The piece had been a housewarming gift that Ashabi chose to interpret as an image of Obatalá, the elderly Yorùbá spirit of wisdom, peace, and coolness. Occasionally migrating from back porch to living room, a metal shelf unit kept framed chromolithographs and sequined bottles featuring the saintly Roman Catholic faces of Haitian Vodou gods; before she "made ocha," Ashabi was first initiated into Vodou, although she did not go on to pursue religious seniority.[5]

After seeing the porcelain Buddhas on the windowsill, the winged Egyptian goddess Isis over the sofa, and Janus-faced Nigerian carvings of Eleggua, one could have come away confused at the profusion of artifacts pirated from different, even competing, aesthetic regimes.[6] As Ashabi once told one of her Latina godchildren, "This is the house of whatever. Lo que sea."[7] But "lo que sea" does not mean the petulant "whatever" of popular parlance, implying passive acceptance of future outcomes and a stubborn reluctance to engage beyond this terse response. To translate literally from the Spanish, "lo que sea" is "what may be" in the present subjunctive, the grammatical mood of possibility, belief, obligation, and desire. Its members saw Ilé Laroye as the house of infinite potential and potency. Far from chaotic in décor, the house could be viewed as a North American convolution of the "Vodun vortex," a phrase coined by Dana Rush to denote the unfinished aesthetic of accumulation and assemblage that organizes West African Vodun and Haitian Vodou, along with a number of Black Atlantic religions. The centripetal force of the Vodun vortex is such that any number of influences may be spun into it.

Lucumí's extension of the Vodun vortex is attested by its ability to convert objects, particularly commodities, from one aesthetic regime to another, without requiring that the items countenance "monolithic interpretation."[8] The tradition does not demand that initiates recite a creed—none exists—or observe its ceremonies exclusively, but rather, master a repertoire of ritual procedures and norms of conduct dictated by context. Elegguá is not a jealous god; he will—and does—have other gods before him, although in Lucumí ceremonies he always comes first. Other Black Atlantic religions also allow, and even encourage, objects from foreign traditions to be incorporated into sacred spaces. They are then construed according to local frames of reference.[9] Residential structures are similarly open to resignification, and Ashabi's less-than-private home is exemplary in this regard. She has rallied to the standard set by generations of priests in reconceiving her house's floor plan to capitalize on every square foot of available space.

## The Spirit of the South Side

The contours of Chicago's South Side were hewn during the Great Migration, in what was actually a wave of migrations between 1915 and 1940 that carried tens of thousands to Chicago in search of new beginnings. African Americans in the U.S. South faced lynchings, Jim Crow, and chronic economic problems that combined with environmental crises to render their everyday hardships impossible to bear.[10] For those steeped in the biblical imagery of sermons and spirituals, the South was an Egypt tormented by plagues and the scourge of bondage, or at best a desert in which they were condemned to wander. Migration acquired the aura of a pilgrimage, with the journey itself compared to "crossing over Jordan," a reference to the Israelites overcoming the last major barrier between themselves and the land of milk and honey. Urban areas with established Black populations, such as Harlem and Detroit, beckoned like electrified Zions. Their "second Exodus" would also be a "second Emancipation," an act of redemption for the entire race, one chosen family at a time.[11]

Chicago's South Side emerged as a Black Metropolis with distinctively African American institutions and forms of association. The most important of these were religious. Prior to the First World War, Chicago was already "a religious mecca for African Americans," with historic African Methodist Episcopal (A.M.E.), A.M.E. Zion, and Baptist congregations that remained dominant social and political forces well into the twentieth century.[12] During the Great Migration, these churches grew exponentially.[13] Since the mid-nineteenth century, A.M.E. churches in Chicago had enjoyed a reputation for their proclamation of the Social Gospel and progressive activism. However, their tentative embrace of migrants cost them dearly, as ministers sympathetic to the Southerners' plight abandoned the denomination to establish Community churches.[14] Having let a golden opportunity for congregational growth slip through their fingers, A.M.E. churches steadily increased in size, but their gains lagged behind those of the Baptists.

Newly minted charismatic denominations made impressive gains. The expressive and participatory character of Pentecostal, Apostolic, and Sanctified church services stood in stark contrast with mainline Black Protestant congregations' high-church formality and "high-brow pretensions."[15] Many migrants clamored for revival-style services with "foot-stomping and hand-clapping up-tempo songs," rousing chants, ecstatic shouting sessions, and an immediate connection with a communally defined source of divine power, made manifest through speaking in tongues, faith healing, and the ritual dissociation, or "slaying in the spirit," of congregants.[16] Pentecostals adopted strict prohibitions on behavior, dress, consumption, and spectatorship, practicing corporeal disciplines intended both to purge their flesh of worldly desires and to prepare it to serve as a medium for God's salvific purpose. But their rituals allowed for a much greater acceptance of the Southern body's materiality than did those of more established Black churches.

Residential segregation intensified during the Great Migration, and it was with considerable disenchantment that many heartsick migrants in the "Black Belt" of the South Side—a series of neighborhoods that extended for thirty city blocks along State Street—realized that they had delivered themselves into another type of captivity, that of the modern ghetto.[17] Yet migrants turned to religion not just as a refuge from the "vice districts, gambling houses, unemployment, and racial tensions" of

Chicago.[18] They sought fellowship with others affected by the sojourn north, with comparable experiences of dispossession from their land, vulnerability to mob violence, and racial, gendered, and class-based prejudice.[19] Out of necessity, migrants from smaller denominations convened in spaces designed for business purposes, and in the process gave birth to a new institution: the storefront church. Storefront churches were pedestrian yet approachable, promising a spontaneous, unaffected, and visceral style of worship in a modest space reminiscent of the one-room church buildings of the South.

Although mainline denominations ultimately attracted more migrants than the storefronts did, theirs was a Pyrrhic victory, due to the storefront churches' wholesale overhaul of the city's religious and cultural landscape. Interwar Chicago and its environs were a "gate of tradition" for Black narrative, plastic, and ritual arts, particularly from the Gulf Coast.[20] Storefront churches acted as "institutional bases for conjuring traditions" called hoodoo or rootwork, the medical and magical techniques developed by enslaved people that fused West and Central African, Amerindian, and colonial European ethnopharmacopeias, folklore, and ritual knowledge.[21] In Northern homes, hoodoo doctors or "rootworkers" became Professors, Teachers, and "God sent healers"; in church, the same individuals were rechristened Prophets, Reverends, Elders, Fathers, or Mothers.[22] The clairvoyant, curative, and entrepreneurial abilities of such migrants were mobilized liturgically, with scriptural foundations for their "spiritual gifts" cited chapter and verse if textual legitimization was called for.

In search of a moral-ethical community in which to address the here-and-now, those with a longer history in the urban North also contributed to what has been called "the rise of cults and sects."[23] African American religious historiography has reproduced the mainstream critique of storefront churches as merely colorful and idiosyncratic, their leaders as charlatans, and their followers as gullible rubes.[24] In fact, Southern migrants had a relatively high rate of literacy, and they tended to be skilled and semi-skilled artisans from urban areas.[25] The "vibrant experimental religious scene" they ushered in intermingled far-flung influences from both material and print culture. African Americans of every economic and educational level availed themselves of communal settings in which to explore esoteric traditions such as Freemasonry.[26]

Religious movements such as the Black Hebrew Israelites appealed to Chicagoans conversant with scripture, responsive to Garveyite claims of the African American *Volk* as a new Israel, and disposed to view themselves as a Lost Tribe. Committed to racial equality, Father Divine's Peace Mission broadcast a message of prosperity, self-sufficiency, and cooperative living, along with the gospel of a flesh-and-blood Messiah.[27]

Derided as "primitive," "hysterical," and "frenzied," the worship styles of the storefront churches violated middle-class models of female virtue, restraint, and decorum.[28] Yet churches were often among the few "safe spaces" available to migrant women, in which their humanity as both Black and female was acknowledged.[29] The Black Spiritual Church provided perhaps the greatest degree of authority and prestige for women, as well as gay men.[30] Born in Chicago, Alethea "Leafy" Anderson founded her Eternal Life Christian Spiritualist Church on the South Side in 1913. About seven years later, Mother Anderson established a second, racially integrated church in New Orleans. Spiritual Churches spread throughout the Midwest along with Southern migrants. From the beginning, they incorporated Roman Catholic devotional practices and material cultural artifacts, including votive candles, statuary, and brocaded ceremonial vestments for ministers. Worship services bore strong traces of Pentecostalism, such as an emphasis on ritual anointing, a declamatory mode of preaching, and a "verse by verse" exegetical style.[31] Members sang Methodist and Baptist hymns from the late nineteenth-century revival period.

Chicago was one of the cities, including New York, New Orleans, and Philadelphia, with a dense concentration of manufacturers specializing in healing and magico-religious products such as charms, talismans, candles, and hex-removing items, sold primarily through mail order. The same social and cultural currents that buoyed the popularity of these products—the desire for self-improvement and refashioning; insistence on this-worldly solutions for problems in the here-and-now; the discovery of the autochthonous in the exotic; the impatience with white models of religiosity and master narratives—combined with a thoroughgoing critique of the political status quo in the African American encounter with Islam. The Nation of Islam moved its headquarters to Chicago in 1934, but the foundation for its success among migrants had been laid in the 1920s, with the establishment of the Moorish Science Temple by Noble Drew Ali.[32] Turning the Orientalism of the day to his advantage, Drew Ali instructed his Black followers that they were descended from the same exalted racial heritage as the urbane and accomplished Moors. His temples also welcomed female leadership.[33]

Despite its depiction as parochial and insular, the South Side has served as a nexus point of Black intellectual sophistication, born of a kaleidoscopic print and material culture blossoming in the midst of economic disparity and racial discrimination. The sociologist and Chicago-based Muslim community activist Rami Nashashibi has called this "ghetto cosmopolitanism."[34] The Black Metropolis has bred cosmopolitan virtues such as tolerance and ecumenism; both anecdotal and sociological evidence suggests a widespread exchange of tropes, techniques, materials, and personnel between religious communities.[35] The historian of religions Charles Long writes that "extra-church orientations" such as conjure have historically offered "great critical and creative power" as a complement to regular participation in mainstream Black Christian congregations.[36] The religious studies scholar Tracey E. Hucks describes African American religious history more generally in terms of "religious coexistence and dual or multiple religious allegiance."[37] The heterogeneity of the religious sphere has been an accepted part of the cultural landscape in Chicago, facilitating dialogue and energetic activity across denominational lines, as well as augmenting the number of resources for crisis management, emotional satisfaction, intellectual stimulation, and corporeal well-being that African Americans have had at their disposal.

Most of the elders of Ilé Laroye are the children and grandchildren of those propelled north during the Great Migration, and the religious culture to which it gave rise went to condition potential members' receptivity to Lucumí. Many members of Ilé Laroye had been christened as Roman Catholics, although an equal number began their religious lives as followers of the Black Spiritual Church or in the Black Nationalist Pan African Orthodox Christian Church, established by the theologian Albert Cleage in 1967 (as the Shrine of the Black Madonna). I was told by more than one male member of the ilé that his first exposure to religious disciplines of the body—head covering, abstaining from pork—came with an introduction to some form of Islam, through flirtation with a local gang; El Rukns, or the Almighty Black P. Stone Nation, had long been affiliated with Moorish Science. This is the complex urban land-scape in which Ashabi has negotiated the survival of Ilé Laroye. And just as the storefronts have, her house of worship has converted impedi-ments into conditions of possibility.

## Head of the Household

Born and raised in Chicago, Ashabi is the eldest of eight sisters. Her youngest sister is also initiated into Lucumí and has her own godchil-dren, several of whom participated frequently in Ilé Laroye's rituals and other events. At the end of the ritual in March 2004, one of the first I attended in the ilé, her friends, godchildren, and family members toasted Ashabi with champagne, and I got a glimpse of the esteem, loyalty, and affection she inspires. Her godchildren told her, "If it weren't for you and orisha, I wouldn't be here"; "Thank you for being the mother I never had"; and "You teach me to be a better mother." A godchild visiting from Michigan said of their relationship, "I can't believe it's been twelve years already," and conferred the blessing, "*Money, Money, Money, Money, Money!*" (whereupon others called out "Health!"). One of Ashabi's peers called her "the hardest-working woman in [regla] ocha in Chicago." A young woman described Ashabi welcoming her into the fold when her first godparent abandoned her. Almost everyone referred to her by the honorific "Iyá," the Yorùbá term for mother, referring to both her mater-nal nurturance of godchildren and her cultivation of Lucumí spirits.[38] These comments expressed the respect she commanded, and conveyed the weight of the expectations invested in her.

While perhaps not typical, Ashabi's upbringing at midcentury was shaped by the same struggles faced by many other African Americans in Chicago. She and her siblings were brought up in a housing proj-ect that had once been racially diverse, but as they got older, the white residents began to move away into surrounding homes, so that eventu-ally the Black residents resembled "flies in the buttermilk."[39] Baptized and confirmed as a Roman Catholic, Ashabi attended parochial school half-time in the eighth grade while continuing to go to public school. This arrangement turned out to be another ordeal, since traveling to her classes from home was an exercise in running the gauntlet. No mat-ter what route she chose for her journey to school, every day she "[got] beaten up on" verbally, with whites calling her the "n-word" and shouting "Go back to Africa!" Although always "sensitive," Ashabi once wondered whether such traumatic experiences caused her to "feel things so deeply" in adulthood. To this day, she will not see a movie that contains scenes of racial violence and segregation if she can help it, and she still does not feel entirely safe going into what she anticipates will be an all-white neighborhood.[40]

Ashabi was initially drawn to African-inspired traditions that appeared to offer both symbolic resistance to mainstream society and tools for its transformation: Haitian Vodou, the Black Hebrew Israelites (even going so far as to change her name for a short time), and an African American form of orisha worship that sought to strip Lucumí practice of any vestiges of European influence. In 1959 Walter King, a Black professional dancer, was initiated into Lucumí in Matanzas, Cuba, and became a babaláwo in West Africa in 1972. At roughly the same time, under his direction, African Americans from the Northeast and his hometown of Detroit organized the Kingdom of Oyotunji African Village in South Carolina.[41] Oyotunji went over the heads of Cuban elders—literally and figuratively—to remove the creole elements and Christian symbolism from "Afro-Cuban" traditions. Oyotunji developed its own neotraditional, anti-syncretic, pro-Black ritual protocols derived from contemporary transnational exchanges with Nigerian elders, ethnographic studies, and historical texts that had been seminal in the Yorùbá ethnogenesis of the late nineteenth and early twentieth centuries.[42]

In reevaluating their collective past, many African Americans of King's generation had come to associate Christianity with a history of enslavement, colonization, and continued domination. Black identity was often telescoped into an African one.[43] By the mid-1980s in cities such as Chicago, Lucumí, Palo Monte, and Oyotunji-style "Orisha-Voodoo" provided African Americans with the opportunity to worship gods whose faces resembled theirs, venerate their ancestors, and foster Black solidarity by broadening kinship ties. Ashabi took it. She had a falling-out with the leaders of an Oyotunji-style group based in Gary, Indiana—precisely over the fact that she chose a white man to be her godfather—yet she described Afro-Cuban religions as "a total revamping of what we learned under a Western premise." Her initial contacts with diviners and other religious virtuosi reaffirmed her sense of self and instigated what the anthropologist Tanya Luhrmann has called a process of "interpretive drift: the slow shift in someone's manner of interpreting events, making sense out of experiences, and responding to the world" that characterizes conversion.[44] Ashabi said, "What religion does is help give validation to our reality. You find things to help you give a frame of reference to cope with everyday living. . . . In my process of conversion to find myself, I found out it helped me to be myself more than these other conversions."[45] She had been steeped in the rich family traditions of distinctively African American forms of religiosity, but turned away from them long enough to see the validating possibilities of Afro-Cuban traditions.

For Ashabi's godchildren and others in the Chicago orisha community, Ilé Laroye passed the test of legitimacy by dint of its inclusivity. African American members represented Ilé Laroye as a house in which they felt they had an undeviating route to religious knowledge without the language barriers or cultural misunderstandings they had confronted in predominantly Latino/a houses. Yet conceptually extricating Africanity from Blackness, Ashabi frequently collaborated with a Michigan-based ilé composed mainly of white practitioners; she traveled to assist in their initiations and hosted their members when they drove in to help her. Close ritual and interpersonal ties among practitioners acted to diminish social divisions, while a nonnegotiable hierarchy mediated complex identities and ensured cooperation. For Ashabi, carrying on a living relationship with Africa meant worshipping side by side with Poles and Guatemalans, since Lucumí's African-born founders retained the convention of privileging rites of passage over ethnicity, race, and familial descent as grounds for religious affiliation.

During the period of my research, Ashabi was pursuing a master's degree in information technology, and often to be found typing up assignments on a laptop when not attending to religious responsibilities. She taught classes at the same institution of higher education where she served as a high-level administrator. For several years, she was part of a group that specialized in singing Afro-Cuban rumba, Puerto Rican bomba, and songs for spirits in the Lucumí, Palo Monte, and Arará traditions, providing music for both religious events and secular engagements. She led praise-songs at drum ceremonies in Chicago from time to time. She occasionally left home for business trips, but remained in close contact with her godchildren via cell phone and e-mail. She had traveled widely, visiting Cuba with her sister and other family members for rituals and in order to learn more about her religious lineage. In 1992 she went to Nigeria to perform in a show on the American civil rights movement. She had gone to try to untangle, for her own edification, the Yorùbá roots of her religion. Souvenirs from the journey trimmed the walls of her home, combining with the wooden clock in the kitchen— carved in the shape of the African continent—to symbolize the possibilities of living in another time and place.

## The Home as Temple: Cuba Comes to Chicago

Ashabi met her godfather on the North Side of Chicago. Born in Havana, he was the proprietor of an eclectic religious supply store, and she was in the midst of exploring her interest in Afro-Diasporic religions. She had come to an intellectual and emotional impasse with the African American and Haitian practitioners she consulted throughout the Midwest—in Chicago, Detroit, and Gary—yet she initially felt considerable ambivalence about turning to a "white Cuban" for religious guidance. Her godfather had been the properties manager of an opera house in Cuba, and affected an idiosyncratic, even flamboyant, personal style. Under his tutelage and that of her other elders, she patterned her home on the classic Cuban *casa-templo*, or "house-temple." Her doing so should not be seen "as a simple process of transcription," however.[46] Ashabi incorporated innovations that reveal a shift in everyday priorities. These modifications addressed the challenges inherent in the mentorship of existing godchildren and in the development of a growing clientele.

Historically, house-temples arose alongside *cabildos de nación*, and eventually became the primary site of Lucumí religious identification. In early modern Spain and the colonial Americas, cabildos de nación were mutual aid societies originally intended to regulate the circulation of manumitted slaves and freeborn Africans—whether of Yorùbá, Kongo, Cross-River region (Carabalí), or other ethnic affiliation.[47] Cabildos furnished room for African-derived rituals and pooled funds to pay for compatriots' funerals.[48] In Lucumí cabildos, associated with Yorùbá ethnic groups, the leadership poached from Spanish and Cuban

aristocratic iconography, acquiring imported porcelains, gilded adorn-
ments, and opulent fabrics to create sumptuous altars for patron orishas.
Cabildos decorated both elected and hereditary officeholders with royal
titles such as queen, prince, and courtier. They also paraded through
the streets, staging festivals for the spirits on saints' feast days. As the
cultural historian, scholar of Afro-Diasporic arts, and *olorisha* David
H. Brown writes, "Cabildo processions . . . presented subversive public
models of royal wealth, order, power, and alternative authority."[49]

Ostensibly differentiated along ethnic lines, Lucumí cabildos followed
the precedent of indigenous orisha cults and became "'cross-cutting' institutions . . . based on initiation rather than [Yorùbá] descent."[50] But
after almost a century of repression, in the 1880s cabildos started to
die out as a result of repressive legislation, and increasingly began to
be located in private homes.[51] As the Cuban cabildo gave way to the
house-temple, both West and Central African influence extended into
the most intimate crevices of the home. Initiates devised new ritual settings that would replicate preexisting spatial paradigms. In precolonial
Yorùbá villages, families had conducted rites of passage in woody, un-
inhabited clearings called *igbodún*, reserved the outdoor courtyards of
family compounds for drumming and dancing rituals, and maintained
lineage-based shrine rooms.[52] When Lucumí initiates moved into semi-
private dwellings, they substituted agricultural fields for the bush and
streets and squares for courtyards. They transformed living rooms, par-
lors, and patios into courtyards, small yards into "ethnopharmacological
garden[s]," and cabinets, closets, and bedchambers into shrine rooms.[53]

During the Mariel boatlift of 1980, over 125,000 Cubans emigrated to
the United States between April and October of that year. Many practitioners of Lucumí, as well as Palo Monte and Espiritismo, were among
the refugees. They joined flourishing communities and established others. In both cases, they arrived with the blueprints for casa-templos still
very much in mind, mapping a familiar urban topography onto their
new homes.[54] David H. Brown has drawn from the insights of Roger
Bastide—himself greatly indebted to Maurice Halbwachs—to analyze the miniaturizing and concentrating of space that occurred as the
Lucumí religion moved transatlantically from African village to Cuban
ilé to tri-state–area apartment.[55] As seasoned initiates settled along the
East Coast, newcomers no doubt absorbed much during ritually man-

dated visits from their godparents to their homes, twenty-one days after ceremonially receiving the aforementioned Warriors in a rite of passage, and every year on the anniversary of their protégés' initiations, often to supervise the assembly of commemorative altars.[56] Initiation is understood to be the wedding of a human wife to a deified husband, and with the assistance of their elders, practitioners have brought into these marriages a "spiritual trousseau" of instruction in the processes through which sacred spaces are constructed.[57]

Ashabi's house-temple was a split-level bungalow probably among those constructed in the last quarter of the nineteenth century, when the neighborhood was still almost 90 percent white, with many German and Irish immigrants in the neighborhood employed in nearby factories and by the shipyards. Since the early 1990s, Ashabi's neighborhood on the South Side had been almost 99 percent African American. White flight, residential discrimination, the decrease in domestic industries, and government disinvestment in urban infrastructure all contributed to the persistent segregation of the South Side.[58] Although living in one of the more stable, secure, and middle-class Black neighborhoods in Chicago, its residents had to contend with relatively high rates of violence and property crime, according to local law enforcement statistical indexes. Despite this fact, Ashabi's door was usually unlatched unless no one was home, suggesting the amount of foot traffic she, her son, and 'Tunde had become used to accommodating. Most godchildren simply opened the door to come in, announcing themselves upon entry, and strangers could be identified by their tendency to ring the bell first.

## Everything but the Kitchen Sink

Most of Ashabi's time and energy was bound up in the maintenance of her home as Ilé Laroye. The early twentieth-century image reproduced in figure 10 resembles its first-floor plan. I present this approximate blueprint with some ambivalence, since it is emphatically not the means through which its inhabitants or ilé members navigated the home. They did not locate themselves in that space with reference to some inscription of a previously made journey. The terrain was always changing. For a significant period of time during my research, Ashabi's niece Berta and her three children lived with Ashabi, 'Tunde, and Fadesiye. They often accommodated overnight guests when the latter arrived from Detroit, St. Louis, and Miami to assist in, or serve as the occasion for, ritual activities.[59] And the house was coordinated around those whose names did not appear on the mortgage, the orishas as well as other spirits, all seen to have their own need for ample berth in accordance with their natures.[60] For Ashabi, her house was her "sacred space," and the sacredness of any given area pivoted on material and temporal contingencies, with space itself always in the process of production.[61]

Past the front steps, the living room at the front of Ashabi's house was a space partially bisected by a lintel, the second half of which was probably intended to be a dining room when the house was first built. The living room regularly functioned as a waiting room for Ashabi's clientele and, with less regularity, as a salon for divination sessions. When she deemed the basement too chilly, she used the living room for Spiritist rituals in which multifarious spirits of the dead—both ancestors and the cosmopolitan, frequently non-African entities called "spirit guides"—were invited to contact the living.[62] During these bimonthly meetings, Lucumí elders prayed, sang, prognosticated, and "cleansed" participants by sweeping their bodies with flowers, multicolored cloths, rum, cigar smoke, and Florida Water cologne. Perhaps once or twice a year, Ashabi rearranged the coffee table, chairs, and shrines to create an open space for the dancing and drumming ceremonies called güiros and for recitals of violin music dedicated to Ochún, goddess of sweet water, sensual and romantic love, prosperity, and pleasure. At annual parties in honor of the Ibeji, or divine twins, children were encouraged to do the normally forbidden: toss popcorn, pop balloons, tear crêpe paper, and eat their fill of candy.

A door to the side of the living room opened onto a shrine room about half its size that held the lion's share of the residents' ritual paraphernalia. This space held the five or six orishas that Ashabi, her son, and her husband each received in initiation, when they were not installed in altars in the living room, porch, or basement. This had originally been Fadesiye's bedroom; throughout his high school years, the orishas had stayed on the porch, then for a very short time, upstairs. When Fadesiye left home for college, the orishas moved in. They were housed in soup tureens and other vessels along with their favored implements: Shangó in a covered wooden bowl called a batea, Olokún in an ornamental vase, and so on. The ritual sacra of Obatalá, Lucumí's creator deity, was elevated above those of other orishas, with additional or *addimú* orishas—acquired over time as necessity and divination called for them—arrayed closer to the ground.[63] This was a living room for the orishas, parallel to that of the human members of the home. It was a primary site of ritual activity, where godchildren left offerings of food and candles in supplication. In an open space in the middle of the floor, elders performed cleansing ceremonies and head-cooling rituals called "rogations." New recipients of the consecrated beads called elekes sometimes ate and slept there for a day and a night, thus cementing their affiliation to the ilé.

Beyond the shrine room, a door opened onto a closet-sized storage area that served as a library for films, compact discs, and Lucumí-related texts, including volumes published by William Bascom and Robert Farris Thompson, commonly consulted by practitioners as a means of contextualizing their practices.[64] Across the living room from this space was a medium-sized bedroom. Ashabi repaired to it on the nights she had the luxury of retiring rather than falling asleep on the sofa, which was seldom. This bedroom and others in the house were inconsequential in comparison to the architecturally and practically central kitchen, about which much more will be said. The growth of her blood family, not her religious following, had been critical in convincing Ashabi to buy the house. Yet her decision bore out the grim truth—variously articulated—that to be a godparent is to lose sleep.

Before reaching the kitchen, one encountered a bathroom, then a door leading to the basement, where wooden shelves built into the masonry fairly heaved with imperishables (mostly dried herbs, candles, and beads) labeled and sealed into transparent plastic containers. Ashabi and her son often sent godchildren under the stairs to fetch white candles and tiny white paper cups of *efún*, a white chalk made from eggshell powder, used for demarcating spaces, cooling objects, and pacifying spirits. At the bottom of the stairs, the ivory-painted floor in the first half of the basement supported communal rituals, such as initiations; annual cleansings dedicated to the orisha of illness, Babalú Ayé; the confection or consecration of a ritual object called Ori; feeding of the Warriors and other orishas; and the "Middle Day" celebrations during which newly initiated priests were dressed as their patron orishas and, for an afternoon, greeted visitors from within dazzlingly spectacular altars called "thrones." Most importantly, perhaps, this area excelled as a sacrificial abattoir, since a basement door opened into the yard, where animals could be delivered by the vanload.

In the second half of the basement, past the refrigerator and before yet another set of cabinets, was the ancestor, or *egún*, room. Photographs of Ashabi's forebears—those acquired through both bloodline and ritual lineage—were arrayed on the ground and wall, separated from the rest of the room by a semicircle drawn on the floor with eggshell chalk. Sometimes the altar was organized against the walls, and at other times, in a corner.[65] It would shift again for rituals in honor of Ashabi's ancestors and those of the entire religious community. During initiations, the room was lined with short banquettes, where godchildren squatted to pluck poultry. Every day, Ashabi or one of her godchildren gave the ancestors nine beverages, including coffee, liquor, and water mixed with sugar or molasses, as well as nine square pieces of coconut topped with dots of red palm oil and guinea pepper. The ancestors were entitled to a taste of each meal eaten communally within the house, and any food that happened to drop onto the floor; the fact that the food had fallen was interpreted as a sign that the ancestors wanted it. But their plates and cups were not the same as those of the rest of the house; the dishware used for the ancestors' food and drink had to be chipped, the chinks in the china symbolizing the rupture between their mode of existence and that of the living.

Cater-corner from a bathroom, washing machine, and drier, an aperture in the concrete led to a modest alcove. In this pantry-sized recess Ashabi kept her *nganga*, a cauldron that contains the organic, mineral, and manmade sacra of the Afro-Cuban religious formation called Palo Monte Mayombe, in which she was initiated prior to Lucumí.[66] Initiation into Palo is usually not a prerequisite for initiation into Santería but must precede it, partly because of the bodily incisions made in Palo initiation, upon which the orishas are said to frown; bodies are thought of as vessels that must be undamaged in order to contain the Lucumí spirits' divine energy. Although Ashabi sometimes held drum parties in the basement to propitiate Palo spirits, or *nfumbi*, she yielded to the "*indigenous* Afro-Cuban historiography and social analysis" that cast this Kongo-inspired tradition as wilder, fiercer, and more morally ambiguous than Lucumí.[67] Practitioners separate the orishas' and nfumbis' ritual objects spatially and their ceremonies, temporally. The placement of the nganga in a marginal space in Ashabi's home reflected the hierarchical position of Palo in Ilé Laroye vis-à-vis the Lucumí tradition. It also reinforced the secrecy that attended the worship of Kongo-derived deities, as opposed to other Afro-Cuban spirits.

Upstairs, past the kitchen, the back porch was a windowed space about the size of the shrine room. One corner was usually devoted to the storage of beadworking supplies. Anything that happened in the living room or basement went on in the porch, at one time or another, on a smaller scale; at least once during my research, a small private misa blanca was held in it. The porch's distance from the rest of the house made it ideal for rituals requiring privacy, such as divinations and the confection of the sacred herbal infusion called *omiero*. For ocha birthdays and drum ceremonies, altars were built against the right wall, from floor to ceiling. New initiates occupied about a third of the back porch's space in the altars built for them, also called *ilé*, in the long, uneventful days after their ochas, eating, sleeping, and coping with their boredom in virtual isolation. When the room was not in use for altars or major rituals, a table held seven glasses filled with water for the refreshment of the spirit guides mentioned above, along with a trio of objects that represented Ashabi's own protectors: a statue of a Plains Indian with a feathered headdress, a brown-faced rag doll wearing her own elekes, and a fine-featured Romani figurine.

Ashabi credited her ability to organize her home as a temple and live cheek by jowl with a host of deities to "training, [when] over time you start to learn how to work with the spirit."[68] But not everything in Ashabi's home was determined by the needs of spirits. For instance, her desire for relaxation and at least the illusion of leisure was satisfied by the single most conspicuous object in the living room: a large flat-screen television. She harbored a lifelong passion for Broadway musicals and classic cinema, particularly Hollywood movies from the 1930s, '40s, and '50s. Sound traveled easily through the house, and the sonic ubiquity of "talkies" made for arresting juxtapositions: Elaine Stritch belting out "Ladies Who Lunch" while I lined up bananas and apples in front of an altar for Elegguá; opening coconuts to the sound of dialogue from *All about Eve*; Bogart and Bacall falling in love in *To Have and Have Not* as Ashabi tapped away on the laptop, and another elder and I ferried plates from the kitchen to the basement for the ancestors. Ashabi's control over the channel changer was absolute, to her husband's chagrin, and in spite of some godchildren's vocal dismay. Nevertheless, even the television moved—from the left side of the living room to the front of it, against the windows, to the wall next to the storage room—according to the placement of the altars. The orishas dictated where everything and everyone else would go, stating their preferences in divination, in response to elders' inquiries.

Ashabi sought to move the altars not only as a matter of simple logistics—the domestic Tetris game of relocating an altar to the porch because drums would be played in the living room, and dancers had to fit somewhere—but as a deliberate effort to convert the area occupied into the most receptive, auspicious, and fortified space possible.[69] The mention of fortification may sound hyperbolic, yet Ashabi saw her home as her "personal temple." The shrewd exploitation of physical space has been indispensable for the continued existence of Lucumí, and initiates have employed defensive tactics designed to repel intrusion and safeguard ritual activity. On the South Side, a "word to the wise" has ensured the safety of residents when local authorities and police services could not be counted on. Yet informal webs of communication constantly threatened to ensnare the ilé, located in a neighborhood where nearby Christian churches were a formidable presence. Its existence was an open secret: as Ashabi left the house one day, a hobo shambling down the sidewalk called out, "Hello, godmother!" The neighborhood had its rules, in addition to Chicago's laws, and both were beyond any one person's jurisdiction.

To avoid exacerbating neighbors' suspicions about practitioners' (real and fancifully imagined) activities, Ashabi requested that her godchildren—often wearing white clothing, head-wraps, and caps—not gather in front of her home. Legal concerns were never far from elders' minds during major rituals, even if their fears were aired in jest. Although the members of the ilé were aware of the 1993 Supreme Court ruling in favor of Ernesto Pichardo's Church of the Lukumi Babalu Aye and the right to sacrifice animals under the First Amendment, none were eager for a pitched legal battle.[70] Few failed to appreciate the consequences, including jail time and ruined reputations, of behaving indiscreetly or discarding ritual substances in a manner that could implicate the house. Ashabi's husband had not forgotten the time several years ago when the neighbors of another Chicago priest tipped off the police and on the night of an initiation, he lost his animals in a raid. They later wound up at a petting zoo.

Although the stereotyping of Lucumí as witchcraft has generally been cause for lament among practitioners, the members of Ilé Laroye sensed that a certain amount of apprehension insulated it against censure. Neighbors were probably less inclined to lodge official complaints if concerned that Ashabi's godchildren could "put some hoodoo on" the tattletales.[71] A voracious reader and cineaste, Ashabi was well aware of the voodoo stereotype and the history of Lucumí's persecution. She playfully referred to herself as a *bruja*, or witch, and seemed to relish the reaction; for more than one member of the ilé, being branded as a witch was a small price to pay to be left in peace.[72] During the Halloween season in 2005, for example, the door was decorated by a sash resembling police tape that read, "WARNING: THIS HOUSE IS HAUNTED"; outside, a terracotta calabash held two disheveled children's dolls, a wooden artist's mannequin, and a concrete Elegguá, among other items. One night, a godchild alerted Ashabi that a suspicious vehicle was idling out in front of the house, perhaps awaiting someone's departure, or in hopes of procuring drugs nearby. Rather than call the police, Ashabi approached the passenger's side window of the car waving a maraca and chanting at the top of her lungs in the Lucumí ritual dialect. As the house erupted in laughter, the car peeled away.

Such games of hide-and-seek, concealing through false revelation, have characterized the mythology of Elegguá. In like fashion, the members of Ilé Laroye played pranks as a guerrilla tactic. They made room for their practices in an inhospitable environment by drawing on a range of "already established forces and representations."[73] During an initiation held in October 2005, I was intrigued by the sly references made by participants to getting caught wearing blood-spattered aprons fringed with downy feathers, rehearsing the comically unconvincing excuses they would sputter if put on the spot ("pillow fight," "painting party").[74] When I asked how the ilé manages to forestall complaints to the authorities, Samantha, a teacher, attributed its ability to carry on under the official radar to "a cultural thing in the Black community." More specifically, she invoked the "G" or "gangsta" code, explaining the attitude as, "I didn't see nothing, I ain't saying nothing . . . I ain't ratting anyone out."[75] The G-code has come under fire since the late 1990s for fostering an atmosphere of witness intimidation that has hampered efforts to solve gang-related crimes.[76] However, for those sensitized to ongoing mechanisms of surveillance and oppression such as racial profiling, wiretapping, drug convictions in the absence of physical evidence, and mandatory sentencing laws, the G-code represents a form of street solidarity that extends to the threshold of the casa-templo.

## Where Ache Becomes Aché

During the ocha birthday of his godfather Fadesiye, Ashabi was telling the new initiate, "You are a servant of Yemayá. You are here to serve her. Yemayá gives people the fruit. You are here to carry out her wishes." Ashabi was very specific about the order: he was to stand and wait until visitors say they are leaving, then bag up fruit from both sides of the altar for them to take home.

I asked Ashabi whether he was doing this for his training as a priest. "No. It's slave work," she said. She said that it's for him to develop discipline and patience, "To be able to know to respect his godparents and do these things for them." It's about him working for his godparents this year and being available for whatever they need.

Afterward he joked that before he was asked to bag the fruit, he heard a little voice saying, "Leave now, brother."
—Fieldnotes, December 12, 2005

Berta said in the wee hours that she had learned how everyone walks up the stairs from the basement: Fadesiye walks with a shuffle, shuffle, run, run; Billal always comes up dragging his feet, as if he's dead tired.
—Fieldnotes, July 24, 2005

It is tempting to say that rituals were performed at Ashabi's house "all the time." But this is not sufficiently precise. As in other Lucumí communities, in Ilé Laroye the ceremonial calendar alternated between highly structured, labor-intensive ritual time (around initiations, for instance, or the drum feasts called *wemilere*) and a temporal period that was not profane. It was loosely analogous to the Ordinary Time of Roman Catholic liturgy, as opposed to its "strong seasons" of Advent and Lent. During the Ordinary Time of the ilé, arrangements for ceremonies did not greatly precede the actual events, and those anticipated did not change the quality of interactions within the community in the manner that larger, more complicated happenings—such as initiations and drum rituals—did. Although misas blancas, rogations, and ancestor rituals required trained personnel and special materials, their scale was much smaller, and less time and money was needed to prepare for them. They did not necessitate a plethora of e-mail messages, telephone calls, overnight shipments, or plane flights the way that ochas or the playing of bàtá drums did. The scheduling of rituals differed in their regularity and placement during the year as well: rites of passage and drumming and dancing rituals occurred throughout the year, at participants' convenience, whereas the dates of large communal offerings were fixed according to long-standing convention.

Time is the most elusive element of social practice. It flies. Many behaviors can be described in phrases certain to paint an image, but pace, duration itself, and the infinitely subtle calibrations of mood and tone according to sensations of the passage of time are beyond my talent and perhaps the limitations of this medium to capture. The problem of representing temporality in the ilé is not a trivial one, since it was the cumulative sequentiality of micropractices that rendered them socially productive, for the most seasoned initiate as well as the greenest beginner. The sedimentation of experience over time is what made religious subjects of practitioners. To the extent that social processes can be objectified for the purpose of synchronic analysis, it is by artificially isolating—and thereby seizing up, or bringing to a halt—moments and events. Yet to detemporalize an account of practice, even of the most banal and everyday type, is to misrepresent it as timeless. Time does not exist outside practice, any more than space does.[77]

I raise the issue of time here to stress that the ritual cycle in Ilé Laroye, along with the ceremonies themselves, had a history shaped by human actors. Behind every appointment of a date was a set of individuals negotiating their interests in the context of an emergent tradition, not only dividing time into increments, but also arranging persons, objects, and concepts into hierarchies.[78] For instance, the timing of an annual lakeside offering for Yemayá signified Ashabi's decision to hew to African models—especially as operationalized in Black Yorùbá "Reversionist" communities—over Cuban precedent for the date of the celebration. Nigerian festivals for this orisha customarily have occurred in the summer, according to many published accounts, whereas Yemayá has been commemorated in Cuba on the feast day of the Virgin of Regla, September 7 or 8, for well over a century.[79] The choice to emphasize Africanness as an index of authenticity and welcome all orisha communities in Chicago to the ilé's event was reinforced in the Yorùbá spelling (Yemoja or Yemonja) of the deity's name in its public announcements. Conversely, setting the date of the Babalú Ayé cleansing on or very close to St. Lazarus's feast day, December 17, publicly affirmed the house's connections with Cuban tradition and living Latino/a practitioners, while nodding to the Catholic upbringings of several Ilé members.[80]

The ritual calendar began at the start of the civil or Gregorian calendar, in January, with an annual Elegguá party that often involved a *tambor*, or drumming ceremony, with unconsecrated congas played by local drummers. It coincided with a communal sacrificial "feeding" of Warrior orishas received by Ashabi's and Fadesiye's godchildren. Sometime during the month of January, Ashabi and Fadesiye issued a "reading of the year," a divination performed for the community, which carried some predictions and sartorial, gastronomic, and behavioral prescriptions and proscriptions meant to be observed by members of the ilé for the next twelve months. This reading assisted members in setting their personal ritual calendars for the following year since it often contained instructions, such as to perform a ceremony or give specific orishas offerings before a certain date. Although practitioners decided to schedule rituals separately from one another, the directives issued in the reading of the year influenced them all, since it created momentum for some rites to occur more often than others and set a tempo for labor within the house.

Initiations in the ilé tended to be scheduled in spring, summer, and autumn due to the inclemency of the weather in winter. This affected travel for visiting priests necessary for the proper execution of the ordination ceremony and the well-being of the initiate made to sleep for seven days on the floor of an altar space in the basement or on the indoor back porch. The month and a half immediately prior to an ocha was a time of intense discussion concerning the logistics of the operation, and often brought ilé meetings in which members came together to determine the roles to be assumed within the house during an initiation. Sometimes Ashabi held meetings restricted to priests to discuss matters of a confidential nature regarding the ocha; at others, the uninitiated committed to shifts cleaning, cooking, plucking, butchering, or taking care of other business within the house, like serving food and beverages to priests seated for ceremonial meals. In the weeks immediately prior to and after an ocha, small talk at Ashabi's house turned less often to the news of the day and private affairs than to details concerning the upcoming or recent initiation.

Among the most frequent annual events were the ocha birthdays, or anniversaries of initiation, of Ashabi's and Fadesiye's godchildren. In 2008, for example, there were three in April, one in May, two in June, nine in July, three in September, five in October (including Ashabi's own ocha birthday), two in November, and four in December, counting Fadesiye's. These were always celebrated on, or very close to, the dates of priests' ochas. On these days, initiates constructed altars for their orishas, hosted visitors, accepted gifts, and handed out refreshments for well-wishers from the community. During ocha birthdays, initiates' homes rang with laughter and occasionally song, and they became a prime site for the relation of initiation stories. The godparents of priests addressed the orishas in *obi*, or coconut divination, while the assembled guests knelt on the floor before them, beseeching the spirits to bless their godchildren and inquiring whether they wanted anything further to be done.[81] On a couple of occasions during the course of my research, orishas requested honey, "speaking" through the pattern made by coconut pieces thrown at the foot of their altars; at one ocha birthday, a spirit stated her desire to vacate a broken porcelain tureen containing sacred objects. In these situations, practitioners demonstrated their obedience to the orishas and to their living elders.

Rounding out the ritual calendar were the annual offering for Yemayá that occurred during the summer, and the mid- to late-December cleansing dedicated to Babalú Ayé.[82] These events attracted members of other Lucumí communities, not only in Illinois, but also from Indiana and Michigan; they thus became part of other ilés' ritual calendars as well. Elders emphasized the efficacy of such events in removing illness and promoting well-being, themes with broad appeal among practitioners often without medical insurance even if employed full-time, and drawn to the tradition partly due to the spirits' reputation for arresting corporeal affliction. The longevity of these two celebrations within Ashabi's house, as well as their success—as gauged by the volume of volunteers for and attendees at the events—indicates practitioners' interest in supporting ritual practices that addressed bodily distress and joining fellow sufferers in petitioning the gods for healing.

The events that made up the ritual calendar could be regarded as interventive practices, the term coined by the sociologist of religion Martin Riesebrodt to refer to human intercourse with divine beings. Viewed as "liturgies," or "staged performances" of worship, they set the parameters for access to gods and ancestors by revealing the privileged means of communication with them. These interventive practices created a spatiotemporal place for the dramatization of the spirits' reality and power. By exemplifying the protocols for engagement with them, interventive practices in the ilé carried out a vital pedagogical function: to educate practitioners in the approach to the spirits that the elders deemed competent and proper. The more complex the rite, the greater the opportunities for priests to teach the favored manner of interacting with the spirits, and foster an appreciation for the tiny number of options available for doing something correctly, as opposed to the myriad possible ways of doing it wrongly.[83] By demonstrating the orishas' responsiveness to them, and their ability to mediate between the gods and the community, elders constructed the authority widely perceived to be acquired by virtue of initiatory status alone.

It is important to emphasize the extent to which the religious knowledge accrued and transmitted through the ritual calendar was embodied. As I show with reference to kitchen work, the learning process that unfolded in interventive practices did not merely involve the senses, attitudes, and emotions; it strove to remake them in the image of the elders'. The aptitudes to be mastered were not always amenable to verbal explanation, for becoming part of the community was also a matter of comprehending haptically the sensorimotor deportment and comportment suitable to the ritual contexts that presented themselves throughout the year.[84] Through repeated attempts, practitioners strove to grasp appropriate modes of relating corporeally to others. An example often given in the literature on Afro-Cuban religions is that of ritualized prostration before Lucumí elders, yet even greetings among peers required some rehearsal: ilé members crossed their arms in front of their chests, touching their right shoulders to others' right shoulders and left shoulders to others' left shoulders, before embracing. Those initiated in Palo Monte shared another, more vigorous and intricate, elbow-tapping, torso-bumping, digit-entwining salutation. Quite apart from what these tactile gestures signified in mythological and theological terms, socially they assisted in binding visitors to Ashabi's home into a group with shared bodily capacities.

The practice of Afro-Cuban religions on the South Side of Chicago changed participants' habits to the point that they became equipped with a new habitus.[85] The sociologist Pierre Bourdieu defined habitus as "an acquired system of preferences, of principles of vision and division (what is usually called taste), and also a system of durable cognitive structures . . . and schemes of action which orient the perception of the situation and the appropriate response."[86] Rites of passage and other highly formalized ceremonies contributed to the generation of a religious "structuring structure," yet it was not engendered solely—nor, I would argue, even primarily—in the rituals analyzed thus far as productive of Afro-Cuban religious subjectivity. While the chapters that follow proceed to make this case, one example of everyday bodily training may be helpful. Both male and female ilé members tended to greet strangers as well as friends with hugs and kisses on the cheek, as has been customary in Cuban and other Caribbean households. These tokens of affection sometimes startled newcomers not accustomed to anyone puncturing the invisible bubble of personal space that surrounded their bodies. Regular exposure to this level of contact was not an item listed on the ritual calendar, yet it may be enumerated among the micropractices that turned individuals into religious subjects.

The adoption of Cuban social etiquette by a predominantly African American religious community raises the question of cultural boundaries, and the degree to which involvement in "Afro-Cuban" religions altered practitioners' understandings of themselves as Black, or led them to reenvision Blackness as encompassing of Latino/a modalities. The latter was suggested by the dating of the Babalú Ayé cleansing on December 17 and by the incorporation of Spanish words in interventive and discursive practices, such as the ritual substitution of the word *basura* in place of "garbage" by some elders. It was also de rigueur for budding practitioners to learn to fix Cuban-style espresso—complete with whipped sugar coffee foam—to fuel initiates' long days of ritual labor.[87] Afro-Cuban religions have been altered by their practitioners, as much as the reverse is true. The anthropologist Stephan Palmié, among others, has interrogated the descriptor "Afro-Cuban" as affixed to Lucumí and Palo Monte, since both are rapidly globalizing traditions, and scholars continue to essentialize racial/ethnic designations at their peril.[88] For example, Ashabi's innovations in the house-temple format gave birth to a domestic religious space that now inspires the fabrication of other ilés. To disregard the African American cultural contribution to the institution of the casa-templo is to deny the historicity of "Afro-Cuban" traditions.

We may clarify this point by returning to ritual time, and the sensation of it as expressed between stretches of intense religious labor. Practitioners often toiled early into the morning, and they conveyed their tiredness in idioms informed by their sensorimotor repertoires and sociocultural norms. A typical late-night conversation could be epitomized by my exchange with Oshunleye in the kitchen, instigated when I remarked, "You must be exhausted." She replied, "I *been* exhausted," as if to say that she had been exhausted before, and her current state far exceeded exhaustion. Her statement implied that words could not capture her weariness.[89] Rather than pain, fatigue was sometimes portrayed as imparting a disconcerting numbness: "Sometimes I'm so tired, I don't feel nothin'."[90] Priests often exclaimed that they were "working like Hebrews" or "Hebrew slaves," alluding simultaneously to Old Testament Israelites and their enslaved ancestors. The comparison between African Americans and Jews as chosen peoples—reinforced by centuries of sermons and spirituals—was lost on very few. The implicit parallel between the orishas and Pharaoh hinted at the widespread perception that practitioners' labor was not entirely free.[91]

Because most elders were raised as Christians before becoming immersed in Lucumí and related traditions as adults, they often used the language of sacramental suffering to convey the value of work that tends not to be valorized. In reflecting on the holy tedium of the kitchen one night, Arlene Stevens said, "The work of the religion doesn't allow you to circumvent your problems, but [acts] to prevent you from being consumed by them—[you can] work off your angst, despair, suffering, negativity, and pain."[92] Arlene, the ilé's main *alashé*, or ritual cook, during the time of my research, often appealed to the memory of her grandmother, "M'dear." A Mississippi-born elder in the Black Spiritual Church, one-time pastor of Chicago's First Deliverance Church, and domestic for a prominent Chicago family, M'dear was "ghetto-ignorant profound" when that brand of profundity was needful.[93] Arlene told me, "M'dear used to say you need opportunities to work out your soul's salvation—this is what the [Lucumí] religion is for. Sweeping the floor [at the ilé] isn't the same as sweeping your own floor. It is elevated, for a higher purpose, for God."[94] Lucumí does not possess a formal soteriology and, due to practitioners' Yorùbá-derived belief in reincarnation within families after death, the question of what her "soul's salvation" means to Arlene should not be generalized. Her statement on the edifying power of toil would still ring true for many, although others couch the same sentiments in terms of aché and its accumulation through labor.

Providing a definition of aché in the context of Yorùbá traditional religion, the art historian Rowland O. Abiodun writes,

> The word, *àṣe*, is generally translated and understood as "power," "authority," "command," "sceptre," "vital force" in all living and non-living things and as "a coming-to-pass of an utterance" in the Yoruba cosmos. To devotees . . . the concept of *àṣe* is practical and more immediate. It includes the notion that *àṣe* inhabits and energizes the awe-inspiring space of *òrìṣà*, their altars . . . along with all their objects, utensils, offerings, and including the air around them.[95]

Aché resides dynamically in both subjects and objects, animate or inanimate: humans, animals, plants, rites, among other worldly phenomena. Aché represents the power to turn mere words into speech acts, to convert desire into endeavor. In parting as in greeting, aché means the same as *amen*, "so be it." Physically working the spirit through ritual labor was the main avenue for the acquisition of aché in Ilé Laroye.

The ritual calendar was not only written on almanacs and webpages, it was etched into practitioners' "social skins."[96] Their perception of the scheduling, duration, and pace of rituals was molded not solely with reference to West and Central African precedents, but also by their gender and class identities, as well as their racial and ethnic locations. "We are not a commune, meditating on lotus blossoms," Ashabi said. Samantha once commented trenchantly on differing conceptions of temporality in terms of class: "With rich people, it's 'stay in the moment'; with poor people, it's 'get past the moment.'"[97] By and large, practitioners credited the spirits with getting them past the moment, as when Theo's goddaughter Caroline, an employee at his shop, said of him in the context of an interview,

> CAROLINE: He is one of the hardest-working men that I know. He will take a nap, get up, and work [again]; I've seen him just sleepwalking [to go to] work, but he has—and I tell him all the time—"you have aché!" . . . I've never seen anything like it . . . it's just, you know, a give-and-a-take thing. . . . I think [aché] strengthens him, it gives him something to roll on: *uhuru*. That's a word I conjured up out of my own vocabulary. And that means "strength," you know, only because I'm an African American, and I've heard that term in the community before, and it's just my own personal word that means "strength." Something . . . given to you that helps you go on. *Move.*
>
> ELIZABETH: Is it like "mojo"?
>
> CAROLINE: Something, yeah. Uhuru! I don't know what it means, other than: he got it, and it helps him, whatever it is. But when I say it to my friends, they just crack up.[98]

In Swahili, the term *uhuru* means "freedom (from slavery), liberty, emancipation," and it has been used as a nationalist slogan, particularly in the Black Power movement and in East African national independence struggles.[99] Bridging the concept of aché with uhuru was a daring yet not unforeseeable feat of translation. It was emblematic of the innumerable interpretive acts that had been necessary for the members of Ilé Laroye to accept novel ways of coordinating space and time, and to find themselves within them.

2

## Kitchen, Food, and Family

"Where's my money, honey?" asks the delivery man, before looking up. I pay for the herbs sent express from a botánica in Miami and walk back to the kitchen. In the sink, banana leaves—glossy black and packed in sheaves like continuous-feed computer paper—are defrosting. The stove stalls coming on, so it's off to the grocery store for matches, sponges, and coffee. By the time I return, Ashabi has arrived and, having turned the burners on with a lighter, is stirring translucent shrimp into an omelet for Ochún. With her goddaughter Fulani, I pat toasted wheat into round clusters. Uninitiated but not new to the house, Berta and Imani jeer at our technique for making gofio. They say we put in too much water and too little molasses to bind the mixture into balls. We mash root vegetables into fritters, blanch sweet potatoes, and whisk batter for black-eyed pea cakes. Next up: rice and beans, Puerto Rican–style.

*food brings people together through cooking together, sharing reciples*

Ashabi promises me her recipe for escovitch fish with all-spice and scotch bonnet peppers. I later overhear her on the kitchen phone with someone from Michigan. She put elekes on him when he was sixteen, then he left the religion. That was about seventeen years ago. Now he wants to receive his Warriors and Olokún ceremonially at the end of the month. Ashabi tells him that rituals are not "earth-shattering," they are about giving him "keys" to work with. Palm oil pops in a skillet behind her. "The orishas are not hung up on perfection."

The kitchen was located between Ashabi's living room and back porch, above the basement, past the shrine room and a bathroom. It was at the bottom of another set of stairs, leading up to two small rooms and an attic. The kitchen had thirty-odd square feet of parquet tile and several pairs of oak-stained wooden cabinets. A stove with four gas burners and an oven fitted with two metal racks stood to the right of the main doorway. To the left sat a long mahogany dining table, surrounded by long-backed chairs with muslin-covered cushions that tied at the legs. The stainless-steel refrigerator was unexceptional, except that it was never quite large enough. Next to it, a microwave rested on the counter. A selection of spices, sauces, and condiments abutted the stove. The windowsill in the middle of the counter held figurines and, sometimes, bottles of vitamins or plant cuttings in jars. There was a birch kitchen cart from a certain Swedish furniture retailer that this ethnographer assembled on the living room floor. Above the dishwasher, a sink with two basins had one faucet that occasionally let out a stream of liquid so hot that it was dubbed "Shangó water," in honor of the fire-eating god. Otherwise, the kitchen was ordinary.

Although no one would suspect it from this description, the kitchen clinched Ashabi's purchase of her home in the early 1990s. Driving past the house one day, her sister—with whom Ashabi and her husband, 'Tunde, were living at the time—saw it was for sale. 'Tunde is initiated to Ochún, the orisha of prosperity and sweetness, whose favorite offering and preferred medium is honey. On his first visit to the property, he spied bees buzzing in the yard and inside the back porch, their nests lodged in the very walls. He interpreted them, along with the pear tree growing in the yard, as a welcome sign; the fact that the house was yellow, Ochún's color, sealed the deal. For their part, Ashabi and her sister "fell in love with the kitchen."[1] Their last home had proven unsatisfactory precisely because the kitchen was tiny and its awkward design inimical to the flow of ritual activity. Since her religious following was beginning to grow, Ashabi settled on the bungalow as the new site of Ilé Laroye. She hesitated only because the space set aside for bedrooms—and more importantly, private, uninterrupted sleep—seemed woefully inadequate. They sometimes still wonder whether this architectural defect should have prevented them from buying the house. But the kitchen's centrality has never been in question.

Holy Hungers

I got to Sphinx Cleaners just before seven o'clock at night to see Caroline. Theo was still behind the counter. His many-

eyed Eleggguá was at the door and the shop was decorated with pencil portraits of Sojourner Truth, Malcolm X, and one composite of Michael Jordan, Rosa Parks, and Billie Holiday, among other icons. Caroline asked about my love life when we went in the back, where she had been doing some bookkeeping, smoking, and listening to the radio. There's a guy at Tropical Island Jamaican jerk restaurant who always tells her he loves her, although he doesn't know her. The last time he said so she asked him, "If you love me then where are my oxtails?" She said that ten minutes later, the oxtails were waiting for her at the cleaners.
—Fieldnotes, July 20, 2005

*food is used to show love and build relationships*

To explain why the orishas need food from human beings, practitioners turn to myths with origins in oracular verses called *odu*. These myths detail the reasons for almost every aspect of the orishas' consumption patterns, from Elegguá's insistence that he receive his offerings at the front door of practitioners' homes and eat first on ritual occasions, to the orishas' choice of dining companions.[2] In one oft-cited narrative recorded by Lydia Cabrera in her 1954 magnum opus, *El monte: Igbo, finda, ewe orisha, vititi nfinda*, Elegguá acts as the doorman and receptionist for three female orishas with a lucrative divination business. They feast on the poultry their clients leave as payment and share their banquets with the other orishas; for his trouble, Elegguá is rewarded with bones. His teeth chipping and his guts rumbling, Elegguá turns away the orishas' customers, saying that the diviners moved house or went on vacation. When Shangó finds out that the orishas have put Elegguá "on a diet," he reminds them that Elegguá owns their door, and they resolve to split their earnings with him in return for his renewed assistance. Soon their house is full of so many hens, doves, and other tasty birds that they all decide to "get fat and relax" for a while.[3]

*teaches that you should share wealth w/ people that help you achieve*

*food used to celebrate you*

This myth echoes others that attest to the significance of the tongue in Afro-Cuban tradition as an opener of doors to both good (with the orishas' support) and ill (without it). Food offerings are called *addimú*, and they are presented to the orishas by being placed either in front of or on top of the vessels that hold their consecrated objects. Practitioners depict the orishas' consumption as a rather straightforward affair, instead of a pretext for regular theological speculation. A couple of my interlocutors claimed that the orishas did subtract their portion from the meals made for them in concrete material terms, and that those dishes would weigh less when removed from the orishas than when they were first set down. This opinion would have been strongly reinforced by myths like the one summarized above that portray the orishas as shedding or putting on pounds based on the amount of offerings garnered. Others maintained that the orishas extract only the subtle essence of their food, and no objectively verifiable transfer of substance occurs when giving addimú. A comparable diversity of opinion would be found among practitioners of other religions that encourage the offering of food to deities and ancestors.[4]

Among Lucumí and related traditions in the Afro-Atlantic world, metaphors of seeing and eating overlap, as if the taste buds of the spirits were in their eyes: neglect is "hunger," the spectacle of ritual activity, "food."[5] Yet nobody in Ilé Laroye suggested that giving addimú to the orishas was symbolic, in the sense of solely figurative.[6] Practitioners treat the orishas as entities similar to themselves, crediting them with desire, agency, sensitivity to sensory stimuli, and aesthetic sensibilities. In other words, they grant the spirits habitus. By assigning this embodied "practical sense" to orishas, practitioners manage to render impersonal forces vividly anthropomorphic, in effect creating them as subjects with whom they may enter into relationships.

When practitioners say the orishas want food, it is no mere metaphor, but neither is it as complicated a proposition as the preceding paragraph may imply. In the fieldnotes excerpt above, the behavior of Caroline's would-be suitor mirrors that of the ideal religious subject. She requests a token of affection that will cost him something in time, money, and effort, yet is relatively easy to obtain. He acts with dispatch to send the exact dish she craves—rather than a random item from the menu—to her place of work. Similarly, practitioners may be bidden through divination to deposit addimú where the orishas reside in the natural and manmade world: in their house of ocha; at the gates of a cemetery or edge of the forest; beside railroad crossings; on beaches; and in rivers, among other places. When Caroline's admirer complies with her wishes, the oxtails serve as not only proof of his devotion, but also a gateway to knowledge about her. His trip to the cleaners might well have yielded the brand of cigarette Caroline smokes and the radio station she plays. This information would have paved the way for further interaction and the possibility of an ongoing relationship, assuming that the oxtails hit the spot.

*food as starting point for relationships*

By offering food in addimú to the orishas, whether on festive occasions or somber ones, practitioners today attempt to cross the divide thought to separate divine other from human self. The food does not merely communicate a desire to build a relationship with the gods, it "can be held to constitute objects of devotion."[7] Practitioners come to recognize the orishas through learning their preferences. They materialize the spirits by repeatedly trying to anticipate their desires and preparing food in the manner defined as proper by elders. In this process, practitioners become accustomed to the idea that orishas possess multiple, non-mutually exclusive modes of existence, yet are not reducible to any one of them. Orishas dwell in their respective environmental or geographical domains: Shangó in fire, lightning, and electricity; Yemayá in the ocean; Elegguá in the street and at the crossroads, and so forth. They are also believed to be embodied in ritually prepared substances (a combination of herbs, minerals, and animal matter) that, during the ordination ceremony, are applied to incisions made on the novice's shaved scalp. These substances install the protective sacred energy of an initiate's patron orisha in the crown of her physical head.

*two principle sort of similar to Devi*

Upon initiation, Lucumí priests receive consecrated stones, or *otanes* (from the Yorùbá word for stone, *otán*), that embody a set of the major orishas, in addition to their personal patrons. The stones of these orishas remain ensconced in porcelain soup tureens and other lidded containers, shielded from the gaze of the uninitiated.[8] To be ordained is to accept the responsibility of nourishing these stones periodically with sacrifices, herbs, and consecrated infusions. Initiates require the presence of elders' otanes to transform new stones into orishas; as Alfred Gell writes, "They are physically detached fragments of the [spirit]'s 'distributed personhood'—that is, personhood distributed in the milieu, beyond the body boundary."[9] As a resource for present and future practitioners, otanes offer the sacred substance for the maintenance of religious families. One individual's mortality does not threaten the longevity of the community but furnishes an opportunity for its reproduction, since her otanes may be transferred to a living initiate.[10] Elders

*similar concert to baptism?*

thus simultaneously prevent otanes from losing the origins ascribed to them, enmesh the agency of the orishas in that of humans, and confirm the hierarchy of ritual descent relating godparents to godchildren.[11]

Feeding with sacrifice can bestir the oldest of stones, yet they can—like Elegguá—go on strike. More is at stake in their loss than the fate of one house of ocha. If starved, the spirits will cease to dwell in the otanes, disrupting the continuity of the religious lineage and jeopardizing the foundation of the religion itself. Although orisha priests in Yorùbáland have featured stones on their altars, they have not assumed nearly the same importance that they have among Lucumí practitioners, who view them as tangible reminders of, and connections to, the Afro-Diasporic past.[12] Oral tradition holds that stones with the most aché came from Africa under the tongues, and in the bellies, of slaves carried to Cuba aboard slave ships.[13] Otanes bind practitioners to the memory of the Middle Passage as well as to the royal Yorùbá symbolism mobilized in Lucumí iconography and material culture.[14] Lucumí altars bearing otanes are called "thrones," and devotees place straw mats before them where visitors are bidden to prostrate themselves, performing acts of physical obeisance to both orishas and human elders. Priests arrange otanes in order of relative seniority on shelves or behind the doors of cabinets, replicating the familial hierarchy at the heart of Yorùbá social structure.

The orishas also live elsewhere, in human bodies transformed into containers for the gods by spirit possession. Regarded as a moral-ethical practice that maintains communal cohesion and promotes individual welfare, possession in this and other Black Atlantic traditions scarcely resembles its mainstream portrayals in films and on television. Trances normally occur in the context of a *bembé*, or drum party. The orishas each rule and respond to distinct drum rhythms; elders specify the property of music that induces spirit possession as Àyàn or Aña, a female deity and patron of drummers. In Cuba, the tonal language of Yorùbá became the dialect Lucumí, deployed in divinatory verses, song lyrics, and rituals. Because drums can reproduce tones, they encode speech in rhythm beckoning the orishas to materialize in the midst of their subjects. Through possession, the spirits temporarily adopt the characteristics of mortals—experiencing hunger and thirst, among other sensations—in order to become subjects with whom communities may interact.

Upon arrival in the bodies of the possessed, the orishas spend most of their time listening to problems, delivering advice, diagnosing illness, and bestowing blessings on their worshippers. Scholars have argued that possession in Lucumí and other Black Atlantic religions assumed the role that other types of ceremonies had played in West and Central Africa. Sensitive to new religious needs created by enslavement, practitioners of Black Atlantic traditions may have altered the level of personal contact with the spirits afforded by ritual. In her study of Vodou in Haiti, the ethnographer Karen McCarthy Brown writes,

*[handwritten margin note: historical possession was popularized in environments w/ no forms of physical spirituality (objects)]*

> When the elders, the priests, the institutions, the musical instruments, the images, the altars, and the sacred objects are absent, where do you turn for spiritual aid? In an African-based religion, possession seems an obvious answer. In Yorùbáland and Dahomey . . . most possession-performances were formulaic affairs with more or less predictable words and gestures. In the New World, however, in that early time when the body and the voice were the slaves' principal mnemonic devices, possession could well have received much greater emphasis, and . . . become much more extemporaneous and expressive.[15]

Possession reinforced the spontaneity and tangibility of the spirits, so that in the person of the possessed, the community could feel, hear, see, and smell the gods, suddenly so close that one could almost taste them as well. Possession made use of a sacred object no white person could destroy without destroying the slave: the human body.

*[handwritten margin note: numerous cultures + religions all altered from origin b/c of white people]*

According to Lucumí theological discourse, at the moment of spirit possession, the orisha simultaneously enters the everyday world while the animating force and personality of the initiate leaves it. After an orisha inhabits an individual, he or she will dance in a set of choreographed movements before engaging on a more private level with practitioners. Since orishas want to wear their favorite colors, fabrics, and patterns, sacramental clothing must be fashioned and readied for the coming of the orishas. More importantly, thrones must be arrayed with foods prepared to their taste in the custom-made assortments of fruits and special dishes called *plazas*, spread out for the orishas in front of elaborate celebratory, commemorative, or initiatory altars. Brown writes of the plazas, "That which is cool, refreshing, and sweet should produce a dis-

position conducive to positive divinatory responses and is metaphorically consistent with the desired result: tranquility, advancement, health,
and well-being."[16] Because spirits are thought to derive aché from their
preferred foods, initiates must refrain from offering prohibited items.
The gods may choose to approach altars with an appetite, and not just
academic curiosity.

Possessed initiates are shadowed by attendees bearing beverages in
dried gourds and plates of honey, sometimes mixed with palm oil, for
the orishas' refreshment. This practice epitomizes human service to the
orishas. Although subordinate, even subservient, practitioners strive to
attain a degree of intimacy with the gods that demands a firm grasp of
their professed habits and proclivities. Newcomers to a house of worship soon learn that an orisha's diet reflects his or her temperament, ac-
complishments, feuds, and bonds with other spirits; favorite dishes are
shorthand for personae. Whether the orishas are immanent in stones,
the body of the possessed, or consecrated substances, a set of protocols
governs both ordained and uninitiated practitioners' intercourse with
them. This regulatory system operates according to what one could call
a theory of moral behavior, in which "moral" (as in the phrase "moral
law") designates the requirements an action must fulfill to be right or
virtuous.[17] As the dance ethnographer and filmmaker Maya Deren
observed of Haitian gods that are similarly envisioned, "The [spirits],
themselves non-physical, . . . are a moral essence; they answer to moral
movement, moral sound, to moral matter."[18] And what matters most is
food.

## Innovation and the Gastro-Geographic Imagination

[Black women chefs] were "turbaned mammies" and "voodoo magicians" and "tyrants" who ruled the back rooms
with simpleminded power; they could work culinary mira-
cles day in and day out, but couldn't for the life of them tell
anyone how they did it. Their most impressive dishes were
described as "accidental" rather than planned. Their speech,
humorously conveyed in demeaning dialect in many an old
cookbook, came across as illiterate folk knowledge and not
to be taken seriously.[19]

*[handwritten margin note, left: relates to a previous reading from fem. philosophy about]*

*[handwritten note, bottom: the categories all black women are unfortunately put into by white men → "mammy" is one of them]*

Many sacred objects in Black Atlantic religions have their origins in vessels used for cooking, from the cauldrons of Palo Monte to the ceramics of Vodou. Such items point to the role played by women historically in transmitting these traditions. Apropos of Candomblé, the anthropologist J. Lorand Matory writes, "Since female domestic slaves had free time and both the competency and the option to cook, they were also uniquely able 'to continue practicing their original religion.' Indeed, something in the experience of enslaved and freed Afro-Brazilians encouraged an extraordinary elaboration in the votary cuisine of the gods."[20] In the context of Lucumí, Brown has tied the use of soup tureens (*soperas*) to hold the orishas' stones, and the shelved cabinets (*canastilleros*) that often house them, to the domestic service performed by prominent female initiates in the late nineteenth and earlier twentieth centuries; the tableware and furniture passed down to them from masters and employers deeply influenced the tradition's "creole style."[21] In the ordination ceremony, novices sit on a large mortar, or *pilón*, charged with healing herbs. New priests' bodies are thought to imbibe "sacred nourishment" and mystical fortification from this goblet-shaped seat.[22] As a pestle within a mortar pulverizes ingredients for meals to be made, their lives prior to ocha are meant to be ground down so they can be reborn.

The emphasis on feeding the gods in Black Atlantic traditions has usually been glossed as a retention of African cultural patterns in the Americas. The pioneering anthropologist Melville J. Herskovits, coiner of the term "Africanism," admonished readers in his volume on Haiti, "It will be remembered that it is held to be more essential to 'feed' the gods than to dance for them."[23] Herskovits connected this feature of everyday life for the rural peasants in his study with their descent from ethnic groups accustomed to using food as a medium of exchange with their deities. Herskovits need not have used quotation marks, for feeding is less a root metaphor than a social fact for practitioners. As the anthropologist Karen Richman puts it, "When a member [of a Haitian family] says . . . 'I serve my spirits (*mwen konn sèvi lwa m yo*),' s/he means hosting them with food."[24] This is abundantly clear in the literature on Bahian Candomblé that places food at the center of this tradition, and connects both the techniques and components of its cuisine to the African past. An important ingredient in cooking for the *orixás* associated with Yorùbá peoples, red palm oil, has become metonymic of Candomblé itself: "So important is this principal item in the cuisine and rituals of Candomblé that one way of describing a person as a member of this religion is to say that he or she is 'in the oil' (*no azeite*)."[25]

In his seminal study of criminality among members of Afro-Cuban cults, *Hampa afrocubana: Los negros brujos*—"the black witches"—Fernando Ortiz portrayed his informants as presenting their gods with dishes exclusively of African origin: "It seemed, to the witches, that to offer their gods the same foods as those of the whites who ridiculed them, would have been to offend them gravely."[26] Precisely, one suspects, because it has been in printed circulation since 1906, the sample bill of fare cited by Ortiz would be familiar to most Lucumí practitioners today: coconuts, red palm oil, roasted and ground whole wheat or maize rolled into balls (*gofio*), black-eyed pea fritters (*ocra/akará*), a fermented corn beverage (*chequeteque/cheketé*), and the legendary pan-Caribbean *calalú* (one of the delicacies prepared for Shangó), just to name a few. It is here that Ortiz debuts the comparative philological method he would continue to embellish throughout his career. To decipher the significance of the Afro-Cuban religious cuisine, he consults the literature on Dahomey, Brazil, and the ethnic groups beginning to identify as Yorùbá in the early twentieth century, proceeding as if the foods' meanings are transparently translatable across related traditions (for example, calalú "es el *Obbé* de Yoruba . . . que en el Brasil llaman *carurú*").[27]

Ortiz is much better known for having formulated the famous analogy comparing the Cuban nation to the hearty, tuber-rich, garlic-fragrant stew called *ajiaco* in an essay published in 1939, "Los factores humanos de la Cubanidad."[28] Ortiz had initially advocated the eradication of such traditions as Lucumí and, according to the ethnomusicologist Robin D. Moore, in the 1910s Ortiz became an employee of the Cuban government, establishing himself as an expert and "witness for the prosecution of Afrocuban religious leaders."[29] Over the decades, Ortiz's disdain yielded to a fervent advocacy for Afro-Cuban cultural forms as the island's contribution to civilization.[30] In view of his astonishing trajectory and coinage of the neologism "transculturation" to designate the process by which cultures mutually (if asymmetrically) influence one another, some scholars have cast the concept of ajiaco as a sort of equal-opportunity "melting pot." Yet Ortiz insisted that some tastes had to come to the fore in the dish's preparation, while the less savory ones had to recede from the palate. He postulated an evolution from the earliest, least hygienic form of "that primitive single-course meal" to a state of modern enlightenment in which the Cuban pot "now contains cleaner ajiaco, and it has better seasoning and less hot chile."[31] For Ortiz, Cuban culture had once included too much African meat and "putrid or otherwise undesirable flavors needing to be covered up with strong spices."[32]

The first popular appearance of the term *ajiaco* in Cuban letters underscores Ortiz's complicated legacy. *Un ajiaco, o La boda de Pancha Jutía y Canuto Raspadura* (1847) was a minstrel show written by Bartolomé José Crespo y Barbón that sought to ridicule the social pretensions and affectations of "ultrarefined, citified" Afro-Cubans.[33] These and other blackface burlesques played to sold-out crowds at a time of profound censorship for antislavery literature. In *Un ajiaco*, the enslaved African-born protagonists declare, "Blessed be the hour that the white [man] / Brought me to this land," a verse to which Ortiz appears to have responded with incredulity in *Los negros brujos*.[34] Even at his most racist (if the context justifies the anachronism), Ortiz's contention was not that Afro-Cubans themselves were an infectious lesion on the body politic, but rather, that the mixture of Blacks and whites on the island had exposed both races to degeneration.[35] In *Los negros brujos*, Ortiz suggests that while Africans in Africa are entitled to their beliefs and practices, some of these became corrupt through contact between slaves and whites and "yellows" (and here he refers to Chinese indentured servants, approximately 120,000 of whom were brought to Cuba in the nineteenth century). For Ortiz, religious formations in Africa resembled an appendix—a useless yet innocuous organ—that ruptured once in the fledgling Cuban Republic, spreading filth throughout the island and requiring excision.

It is against this background that one should read Ortiz's assertion about foods for the orishas:

It is worth noting that the gods are not offered other foods than those belonging to the meager African culinary art. This fact, like so many analogous ones, can be explained by the resistance that [the witches] demonstrate against innovations and reforms of religious rituals, always frightened of losing the prestige that formulas consecrated by time have for uneducated minds [*conciencias incultas*].[36]

Ortiz's analysis of what today are Lucumí staple foods was not intended to advance knowledge about their origins and identity disinterestedly. It is no coincidence that the *calabaza* (Spanish squash), *ñame* (yam), *plátanos* (plantains), and *malanga* (cocoyam) placed by Ortiz on witches' altars in 1906 reappear as ingredients in his 1939 ajiaco, recoded as emblematic of the European, African, and Indian stocks that combined to create the Cuban nation. We should be wary of Ortiz's hypothesis that Yorùbá and Dahomeyan dishes survived intact in Cuba and Brazil among hidebound religious practitioners. Like many scholars after him, Ortiz turned to religious foods as a means of bolstering his larger argument about the Africanity, and therefore the purity, of some New World practices, while anathematizing others as contaminated.

That said, there is some truth to Ortiz's words, whether due to the acuity of his observations or the fact that practitioners have been engaging with his quadrant of the "ethnographic interface" for over a century.[37] The elders of Ilé Laroye did hold up the kitchen as a locus of authenticity, a proving ground for the preservation of African tradition in the Americas. The discourse of cultural continuity surrounding other "survivals" has been championed as a means of grounding Black Atlantic religious systems in those of the African continent and confirming that Black peoples in the Americas more generally—nodding to Du Bois and Herskovits—have had histories worth remembering. The emphasis on the kitchen as a "cultural archive" in the ilé could be attributed to several factors, including the wide availability of information on Afro-Diasporic religions, against which practitioners may compare their experiences with those of others in the past and present day. With the relative ease of travel to Africa, the Caribbean, and Brazil, practitioners could see different styles of worship and institutional organization unfold in real time.[38]

The ilé's dynamic approach to historical memory infused the pedagogy of the kitchen. While cooking, elders personified the precept "The only way to learn is by doing."[39] Yet they relied on what they perceived to be the most old-fashioned routes to learning: bodily engagement and repetition. More than once, I attempted to jot down notes while Arlene demonstrated a butchering technique, and she told me to watch instead. She wanted me to look without thinking about paraphrasing her statements in my transcriptions, or withdrawing my gaze periodically to write. Writing was also distracting for elders attempting to focus on anticipating questions from their students by reading the expressions on their faces. While uninitiated practitioners were never privy to secrets that could, in disclosure, compromise the integrity of a ritual, textual inscription was consistently discouraged. Elders did not advocate simple rote memorization; they urged their protégés to synthesize information by exercising muscle memory and using mnemonic devices to promote semantic associations. Scholars of cognitive and educational psychology call this affectively laden, task-oriented coaching "scaffolding."[40]

An excellent example may be found in the preparation of items for rituals such as "rogations." The term is a loan translation from the Spanish *rogación de cabeza*, "prayer (or petition) of the head." Rogations have been one of the first ceremonies experienced by newcomers to houses of orisha worship.[41] The elders of Ilé Laroye glossed rogations as a feeding of practitioners' *orí*, a concept that encompasses the top of the physical head and the destiny immanent within it; orí combines an individual's fate, character, and enabling power. In rogations, white substances are ceremonially applied by elders to the crown of the recipient's head, including shredded coconut, wads of cotton, lengths of white cotton fabric long enough for a head-wrap, and cocoa butter.[42] These items are associated with Obatalá, the orisha of wisdom, peace, and purity, credited with molding heads from clay to create the human race. He "owns" such products of civilization as woven cloth, and the cost of rogations in the ilé was twenty-four dollars, three times eight, the number Obatalá "rules."[43]

Busy elders often turned to the uninitiated to compile the ingredients for rogations. Their assembly involved opening coconuts with a hammer or mallet, then digging out the meat at the point of a blade. The segments had to be cut into at least four pieces, so that a divination (called *obi*, for coconut) could be performed after the rogation to ascertain its felicity and determine where and how its recipient should dispose of the offerings to her head. The brown rinds from the other pieces of coconut had to be removed, then scraped against a grater for shavings that would be scooped up and tapped onto the cardinal points of the recipient's body. Cocoa butter had to be grated for the same purpose, and a handful of cotton, torn from a medical-grade roll and neatly folded. A paper cup of eggshell chalk had to be fetched from a box next to the stairs leading down to the basement along with two candles, if the recipient of the rogation had forgotten to bring his own, or the weather was too inclement to permit a trip to the drugstore. All of the items needed to be arranged to fit on a single white china dinner plate, then covered by another white plate.[44]

Rogations normally occurred in the shrine room, the back porch, or basement, depending on the space available for the ritual. The recipient of a rogation was seated on a small banquette, with closed eyes, bare feet on a fiber mat, and hands resting on her thighs, facing up. The rogation started with the usual invocation of ancestors and orishas called the *moyubá*, and the presentation of the objects collected for it to the recipient's head.[45] The plate was touched to the recipient's crown, nape, the middle of her chest, the insides of her elbows and palms, and the spaces between her big and second toes. The elder performing the ceremony then began administering small doses of each of the ingredients on the plate to these sites. The layering of these items should be read as a narrative progression, rather than as a procession of interchangeable components. The ritual normally began with the most primordial, wet, and raw substance (water from a gourd, then coconut) to those increasingly more complex, refined, dry, and difficult to produce (cocoa butter, then chalk, culminating in two types of cotton: bleached yet uncombed, followed by dyed and woven). This sequence from nature to culture has referred both to precedents in Lucumí mythology and to the process through which human beings become "cured"—in the sense of seasoned—as vessels for the orisha.[46]

The folklorist Michael Atwood Mason argues that rogations have instilled new modes of somatic awareness and behavior in their recipients.[47] I would assert that the same is true for the practitioners charged with preparing them. The exercise of assembling rogations in the kitchen afforded an opportunity for the fundamental homology between heads, coconuts, mouths, and round ceramics to be constructed. For instance, one day an elder named Billal pointed out that the plate someone had planned to use for her own rogation was chipped and therefore could not be "put on her head," because only the ancestors (egún) are supposed to use damaged plates. "You're not an egún yet!" Billal told her with a laugh, thus comparing the ancestors eating food from a plate to her head's consumption of ritual substances.[48] In this way, elders thickened the substance of their juniors' religious knowledge. They also clarified the extent of the convergence between ritual micropractices and macropractices, such as rites of passage, in impromptu teaching sessions:

> Ashabi thought I could help by fixing the rogation. When we finally found a hammer, Billal leaned over the sink with an unlit cigarette dangling out of his mouth, showing me and a young godson of Ashabi's in middle school how to crack open a coconut—*thwack! thwack! thwack! thwack! thwack!* I had been joking with Billal that we could just throw the coconut off the stairs onto the concrete in the back yard and he said gravely that that can't be done, because the coconut—*obi*—is an orisha. This is why we ask permission before we hit it: *"Ago obi?"* He explicitly likened this to posing the question *"Ago ilé?"* before entering a sacred space—for example, going behind the white sheet and curtain of raffia hung from a doorway during an initiation—and waiting for the response: *"Ilé ago!"*
>
> The brave 'tween was keen to open a coconut himself. First he had to pry the meat out of the first one, easier said than done. I thought the problem was the dullness of the blade until Fadesiye stopped at the counter before rushing out the door, put his ironed clothes in my hand, and in no more than five seconds had popped out the section of flesh I'd been worrying for almost half an hour. A goddaughter of his named Bobbi swore that the key is keeping the knife moving around the sides. One of Fadesiye's childhood friends was home from college and he gave another expert coconut-opening demonstration, telling us to strike the eyes and seams as often as possible.
>
> Mostly he taught by doing, and I was impressed how everyone who knows how has control over the coconut even during the impact of the hammer on the shell. One elder tapped at coconuts almost musically, as if playing the vibraphone, asking "Ago obi?" over and over again. When I inquired into her gently percussive method, she told me that the meat will sometimes simply fall out of the coconut if loosened before the shell splits. She hastened to add, "This is how *I* was taught; everyone has their own way of doing it."[49]

Elders trained the uninitiated in bodily comportment so that their gestures would become mnemonics. But in the kitchen, "comprehension of the body" did not always precede "full visual and mental cognizance" of what it was doing.[50] Elders occasionally emphasized "practical mastery of the practical rules" by encouraging an apprentice, under supervision, to demonstrate proper techniques to others. Obligated to assume the role of instructor, the apprentice relived her memory as a lesson for others. Elders placed more emphasis on producing teachers than creating good students; as initiates acquired seniority, they came to realize that teaching others, inside and outside the kitchen, is integral to priesthood. Occasionally, they rendered explicit the principle that forgetting is an index of memory more fundamental to ritual practice than conscious recollection. A compliment that Fadesiye paid to his godchildren exemplified this: "What you have forgotten, [others] don't even know. Pat yourself on the back."[51]

Practitioners always had to consider future applications of the coaching they underwent. Paradoxically, their cultivation of a future-directed memory was one of the most tradition-bound aspects of cooking rituals. Ilé members did not encounter the same ceremonies time and again year after year, merely accumulating discrete fragments of data about them and the orishas—for example, that Yemayá eats watermelon, rather than citrus—as if flipping flash cards to learn multiplication tables. Even in an act as simple as opening a coconut, practitioners synthesized their remembrance of past performances with their experiences of the present as it was happening, and projected their recollections into the future, as elements of a religious *imaginaire* never to be fully actualized.

One innovation was the degree to which Ashabi and Fadesiye offered opportunities for instruction on kitchen work outside the context of immediate ritual practice. The classes, lectures, and meetings held in advance of major rituals brought inexperienced members up to the requisite level of competence. The elders of Ilé Laroye wanted to maintain their reputation as a "teaching house," inspired partly by the model of role-based discipline documented in Bahian Candomblé and partly by scholarship on the aforementioned cabildos. In describing the ilé as a community to others, members cited historical precedents to emphasize its legitimacy as a corporate body. Fadesiye went so far as to say to his assembled godchildren, "We are a cabildo," in reference to the house's stated intention to be a source of mutual aid where ceremonies are held, and to promote "health" and "spiritual or mental evolution."[52] Using the model of the cabildo recalls the strategic claims of Yorùbá origins made by Nagô Candomblé cult centers in the early twentieth century to obtain legal recognition, and distance their temple compounds from stereotypes of witches' covens.[53] By casting the ilé as a modern-day North American cabildo, Fadesiye sought to define it as a site of hard labor, where both the spirits and their servants work.

The precipitous inclination of the learning curve in the kitchen of Ilé Laroye reflected a sense of urgency among elders to educate the upcoming generation of practitioners, teaching the same information but employing a distinct pedagogical approach. Many elders cut their religious teeth in Cuban ilés where the flow of information was obstructed by a combination of ritual secrecy, language barriers, and cultural misunderstandings. As Ashabi recalled, "In my day, you came in and sewed and scrubbed until someone gave you a *tidbit* of information," describing the payments of labor in exchange for knowledge that she routinely disbursed at the beginning of her career in Lucumí. She tacitly contrasted this arrangement with her ilé's attitude toward teaching.[54] Ashabi acknowledged her debt to her lineage by continuing to call items employed in ritual contexts by their Spanish names, a practice adopted by others within the house; for instance, ritual sacrifices—especially as part of an initiation ceremony—were called *matanzas*; dried gourds, *jicaras*; and large plastic and aluminum bowls, *palanganas*. She reminisced about the time spent with her godfather as an invaluable apprenticeship and lesson in obedience, particularly with regard to kitchen work: "If he said, 'Cook [something foul],' we would've said, 'This is the best thing we've ever had in our life!'"[55]

## What's on the Menu

On some ritual occasions, one orisha is presented with multiple dishes. Other ceremonies require food for a number of spirits, such as ocha birthdays and drum rituals. For one such ritual event that took place during my research, pans of dry corn kernels and black-eyed peas were first sautéed in red palm oil. Five eggs were scrambled into a mix of spinach and freshwater shrimp to create *oshinshín* for Ochún. Ogún's stewed black beans were topped with a whole yam roasted in the oven over the course of an afternoon. For Ochosi, onions and flaky grated shrimp were stirred into yellow corn hominy, then garnished with a spiral of coconut. For Yemayá, five boiled eggs were carefully shelled and slipped into a bowl of black bean soup. Obatalá's plate of maize kernels was dotted with plump green kalanchoe leaves. For Shangó, there was *amalá ilá*: cornmeal pudding in a mantle of tomato sauce studded with de-seeded okra pods. When the elder picking the seeds out from the okra remarked that the small pods have larger seeds than the bigger ones, it became apparent that she had undertaken this task many times before.

It is tempting to introduce a shift from the passive voice to an active one, and assign specific agents to these actions, by lingering over the flavors of the foods: the crunchy edges and earthy fragrance of bean fritters, nibbled out of paper napkins translucent with oil; the bright tang and lush slipperiness on the tongue of Shangó's scarlet sauce; the bracing vegetal insipidity and ashy foretaste of Obatalá's hominy; the gritty soapiness of raw, chopped kola nut. The presence of a large Nigerian expatriate community in Chicago meant easy access to historically resonant food products associated with the precolonial and contemporary Yorùbá diet, granting Lucumí practitioners a taste of what they visualized as their lineage ancestors' everyday lives. One stretch along 89th Street and Commercial Avenue on the South Side had changed in recent years from predominantly Mexican to Caribbean to African, and was the source of cassava, yam, and black-eyed pea flours, red palm oil, coconut oil, banana leaves, alligator pepper, kola nuts, and smoked fish, among other ingredients. Ashabi said of the neighborhood, "It doesn't feel like 'here,' but it feels like home."[56]

She once described priests as her "royal tasters," since they ensured that foods for the orishas—kings, queens, and warriors—were unadulterated by taboo substances.[57] But bites of addimú were taken either to check the consistency of a recipe's components or to determine whether a dish could be counted as done. These bites were not savored, as if in a montage from the cinematic adaptation of a magical-realist novel. In Black Atlantic religions, food offerings to the gods in Lucumí come under the rubric of sacrifice (*ebó*). The theological rationale for ebó has been laid out in the following manner:

> Human beings should always live within the bounds of iré [blessings]. Nonetheless, iré is only one power, while osobo [misfortune] is a multi-

plicity of forces: *arún* (sickness), *ikú* (death), *ofo* (loss), *eyó* (tragedy), *iyán* (fight), and so forth. Osobo lives in a constant and unending war with iré, battles that can only be placated with the help of ebó and Elegbá's aid.[58]

According to one taxonomy, ebó falls into five different categories: votive, propitiatory, preventive, substitutive, and fundamental. Votive ebó curry favor and express gratitude; propitiatory ebó placate the orishas after a practitioner has caused offense by committing an unethical act; preventive ebó avert disasters and ensure safety during travel; substitutive ebó foil the plots of human enemies or angry spirits; and fundamental ebó entail feeding the sacred stones that embody the orisha.[59]

The sensory experiences that came to the fore in my research had to do with the production of meals rather than the consumption of them: diced onion fumes suffusing sinuses and flooding the eyes with water; the flabby tackiness of mashed plantains massaged into spheres, sixteen at a time; the dark chocolate and chicory aroma of whole wheat crumbs rolled in molasses. One of the foods often prepared for ritual occasions in Ilé Laroye was the cone-shaped dumpling called *akasá*. Akasá contained white hominy—grits boiled to a custard-stiff consistency—within a banana-leaf pyramid. The banana leaves had to be cut into squares with scissors, then roasted over a gas burner to burn off their moisture and render them flexible. They smelled of freshly mowed lawns and English breakfast tea. Arlene said that these midnight-green envelopes occasionally resembled "mail from the underworld," an unforgettably apt phrase considering the difficulty of keeping the veins from splitting once singed. The hominy had to be scooped into the leaves prickly-hot, before it cooled into an impenetrable block, and members of the ilé with a knack for making akasá were pressed to share their tricks for doing so. Sometimes the need for an open flame required them to be quite creative. When Ashabi's stove was under repair in 2006, the banana leaves were roasted over a candle.

There was one exception to the rule of feeding orishas foods with ingredients and methods evocative of an African past. This was addimú containing sugar. Miguel "Willie" Ramos writes that cakes and pastries for the orishas are "definitely a Cuban phenomenon, especially the addition of sweets and desserts to the *orisha*'s food preferences, a practice that is unknown in Yorubaland. This practice results from the ingenious methods of food preparation encountered and/or developed by enslaved Africans for their survival."[60] Several orishas prefer white sugar in pastries and a handful favor brown; others clamor for cane syrup and molasses; joints of raw sugarcane and cane liquors suffice for a few. Although the gastronomic preferences of the orishas may seem randomly distributed at first glance, their tastes are structured in part according to the discriminatory racial discourse of colonial Cuba, which sought to arrange bodies in a hierarchy according to gender and color—a concept elaborated more thoroughly in "slave societies" such as colonial Cuba than in "societies with slaves," including precolonial West Africa.[61] The degree of sugar's refinement became metonymic of class and race.[62]

Whipping up desserts for the orishas sometimes happened late at night before an ocha birthday celebration. They did not suffer too severely from last-minute preparation, although the preparation of even simple dishes was far from foolproof. Turned out elegantly, they were valued above readymade desserts. But the transmission of cultural information about crafting the sweets was minimal, bearing in mind their replaceability—in an emergency—with store-bought desserts. Conversations while cooking them drifted into personal territory not traversed during the execution of more recondite dishes:

> At about 11:30 p.m. Ashabi started the puddings to be presented to the [new initiates'] orishas tomorrow: rice pudding, with white sugar, condensed milk, cinnamon sticks, and milk for Obatalá; *dulce de coco*, with shredded coconut, butter, brown sugar, and vanilla for Yemayá; corn meal pudding for Shangó, with nutmeg, butter, milk, and raisins that had been marinated in white wine; and flan from a mix for Ochún, "just add milk." When I asked Ashabi about the puddings she said that a lot of people buy a cake for the occasion and leave it at that, but making homemade things was the way she was taught by her godfather. The first pudding for Obatalá was a bust because the metal pot got too hot and scalded the milk for long enough that it tasted burned. Back to the drawing board, this time with a cast iron pot.
>
> For a long time Theo and I just stood and stirred, staring down at the food on the stove. Then he said that when he got initiated, his brother talked down Theo's decision to their mother. They both thought his religion was "backward" because it's "African." When Theo completed his

initiation year and stopped wearing white, his brother told him he had
"come to [his] senses," because he had stopped looking like a priest. His
mother's attitude improved when she saw the "Sacred Arts of Haitian
Vodou" exhibit at the Field Museum, and she even went to one of his
ocha birthdays.[63]

*offering food to dieties is history*

Food feeds memory. Redolent of Thanksgivings and Christmases, the *but also*
cozy aroma of cream mingling with spices may have triggered painful *pedagogy*
feelings of family togetherness, lost as the result of participation in the *of kitchen*
religion. Theo's comments bear witness to the way that stereotypes about *&connect*
Black Atlantic religions have damaged the social relationships of prac- *to history*
titioners, and the ability of positive representations to help in mending
them.


## Food Makes Family

Celebration leads to feasting at drum rituals and other religious functions. After the music ends, host communities spoon out rice with
pigeon peas, fried ripe plantains, collard greens, braised chicken, barbe-
cued beef, cassava with garlic, vinegar, and green onion, and a multitude
of other dishes. They feed all and sundry with generous portions, even if
possessed initiates remain on their feet in the corners of the same rooms
as the cooks. During my research, ceremonies were increasingly catered,
yet the dishes often still came from Cuban, Puerto Rican, and Black family recipes, seasoned to the taste of Chicago's diverse orisha community.
These meals set the stage for those preparing food to hear praise, and for
guests to reminisce about the classic dishes once interpreted by departed
female ancestors.[64] Sitting around a table (or, in the case of new initiates
and children, on the floor) built camaraderie in houses of orisha worship while reinforcing the hierarchy that placed priestly elders above
godchildren. Eating together gave elders the chance to instruct novices
in the observance of taboos prescribed in divination, and correct common errors in food selection or handling.

One should not underestimate the importance of assimilating the
aché from fruit present at drum rituals and ocha birthdays. Practitioners
arrange dozens of bananas, oranges, apples, pears, grapes, pineapples,
mangos, watermelon, and other fruit in plazas before such ceremonies

commence. Consecrated through the orishas' acceptance, the fruit is handed out from the altar as the events come to a close, "often in the same shopping plastic or brown paper bag used to purchase the fruit in the first place," and eaten at home as an "exponential spreading of the *oricha*'s blessing."[65] According to the ritual discourse of Lucumí, this fruit becomes an extension of the orisha's body, and consuming it acts to redistribute the aché coursing through it; practitioners "depict access to power as ingestion/incorporation rather than occupying a position or territory, or imposing order. Once ingested, as it were, power is internalized; it becomes [analogous to] a person's weight, a property rather than a function."[66]

In Ilé Laroye, the best examples of culinary abundance and blessing through plentiful food may have been the lavish parties thrown in Ochún's honor. For instance, in January 2006, the divination performed for the ilé established that the new year would be ruled by her, and advised those with special obligations to Ochún to fulfill them. That July, a devotee of the orishas Obatalá and Ochún gave her a celebration that aspired to redefine the notion of luxury. A classically trained harpist and a violinist played throughout the afternoon in front of an exquisite gold and yellow altar. In addition to the melted chocolate and sparkling cider flowing from two mechanized fountains, guests—instructed to don their most elegant finery—could enjoy salmon croquettes with black bean and mango salsa; smoked salmon wheels with caviar and crème fraîche; salmon fumé on garlic toasts with cucumber slices; crispy chicken wings; semisweet and white chocolate truffles; petits fours; and mini-cheesecakes, to mention only a few of the rich foods to be sampled. There was nearly enough food for Ochún—or anyone present that day—to forget that she had ever gone hungry.

Many times at the ilé, I heard some version of Ashabi's statement, "[Lucumí] is not a religion of the rich, although you almost have to be rich to practice it."[67] Most members of Ilé Laroye were not wealthy. Among ilé members, a disproportionately high number were teachers, entrepreneurs, artists, and adult education students paying their way through school with day jobs in retail or business management. When practitioners prayed to the ancestors "never to see a hungry day," the appeal was sincere. During one interview, I asked an elder to place herself in an economic bracket: working-class, middle-class, et cetera. "Poor!"

was the response. Another elder confided that when her children were growing up, she would announce a special "egg drop soup night" to entice them to the dinner table, and while chopping celery and carrots, try to convince them that they were about to have a Chinese delicacy. The truth was that eggs and sachets of chicken noodle soup were all she could afford.

In her Lucumí myths and praise-songs, a picture emerges of Ochún as a multifaceted figure with several "roads" or manifestations, both moneyed and penniless.[68] She is renowned for transforming the sweet food offered to her into material blessings.[69] In 2008 a drum ceremony was held to commemorate Ashabi's twenty-first year of initiation, and Ochún possessed a visiting priest. She was escorted away to be dressed in a shimmering blouse and rejoined the gathering with a dancing gait while balancing a plate of honey on her head. Ochún then commandeered the large sheet cake from beneath Elegguá's altar, covered in white buttercream with red and black piped lettering. She smeared handfuls of the cake over Ashabi's face, hair, and upper body, wiping her frosting-covered fingers on the face of her first godson, Theo, and another honored guest. Ochún deployed the cake as media for aché, in the same manner that orishas use the sweat they have wiped from their faces to coat the foreheads, eyelids, cheeks, and chins of their children. For the rest of the evening, Ochún sported a frosting-encrusted ribbon from her cap as if it were a renegade tendril from a baroque coiffure.

The theme of food as media for cleansing, and its relationship to the body, may be further illuminated with reference to the figure of Babalú Ayé. Although communicable diseases and leg ailments are the specialties of this orisha, he is hailed as the orisha of all illness, and closely associated with those brought low after hitting the trifecta of infirmity, poverty, and old age.[70] During one drum ceremony held in a ballroom on Chicago's North Side in 2004, Babalú Ayé seized one of his mounts, a stooped, grandfatherly man whose near-acrobatic dancing—once possessed—belied his advanced age.[71] After a while, he motioned for a small group of guests to huddle under a white sheet, and directed an initiate possessed by Obatalá to dance with a dove. He stopped dancing with it only to cleanse two small boys with the bird, passing its white feathers, as if a bundle of living cloth, over the surface of the children's bodies. A priest later told me that the people under the improvised tent had been cleansed, and that Babalú Ayé had motioned for everyone else to cover their heads to protect them from the misfortunes he had released. The same priest did not comment on another more stunning act of Babalú Ayé's: after the cleansing was complete, he swept his gaze around the room in a gesture kabuki-like in its intensity, and started in on the bird.

This act could be said to dramatize what Babalú Ayé was thought to do in the yearly *agban*, or cleansing ceremony, that Ashabi held for him in the basement of her home.[72] Members of the ilé donated plantain chips, grains, beans, rice, candy, cornmeal, fruit, and meat, among other foods, to be placed on twenty-one plates. Since pustules and lesions have been depicted as dotting Babalú Ayé's flesh, the foods in the ritual bore both a metaphorical and metonymic resemblance to him.[73] On the night of the agban, the foods were arranged in a circle around a basket lined with purple fabric and burlap.[74] Participants draped their shoulders with *cundiamor*, the vine of the bitter melon plant, one of the fragrant herbs belonging to Babalú Ayé.[75] They moved counter-clockwise around the room scooping up fistfuls of the items on the plates, passing them over their bodies, and tossing them into the basket. Elders then brushed down participants' bodies with Babalú's favorite birds and the decorated broom (*ja*) sacred to him, before briefly rubbing their eyelids with a pair of eggs.[76]

"Everything goes," elders said, because nothing was reserved from the ritual. Afterward, a priest deposited the basket's contents in a spot chosen by Babalú Ayé through divination, usually a forested area. No one was allowed to leave the house until the priest returned. In the agban, Babalú Ayé symbolically destroyed illness and affliction by fearlessly devouring it—as the possessed initiate had at the drum ritual—thus integrating it into himself, the mythological source of the very ailments that practitioners sought to eradicate. They did not expect to be healthy for the rest of their lives, but instead to be freed from chronic complaints and apprised of latent conditions. For example, after one agban, an elder credited the detection and swift treatment of her appendicitis to her participation in it. The agban was a communal ebó of the sort performed in Ilé Laroye routinely on a smaller scale, on behalf of individual practitioners, entailing the application of cleansing substances (often foods specified in oracular speech) to the body and the subsequent disposal of them.

Participants' perceptions of the agban reflected the logic of gift exchange operative in other ebó: "I give you so that you may give me in return."[77]

The importance of food and eating in Lucumí may be impressed upon practitioners most strongly in initiation and the first year of ordination, called *iyaworaje*. A classic rite of passage with sharply demarcated periods of separation, liminality, and reaggregation, initiation involves a temporary loss of control over the most basic aspects of one's existence. To facilitate their entry into a liminal state, elders observe a tradition of "snapping on the *iyawos*," or new priests, that involves a measured nonresponsiveness to their immediate desires when their godparents place them in initiatory seclusion. The customarily affectionate and "earth mother"-ly Ashabi has said that she metaphorically sits "watching T.V. and eating bonbons" during iyawos' stay in her home in order to heighten their awareness that the ritual process "ain't about them," but about their lifetime of duty to the orishas.[78] The image of a godmother savoring bites of imported chocolate while her iyawo presumably goes hungry—having no say in what, when, how much, or whether she eats—is one that exemplifies the prerogatives of seniority within the tradition.

It is no coincidence that the disciplining of iyawos into docility—particularly during the most solemn stages of the initiation ceremony—entails the mandatory consumption of unaccustomed substances. The transition into priesthood depends largely upon iyawos' ability to literally and figuratively "suck it up." Iyawos are bidden to eat portions of the same animals sacrificed to the orishas in order to incorporate their aché. After the meat has been cooked, iyawos must swallow at least one bite from each plate that has been prepared. As Ashabi said to future priests, "[In initiation], you're going to eat everything about the animal but the sound it makes."[79] Calumny and reprimand await those who would turn up their noses at unfamiliar dishes. While elders may refuse to eat the farm-raised—as opposed to factory-farmed—meat in the stews and Yorùbá-style fricassees prepared after an initiation, iyawos' absorption of aché through meat is a crucial part of the ritual, without which it cannot be considered efficacious. Because the cooks in the kitchen work to make their food as appetizing as possible, the refusal to eat can seem childish. It can also signal that, clinging to the prerogatives of autonomous adulthood, the iyawos are not yet childish enough.

Food taboos, or *ewos*, are often among the lifelong strictures imposed in the lengthy divination session, called *itá*, that occurs two days after the major sacrificial ritual of ordination. The priests participating in an itá instruct the novice on what she can eat and drink (sometimes forbidding different colors and types of foods and beverages), where she can live (in the city, country, inland, near to or far from the ocean), and what she can wear (most often ruling out red and yellow clothes, although hair dye, particular shapes of jewelry, and clothes with holes, fringe, and patterns such as stripes or calico may be banned too). The itá sets limits to what an iyawo can do and where she can go; among the proscribed activities may be entering any large body of water, visiting a nightclub, and keeping certain pets. What is verboten for some may be decreed for others. The results of the divination are inscribed in a notebook, sometimes adorned with lace and ribbons. While myriad initiates may share the same divinatory sign that the iyawo is proclaimed to have, every itá is singular, more so than a snowflake or fingerprint, both of which have been known to recur in nature.

In the itá, it is not uncommon for the consumption of particular fruits, vegetables, legumes, meats, or the flesh of certain sexes of animals to be forbidden, or conversely, compelled. Forbidden foods may be the practitioner's favorites. The ethnomusicologist Katherine J. Hagedorn was told in a cautionary tale about a disobedient practitioner, "His santo [orisha] say he not supposed to eat red beans. But that guy he like red beans, so he eat them. And then all sudden red beans come out his eyes, his ears, his mouth, his nose. And he get sick! Real sick! The *santo* is a mischierf [*sic*], big big mischierf."[80] Hagedorn glosses, "The santo as 'big mischierf'—mystery and mischief combined—points to the awesome, arbitrary power of the divine: pure aché, the theological crux in Santería that is the power to make things—anything—happen."[81] At her itá, most of what Ashabi calls her "cultural foods" became taboo. Since her father's side of the family hails from Louisiana, almost every Wednesday when growing up, she would eat red beans and rice. At her itá, red beans were "taken away," followed by cornmeal. Sensing Ashabi's distress, another elder requested a clarification from the officiating diviner, and he determined that only white cornmeal was disallowed. Ashabi was elated not only because she would still be able to eat muffins, spoonbread, and other popular dishes, but also because yellow cornmeal appears in preparations for countless foods. Removing it from her diet altogether would have altered her eating habits beyond recognition.

This is what happened to Alaafi. Alaafi was in his early twenties at the time of his initiation as one of Ashabi's godchildren. He was born with his umbilical cord wrapped around his throat, so for many years his mother, Arlene, believed him to be a son of Obatalá, the divine patron of children born with birth defects or in unusual circumstances. Arlene said she sometimes regrets giving him a name with royal Yorùbá connotations because it may have affected the way Alaafi carried himself, with a sense of entitlement at odds with the humility she had hoped to instill in him. Alaafi possessed considerable charms, and when he wanted to seem too "hard" to smile, he would deepen the one comma-shaped dimple in his face while trying to immobilize his lips, usually without success. He had a mermaid tattooed on one arm and the name of his son inked in cursive on his neck. When Alaafi found out that he was a son of Ochún, he was not best pleased: "Every man wants to be the son of Shangó." He was among the men who did not want to wear jingling bracelets around their wrists for at least a year after they made ocha, or prostrate before elders with one hand on the hip and another under the chin, to signal patronage by a female orisha. Ochún claimed Alaafi as her own when he was ignorant of her manifestations.

Alaafi would say, "Ochún humbled me," meaning that his patron deity had shown him the need for self-discipline and compliance with divinatory mandates. Alaafi's itá brought a series of surprises. He was to stay in initiatory seclusion at Ashabi's house for almost a month, not just for seven days. He was never again to eat sugar or any yellow foods; he should avoid red meat and all food not made with his own hands; and he should never be outside his home after nightfall, unless necessary for his job. His inability to come and go as he pleased was a burden, as was the sense that he had to beg permission from his elders "for everything." Yet after initiation, Alaafi professed to experience severe stomachaches and cramps if he ate sugar, and construed the need to fix his own meals in terms of what he perceived to be his vulnerability to parasites, bearing in mind the lax sanitary conditions of many restaurants. By the end of his iyawo year, Alaafi had earned himself the titles of "Iyawo Police" and "Eternal Iyawo," due to his vigilance over the minutiae of religious protocol. He was fiercely attuned to others' unhealthy dietary habits, not hesitating to pronounce sugar "poison." He hardly balked when for his birthday, he got one cookie instead of a cake.

In contrast to the dietary prohibitions outlined in the Torah, those of Lucumí do not set practitioners apart as a group with firm boundaries.[82] Proscribed foods are not associated with any religion against which Lucumí defines itself. In fact, taboos reinforce practitioners' individuality and repudiate the notion that every substance or situation affects people in the same manner. On the other hand, observing taboos and consuming food in ritual contexts makes for kinship between initiates. Practitioners tend to hold conventional ideas concerning genetic parentage, but they also adopt tradition-specific understandings of consanguinity—blood relation—through the consumption of shared substance. The classical anthropological definition of kinship has privileged reproduction as a sexual and biological universal, positing that social groups invest this purportedly ineluctable fact of nature with meaning through representation. The assumption that kinship has irreducibly to do with procreation has adversely influenced accounts of Lucumí to the extent that the ritual paternity of godmothers and godfathers has been viewed solely in terms of their quasi-reproductive role "giving birth" to the orishas of their protégés. This perspective has failed to link godparents' actual material nurturance of their godchildren to kinship through eating together, or commensality.

The obligation to ingest food in rites of passage acts as a social leveler and acts to introduce novices not yet fully bereft of their identities into the disorienting liminal stage of their initiations. A remark of Ashabi's may illustrate the extent to which priests construct obedience, ritual efficacy, and absorption of the orishas' energy in terms of diet. Once, after an iyawo repeatedly grumbled at a series of ritual foods, Ashabi pointed out that if a godparent told him to eat "a pork sandwich with a crayon in it" because it had aché, he would have no choice but to comply.[83] Melding the inedible with the unappetizing, Ashabi's formulation was especially striking because several African American religious formations—like the Nation of Islam and the Black Hebrew Israelites—condemn the pig as an unclean animal and pork as "slave food."[84] It was not uncommon for Black members of orisha communities in Chicago to have a personal policy of "no pork on the fork" for a combination of religious and ideological reasons, as I learned when handing out plates of food after ceremonies. Ashabi conjured the nightmare of a crayon-packed pork sandwich to warn that refusing food jeopardizes incorporation into the Lucumí tradition.

The implications of this statement go beyond the time-honored observation that affective bonds are strengthened by eating together and alike. The orishas are seen as practitioners' parents, with the phrase *omo orisha*, or "child of the orishas," serving as a synonym for initiate. It has not been uncommon, when inquiring about the orishas to whom priests are initiated, to hear the words "mom" or "daddy" uttered to describe them. This idiom indicates an everyday intimacy with those entities that live in the bosom of initiates' homes and supply them with positive role models in the absence of supportive, accepting human parents, whose bitter rejection can be felt in the most unexpected moments. In consuming the aché from the deities' favorite animals, iyawos become the kin of the orishas themselves, as well as other members of their religious lineages. It is to practitioners' own cooking that the next chapter turns.

PART II

Kitchen Work

# 3

## Engendering Knowledge

Taking my arm, she went round introducing me. "This is my new godson. . . ." There must have been fifteen people crowded into that little kitchen. At a table in the corner two young women in white blouses and turbans were carefully cutting the centers out of a heap of black-eyed peas. Some men in loose-fitting white suits were gathered about the icebox drinking beer. Out on the glassed-in back porch, an immense and very black woman with red head-cloth and suggestion of goatee was vigorously leading a team of chicken pluckers.[1]

Ritual sacrifices and their consumption have preoccupied scholars since the history of religions first emerged as a discipline in the nineteenth century. Despite the importance of religious cooking, it has not inspired the same degree of analysis once lavished on "the cooked" as a conceptual category, or on rituals controlled by men and characterized by violence. Ceremonial labor in the kitchen has remained in the shadows, although it goes on longer than most sacrificial rites, and often requires expertise in drawing distinctions between sacred and profane that cannot be obtained except through firsthand experience. The reason for this is threefold. First, domestic space within the private sphere of the home has only recently been flagged as fertile ground for the exploration of religious imaginaries. In addition, the naturalized, cross-cultural relationship of women to domesticity has hindered consideration of cooking techniques as generative of religious subjectivity.[2] It has been assumed that women are cosmologically subordinate if they fulfill roles customarily assigned to them, and that by performing "unskilled" labor such as kitchen work, they perpetuate what has been determined in advance to be their subordination.

Food preparation has garnered only passing mention in comprehensive published accounts of Black Atlantic religions.[3] The reluctance to discuss it—above all in Afro-Diasporic sacrificial contexts—can also be traced to the identification of cooking by people of African descent with violence, sorcery, and magic. This has been the inverse of its association with maternal submission within the household, closely linked in the Americas with Black mammy figures ("an immense and very black woman"). Think of the countless cartoons with bloodthirsty "savages" stewing pith-helmeted explorers over bubbling cauldrons, witch doctors mixing up potions in steaming pots, and slaves dropping poison into their masters' dinners. These caricatures have their origins in travelers' diaries and literary fiction from the colonial era that strove to titillate readers while promoting European imperialism as a civilizing mission. Projected onto Black populations, fantasies of Caribbean cannibalism fed off the bodies captured, bound, and "gobbled up" by the transatlantic slave trade and colonization of Africa.[4] The comic-strip cauldron is the exact duplicate of the enormous wood-fired vats used to refine sugar on plantations, engravings of which circulated in Europe as early as the sixteenth century.[5]

Since Black Atlantic religions still summon such stereotypes, particularly in pop culture, to speak at length about sacrificial food preparation within one of them is bound to touch a nerve. Were the historical vilification of these traditions not egregious enough, the language of culinary endeavor conspires to equate cooking with aggression:

> Look at this list of verbs associated with the preparation of food: pound, beat, strip, whip, boil, sear, grind, tear, crack, mince, mash, crush, stuff, chop. Images of torture occur: *sauter* is to make jump in the pan by applying heat, there is skinning and peeling and bleeding and hanging and binding, not to mention skewering and spitting, topping and tailing. . . . The process of turning raw materials into stuff fit to eat is a series of bloody battles and underhand tricks.[6]

In nevertheless seeking to dwell on what transpires in the kitchen, I am mindful of the respect due to my interlocutors, and the inability of racked nerves to say whether it has been given.

## In the Thick of Cooking

Never in a million years would I have thought—hear me?—
that I would be cooking some chicken heads, tails, gizzards,
chicken feet. . . . I would've said you was lying.
—Diahann Meyers[7]

Several Black Atlantic religions developed terminology to designate the
people in charge of cooking sacrificial remains. In Lucumí, the word
used (along with the Spanish *cocinera*) is *alashé*; in the Afro-Cuban
tradition of Abakuá, the cook has occupied the office of *nkandembo*.[8]
Vodou temples have had *hounsi cuisinière*.[9] Candomblé communities
have been known to keep a kitchen manager called *iya bassê, iabassé,* or
*ayabasè*.[10] Those responsible for the food at ritual events may be hired
for the purpose, or be existing members of a house of worship. In both
cases, they are obliged to obey sartorial and other taboos, sometimes
concerning menstruation or sexual activity, and meet high standards
of cleanliness, hygiene, and conduct. They should be "cool," meaning
they can be trusted not to bring the polluted "heat" of the street—where
violence, accidents, and disease run rampant—into the midst of ritual
practice.[11] Cooks may press members of religious families into service
to dress animals and butcher meat.

Throughout the course of my research, the main alashé in Ilé Laroye
was Arlene Stevens, Ashabi and Fadesiye's godchild. It was under her
direction that, after the ritual slaughter of fowl and four-legged animals,
their blood, organs, and extremities were classified as *iñalés*, meaning
"food for the gods." In Latino/a houses of orisha worship, iñalés are often
called *ashéses*; in Ilé Laroye, they were referred to collectively as *ashés*
(plural), no doubt because they were viewed as aché in a particularly potent form.[12] Blood sacrifice, called *ebó eyé* or *ebó woni*, has been understood to transfer the primordial energy called *aché* (singular) from the
blood of animals to the orishas' implements and other sacra.[13] As Theo
once said of the orishas' paraphernalia, "It's blood that brings them to
life."[14] Aché is thought to emanate from speech and saliva, thus further
accounting for the perceived efficacy of ceremonial incantation. As we
have already seen, aché may be immanent in or imparted to objects—
for instance, money—in the mediation of exchanges between human

practitioners and the spirits. By eating portions of the animals sacrificed on their behalf, the subjects of rituals are believed to incorporate their aché, while aché spreads to other practitioners through the preparation and consumption of food from the same animals.

During major rituals such as *matanzas*, the slaughter performed as part of an initiation, at least five goats and almost three dozen fowl were usually sacrificed. The animals were put down rapidly, with consecrated instruments, so as to minimize their suffering. After sacrifice, the rams and goats were put aside to be flayed and disemboweled in the basement, while the larger pieces of the carcasses were disarticulated in the kitchen. Elders labeled each four-legged animal according to the orisha to whom, and the initiate for whom, it was offered.[15] Birds were placed in plastic or aluminum tubs, and separated according to the orisha and practitioner on whose behalf they met their ends. The roosters, pigeons, and so forth of Elegguá would thus be placed in one tub, labeled perhaps "Elegguá Eshubi," meaning the "[birds for the] Elegguá that belongs to Eshubi [ritual name of an Ilé elder]."[16] A portion of the blood shed for each orisha was collected in its own dried gourd, then marked— preferably with a laminated tag—and later added to the ashés when they were to be roasted. Although the sacrificial animals for different orishas could come into contact with one another, they were not to be confused or commingled; for example, at no cost could the guinea hen sacrificed for Oyá be mixed up with the one for Ochún.

Ashés had to be set apart from both meat and offal. The physical exertion of preparing them to be cooked according to Arlene's rigorous standards rivaled the mental labor required to remain cognizant of their identity throughout the cooking process. The bodies of birds were dipped in boiling water to loosen their feathers, and their feet were briefly scalded so that the epidermal scales, footpad, and skin could be more easily peeled away and the outer nail detached.[17] For plucking, initiates and non-initiates alike usually sat on white benches less than six inches from the ground, and each person had access to a bowl into which feathers, down, and other waste matter could fall. Shoulders tended to roll forward, spines to hunch, and legs to splay, necessitating periodic stretching and adjustments in posture. Those removing the ashés from both goats and birds either stood at the kitchen counter or bent over improvised tables that sometimes were no more than wooden boards laid across two benches. Although knives were sharpened prior to and throughout the duration of the sacrifices, they quickly grew dull. The added pressure necessary to make incisions—to say nothing of chopping goats' ribcages into ribs, or bisecting the spinal columns of guinea hens—led to sore digits, palms, wrists, and shoulders. During the course of a night, someone helping in the kitchen or in any space designated as the proper area could expect to clean eight to ten birds of diverse types, depending on experience, speed, and tolerance for the visual, auditory, olfactory, and tactile sensations that presented themselves in the course of this endeavor.

Arlene and other elders advocated a single method for dissecting poultry that begins with placing the bird belly-up on a cutting board and carving beneath the ribcage from wing to wing, driving the tip of a blade deep enough to create a cavity but not so far in that any organs may be slashed. After the top and bottom ends of the bird are tugged apart, entrails are pulled gently from the esophagus downwards so that the gallbladder, attached to the liver, does not burst, corrupting the other organs with bile.[18] The heart is detached from what appears to be a wet ribbon holding it aloft; spongy lungs, nudged up and scraped out from the ribcage; intestines and stomach, discarded; gizzard, slit up the side, pried open, then emptied of its sandy, fibrous contents, in order to reveal its lining's otherworldly opalescence.[19] Sometimes there are eggs or testes, and these are set aside, along with the kidneys and pygostyle, referred to in the ilé as the "butt" although it does not include the anus. Located at the end of the butt, the papilla of a bird's uropygial or preen gland is sliced off and discarded. The wing-tip is severed by cutting just above the spur of bone called the alula, visible on the wing as a tiny ridge, and reserved for roasting, along with the feet, after the sharp point at the end of the wing has been clipped off. Roosters' coxcombs and wattles are excised and thrown away.[20]

Ashés were rinsed by someone willing to grip them firmly as they danced under the tap, threatening to escape down the drain in a torrent of waste. Once washed, ashés were heated on medium-high in cast iron pans on the stove or outdoor barbecue grill.[21] Finished ashés differed conspicuously from food made in the ilé for human consumption and from offerings to the orishas made from nonsacrificial meat, since the latter are customarily of Yorùbá provenance and rich with flavorful combinations of legumes, vegetables, and grains.[22] Ashés' roasting could not be rushed, because if heated at too high a temperature, they would smolder and burn on the outside while staying raw on the inside.[23] Some ashés could be combined, such as those of the Warriors, or of the god Shangó and his mother, Yemayá, but most often they were separated, and the oils and other substances used to roast them remained completely distinct. In Lucumí mythology and ritual practice, geographical locations are homologous with dietary codes: the robust, emotionally "hot" Warriors who reside in the forest and at the margins of polite society have their ashés cooked with red palm oil. It is thought to be warmer and less refined—literally and figuratively—than oils belonging to the chromatic category of "white" and employed for cooler orishas.[24]

To prevent contact between the ashés of hierarchically, spatially, and temperamentally divergent orishas, cooks either used spoons color-coded with electrical tape or positioned utensils so as to indicate the pots in which they belonged. The round-bottomed dried gourds were in constant danger of not only being confused but of tipping over and spilling, so those working at the kitchen counter had to exercise composure and an extraordinary economy of movement. It helped to possess "presence of mind"—that special blend of equanimity and alertness to the potential need for swift action—especially after midnight, when it would be toughest to preserve.[25] Members of the ilé scrubbed pots and utensils between uses to minimize the possibility of any transfer of food particles, as if maintaining the illusion that each orisha had a personal set of vessels.[26] Elders demanded scrupulous care in the preparation of ashés, and they seemed to serve as the material embodiment of the ilé's observance of tradition; once cooked, they were not presented to the orishas ceremonially until the initiates in Ashabi's house had all touched the edges of the vessels that held them and approved the contents by kissing their fingertips.[27]

## They Are How They Eat

Culinary styles spring from and express social relations. The previous description of the ashé-roasting process reveals the three roles played by the orishas that are most salient in Lucumí: they are simultaneously parents, strangers, and monarchs. While the exotic and regal aspects of the orishas are most dramatically displayed in events that require the construction of thrones, they are marked as noble foreigners on a more regular basis by the foods that they are offered.[28] Ashabi herself has made this point when prompted to speculate on the origins of ashés, citing her trip to Nigeria in the early 1990s. As a guest, she was often served what at first she regarded as offal. She soon learned that her Yorùbá hosts saw the internal organs as the choice bits and more appropriate than flesh for esteemed strangers and royalty. The supremacy of the "choice bits" is homologous with that of monarchs, divinely descended and central to the operation of sociopolitical units. The choice bits taken for ashés are perceived to be senior to the rest of the body by virtue of their indispensability and temporal primacy. A bird may survive a flesh wound, but cannot live for long without its head, wings, feet, or vital organs; these also appear in an embryo prior to the development of its musculature and epidermis.

*[margin handwritten: vital organs served to important people b/c organs are important to the animal's life]*

Although it may be suspect to suggest a causal relationship between indigenous Yorùbá dietary regimes and Lucumí ones, practitioners themselves view it as self-evident, in light of the understanding that food represents the character of its consumer. Orishas dine at the first two vertices of what the anthropologist Claude Lévi-Strauss called the "culinary triangle" of raw, cooked, and rotten.[29] They are first fed ceremonially by the blood of the animals sacrificed for them, and later feast on their bodies, converted by arduous human labor into containers of the orishas' divine power. While not directing this semiotic process, those removing, cleaning, and roasting ashés in the kitchen submit themselves to it. As the anthropologist Dimitri Tsintjilonis writes of sacrifice among the Sa'dan Toraga of Indonesia,

> By utilizing different kinds and cuts of meat, a set of sacrificial offerings is both a sign and material instantiation of the way in which particular bodies are arranged and constituted. . . . Thus, recasting the body in the flesh of animals, the various sacrificial offerings represent signs taking hold of the body in a despotic fashion.[30]

*[margin handwritten: implies that women cooking for ritual are temp. possessed in their devotion & submission to food prep.]*

The "despotic fashion" in which Lucumí sacrificial bodies are reduced to their rudiments and redefined as vessels parallels the commandeering of human bodies by the spirits in possession.[31] In both cases, bodies are left unconscious (permanently in sacrifice, temporarily in possession) and apprehended by religious communities as repositories for the spirits.[32]

Cooked ashés show not only what the orishas are thought to prefer, but what they are believed to be able to do: turn anything into a container of aché by transforming it in both internal substance and outward appearance. The orishas all lay claim to the same body parts of their favorite animals—the vital organs and extremities—and leave the undifferentiated flesh for human consumption. Contrary to such classics as the anthropologist Godfrey Lienhardt's study of Dinka cattle sacrifice, in Lucumí, the division of the sacrificial body does not show "the ordered social relationships of the sacrificing group" according to distinctions of age and sex.[33] Although meat prepared for initiates is apportioned by seniority when served out, with the eldest in order of ordination eating first, what is "'put together' in each beast" is the relation of orishas to human subjects. Whether the orishas are viewed as foreigners, royalty, or family, a hierarchical relationship with practitioners obtains, one encoded in the prioritization of ashés over meat. As in the case of ancient Athenian sacrifice, what is intended for the gods' consumption is prepared and presented first. To reverse this sequence would be to contest the order that places divine needs above and before the human.[34]

One explanation for roasting ashés never far from elders' minds was that scorching burns off stray feathers, hair, and any waste matter, should someone become possessed and be moved to gorge on them. Ashabi credits her godfather with raising this possibility when she was a newcomer to his community; to give her instructions greater force, Arlene once used herself as an example, and stated that if she got mounted by an orisha, she didn't want to find feathers between her teeth later.[35] The idea that orishas might assume human form and taste their ashés informed every step of the animal cleaning and cooking process. No one wanted to be responsible for an orisha's disgust or initiate's post-possession bout of botulism, but ensuring that neither came to pass took some effort.[36] For instance, as noted earlier, the heads of chickens and roosters were also dressed, with difficulty, before roasting, and one could spend an untold amount of time pinching off the sheer feathers called "coverts" that tuft over the ear canal, and those that sprout in wispy fuzz under the jaw. Time stood still; tips of the fingers grew numb and palms began to seize; the birds' eyes—now open, now closed—appeared to wink in mockery of one's frustration. It would be tough to justify such meticulous attention to detail without feeling that the alashé inspecting the heads represents the orishas and thus has the ability to anticipate correctly their desires.

When elders connected the dirt and drudgery of kitchen labor with possession, their protocols became more soberly weighted with religious significance.[37] In possession, initiates become embodied altars, through whose eyes the gods peer out into the world. Elders' reminders that the ashés were destined for the orishas' mouths, and thus must be at least as sanitary as the food one would present to a person, underscored the fact that their aesthetic imperatives—to turn out ashés that conform to certain criteria visually and texturally—were ethical ones. Correctly prepared ashés were "right" and "good" rather than merely "beautiful," for values materialize in aesthetic forms.[38] Cooking ashés is an art, according to the anthropologist Alfred Gell's definition of the term: "a system of action, intended to change the world rather than encode symbolic propositions about it."[39] An analogy could be drawn between cooking ashés and executing the movements specific to each orisha in dance; both involve producing a subjective state in a creative process governed by religious principles. As Deren explained, "It is not only the attitude of reverent dedication, characteristic of all ritual action, which distinguishes ritual dance from secular dance; for just as the ritual does not symbolize a principle but is an exemplary demonstration of that principle in action, so the actual dance is itself principled."[40] Elders enforced "the attitude of reverent dedication" in cooking among their juniors, most often by stressing that too much conversation slows down the process.[41] This was as much a pedagogical concern as a pragmatic one, because the principled composition of ashés must be taught through studied practice.

## Teaching Cooking

[The Lucumí religion] revolves around cooking.
—Alfons Szycman[42]

It was with some hesitation that I elevated the quotation above to the status of an epigraph; this statement was only a single expression of the same sentiment verbalized, at one time or another, by all of my initiated informants. Yet the common spatial metaphor of revolution fits with my experience of the kitchen as exerting a centripetal force that draws religious personnel to it in an orbit shaped by the exigencies of a given ritual. Although for reasons to be addressed in short order, not everyone in Ilé Laroye cooks, its survival has depended on *someone* cooking. Without ashés there are no orishas, at least in a form that renders their aché accessible to a religious community for its reproduction as an institution. Practitioners of other Black Atlantic religions have voiced similar sentiments; Mãe Stella de Azevedo writes, "Without a doubt, in Candomblé everything starts in the kitchen and nothing can be compared to the energy that emanates from the offerings to the orixás. . . . The kitchen, therefore, is the great sacred laboratory where know-how, faith, respect and physical beauty meet each other for the enchantment of the divinities."[43]

The space of the kitchen in Lucumí has furnished a site for the acquisition of technical proficiency and dispositions indispensable for the continued practice of the religion, in a manner that may be adjudicated by elders to conform to historical precedent.[44] Since records concerning the removal and roasting of ashés are partial at best, it is impossible to state with certainty that "kitchenspaces" have consistently met these needs.[45] Domestic butchery was more common in the nineteenth and early twentieth centuries, yet the crystallization of Lucumí in urban Havana probably meant that some instruction—as attested by the presence of anatomical charts in the few initiates' handwritten manuals, or *libretas*, published to date—was always necessary. Practitioners have had to learn the preferred style of cleaning and cooking sacrificial victims, as well as what parts, types, and numbers of animals pertain to each orisha.[46]

In Ilé Laroye, the challenge delivered to the uninitiated and the inexperienced, "Sit down and train on proper protocol," dovetailed with the one issued to priests: "Step up and teach."[47] Lucumí initiates are not only responsible for the care of their own orishas and other ritual objects after ordination; they are frequently called, in their post-initiatory itá, to accede to the future tutelage of godchildren, or at least act as ritual sponsors. For many elders, religious obligations have included showing their juniors how to deal competently with the end products of sacrifice, educating them in butchering technique, anatomy, and morphology, as well as viscera and tissue differentiation. Since none of the elders in Ilé Laroye earned a living as a ritual specialist or butcher—among the elders I knew best were a dry cleaner, a real estate agent, and a massage therapist—the expertise they wielded had been accumulated slowly over the course of years, in Ashabi's kitchen and others. Their labor converted the kitchen into a classroom for minute instruction in the exceedingly complicated taxonomic enterprise of what might be termed Lucumí butchery, and a site for the elaboration of a dynamic and largely unanalyzed religious pedagogy. It is a pedagogy rooted in bondage, for to be an initiate is—in the religious ideology of Lucumí—to be the property of the orishas, envisioned as masters, as well as strangers, monarchs, and parents.[48]

This training was seen to require surveillance by elders, since the "signifying action" of ritual always contains the possibility of "signifyin'" in the African American vernacular definition of the term: critique and subversion.[49] An error made often enough becomes its own ritual, one that may pose a challenge to the act it parodies in failing properly to replicate.[50] Elders' pedagogy, then, moved to ensure that traditions would be maintained by their accurate repetition and any improvisations could be accepted as upholding precedent. Elders wanted the enactment of variation in the kitchen to yield a species of uniformity and corrected actions seen to deviate from the norm. As Mason has cogently argued, the acquisition of bodily habits has been central to the production of Lucumí religious subjectivity; for instance, upon greeting elders, an initiate must salute them according to the gender of the orisha that rules her head, with the child of a male orisha lying straight down on her stomach with her arms to her sides, and the child of a female orisha lying down face-forward with bent legs then quickly shifting her weight from one hip to the other.[51] Cooking has been monitored no less exactingly.

Newcomers acquired the ability to take out and cook ashés both at a conscious discursive level and through the education of the "corporeal sensorium," without which the learning process is over before it begins.[52] Ilé Laroye's physical drills included having the uninitiated mirror the actions of elders in the kitchen as they completed jobs that, in the context of instruction, became examples of how to do those jobs according to senior priests' religious ethos. Training involved the sensuous internalization of the elders' sensibilities through acts of what the anthropologist Rane Willerslev has called "mimetic empathy," a type of cognitive and embodied projection that, beyond "imply[ing] simply representation or imagination, . . . has a decisively corporeal, physical, and tangible quality from which the former ultimately emerges and from which it derives its 'material.'"[53] Practitioners had to apprehend—in the sense of both capture and understand—the sensorimotor attitudes of the ideal religious subject as modeled by elders. Elders highlighted the difference between the template (elders' behavior) and the copy (that of their apprentices) so as to transform the latter into a more accurate facsimile of the "original."

During kitchen work, elders apprised newcomers that no matter how alien the acts of plucking and disemboweling may seem, until relatively recently they were a routine part of both agrarian and modern urban life. To eat chicken was to have killed a chicken, or to have gone where the killing was done, or to know someone whose livelihood derived from slaughter. This is obviously no longer the case. Consumers' distance from the origins of meat is evident in both the end product—the nearly bloodless plastic encasement of animals into jigsaw-puzzle portions at grocery stores—and the manufacturing process, since minimally regulated factory farms and slaughterhouses are often staffed by migrants, recent immigrants, and other legally vulnerable workers today. When the uninitiated came into contact with animals in Ilé Laroye, they might be informed that they themselves would not exist unless their ancestors had been willing to get their hands dirty to feed their families. This perspective underwrote the ritual invocation of the ancestors in Ashabi's ritual lineage, whose sacrifices long ago brought her ilé into being. This could be one interpretation of the common Lucumí saying "Los muertos paren santo" (The dead give birth to the orishas).

Although priests sometimes recommended ordination to the uninitiated, they recognized that no ilé could function in the absence of junior practitioners, especially in the kitchen, due to the restrictions imposed on elders during ritual functions. According to Ashabi, "We are just invalids without [uninitiated people]."[54] At certain moments in rites of consecration, every ordained person had to be present in the ritual chamber, and strict restrictions hampered the movement of seated priests during meals at major ceremonies, because no one can rise until the eldest initiate has stood up from her chair (although, in case of an emergency, she may grant permission for someone to depart by rapping on the table three times). "Priests are prisoners of that table," Ashabi has said; the uninitiated must "anticipate the need" by serving from bowls and chargers that must not leave the table once placed there until the meal is over; replenishing beverages automatically, without requests for refills; and remembering that, when the traditional dish of red snapper arrives, its spine is not to be fractured. In such situations, where the uninitiated were told, "Don't ask questions: *do*," unforeseen error often had a greater role to play in learning than flawless execution. Missteps offered opportunities for correction, reinforcement, and the creation of memories steeped in emotions—of embarrassment, disappointment, or pride—through which to assimilate physically the directive to improve one's future performance.[55]

Sometimes questions in the kitchen delved into the mythological rationales for cooking protocols. For instance, if prompted to explain why the ends of birds' toes, wings, and beaks are cut off and thrown away, elders said that the orishas should not be presented with anything sharp or tapered that could symbolize aggression.[56] For practitioners, rounded food communicated the intentions for which it was offered, such as the removal from the community of sharp misfortunes that interrupt the smooth cycle of life: illness, strife, obstacles, and accidents. Like stones, heads, soup tureens, and calabashes in Black Atlantic religions, ashés were seen to convey the fundamental reality of their purpose through their shapes. Recall that soup tureens not only stand for the nourishment provided by the orishas to their followers, they hark back to the maids and cooks among those now remembered as Lucumí lineage founders, and retain the connotations of bourgeois domesticity they acquired in colonial Cuba.[57] In the kitchen of Ilé Laroye, ashés added one more vinculum—in the sense both of "link" and, as in anatomy, of "a ligament that limits the movement of an organ or other body part"—to the chain of associations connecting roundness to the containment of aché.

Elders thus taught newcomers sensory modalities essential to following the overarching aesthetics, ethics, and poetics of Lucumí ritual acts. It may be useful to pause here and pose two questions: What is re-membered in the kitchen? And what is in danger of not being re-collected? Other pertinent queries are posed by the historian of religions Charles Malamoud in his study of ancient Indian cooking rituals:

What does it mean to begin? . . . How is one to understand that the same act can be both single and multiple? What is meant by "too much" and "not enough"? What is the relationship between parts and wholes? What does it mean to measure? How are repetition and difference to be understood? How does one tell creative reiteration apart from harmful redundancy?[58]

As Oshunleye once put it, "How can you separate the part from the whole, and still have it be the whole?" Motivated by a concern to honor the orisha with "moral matter," such inquiries were made with regard to any number of variables in the kitchen: the amount of oil to use in roasting an orisha's ashés, the length of the wing-tip to be severed, the angle at which to grip a paring knife so as to guard against impalement.

Like practitioners' understandings of other rituals, their grasp of kitchen work was cumulative and intertextual. Only years after starting my research did I realize that the points of the body addressed during the rogation ceremony are those at which a sacrificed rooster is cut by a knife before its ashés are roasted for the orishas: at the cockscomb (head), the neck (nape), the breast (throat), the wing-tips (elbows/palms), and the talons (toes).[59] The idea that Lucumí ebó—sacrifice as a category of ritual action—substitutes the bodies of animals for those of practitioners is not a novel one. Yet in the rogation, one finds a profound identification between its recipient and the paradigmatic sacrificial victim in a setting far removed from the initiation chamber and the abattoir. The ceremony refers beyond itself to a vastly more intricate religious schema, in which ashés symbolize the orishas' ability to disarticulate human bodies ritually and rearticulate them as sources of sacred nourishment. In juxtaposition with everyday kitchen work, the rogation generates meanings that could never be gleaned from analyzing its micropractices in isolation. A client may enter into it casually, just to have her head "refreshed," only to find that the seasoning has already begun.

## Strangers to Servants

And you want to get initiated! . . . Before initiation, you chop wood and carry water. After initiation, you chop wood and

carry water. *There is no glamour.* It's for longer periods of
time, and now [once you get initiated] you have to.
—Ashabi Mosley[60]

It was nearly dawn when I scurried from the room to scribble down
Ashabi's words with black permanent marker, on a square of lined paper
about to be used as a label for ashés. The kitchen resembled an abandoned army camp, with the last few soldiers left standing surrounded by
carnage, and no words of praise uttered for the deserters. The previous
afternoon, a series of delays had forced two initiations to start much
later than usual, and there was still so much guinea hen to eviscerate
and quarter at five in the morning that Ashabi announced there was
nothing short of "guinea's mammy"—roughly translated as "the mother
of all guinea." The comment quoted above was directed toward a young
man known to be saving money and gathering the necessary items for
his initiation. He had spent the night running ashés between the kitchen
and the grills in the backyard, up and down narrow porch stairs in the
dark, with admirable diligence, stamina, and humor. Ashabi addressed
him not only in the context of the hour, but out of over twenty years of
her own chopping and carrying.

It may seem odd, then, for Ashabi to suggest that anyone would see
Lucumí eldership as glamorous. However, she felt that the amount of
money paid to godparents for officiating rituals, and the status accrued
through their performance, led newcomers to underestimate the intensity of the work elders continue to do after their ordinations. "People
see the glamour. . . . Nobody sees the 'behind the scenes,'" Ashabi once
told me, implicitly comparing the micropractices of the kitchen to the
stagecraft that enables a theatrical production to be mounted but remains invisible to mere spectators.[61] Her words may sound like a poor
advertisement for Lucumí, embedded in a description that reinforces
the most sensationalistic stereotypes associated with Black Atlantic religions while simultaneously robbing them of their lurid—or indeed any
discernible—allure: blood without lust, sacrifice without frenzy. While
stopping short of analyzing Ashabi's statement as an instance of what
the literary theorist Roland Barthes called "operation margarine"—a
politico-cultural institution's strategic admission of its negative aspects

as a way of gaining the ideological upper hand—I would imagine that the comment was designed to elicit agreement from its hearers.[62]

It underscored the paradoxical conclusion I eventually reached, that the more work a newcomer does, the greater the probability that he or she will get initiated.[63] Although newcomers may enter the ilé to attend a drum ritual or to have a rogation, they stay after developing a sense of solidarity with and investment in the community, forged in the singular intimacy and camaraderie that toiling in close quarters provides. In the kitchen, customarily unpaid, widely denigrated domestic labor—such as washing, cooking, and serving food—is converted into an endeavor of enormous religious value.[64] I would argue that this lowliest of undertakings is vitally necessary for the internalization of dispositions and relationships to the orishas that lead to initiation, contrary to most accounts of Lucumí that emphasize rites of passage as the basis for the tradition's survival. As Arlene put it, "If you go into the kitchen, things will happen to you."[65]

We may understand this point more clearly by considering the opposition of clients and godchildren. The most common word for newcomer, *aleyo* (stranger), expresses the relationship of the outsider to Lucumí from initiates' point of view. Elders distinguished between the aleyo interested in finding a definite resolution to a problem, and a person committed to staying indefinitely and bowing to the will of the gods. As Ashabi said, contact with a Black Atlantic religious community "starts with someone not being happy," usually after losing a mate, contracting a disease, or facing persistent misfortune. Unhappiness acts as the impetus to request a divination, often subsequently drawing the client into further dealings with the ritual specialist as well as other members of her ilé.[66] However, whether a client turns into an *aborisha*, or "servant of the spirits," has little to do with her finding happiness. There are children never to be born, paralyzed limbs that will not budge, and the lover's heart, once split in two, may be no more receptive to chants in Lucumí than to topical applications of Krazy Glue. The aleyo, happy or unhappy, moves on; the aborisha sticks around. The aborisha accedes to a habituation or "seasoning" into virtue as defined by her elders, through cumulative engagement in ritual labor that comes to make sense for her even as it remakes her senses.

The stranger becomes a servant through participation in ilé activities and through ritual interventions, such as receiving sacred necklaces and the Warrior orishas. The servant heeds the orishas' responses to aesthetic forms and other sensory stimuli in ritual contexts. When enthroned in altars for special celebrations, the orishas are surrounded by food, but their desire to see acts of obeisance and hear praises is almost as pronounced as their need to eat. In these luxuriant displays, the details of the orishas' personalities are rendered visible through the arrangement of colors, fabrics, and objects in characteristic numbers and patterns citing episodes in their interconnected mythologies. Practitioners encountering thrones are obligated to prostrate to them as if meeting an elder face to face; in Lucumí and other Black Atlantic religious formations, altars are described as the faces of the gods.[67] Such visual, verbal, and gestural exchanges contribute to understanding individual orishas as having predilections, idiosyncrasies, sentience, and agency.

Service to the spirits in Black Atlantic religions not infrequently equates to unpaid labor in houses of worship. Practitioners become deeply implicated in their ritual economies by assisting in ceremonies. In Lucumí, even minor ceremonies cost money, and while the *derecho*, or ceremonial fee, in Ilé Laroye often did not cover elders' expenses, for rites of passage the cost could still amount to a week's paycheck. Receiving sacred objects did not confer the privileges of seniority on the uninitiated, yet it did authorize them to carry out time-consuming tasks that might otherwise fall to priests. For instance, after obtaining their Warriors, recipients could be entrusted with ritually cleaning those of others in the wake of matanzas. As one of Ashabi's godchildren once said, "If you have elekes, you can string elekes."[68] Rather than casting their lack of a wages as exploitative, however, practitioners reckoned knowledge to be the compensation for their work. In undertaking it, they developed technical aptitudes, sensibilities, and moral-ethical qualities—of perseverance, for instance—available only through their progressive embodiment.

## Schooling the Senses and Sensibilities

Dreamed last night I was with elders from the ilé. They lead me across a narrow, rusty bridge that reminds me of an old fire escape. I come to a place where there is a small house, like a storage shed. I am told that in order to be well, I need

to take the pudding. They laugh, it's a joke. Tre, the son of
Shangó, goes in the shack and when he comes out, in his
hand there is bloody matter the size and shape of a fig, with
fat and flesh where seeds should be. I gag, so nauseous I fall
to my knees. I apologize, I know in the dream this is what is
meant by aché. They say once a month when I am initiated
I need to eat this. I start to think of how I would cook it and
I wake up.
—Fieldnotes, June 18, 2005

Vital to the transformation of clients into godchildren is the mastery of
seemingly involuntary bodily responses by the uninitiated. Since priesthood demands periodic feeding of the orisha with blood throughout
one's lifetime, raising one's threshold for discomfort is crucial for the
normalization of sacrificial rites that might strike newcomers as both
primitive and convoluted. Sometimes the adaptation to them occurs
outside the kitchen. For instance, Oshunleye's son Billal underwent initiation in Chicago with scant exposure to the everyday operations of
an ilé. Raised in the Black Nationalist Church of the Black Madonna,
Billal had to learn the theological rationale for the sacrifices to reconcile
himself to the bloodshed, which he had deemed excessive to the point of
grotesquerie. Told in his itá that he had to move and change jobs, Billal
spent much of his first year as a priest under the tutelage of a Lucumí
priest based in another city. Billal has often said that at the first matanzas he attended, he judged his mentor be a "sadist," since he was to be
found laughing and singing ditties immediately prior to and after the
sacrifices. Billal said he now manages to deal with the anxiety of highly
charged rituals through similar expressions of levity, trusting that others
do not doubt his level of commitment to the orishas.[69]

Ethics and synaesthetics are united powerfully in Billal's attitude toward humor in the sacrificial chamber. Although comedy may commonly be regarded as too subjective to admit analysis, laughs are no
more "natural" than tears.[70] Individuals are conditioned socially to recognize the metapragmatic cues that accompany the telling of jokes—
raised eyebrows and changes in verbal intonation, among dozens of
other gestural and vocal signals. Understanding the gist of a joke and
its punch line depends on the hearer's degree of cultural competence,

among other factors. "In the fraught moment of response is a micro-process of sociality, of emerging consensus or lack of it: the division of the respondents into those who laughed and those who didn't," the an-thropologist J. Lowell Lewis writes.[71] As Lewis implies here, the sponta-neous decision to laugh is as much an ethical as an aesthetic one, hence the pained reaction to a "dumb" or "tasteless" but funny joke. Billal's synaesthetic exposure to "gallows humor" altered his opinion of it as morally abhorrent, and he grew to accept what one might call his dis-positional disciplining.[72] Such dispositional disciplining was evident in the response to Ochún's use of cake in the previous chapter, when priests took the sensation of buttercream and crumbs spread on their faces as a welcome blessing rather than a source of distress.

Billal had to become socialized into Lucumí while "on the job," but most practitioners have ample opportunity to do so prior to ordina-tion.[73] The uninitiated must adhere to the kitchen's dress code (white head covering and clothing, whenever possible), and the taboos that transform the kitchen into a sacred, and dangerous, space. For instance, neither Ashabi nor Fadesiye have allowed godchildren to prostrate to them there because, since ashés are cooked in the kitchen, to lie on the floor is tantamount to offering oneself up for sacrifice. Sensory training may also be more subtle. One had to become inured not only to seeing unconventional sights, but to touching objects of a texture and consis-tency that could feel repellent, and to hearing sounds—such as the un-cannily infantile cry of goats about to be slaughtered—that challenged the hardiest of contemporary North American sensibilities. Part of this education entailed becoming comfortable with the "smellscape" of the kitchen: its olfactory perimeters as delineated by, among other factors, the crisp yet vaguely diesel-tinged air let in through open windows; the slight putrescence of the leaves collected downstairs for rituals; the min-eral rancidity of the abattoir-cum-basement when blood started flowing; the grassy damp notes brought into the house on goats' hooves; and ripe, split coconuts' sweet richness.[74]

Elders taught that emotions such as disgust are learned at an early age, not inborn—in other words, cultural constructions, with histories and sociopolitical contexts that are not readily apparent.[75] They cast the display of emotions as an acquired behavior, and coached practitioners in discerning the appropriate affective states to inhabit in the kitchen. As

clients-turned-godchildren grew aware of the mistakes they were making, their emotional repertoires expanded to encompass a broad range of
attitudes, including humility. The first time I plucked poultry at Ashabi's
house, I wrote, "My guts got twisted into knots when I realized that the
tubs had been moved, and I'd momentarily forgotten to which orisha the
pigeon I'd finished plucking had been dedicated. . . . Thankfully Oshunleye remembered the number of birds each had received and spared me
having to bluff my way through the awkwardness."[76] Such lapses could
bring on anxiety and shame, mingled with the uncomfortable knowledge of oneself as susceptible to dishonesty. From the elders' point of
view, these gut feelings and moral judgments would ideally lead to the
formation of virtues: self-control, attentiveness to detail, timeliness—
not speed, because there is such a thing as going too fast—and poise, in
service to the orishas.

During one initiation in April 2007, I became privy to three situations that illustrated the way preparing ashés dismantles and recon-
stitutes practitioners' corporeal sensoria.[77] Early in the evening, one
aborisha long affiliated with the house suddenly felt so ill at the odor of
the chicken she was holding that she excused herself from the kitchen,
closed the bathroom door behind her, and vomited. Sometime after 3:00
a.m., another uninitiated but experienced member of the house working
in the ilé since that morning was so disturbed by the sight of coagu-
lated blood inside a bird that she asked Arlene to look at it for her. After
testing her resolve with a few passes of the blade over the carcass, she
decided on the spot that she needed to go home. In between these two
incidents, Ashabi's goddaughter Fulani decided that she would help to
pluck for the first time. Fulani had grown up in the religion; her mother,
Cleopatra, is one of the first priests Ashabi ordained, but she had always
promised her daughter that she wouldn't have to pluck chickens at the
ilé. In fact, even while living in Ashabi's home for a while, Fulani had
avoided it.

As Fulani confided to me, contemplating sacrifice had summoned
gruesome stereotypes about Lucumí, and the example given by her
mother had not been compelling enough to inspire her to follow in her
footsteps. When Fulani decided to try plucking, she squatted down on
one of the small stools lined up in the basement room usually occupied
by Ashabi's ancestral shrine. As part of a kitchen work crew, Fulani had

to learn everything from where to hold a bird's wings to access the down underneath them, to how to pull the feathers against the direction of their growth so as to extract the shafts most efficiently. At one point, Fulani had the misfortune of picking a chicken to pluck that, while headless, began clucking, and she could not refrain from screaming twice. Ashabi told her repeatedly, "It's just air," to little effect. By the end of the night, though, Fulani's pride in herself and her fellow laborers was such that she proposed designing a line of tee-shirts that would read, "Real Women Pluck Chicken." Her wording suggests that the old-fashioned connotations of plucking, far from rendering it obsolete, validated it for her. She had come around to valuing the job as imparting authenticity to those performing it.

In the first two cases cited above, exhaustion, among other factors, made the practitioners in question especially vulnerable to feelings of disgust. Their training had been adequate enough to get them through their assignments until the introduction of deviations from the sensory norm. It is doubtful that they would have become long-standing members of the ilé had they not experienced realizations similar to Fulani's at some point. In the case of the second woman, leaving the ilé could have been seen as an act of defiance not only against Arlene—who insisted that the clot of blood did not differ substantively from anything else normally seen inside a chicken—but also against the bonds of affiliation with the community that had brought her to the kitchen that morning. Such episodes are common among aborishas; Arlene said that the first time she was supposed to cook ashés, a turtle that had been beheaded in sacrifice started to crawl across the floor, leading her to flee with no more explanation than, "Oh *hell* no. I'm out!"[78] The acquisition of technique went hand in hand with the mastery of an ingrained resistance to the labor itself.

Another aborisha, Berta, gradually changed her attitude toward ashé preparation as well. She cast her growing ease in the kitchen not only as evidence of her acceptance of Lucumí, but as something that separated her from uninitiated family members and friends with more conventional sensory orientations. After one initiation, Berta said that she never would have believed that she would be chopping and cleaning goat the way she had. She added that since her involvement with the ilé had grown, she had trouble spending time with her siblings. Because they were on a "whole other level" from her, activities that used to be fun always turned out to be tiresome. Their criticism had caused Berta to distance herself from them, and turn further to the company of those active within Afro-Cuban traditions. Having rejected plucking and butchering as grimy and debased, she came to appreciate its difficulty as an index of its sacredness. Berta's and Fulani's recurrent proximity to ritual slaughter clarified the connection between their labor and the alimentation of the orishas.

The contribution of Fulani's first experience with kitchen work to her future career in Lucumí might seem to be negligible. By the end of the night, she had not yet become committed to initiation, and her actions could be replicated by anyone similarly trained—say, in a factory—or by a machine. But I would argue that without such moments, in which labor for the orishas becomes naturalized as necessary for the pursuit of a real—that is, meaningful—life, the reproduction of the religion would be in doubt. According to practitioners, the decision to become ordained occurs either after ongoing health problems or at a moment of crisis in which ocha emerges as the only alternative to a more undesirable, potentially life-threatening, outcome. This course of action would be inconceivable, particularly for practitioners without a firm divinatory mandate to get initiated, in the absence of sentiments of affinity for other community members. Such sentiments might include sympathy, trust, and esteem.[79] Although Fulani was not serious about printing the tee-shirts she proposed for her companions, to fantasize about advocating labor widely regarded as menial and filthy suggests her burgeoning sense of solidarity.

## Seasoning Subjects

Practitioners become aborishas through service to both the orishas and the elders. As the result of her experience with kitchen work under Ashabi and Arlene, Fulani might be said to have "matured" in her thinking or "warmed up" to the idea of becoming a priest. These terms convey more than is apparent at a glance. Across cultures, foods are frequently conceptualized as progressing from a raw to a cooked state, becoming less crude through manipulation by culinary techniques. Lucumí joins religious traditions around the world in regarding transformative rituals as raising the temperature of spaces and participants, and equating the civilizing effects of rites of passage with the curing or heating of food. Culinary codes convey sociocultural and cosmological distinctions; these codes correspond to modes of ritual mediation that symbolically cook participants or make them raw as a means of bringing them into communal life.[80]

This much has already been suggested in the preceding sections, or could easily be extrapolated, yet it is possible to go further. I would contend that producing ashés is a ceremony analogous to those in which novices are seasoned in rites of passage. Being prepared for the orishas in the kitchen are not only sacrificial animals, but also the people cooking. As Lévi-Strauss wrote, "The conjunction of a member of the social group with nature must be mediatized through the intervention of the cooking fire, whose normal function is to mediatize the conjunction of the raw product and the human consumer, and whose operation thus has the effect of making sure that a natural creature is at one and the same time *cooked* and *socialized*."[81] So it is in the kitchen. Although Lévi-Strauss referred to cooking in the context of physiological processes, such as menstruation and childbirth—thereby, of course, conflating nature with biology—it is plain to see from the preceding discussion that cooking integrates strangers into Lucumí communities.[82] It could be said that houses of worship are themselves fattened up by the cooking process.

Practitioners are cooked in the sense that they transition from a green, or ignorant, condition to seasoned competence, finding significant roles to play vis-à-vis the orishas and other godchildren, visitors, and elders. More than one of my interlocutors attributed her sense of affiliation with Lucumí directly to the work she did in the kitchen. Arlene often commented that when she went to her first casa-templo, she gravitated toward its kitchen out of timidity, unease as an Anglophone Black woman among immigrant Latinos, and an eagerness to blend inoffensively into the social landscape of the house. She soon found that by distinguishing herself at the stove as a cook, rather than standing at the periphery of ritual practice, she was delving into the midst of it. In becoming responsible for tasks that others viewed as indispensable, she realized that "women's work" was prized as ritual labor of a high order. Her grandmother—idolized by Arlene as a "s/hero," or heroine, whose impact on her life was incalculable—had been both minister and maid, but her religious service contrasted sharply with her domestic service. Arlene discovered a means of fusing the two in Lucumí.

The metaphor of seasoning here and throughout this book refers not only to the transformation of food by the addition of salt, herbs, spices, and condiments to improve its flavor. It is meant to evoke the cultural process called "seasoning" through which enslaved peoples became accustomed to their new legal condition and social environment in the Americas.[83] African captives were not always forced to toil immediately upon arrival; they spent time recuperating from their ocean voyages and becoming familiar with the climates and customs of their new homelands. While seasoning practices were regionally distinctive and not always pursued systematically, they often involved placing "salt-water" Africans under the apprenticeship of slaves from the same ethnic groups or with a common tongue. Seasoned slaves acclimated "outlandish" ones to the types of communication and labor expected of them. Their seasoning reinforced slaves' dependence for sustenance and safety on their owners, in order to render attempts to escape a less attractive prospect. Seasoned slaves brought higher prices at auctions and—especially germane to my discussion here—were described in advertisements as "sensible," meaning acculturated: intelligible, intelligent, skilled in diverse kinds of work, and resigned to their subjugation.[84]

One might object that the comparison between socializing individuals into Lucumí and the seasoning of slaves smacks of anachronism and essentialism. It is possible that the verbal references to slavery in Ilé Laroye were atypically frequent, and that other practitioners consider kitchen work straightforwardly pleasurable: mentally restorative, emotionally uplifting, and so forth.[85] Lucumí rites of passage nevertheless are rife with allusions to bondage. For instance, to signal that the ordination ritual has officially begun, elders lasso the initiate-to-be with a heavy beaded necklace (the aforementioned mazo).[86] This ritual act is called the *prendición* or "abduction." Prendición also occurs after someone has unwittingly or deliberately violated the ritual protocols that separate the uninitiated from secret rituals and sacred substances, as when a child repeatedly stumbles into the midst of a major ceremony. In these cases, the prendición indicates that the one thus yoked must be initiated as soon as practically possible. Personal desire is seen to have no say in the matter.[87] Lucumí priesthood is depicted as bringing the practitioner from a natural, disordered condition to a cultured, orderly one; ocha recapitulates and telescopes this domestication process from the moment when novices are "captured" as a wild animal would be, or enslaved Africans were.

References to chattel slavery in ritual contexts are not exclusive to Afro-Cuban traditions:

> A survey of . . . African and African diaspora initiations known as *kanzo*, *kouche, asiento, kari-ocha*, "flooring," or "mourning" among West Indians and African-North Americans reveals episodes resembling the quintessential African slave ship voyage. These include a number of melancholic and listless victims enduring head-shaving, fasting and other physical and sensory deprivations, incarceration in a hot, crowded room while lying on the floor, on their sides, ankles and wrists tied with raffia, rope or cloth bands, blinded by eye-bands, helpless, unwashed, undergoing physical and spiritual lashing and becoming increasingly somnolent and disassociated.[88]

Suffered in the Middle Passage, these torments have been documented historically as seasoning methods. Since phenotypically white, Asian, and indigenous people—among others from a variety of ethnic groups—have become part of Black Atlantic traditions increasingly within the last century, one might speculate that the translation of such ordeals into religious disciplines has allowed priests of African descent to pass on counter-memories of enslavement to succeeding generations. When questioned about these aspects of ritual experience, Black elders in Ilé Laroye answered that their ancestors had undergone the same treatment, invoking both their religious forebears and biological progenitors. Foundational Lucumí figures may well have integrated the discourses and micropractices of seasoning into rites of passage as a means of absorbing their efficacy through sensuous imitation.[89]

The temporal component of the religious seasoning process should not be discounted. In his study of Afro-Brazilian traditions, the anthropologist Mattijs van de Port quotes one source, an anthropologist and initiate, as saying,

In [C]andomblé it is believed that nothing done in a hurry turns out right. By asking [questions], people will only understand this much of a certain notion but they will not assimilate it. It is only time that will make knowledge sink in. Let's say, it is as with French wine: it gets better by decanting. Intellectually it is the same thing. Things have to get to rest. You learn, but then you leave it at that. And when it has ripened you go back to it, structuring it, balancing it out.[90]

Along with that of decanting, the image of ripening evokes exposure to air and the settling down over time that allows for micropractices to have a "sedimented effect."[91] These analogies complement the seasoning-of-the-self-through-cooking-of-the-other—subjectivation via objectification—that I am proposing as normative for the kitchen. Candomblé initiates have to wait until seven years after their primary ordination rituals to be regarded as elders and initiate other priests; Lucumí practitioners do not have to wait more than twelve months. But these traditions depend on a similar economy of secrecy and power in which hierarchical status comes with corporeal experience.

As David H. Brown and others have argued, Lucumí owes the codification of its institutional and liturgical protocols to a relatively small group of visionaries, some of whom knew slavery and the subsequent seasoning process firsthand. They were determined to regulate divergent practices in the interest of preserving an elevated standard of ritual competence among future initiates.[92] Brown maintains that many of the beliefs and practices now called traditions simply did not exist on the African continent. In the name of reconstituting their pasts, the talented individuals at the root of prominent lineages (or "branches") gave birth to a series of innovations. Even as ashés today seem emblematic of a far distant history, and their continued preparation nothing short of miraculous, innovations in cooking for the gods may have been among the most significant. What is not new—but in fact so routine as to be axiomatic—is that those regulating the kitchen's economy of signification are the women of the house, and men who are either gay, gender-nonconforming, or the children of female orishas. This gendered division of labor is the theme of the following chapter.

4

# Gendering the Kitchen

The preceding pages addressed the emergence of Lucumí religious subjectivity through the micropractices performed in cooking for the orishas. I argued that kitchen work fosters emotions, affective states, and sensibilities that catalyze initiation, thereby conducing to the spread of the religion. In so doing, I referred to the uninitiated as a group presumably younger than elders in chronological age and composed of both male and female aborishas. Yet as in other Lucumí houses, in Ilé Laroye, men and the daughters of male orishas were groomed in the handling of sacrificed goats and rams. Women and the children of female orishas concentrated chiefly on plucking and removing ashés from birds. They also dominated the cooking process, from butchering to roasting to the plating of food offerings. While elders of both sexes were secluded in the basement during ceremonies, a crew mostly made up of female aborishas fixed meals, set the dinner table, and ensured that the house was as welcoming as possible for the benefit of visitors.[1] They controlled "the food axis," the space of food preparation, storage, consumption, and elimination in Ashabi's home.[2]

In Spanish and most other Indo-European languages, the word "kitchen" is grammatically gendered female. In the ilé, practitioners' approaches to kitchen work were highly gendered; for some, as we saw, it was a badge of pride worn by "real women." Their experiences were racialized and marked by class as well, in ways that accentuated the convergence of authority, ethics, and ritual orthodoxy. This is in keeping with the powerful cultural connotations of the kitchen in the African Diaspora. The first publishing house in the United States for nonwhite women was called Kitchen Table: Women of Color Press. One of its founders, the Black lesbian activist and scholar Barbara Smith, said, "We chose our name because the kitchen is the center of the home, the place where women in particular work and communicate with each other. We also wanted to convey the fact that we are a kitchen table, grass roots operation, begun and kept alive by women who cannot rely on inheritances or other benefits of class privilege to do the work we need to do."[3]

When I first interviewed her, Yomí Yomí had been initiated for over ten years and active in Lucumí for twenty-three. She recalled an initiation at the ilé during which Elaina, a visiting Cuban priestess, recoiled at the notion of men joining the house's team of chicken pluckers. Yomí Yomí explained, "It's that Spanish mentality; I don't have to tell you!"[4] When I pressed her to elaborate, she continued, basing her comments on her experience in a house of orisha worship dependent on the male diviners called babaláwos as the main source of ritual authority:

> We were talking about it, that we needed more people, [and] . . . I said, "What about Tom, what's he doing?" Because I brought Tom Layton. "Well," [Elaina said] "he can't pluck, he's a man." I don't think so! [Ashabi and I] both looked at each other and were like, ["What?"] But that's how it is at [Elaina's] house, only the women [pluck].
>
> She's Cuban, you know, she has [a] babaláwo—and everybody does have a role, I mean, like, we cannot sacrifice four-legged animals. We cannot, *women* cannot. That's why the women are the chicken pluckers, and the men do the [animals with four] legs—although I do know there are some women who do chop up those animals now . . . they're kind of making that cross-over. I think it's that everybody has a role, everybody has a role in the ritual.

Yomí Yomí summed up the reason that, from Elaina's point of view, men should not pluck chickens: "Because it's a woman's job." She added, "[Ashabi] says, 'Why not?' And I agree with her. But you'll never find it [in a Puerto Rican or a Cuban house]."[5]

## Divided Labors

Women in Ilé Laroye were often the ones cooking meat produced through sacrificial rituals, yet they were not simply relegated to the stereotypically feminine realm of the kitchen in some Lucumí version of *Kinder, Küche, Kirche*.[6] Female elders engaged firsthand in sacrifice alongside men and skinned goats. This is not the case in every community. As Yomí Yomí pointed out, in Lucumí communities headed by babaláwos, women are categorically excluded from sacrificing four-legged animals and from divining using the Ifá oracle.[7] Women are able to sacrifice four-legged animals after receiving the ritual implement called *pinaldo* in communities where the regnant form of divination involves *diloggún*, or sixteen cowrie shells, and whose ultimate initiatory authority rests on a figure called the *oba oriaté*—the master of ceremonies for ordination and the person entrusted with determining the patron deities of religious subjects. Ashabi's community is of this latter type.[8] The oba oriaté Ashabi entrusts to conduct initiations in Ilé Laroye is male, and this is almost an exclusively male office today, but historically some of the most famous oba oriatés—such as the legendary Timotea Albear—have been female.[9]

Nevertheless, sexual equality in sacrificial practice does not necessarily lead to, or proceed from, gender parity. Although the trope of sacrificial alimentation "suggests an ideology of ritual practice that places it within the realm of female rather than male labor," little scholarly attention has been paid to the actual experience of women upon whom the duty for the orishas' care devolves.[10] Lucumí ritual labor has historically had to be negotiated with wage labor by women dependent for their livelihood upon their ability to toil over the course of long hours, although this aspect of their religious lives has either been downplayed or ignored altogether. Work within the home—child rearing, washing dishes and laundry, sweeping floors—has fallen disproportionately on women's shoulders, rather than on those of their male partners.[11] Women placed in charge of feeding the orishas have had to put dinner on the table for their companions and children as well.

Feminist critiques of Lucumí practice have tended to focus on the prohibitions against women (as well as gay men) performing Ifá divination, or playing the sacred drums called bàtá.[12] Scholars such as J. D. Y. Peel have repeated the anthropologist William Bascom's assertion that the office of the babaláwo was traditionally "male-dominated," and thus anticipated such "world religions" as Judaism and Islam; bàtá drumming has become emblematic of masculine self-fashioning in a religious idiom.[13] Straight and normatively masculine men, as well as those with male orishas as patrons, are socialized into Lucumí communities through learning Ifá, drumming, and engaging with "four legs" sacrifices (as well as by performing wifely work in the communities that allow it).[14] But the most prevalent asymmetry in this and other Black Atlantic religions—and the one that undergirds the others—is the female body's portrayal as the most receptive material container for the gods' sacred power. The scholarship on Lucumí is still coming to terms with the ways that this "female normative" tradition simultaneously reifies and contests "essentialist views of gender."[15] It has yet to sufficiently account for the material and discursive means through which women negotiate their everyday religious obligations.

In Lucumí and other Black Atlantic religions that derive much of their symbolism, leadership structure, liturgical language, and ritual imaginaries from West African Yorùbá groups, practitioners tend to regard women as the ideal religious subjects. Women's domestic careers as wives and mothers form the basis for conceptualizing the proper relationship between people and gods. The orishas, whether male or female, are regarded as husbands in their initiatory marriages to human spouses. This wedding gives new life to an initiate after she has undergone ritual death. During the first stage of Lucumí ordination, elders change the novice's name to *aboku*, "the dead one"; the term used for the priest after he or she has been ceremonially reborn, iyawo, means "most junior wife" or "bride." Throughout the year following initiation, Lucumí priests are called iyawo, sometimes modified by the name of their patron orishas, as in "iyawo Obatalá."

According to published sources, many ordination ceremonies for possession priesthoods in Black Atlantic religions culminate with the newly initiated incorporating their patron deities in possession. This ceremonial act derives much of its religious significance from its gendered metaphoricity.[16] In possession, the deity is understood to assert his dominance by forcibly entering a practitioners' head—the seat of human destiny, personality, and sacred power—to assume control of her body, despite any reluctance to be possessed. Whether in Yorùbá, Spanish, Portuguese, Creole, or English, the term used to describe possession phenomena, *mounting*, retains its double meaning, with the gods consistently compared to husbands penetrating their wives in sexual congress.[17] Among Lucumí practitioners, the initiate's head becomes not only a hollow vessel to be filled by the god, but a womb fit for the orishas' reproduction, pregnant with the potential of their aché.

The central trope of mounting relates to both women and horses. Black Atlantic deities do not descend from above, they climb up from below, then mount, since they are conceptualized as rising from below the earth. Possession priests are called "mounts" or "horses" (in Spanish, *caballo*).[18] The analogy between possessing a wife and riding a horse derives from Yorùbá history; coupled with an administrative bureaucracy, a cavalry allowed the Oyo Empire to convert trade routes into territories in the sixteenth century. The horse came to epitomize the power to demarcate space as property, wealth, and status. While wives are also mounted by men in intercourse and transport infant children from place to place, they surpass horses as carriers by bearing entire human beings inside their bodies in pregnancy. Possession mounts are perceived as both conveying the power of their patron deities and enlarging their religious lineages by "carrying" protégés throughout their religious lives.

It would seem that, bearing this degree of female normativity, Lucumí leaders would emphasize women's presence in Afro-Cuban religious history. But as Brown has shown, scholarship on the religion has relied disproportionately on babaláwos, whose ideologically informed accounts have been inclined to place male diviners at the top of the religious hierarchy as the only initiates competent to consecrate the orishas Olokún (the deity of the ocean's depths), Odudúwa, and the Warriors.[19] This gendered division of labor must be considered alongside the sexual distribution of prestige in the academic literature, which has not tended to valorize female labor in Black Atlantic religions apart from possession performance. Perhaps in an effort to "flip the script" of babaláwos' hegemonic Ifá-centric narrative, Ashabi once said of Lucumí, "Women invented this."[20] Her statement was not a denial of men's participation in establishing the religion, or a repudiation of the heteronormative constructs of masculinity upon which understandings of gods such as Shangó rely. It was meant to recognize those whose contributions are seldom celebrated, even among those profiting from their past and current labor.

Emblematic of women's work is cooking. But if the Lucumí kitchen is a realm ruled by women, this is partly because it is one most men have not wanted to govern. Miguel "Willie" Ramos captures the prevalent attitude toward men in the kitchen in his volume of recipes and culinary techniques *Adimú: Gbogbó Tén'unjé Lukumí*, circulated within the ilé much as the aforementioned libretas have been in casa-templos since the late nineteenth century.[21] Ramos writes that while several women in his family are "excellent cooks" and his mother was an alashé, "they never taught me directly—[because] *men are not supposed to cook*."[22] This sentiment (at some remove from Ramos's own opinion) reflects hegemonic notions of masculinity operative on the Iberian peninsula since the early modern period and dominant throughout the Caribbean.[23] Ramos goes on to clarify, "Although most alashés are women, some men also serve as Orisha cooks. Though it is acceptable for a man to cook the *iyanlés* and other [food offerings], men may not cook amalá ilá—corn meal porridge and okra—or Kalalú stew for Shangó. These must be cooked by a woman."[24] According to Ramos's account, the "hot" and virile Shangó requires not just his own vessel for food preparation. He needs for the preparer of his food to be the ideal type of human vessel, according to the religious ideology of Black Atlantic religions: a woman. Only women, envisioned as constitutionally and temperamentally "cool," can manage Shangó's aché in the heat of the kitchen. Left unsaid but implicit is that Shangó will not countenance the handling of his food by the only men customarily found cooking there: homosexuals.[25]

## Gay Men and Lesbians in the Kitchen

Straight men in Lucumí houses of worship may fix coffee and heat up meals for themselves during religious ceremonies, but gay men do the cooking for everyone. The sociologist Salvador Vidal-Ortiz echoes Gleason's evocation of a "very black woman" supervising kitchen work in the previous chapter as he recalls his ethnographic research in New York City during the early 2000s: "Most of the events I attended had Puerto Rican women, often short, often dark skinned, preparing the food and in command of the kitchen. (The very few exceptions when men were involved were at a couple of houses where the men in the kitchen were gay-identified, many of whom were fieldwork informants.)"[26] Gay men have long been celebrated in Lucumí communities for their rigor, industry, and attention to detail. Mason casts their meticulousness as a sort of defense mechanism: "Gay oricha priests subvert norms about sexuality, but some compensate for their homosexuality's effects on their reputations by becoming severe and rigid about ritual matters."[27] Of course, in view of the "hyper-performed masculinity" of straight men in Latino/a houses of orisha worship, not all spaces are equally welcoming.[28]

Recent research in African American studies posits that the Black Atlantic—the world shaped by the Middle Passage and transatlantic slave trade—has always been a queer Atlantic, pointing to the rich history of sexual crossings, gendered maroonage, and multiple gender identities that have flourished in the Caribbean and Latin America.[29] This approach dovetails with a new emphasis on Black Atlantic religions as "gay-friendly," yet it is important to recognize regional and cultural differences within traditions. The relative openness to homosexual—as well as genderqueer—people in Lucumí is predicated partly on the tacit understanding that sexual orientation is inborn rather than acquired, yet there are limits to straight practitioners' tolerance of LGBT community members. The anthropologist Aisha M. Beliso-De Jesús has deftly analyzed homophobic discourses that circulate in heteronormative Cuban Lucumí communities and articulate with nationalist sentiment in casting the effeminate male as "both a cursed *and* necessary object" within the tradition.[30] Beliso-De Jesús brings to the fore tensions between babaláwos and male possession mounts, the ostracism of transgender and transsexual practitioners, and the perception that Afro-Cuban traditions in the United States have been queered to the point of spoilage by the presence of too many LGBT people.[31]

One of Vidal-Ortiz's Puerto Rican interlocutors, a lesbian involved in the religion for twenty years, rehearsed the selective appreciation of gay men in Lucumí communities:

[People say,] Listen, get that one [to work at a ceremony] because that one, although he might be *loca* [a sissy] and all, man [the way he] kills chickens! Seek out that one. . . . Have you seen the thrones they make? Sissies, the best kitchens; sissies, the best dresses; sissies! Because not even women [can measure up to them. . . . So, they distinguish themselves in that.[32]

Her observations accord with those of the late Clay Keck (a.k.a. Afolabí, a.k.a. Shloma Rosenberg), a Michigan-based gay genderqueer orisha priest and author. In one essay, Afolabí denounced the hypocrisy of homophobic practitioners, charging that almost any nonheteronormative behavior—in choice of clothing, mannerism, or romantic partner—elicits discriminatory treatment:

> Gay Oloshas make the thrones for celebrations and initiations, they sew, they bead, they cook, they divine, they mount Orisha, they lead chants, and they initiate other priests at a phenomenal rate. The number of Gay Oloshas who specialize in the creative or aesthetic arts of the religion *so far* outweighs the number of straights as to be comical. Yet even with all this, there is a seldom-voiced undercurrent of opinion that holds Gays to be less than fully accepted within the religion.[33]

Afolabí noted the bitter irony that no amount of sexual deviance displayed within a house of orisha worship could possibly match the social deviance associated with Lucumí ritual acts from possession to sacrifice, but the onus continues to be placed on homosexuals to act "normal."[34]

That both Afolabí and Vidal-Ortiz's interlocutor mentioned kitchen work is telling. For the same reason that gay, nonbinary, and genderqueer men have been accepted and valued as possession mounts, they have been welcomed into the overwhelmingly female space of the kitchen: they are perceived to share an internally coherent subject-position with women that renders them capable of serving the spirits in the manner appropriate to a wife.[35] In the Caribbean and Latin America, homosexuality has long indicated involvement in penetrative sex with men rather than same-sex affective and erotic orientation. Often only the "effeminate" sexual partner, stereotyped as assuming the "passive" role in sexual relations, may be regarded as gay. Since the wives of Black Atlantic deities represent "the captivity, the riddenness, the hollowness, the penetrability, and, in a word, the mountedness of the self" constructed as the ideal religious subject, men recognized as gay have been thought to occupy the role of possession priest just as capably as women have.[36] Wifeliness in these traditions implies receptivity, and Lucumí privileges forms envisioned as accommodating sacred substances and releasing them without resistance: pots, calabashes, soup tureens, dried gourds, and gay male bodies no less than female ones.

In Afro-Brazilian religions, these ideas inform popular understandings of consumption: "to eat" (*comer*) is Portuguese slang for "to penetrate" sexually, while "to be penetrated" is "to give" (*dar*). As the anthropologist Serena Nanda explains,

> Comer describes the male's active penetration and domination of the female and is used in different contexts as a synonym for the verbs "to possess" (*possuir*) or "to conquer" (*vencer*) . . . Just as comer is used to describe various forms of domination through reference to the relations of gender, dar is also used to imply submission, subjugation, and passivity in varied contexts, from politics to sports, in which victors are said to have "eaten" their opponents.[37]

This relationship obtains between "real," or normatively masculine, men (*homens*) and those they are perceived to penetrate and dominate physically (*bichas* or *viados/veados*). The latter are referred to by the Yorùbá-derived term *adés/adéfontós* in houses of Candomblé and in the traditions of Batuque, Xangô de Pernambuco, and Tambor-de-Mina.[38] As has been analyzed in the formidable body of scholarship on "effeminate" cisgender gay men in Afro-Brazilian traditions, they accumulate prestige through possession performance, especially as mounts for female spirits.[39] While their social deviance redounds to their reputation for mystical power, they may strategically assert their male prerogatives when the opportunity arises, ascending to the leadership of religious communities and stepping in to perform ritual functions usually carried out by straight men (such as sacrifice) when necessary.

Possession as performed by adés is typically discussed as legitimating their gender identities and affective orientations. Adés cook too, yet few sources take up their kitchen work in the vast literature—both vernacular and academic—on food preparation in Afro-Brazilian religions.[40] As gay, nonbinary, and genderqueer men do in Lucumí houses, adés execute tasks marked as feminine, like washing dishes, laundering, and embroidering ritual vestments. They give themselves up to be "eaten" by the gods in possession, and feed them and the communities defined by their service.[41] One tantalizing link between urban sites of orisha/orixá worship and the "queer" social margins is that effeminate gay men were historically hired to cook, clean, and sew in both Brazilian and Cuban brothels, where they also occupied a mediatory position between men and women.[42] Despite the lack of a male counterpart in Candomblé for the *iya bassê*—"mother of the kitchen"—it is clear that adés have distinguished themselves as disciplined citizens of "Kitchen Women Nations," religious and secular alike.

In *El monte*, called "one of the queerest books ever written by a Cuban author," Cabrera lists the terms that Afro-Cuban religious practitioners used for homosexuals in the early twentieth century—"Addóddis, Obini-Toyo, Obini-ñaña, Erón Kibá, Wassicúndi, Diánkune"—and details gay and lesbian relationships between both orishas and their worshippers.[43] Yet if gay men are hypervisible in Lucumí to the point of notoriety, lesbians suffer from a corresponding erasure. Lesbians in communities of orisha worship do not occupy different ceremonial roles from straight women's, unlike in Candomblé, where lesbians' resistance to possession recommends them for the position of *ekedi*, ritual assistant to possession mount.[44] But lesbians in Lucumí are known for having violated the prohibitions against the playing of bàtá drums by women, and traces of their historical presence surface mainly in counter-memories transmitted through oral tradition.[45] According to the anthropologist Jafari Allen,

> *Oremi* means "close friend" in Yoruba. According to my respondent Yanire, Oremi is also the name by which a group of nonheteronormative 19th-century Cuban women adherents to Lucumí (Yoruba religion in Cuba) were known. Yanire learned through a local *santera* (Lucumí priest) in Regla that these women loved one another sexually and formed a mutual-aid society. Their reported sale of tortillas has become a bawdy sexual double-entendre, leading some to claim that the colloquial term for lesbians, *tortilleras*, references these women.[46]

Textual inscriptions of oremi are virtually nonexistent, however, and few practitioners today would be conversant with this history.

In Ilé Laroye, Ashabi and Fadesiye accepted openly gay men and women, a decision that both attracted godchildren and repelled potential members. Many in the Black American Yorùbá movement have espoused more conservative opinions, supporting the exclusion of gays from leadership positions in communities of orisha worship by citing divination verses to condemn them and casting homosexual activity as a European aberration without sanctioned precedent in Africa.[47] While in many ilés, gays and lesbians have been bound by standards of propriety more stringent than those applied to their straight godsiblings, in Ashabi's house, queer godchildren freely showed affection for their partners. They employed spousal terminology to refer to them and did not bowdlerize discussions of their personal lives. One godchild said that after his post-initiatory itá, he realized he had never felt as completely accepted as he did among the elders surrounding him, bestowing their blessings on him just as he was, instead of framing his sexual orientation as a defect to be fixed. This confidence in self-presentation extended to men and women whose appearance, comportment, or relationship status fell short of hegemonic heteronormative ideals.[48]

One anecdote may suffice to illustrate this point. In October 2006, two of Ashabi's gay godchildren, André and Brian, traveled from the Detroit area to assist in the initiation of a young woman to Obatalá. They rose every morning shortly after dawn and cheerfully attended to the assignments set before them over the course of three long days with competence and aplomb. The initiation was judged to have gone exceedingly well.[49] Ashabi lavished praise on André and Brian before they left the house, and other elders' compliments rang in their ears as they carried their luggage outside. Upon opening the door to his car, André declared, with a toss of the head, "Michigan faggotry has left the building!"[50] By borrowing the phrase that would announce Elvis Presley's departure from concert venues—and notify the audience that he would not be returning for another encore—this godchild ventured to confirm his status as a star in Ashabi's approving eyes. He also underscored his pride in being a gay man whose centrality to the smooth operation of a major Lucumí ritual was undisputed.

Gay men and women came into the ilé as Ashabi's peers and elders, and the respect accorded to them contrasted sharply with reports of their treatment in Christian congregations. To explain this matter-of-fact acceptance of homosexuality, we may find it fruitful to examine the construction of personhood within the ilé. Sexual orientation was deemed not a decision to be made, but an unchangeable feature of the self that was both birthright and destiny. Homosexuality precluded some avenues for the generation of prestige (bàtá drumming and Ifá divination) and opened up others (recognition as a possession mount, aborisha, and alashé). The notion of the self that underwrote this dichotomy is problematic in granting sexuality a privileged place in the construction of identity and asserting a biological basis for gender. As the feminist theorist Rosemary Hennessy writes, "The notion of an authentic sexual orientation keeps us from considering the ways sexual (as well as other) desires and identities are historically organized or how sex-affective relations are infused with ideologies of race and mediated by relations of labor."[51] The essentialist approach to gender that remains dominant in Lucumí houses nevertheless enables a reappraisal of "women's work" that sacralizes the efforts of both women and gay men in the kitchen. It is of a piece with an organization of the self that puts agency in the hands of the spirits.

It might seem that the kitchen has functioned as a sort of ghetto within the domestic space of the ilé, exploiting men whose defiance of heteronormative expectations has precluded their participation in more highly esteemed ritual practices. Yet this would be to project the racialized denigration of women's work that obtains in secular contexts onto a religious milieu. Although aborishas do not officially lose their given names and become wives of the orishas until their initiations, in the kitchen they enact their espousal to the gods. Plucking feathers, removing ashés, cooking—these acts of putting dinner on the table are forms of "citational practice" by which the body of the orishas' servant materializes in a "ritualized repetition of norms."[52] It is, as the theorist Judith Butler defines the type of performance that contributes to subject formation, "a ritualized production, a ritual reiterated under and through constraint, under and through force of prohibition and taboo, with the threat of ostracism and even death controlling and compelling the shape of the production, but not, I will insist, determining it fully in advance."[53] Although Butler bases her analysis on linguistic performance, the historian of religions Amy Hollywood has demonstrated that it may be extended to describe ceremonial action: "It is the process of ritualization that constitutes social beings, social worlds, and the constraints through which identities are maintained and differences enunciated."[54]

In the ilé, despite the rigors of the kitchen's bodily training and elders' control over their juniors' "citational practice" while cooking, gays and lesbians were not bidden to change their gender presentation, much less to terminate homosexual relationships. Divination and other practices were premised on the discovery of a sexual self that preexists one's consciousness of it, rather than an active, ongoing constitution of subjectivity. Turning to Lucumí more broadly, I would hypothesize that ritualized norms in the kitchen have socialized uninitiated women into strictly hierarchically ordered religious communities, along with men whose sexual orientations and close relationships with female spirits render them capable of embodying the ideal of wifely service with which worship of the orishas is synonymous. It is through the "sedimented effect" of doing women's work that individuals have been converted into wives for the spirits; this process has occurred independent of any "religious conversion" in the conventional sense of the term.[55] The formation and reformation of wifely dispositions in the kitchen have been paramount because these are what get the orishas fed.[56]

Despite the "female-normative" ethos of Lucumí, to reproduce a counterfactual discourse of orisha worship as matriarchal—advanced in the seminal scholarship on Brazilian Candomblé—serves only to sideline men at the vital center of Black Atlantic traditions since their inception.[57] Although the historical record is incomplete, I would submit that the kitchen's gendered division of labor has historically equipped those marked as exemplary wives for the spirits with the specialized skills required for the transmission of Lucumí traditions to succeeding generations. By saying so, I am not arguing that the kitchen has historically furnished women and gay men with an unrecognized site of resistance to heteronormative institutions and paradigms, although one could easily picture the outlines of such an argument. I am saying that their work in the kitchen allows us to rethink feeding in the fashioning of religious subjectivities, and speculate on the articulation of everyday micropractices (cooking) with ritual macropractices (possession performance). Far from merely adding a dash of spice to Lucumí, gay men have helped turn generations of green aleyos into seasoned aborishas. Their contributions to the tradition's characteristic temporalities and affective structures live on in "the best kitchens."

## Female Kinship and Sexed Sacrifice

When Oshun was impoverished, she went to live with [Elegba], who had only male goat to eat. He castrated [it] to make her believe she was eating she-goat, which, prior to

that, had been her customary food. From that day forward, she ate only castrated goat, as a pact with Elegba. . . . When I say that Oshun is the Orisha of survival, I mean to say that whatever it is that she does, she does to make life worth living. If she dances, she spins and whirls to make life bearable. If she sews, makes love or cuts someone's throat, it is because she HAS to, in order to survive.
—Afolabí[58]

In her ancestral invocation, or moyubá, and elsewhere, Ashabi traced her lineage to Fermina Gómez Torriente (1844–1950) and to Eulogio Rodríguez Tata Gaitán (1861–1944), "considered to be the only babalawo to be formally invested as obá [master of religious ceremonies] in Cuba," and an adept in Palo Monte as well as a priest of the Warrior orisha Ochosi.[59] Ashabi and other elders saw themselves as upholding a long tradition of female leadership in Ilé Laroye, and narrated the genealogy of the house in a manner designed to corroborate this claim. As has begun to be more extensively documented, some of the first and most influential early leaders in Lucumí were women, most famously Ñá Rosalía Abreú, Timotea Albear, and Ma Monserrate González, called by her religious name Obá Tero.[60] Oral history holds that Obá Tero was born in the Yorùbá region of Egbado, associated in the nineteenth century with the orishas Yemayá, Olokún, and Odudúwa, whose worship she introduced to Cuba (according to her descendants). Obá Tero passed on the secret of Olokún's confection to Fermina Gómez, around whose cabildo in the province of Matanzas, Brown writes, "Olokun masquerade traditions were reinstituted."[61]

Ashabi cited the presence of Gómez in her lineage as the reason that her godchildren receive the ritual sacra of Olokún from her.[62] To assert descent from Gómez is one way that Ashabi's house defended its credentials and wrested authority away from those wishing to claim it exclusively, such as babaláwos, to whom her godchildren seldom have recourse. But it was not only lineage forebears who influenced the ilé's development. The rupture occasioned by the slave trade shattered genres of historical consciousness in which the names of female ancestors had been enmeshed, yet women have been prominent in the familial genealogies there as in other casa-templos—for instance, at the beginning of rituals to propitiate the dead, when participants summoned them by name. Ashabi went a step further; she attributed her earlier initiation in Vodou to a mysterious French-speaking woman whom her paternal great-grandfather rowed home on a boat one day through the bayous of Louisiana, and introduced to the family as his second wife. It had come down through family lore that this woman was Haitian. She died long before Ashabi's birth, yet Ashabi said that she felt her great-grandmother's presence in her life, thereby enlarging the pool of women on whose energies she could draw in trying times.[63]

In Ilé Laroye, more than one Black female ancestor and living matriarch has assumed prominence as a "foremother figure" and, in the narratives of elders, "acts as a moral repository, preserves and cherishes culture, possesses wisdom and intense spirituality."[64] Sometimes foremothers were nameless contemporaries: after Ashabi visited Cuba several years ago, she wistfully recalled "old sisters" going about the ceremonial business of worshipping the orishas in dignified silence, uncomplainingly, without the benefit of first-world privileges and technological conveniences. One of her anecdotes concerned a woman she saw in Havana chopping sacrificed poultry on a marble floor, wielding a fierce cleaver with great force—"THWACK-a-tah!"—yet enough finesse to avoid splitting the antique tile.[65] In telling these stories, elders formulated a poetics of Diasporic relation to women of African descent elsewhere in the Black Atlantic world, reclaimed as formidable kinfolk.

References to the efficacy and power of these foremothers came to the surface in the kitchen, as practitioners' own ritual labor prompted them to envision the transformative work of others. To recall a scene that would not have been out of place in Alice Walker's *In Search of Our Mothers' Gardens*: "Fixing tea for a stomach virus with goldenseal and cayenne pepper, Arlene told me she comes from a long line of healers— her grandmother's father, her grandmother, and down the line. It's her calling, she says; she's the only one in traffic 'looking longingly' out the window at the weeds, wishing she could be on the shoulder, picking them and 'talking to them.'"[66] Arlene's main foremother was her grandmother, the late Gertrude Williams. Arlene had been groomed since early childhood to follow in M'dear's footsteps as a medium in the Black Spiritual Church.

Relying on the family lore that cast Ms. Williams's father as a Native American medicine man and an expert with herbs, she reiterated in an interview that her "family was a family of priests and healers." Arlene reminisced,

> I'm not sure what the nature of her gifts were, but she was best known in the community as a healer; she had the gift of what they call "laying on of hands." So she could put her hand on whatever was hurting, and we used to, you know, everybody who knew M'dear . . . used to say, "She could pray the devil up out of hell," OK? When M'dear got through praying, everything was all right within a fifty-mile radius. It was *cool . . .* 'cause she prayed it *out*, OK? And when she got through *praying* and *touching* and *rubbing*, and calling on whoever she called on, it was *straight*. She had the ability to move things by her sheer will, and with God's input. . . . She would [say]: *"We gon' move it, it ain't gon' be here no more."* Yeah, she was good like that.[67]

In the Black Spiritual Church, there was no glass ceiling on M'dear's leadership as a woman. Female elders donned regal vestments and robes resembling Roman Catholic chasubles as emblems of their sacerdotal prerogatives. Arlene conceived of her ordination in Lucumí as having fulfilled the promise M'dear saw in her and making her "good" in her own skin.

Fictional women figured in elders' self-understandings too. It was from Ashabi that I first heard the Richard Pryor routine called "Little Feets" that describes the best friend of his "Mudbone" character getting "a mojo" put on him by a girl from Louisiana, then consulting a hex-removing "voodoo lady" named Ms. Rudolph.[68] Despite Pryor's unflattering portrayal of Ms. Rudolph's domestic squalor and Rabelaisian physical dimensions (with an eye tattooed on one breast and a pair of lips on the other), she emerges in his tale as a community resource willing to care for clients regardless of their ability to pay. More importantly, Pryor depicts her as a healer whose treatments, no matter how fetid, prove largely efficacious.[69] I heard Ashabi recapitulate "Little Feets" with gusto while preparing a godchild of hers to receive sacred necklaces ceremonially, a process that includes sipping a frothy herbal infusion from a dried gourd.[70] Recognizing the parallels between her godchild's predicament and that of Mudbone's best friend—both of whom had to ingest mysterious liquids as part of a ritual—Ashabi placed herself in the "roots" tradition that Ms. Rudolph represents.

Remembering the past was an ethical imperative among Black elders in Ilé Laroye, as was paying homage to women whose ingenuity has seldom been celebrated—the Ms. Rudolphs of Lucumí. On the night of an initiation, the kitchen became a hearth around which to speak this knowledge.[71] In the midst of other Black female elders, Ashabi once said that she could not get over the way that Yorùbá sculptures of Shangó show his mother and other women holding him up, and brought up the fact that the orisha Dadá has been lauded as both Shangó's sister and his "crown."[72] Cleopatra and Arlene then commented critically on the widespread suppression of goddesses in world religions, lamenting the historical emphasis on male deities. It is important to note that practitioners with Dadá as a divine patron are ordained with the procedures for initiation to Shangó; some priests believe that Dadá was once as prominent as Ochún remains today, before her ritual secrets were lost in the Middle Passage.

These statements do more than mark the wide reach of feminist "goddess theory" and evoke how little is known about the reception of matriarchal prehistories among Black women, apart from what may be gleaned from the reading of womanist theology and philosophy. The elders' remarks could well be understood as disrupting, in a distinctively Black Atlantic religious idiom, the denigration of female labor in the present day. For Ashabi, the denial of women's ritual agency and their exclusion from privileged ceremonial offices fell under the rubric of "Western ideas coming in on African religion."[73] Her sentiments concerning Dadá expressed the conviction that, although a range of historical and sociopolitical processes contributed to the diminution or disappearance of some female deities, they may still be apprehended in African and Afro-Diasporic material culture, if seen through a Black woman–centered lens. She thus supplemented common understandings of the orishas based in mythology and oracular speech with her own speculative-fictional reflections.

Elders also made female orishas more prominent in the Lucumí pantheon by connecting episodes in their mythobiographies to present-day situations in the kitchen. This was particularly the case in discussions of the orishas' food preferences. During the first phase of my research, I had focused on the sexing of sacrificial victims and gendering of spirits—for instance, on the reasons for Ochún's consumption of wether, or castrated he-goat. The spirits' demands for particular sexes of animals are not always consistent across related Black Atlantic traditions; while most accounts of Ochún's preferences from Nigerian Yorùbá religious practitioners and Brazilian Candomblé initiates have her eating only she-goat, Lucumí priests continue to insist that a she-goat cannot be substituted for a wether. To the extent that scholars have attempted to analyze the spirits' preferences, they have surmised that their origins lie in the precolonial Yorùbá sacrificial complex. For example, the scholar, Ifá diviner, and priest of Obatalá John Mason conjectures that Ochún eats wether because her shrine in Nigeria is tended by priests not of childbearing age, such as female virgins, post-menopausal women, or very elderly men—those, in other words, whose fertility has yet to reach its potential or is diminished.[74]

It struck me that there are limitations to relying on Yorùbá history to account for contemporary Lucumí practice. During the next initiation I attended in Chicago, I approached three different female elders separately in the kitchen and posed the question of why Ochún demands castrated he-goat rather than she-goat, as the female orisha Oyá does. I was told three superficially similar, yet intriguingly distinct, narratives. They demonstrated the coexistence of different interpretations and the elders' investment in relating the orishas' travails to their everyday lives. The shortest story was told by Arlene, a daughter of Ochosi and Oyá, while still on her feet. She explained succinctly that Ochún had gone to visit Elegguá one day and, since she only ate she-goat and he had none at his disposal, he decided to castrate a male goat. As someone whose talent as a cook derived in part from her quick thinking and sensitivity to her guests' expectations, she stressed Elegguá's hospitality in observing Ochún's preferences. What stayed with her was his genius for improvisation; he created an intermediate category to bridge what, at first glance, would appear to be irreconcilable opposites (male and female).[75]

When I approached Oshunleye, an elder initiated to Ochún and Shangó, she told the same story while seated at the kitchen table in a rare moment of leisure. In keeping with her personal style, she embellished it with greater detail. She added that the formerly affluent Ochún had "come down in the world" and could not afford she-goat, and thus was not eating properly because she could not bring herself to abandon her extravagant tastes.[76] To get her to eat, Elegguá castrated the only four-legged animal available. This narrative stressed Ochún's vanity and stubbornness; conversely, although Elegguá deceived Ochún in passing off billy for nanny goat, his lie was interpreted as virtuous rather than unethical. Oshunleye also tied Ochún's appetite for castrated goat to the idea that she "castrates men," an assertion that underscores this orisha's reputation for ferocity in dispatching enemies and rogue initiates through another form of amputation: decapitation.[77]

I posed the same question to Ashabi as we marinated the meat from the day's sacrifices and sealed it into plastic bags. While echoing the first two responses, she expounded more fully on the reason for Ochún's poverty, ascribing it to her misguided romantic pursuit of Shangó. According to Ashabi, Ochún's neglect of her household obligations and maternal duties had cost her custody of her twins, the Ibeji, to her mother, Yemayá. Ochún arrived at Elegguá's home after a loss in both socioeconomic and maternal status directly tied to her unrequited love for a man. Only after stressing the nature of Ochún's indigence did Ashabi recount Elegguá's sleight of hand in passing off male goat as female. Her rendition of this story is noteworthy in three respects. It reflected her own view, frequently reiterated for the benefit of her goddaughters and perhaps gained at the price of experience, that women do not need men to be happy, and frequently become financially and emotionally impoverished by them. In addition, Ashabi's story expressed her desire to connect Lucumí myths to larger social issues; Yemayá stood in for the large number of grandparents in African American communities currently raising the children of sons and daughters ensnared in the criminal "justice" system or otherwise unable to be caregivers.

In addition, Ashabi related to this myth as a child of Ibú Kolé, a manifestation of Ochún in which she is destitute, inhabits gutters and sewers, plies a mortar and pestle, and keeps a vulture as her animal familiar. The divination verses associated with Ibú Kolé tell of a dispute between Earth and Heaven about which of them was greatest. To win the argument, Heaven withheld rain from the Earth, leaving the land scorched and every living thing gasping for water. The Earth decided to beg forgiveness. It wanted to send apologies in the form of offerings, but no orisha could fly high enough to reach Heaven except Ibú Kolé, the buzzard initially scorned by the gods for her appearance and status as a lowly carrion-eater. A thunderous downpour heralded the successful completion of her mission to Heaven and established her thereafter as the orishas' messenger.[78] In explaining Ochún's consumption of wether, Ashabi registered the centrality of a carrion-eating, unglamorous avatar to her identity, despite the widespread stereotype of this orisha as a glitzy, somewhat ditzy, "holy whore."[79]

While these responses did not lead me to a definitive conclusion about the basis for Ochún's dietary preferences, it was clear that elders addressed my question from the perspective of their multilayered relationships to her. While teaching principles of taxonomy, they demonstrated the use of Lucumí myths, or *pataki,* as moral-ethical "action guides" that model proper conduct outside the divinatory contexts in which such stories are usually embedded.[80] These elders chose to interpret myths as suggesting "normative trajectories" for behavior and reasoning that run counter to dominant Christian theological and ethical thought. They celebrated conceptual synthesis, the resolution of intractable dilemmas through a mastery of tactics, and—above all—the goal of survival, over obedience to literal or absolute truth.[81] Their retelling of these and other myths in the kitchen bore what the ethicist Katie Cannon calls "the real-lived texture of Black life," highlighting the ludic aspect of maneuvering under oppressive political and socioeconomic conditions, as well as the corresponding opportunity for creativity in the necessary exercise of subterfuge.[82] In making do with what he had at the moment of Ochún's greatest need and feeding her, Elegguá personified the Lucumí tradition.

## Gendered Disciplines

Arlene said that what Lucumí is about is becoming a repository for divine energy, and almost tearing up she said, "It's *hard*. It's hard work. The life of a priest is hard"—elongating the "a" in "hard" and pronouncing it as "awe." She said that she was telling us and reminding herself because no one had told her. She said that iyawos don't have "a name, or a title, or a position"; all an iyawo is, is "a tool, a vessel, and a ser-

vant." She said that when she got initiated, "I became nothing. I was nothing. I was genderless. I thought, 'What am I, a
hermaphrodite?' I didn't know what or who I was." She said
that when you're an iyawo, you've got "your whites and your
ass," and not even these belong to you. That sort of radical
destabilization, she was implying, was the whole point of the
process, and "process" is a word that she uses often to capture what rituals are about, what they aim for.
—Fieldnotes, July 24, 2005

The day that Arlene told us about her experience as an iyawo, Diahann
was driving us both home from Ashabi's house the morning after an
initiation. I was hunched behind them with the side of my face flush
against the windowpane, nearly asleep, until the edge of Arlene's voice
jolted me upright. Diahann had just gone through a significant ritual
experience, and while resigned to wearing white and covering her head
for the next few days, she was pressing Arlene on the matter of jewelry
and perfume. Arlene's response exposed her assumption that Diahann
would go on to be ordained someday—actually, it came sooner than
either of us thought—along with the social isolation Arlene felt in her
first year of ocha. Her brief monologue, a variation on the theme of
"buyer beware," encapsulated the objectives of iyaworaje in the eyes of
elders. It broke down the means through which its disciplines, far from
reaffirming her identity as a Black woman, had reoriented her sense of
self according to the ideal of Lucumí religious subjectivity. Although
indubitably an agentive subject during her iyaworaje, she saw herself
principally as a receptacle for and implement of the orishas' desires,
rather than her own.

Arlene's words bring to light the loneliness, powerlessness, and bewilderment that have tended to be overshadowed by theological issues in
accounts of initiation. Far from feeling invested with purpose and inner
peace, she had to confront an alienation from her own ritually altered
body, and a dread that she was no longer Arlene. The parallels Arlene
drew between her feelings of nothingness and genderlessness merit particular attention. Lucumí may be a "female normative" tradition, yet I
was surprised to be told that women often have a more difficult time
than men in adapting to their iyaworaje. One of my interlocutors once

blurted out in frustration, "Who made these rules? It must've been a man."[83] For Arlene, the "whites," or white clothing, of the liminal period following initiation (particularly the long dresses, and the tights and bloomers that have to be worn under them, even during the summer) constituted an anachronistic, foreign, hyper-feminine form of dress that threw into relief the loss of her most familiar gender-defining attributes, particularly her hair.[84] Black women have historically been the targets of anti-Black misogynist and transphobic discourses. Arlene's invocation of the hermaphrodite as an unsettling anatomical aggregate indexes the degree to which—despite the continued stability of her sexual preference—to be without a secure gender identity was to be without personhood.

The racialized gender identities of practitioners have both circumscribed and expanded their horizons for action within religious communities. Although according to her itá Arlene was able to wear the color red—unlike several others in Ilé Laroye—she was told that she could no longer wear trousers of any sort. As the daughter of a Warrior orisha and the Amazonian Oyá, Arlene was not shy about admitting her preference for pants, but she accepted this rule as dealing with her overabundance of "male energy." At the time of her initiation, Arlene had four children and did not identify as a lesbian; at issue was not her sexuality, but the "heavy" effect on her person of the values associated with masculinity, such as heat and passion, bearing in mind the dominance of martial influences in her religious makeup. Few skirts suited her sense of style or image of herself as "hard," in the sense of tough and strong. On one afternoon, she caught two young women horsing around in Ashabi's living room, trying to lift up and drag each other around the room. Arlene reprimanded them, "Hey! Ain't nobody here harder than me—nobody!—and if I have to sit here and wear a skirt and pretend to be a lady, so do you all."[85]

The force of this rebuke came partly from their knowledge of Arlene's sacrifice. Her choice of the word "pretend" cast ladylike femininity as a role to be played, a subject-position that must be learned to be inhabited, rather than the cultural expression of a biological sex. In the kitchen and elsewhere, Arlene delegated tasks to both male and female charges, and had the last word in any exchange. In short, she wore the pants, an uncommonly apt idiomatic expression because practitioners celebrate Oyá's superior courage, daring, and strength when referring to her as "*obini toto, olo shokoto mesan* (the fearful woman, owner of nine pairs of trousers)"[86] However, in the same manner that sons of Shangó have been warned not to copy his behavior, so Arlene was prohibited from imitating Oyá's war-waging habits.[87] In the wee hours of the morning, she could beckon an assistant to Ashabi's stove with no more than a snap of her wrist and perfunctory third-person address: "*What [is] that baby['s] name?*" Yet she prided herself on humble submission to the will of the gods, on whose favor her authority rested.

For Arlene, the terms of her sartorial surrender had the incalculable appeal of deriving from African precedents; throughout her life, dress had been inextricably intertwined with racial and gendered body politics. An "old-school revolutionary," Arlene received early religious training in the Black Spiritual Church, but in adulthood her political consciousness sought expression in both social activism and artistic collaboration.[88] Born in the 1950s, she felt prejudice "all the time" as a child; her school was mostly African American, but "discrimination came from the teachers, white teachers."[89] One episode was particularly revealing of the white supremacist aesthetic codes that governed everyday life:

> ARLENE: I remember an art teacher being angry with me because she had asked us to do a project. . . . We had these figures that we cut out and she wanted us to dress them, and, well, I drew the figure on the paper, but it took me longer because I couldn't find the right color paper; I wanted *brown* paper, and I found brown paper, finally, you know, and I cut out and drew my figure. Then the way I dressed the figure [made the art teacher say]: "*Who told you to do that? Where'd you get that from? You didn't think that up! Who told you to do that?*"
>
> I'd dressed him . . . and I don't really know where I got the image from, really, I must have seen something or read something or heard something that impressed me, but it was an *African* man. And I had the cloth going from across one shoulder and wrapping, I wrapped the cloth around the bottom.[90] I had the black yarn hair—it wasn't long and flowing, I had it cut short—and [the art teacher] was angry.

Yeah, she was angry and did not believe that I had come up with this on my own, [she thought] that someone told me or said to do this.

ELIZABETH: *As a provocation?*

ARLENE: Yeah, and then, she never even—she took it, and never gave it back and never gave me a grade. And as a kid, you're looking for feedback, you know: "*Well, how did I do? How did I do? You know, you made me do this damn thing, now, how did I do?*"

When I commented on the irony of having a room full of Black children produce white figures, Arlene responded,

[It's] because we're socialized not to see our own beauty and it's—I was very much aware of how that [worked]. I don't know why [I chose] that image, I must have seen it somewhere, I don't *understand* where I even got the image from, but it *impressed* me, this man, because I could see him in my mind as I was making this little doll. 'Cause he looked so beautiful to me, he was so royal and regal-looking, and I'm me, and [in] my little six- or seven-year-old mind—I'm trying to re-create this on a piece of paper *with this funny-lookin' stuff that don't look nothin' like the fabric he had on, but I'm going, I'm going try to make it work anyway.* And I caught *hell* because of that.

Her teacher's confiscation of her drawing—and her erasure of Arlene's labor, by refusing to grade her or return her figure—taught her that

[depicting Blackness] is not dangerous—that was never even a part of the process—it was just ugly. Or not allowed. In other words, "You don't exist except in the context that I give you to exist, and any of your ideas had better be expressing that context." *Or you gon' catch hell.*[91]

The experience of "catching hell" for daring to depict an African man in non-Western garb with dark skin and textured black hair unmasked the normativity of whiteness. It revealed that only the representation of white bodies—metonymic of white North American cultural values—would be tolerated. Arlene sought to present a beautiful image that was, in some sense, a reflection of herself, only to be silenced and have her existence outside the context "give[n] to exist" called into question.[92] For her and other Black members of the ilé, "To conform to this cultural system was, imaginatively, to be elsewhere, aesthetically, to be elsewise."[93]

Arlene had broken from the Black Spiritual Church precisely over the matter of her appearance, when at fifteen she decided that she would no longer straighten her hair. She had awoken to the oppressive nature of Eurocentric beauty standards and declined to waste any more time with hot combs and chemical hair relaxers. After the elders in the congregation noticed the change in Arlene's hair, she was given an ultimatum: straighten it or stop attending religious services. Their concern for attaining respectability in the face of the class-based stereotypes that trailed the storefronts prevented them from accepting her as she was.[94] Arlene's desire for Black figurations of dignity, prestige, and nobility in a religious idiom would be satisfied only years later, when she encountered the royal symbolism of Lucumí material culture.[95] The fashion of her African doll had anticipated the whites worn by Lucumí practitioners as well as the "clothing" of the orishas themselves, the heavily embroidered and appliquéd fabrics called *pañuelos* that are draped over their vessels. But Arlene would not recover the stolen figure from her youth until her iyaworaje, when—"wrapped" in cloth and with hair "cut short"—she accepted both "who" and "what" she would become.

## Wives and Martyrs

"In the religion, there is no gender," Fadesiye once told me in an interview. Later I wondered what he could possibly have meant by this. The asymmetrical relationship between human servants and deified masters in Lucumí is arguably devoid of meaning without reference to gender as a symbolic system reliant on "sexual" imagery as a source for the creation of difference through a masculine-feminine dichotomy. As we have seen, the orishas' preference for animals according to their sex has been a classificatory mandate in sacrifice, and explaining the origins of their tastes has provided an opportunity for initiated women to convert myths into "moral-ethical action guides." Arlene's story pointed to the awesome price exacted by gendered clothing restrictions within and beyond iyaworaje. The ordination ceremony itself has seemed to vindicate the cultural theorist Paul Gilroy's assertion that "gender is the modality in which race is lived"; that is to say, in Black Atlantic religions, the Middle Passage and experience of enslavement deeply mark the kind and degree of strictures imposed on practitioners, including the necessity of ritually assuming women's roles—as construed according to Yorùbá precedents—regardless of sex or sexual orientation.[96]

Metaphors of enslavement and marriage have overlapped to the point of interpenetration in Lucumí initiation. The homologies posited between a master's control of his slave's labor, a husband's over his wife's, and the orisha's over his servant's, have revalorized both the slave and wife as social actors.[97] From the expectation that women wear skirts on most ritual occasions to the convention of prostrating based on the sex of one's patron orisha, gender appears to be working overtime in Lucumí. Yet we can begin to unpack Fadesiye's claim by considering that the term "gender" often connotes bias based on stereotypes of women as inferior to men, and implies the patriarchal oppression of female sexuality. Lucumí practitioners do not take gender—as a hierarchical distinction based on an anatomically defined biological sex—for granted as determining the parts that practitioners play within the community. As discussed above, in Ilé Laroye, elders assumed that sexual identity would not be determined by reproductive organs alone, and the uncoupling of wifely femininity from femaleness was a basic tenet of its religious ideology. Both straight and gay men took up "women's work," and some women engaged in butchering goats and rams. Priests were invested in the sexes as having complementary, rather than equal, ritual roles.

To the extent that gender in a given culture conveys the proper constitution of social institutions, it is a key element of the political imagination. The concept of gender complementarity, then, is far from uncontroversial, and has been accused of promoting reactionary policies. The social theorist Patricia Hill Collins has tied this notion as formulated in Afrocentric scholarship to heterosexism, misogyny, and the marginalization of women in the Black nationalist project, along with a corresponding glorification of African American motherhood. Collins writes, "The notion of complementarity dovetails with an ethic of service in which Black women and men demonstrate racial solidarity by submerging their individual needs, goals, and concerns to those of the Black community as a collectivity. Theoretically, all make sacrifices so that racial solidarity can be maintained. But in actual everyday life, African American women typically sacrifice more."[98] So it is in the mainstream of Black life and myriad other contexts in which gender difference rationalizes exclusion, barring women's access to material resources and giving men a monopoly on decision-making power.

In Ilé Laroye, gender complementarity was linked to a principle of self-preservation developed precisely in response to the violence historically visited on Black bodies. In the kitchen, as if according to Hippocratic dictum, the first rule was "Do no harm," to others or oneself.[99] To this end, elders monitored their own and others' posture and comportment, urging aborishas to take breaks and pausing to adjust their juniors' dangling sleeves when poised over pots of boiling water. One afternoon, I resisted when one elder gave me a pair of gloves with which to wash a set of containers left in the basement after an initiation. She warned me against approaching the task barehanded with a reference to the heroes of her Roman Catholic upbringing: "Ain't no martyrs up in here. Martyrs laying up in the hospital!" The thrust of her remark was clear: self-abnegation to the point of injury may be cast as a virtue by hagiographers, but Lucumí priests will dismiss the same as reckless naïveté. Needless to say, I put on the gloves.[100]

The principle of self-preservation explains Ashabi's pronouncement on the night of an initiation in 2005, after the matanzas had concluded: "There are some aspects of feminism I can let go. One of them is taking out the garbage, and another is killing a goat. I can let that go."[101] Ashabi made this statement in the kitchen with reference to a rite of passage (*pinaldo*) that enables women to sacrifice goats and other four-legged animals. Although the pace was comparatively slack that evening, she had already fixed part of the household's lunch and planned the menu for dinner, in addition to discharging her ceremonial duties. Her hands would soon feel so clawlike from hours of butchering that I would sit on a banquette next to her and massage spices, garlic, and onion into cuts of meat while she poured on the ingredients one by one, choosing her marinades from a soul food cookbook and another subtitled *Traditional Recipes and Fond Remembrances from Alabama's Renowned Tuskegee Institute*. The work she had yet to do was on her mind.

It might seem odd for her to have equated taking garbage out with killing goats, and stranger still to link both to feminism. What she meant by the term merits some elaboration. For white women of Ashabi's generation—influenced by Betty Friedan's book *The Feminine Mystique* and other classics of post-Marxist second-wave feminism—the objectives of sexual revolution included freedom from household drudgery, sole responsibility for childcare, and norms of feminine beauty.[102] They also wanted to gain entrées to professional avenues previously closed to them. Since many women of color and immigrants were historically obligated to work outside the home to support their families, second-wave feminist activism proved to be less responsive to their concerns, and overwhelmingly attuned to advocacy on behalf of middle- and upper-class women.[103] Womanism as an African American feminist counterdiscourse owes its efflorescence to racial and class disparities that have only become more thoroughly exacerbated over the last quarter-century. To quote the cultural theorist Brittney Cooper, "White women's feminisms still center around equality. . . . Black women's feminisms demand justice. There is a difference. One kind of feminism focuses on the policies that will help women integrate fully. . . . The other recognizes the fundamental flaws in the system and seeks its complete and total transformation."[104]

Although Ashabi said that, with her Army shirt, Afro, and granny glasses, she was more of a hippie than a revolutionary, the mainstream women's liberation movement impressed itself on her forcefully.[105] She repeatedly professed her sense of responsibility toward her goddaughters—not to mention her seven biological siblings, all sisters, as well as her nieces. She wondered aloud whether younger women realize how hard those of her generation fought for their independence. She said that her love of classic Hollywood films, such as the original version of *Cheaper by the Dozen*, came partly from her interest in the ways popular cinema has represented controversial feminist issues such as birth control and abortion while aspiring to reach a mass audience.[106] It was not surprising to learn that her favorite movie star is Katharine Hepburn, or to hear her describe the 1953 film of the musical *Kiss Me Kate*—with pride—as "the story of my life," implying that the taming of the shrew in question was far from complete.[107]

Her commitment to women's rights has not prevented Ashabi from formulating critiques of the ways that "equality feminism" has affected her life as a Lucumí initiate and African American woman. To put the sentiment more pointedly: Black religious practitioners like her have been at the intersection not just of race, class, and gender as mutually constituting categories, but of white supremacy, class exploitation, and heteropatriarchy as well.[108] These are large words for big problems. In the words of the critical race theorist Kimberlé Crenshaw, "Because women of color experience racism in ways not always the same as those experienced by men of color, and sexism in ways not always parallel to experiences of white women, dominant conceptions of antiracism and feminism are limited, even on their own terms."[109] Over twenty years after Crenshaw published these words, mainstream feminist discourse has yet to come to grips with its anti-Blackness and complicity with racist misogyny, neologized by the Black feminist scholar Moya Bailey as "misogynoir."[110]

The most fruitful interpretation of Ashabi's striking statement takes into account the intersecting axes of oppression in her life and that of many Black Atlantic religious practitioners. For Ashabi, the fact that men kill goats was not reason enough for her to aspire to do so. Just as taking out the garbage may be seen as a male chore in the contemporary United States, so too, for many Lucumí practitioners, is sacrificing four-legged animals; both are indispensable yet noisome tasks. Drawing on her experience as a Black working mother, Ashabi felt that some restrictions on women in the sacrificial abattoir redounded to her benefit, since she suspected that ritual equality with men would simply lead to more exploitation. She did not relish the thought of cutting throats. She regarded the inequalities to be found in Lucumí—for instance, that only men can prepare and consecrate the Warriors—as matters settled by the legendary women involved in codifying the tradition's protocols in the late nineteenth and early twentieth centuries.[111]

Womanist theologians have pursued complementary approaches. Delores S. Williams invokes the biblical figure of Hagar—impregnated by Abraham as a proxy for her mistress, Sarah, then abandoned by them—to explore Black women's plight as both coerced and voluntary surrogates for white mothers, sexual partners, and Black male workers. She makes the case that, for Black women, existence has trumped the goal of liberation.[112] Decrying the suicidal self-sacrifice asked of Black women, JoAnne Marie Terrell looks to the blood they have shed for her empowering vision of sacramental witness.[113] Their insights would be food for thought in the Lucumí kitchen, where the Ochún that had to be tricked into surviving has been a protagonist in cautionary tales. Practitioners have known suffering, and talked about cooking in Ilé Laroye as rendering thanks to the orishas for keeping them alive. Why and how they said so concerns the next chapter.

Figure 1. Ashabi and 'Tunde Mosley at one of Ilé Laroye's Ochún parties

Figure 2. Altar for Billal Henderson's Elegguás (one of them wearing yellow-rimmed sunglasses) with toys, balls, candy, painted hanging gourds (beside the "E-Z Break" coconut), and clown doll

Figure 3. Violinist playing classical music during Ochún party

Figure 4. Placing sweets on an altar for Ochún

Figure 5. Shangó "throne" for the anniversary of a priest's initiation (ocha birthday), with a sheet cake at the base that carries an illustration of the orisha dancing

Figure 6. Combined Shangó and Ochún altars for the one-year ocha birthday of priests concurrently initiated ("twins")

Figure 7. Yemayá altar, for a manifestation of the orisha associated with dishes, plates, and pots

Figure 8. A godchild waiting to serve the priests after a drum feast

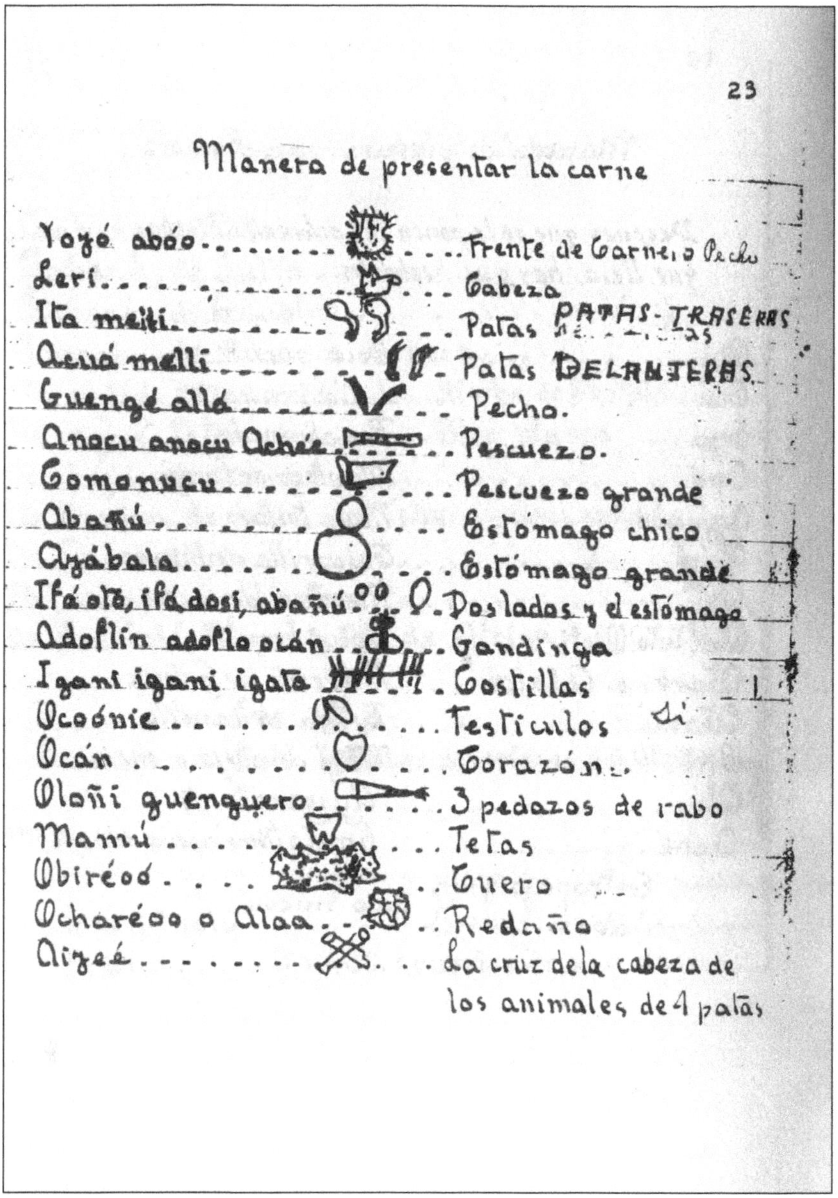

Manera de presentar la carne

Yozó abóo .......... Frente de Carne, o Pecho
Leri .......... Cabeza
Ita meiti .......... Patas [PATAS-TRASERAS]
Acuá melli .......... Patas DELANTERAS
Guengé allá .......... Pecho.
Anocu anocu Achée .......... Pescuezo.
Comonucu .......... Pescuezo grande
Abañú .......... Estómago chico
Azábala .......... Estómago grande
Ifá otó, ifá dosi, abañú .......... Dos lados y el estómago
Adoflín adoflo otán .......... Gandinga
Igani igani igata .......... Costillas
Ocoónie .......... Testículos
Ocán .......... Corazón
Oloñi guenguero .......... 3 pedazos de rabo
Mamú .......... Tetas
Obiréod .......... Cuero
Ocharéoo o Alaa .......... Redaño
Aizeé .......... La cruz de la cabeza de
los animales de 4 patas

Figure 9. Image from Lázara Menéndez, ed., "Libreta de Santería de Jesús Torregosa." The rare image, ca. 1936, depicts a priest's instructions on the presentation of meat from four-legged animals to the orishas.

LIVING ROOMS AND SLEEPING ROOMS SEPARATED

JUST how to separate the daytime part of the house from the nighttime part in the bungalow, where all the rooms are on one floor, is often a perplexing problem. You will approve the manner in which it is solved in this plan. The bedrooms and bathroom are separated by two walls and some eight or ten feet of space from the living room and dining room. This arrangement makes possible a generous vestibule and commodious coat and linen closets. It also gives you a large kitchen with space enough for wide cupboards so you don't need a pantry.

FLOOR PLAN

*The*
*Manson*

56

Figure 10. Sample house plan

## PART III

Kitchen Talk

5

## Tasting Affliction

Men . . . skin, clean and cut up four-legged animals. Women pluck and eviscerate chickens, pigeons and guinea hens. Certain parts of the sacrifices are cooked to be given to the Orisha. (Each Orisha has her favorite foods, taboos and recipes.) Other parts are cooked for people to eat the next day. This is a gargantuan task.

When the sacrifices and cooking are over, the sheet is raised and people sit around and talk.[1]

In the kitchen of Ilé Laroye on any given day, dozens of activities occurred that had nothing to do with food. Even during interminable days—and longer nights—say, on the first full day of an initiation, the kitchen was not simply a place to admire virtuosic knife-work and the attention to detail that makes rituals go right. Being in the kitchen was a chance to savor the exchange of unexpected presents and caresses; clipped recitations of myth; confessions of exhaustion accompanied by impromptu "stay awake" dances; the occasional lyric rapped or sung as if before an audience of thousands; and the delicious gallows humor for which a puddle of blood has always been the best sauce. The kitchen was a preeminently social space in which issues of gender, sexuality, and race merged with those of class.[2] I have in mind here such instances as when a young woman named Berta was forced to substitute one object for another at a moment's notice, then shrugged and said—as if explaining the seemingly preternatural ease with which the improvisation was made—"We Black."[3]

In the kitchen, people also told of how they had come to claim Lucumí—leaning against the sink, fishing for silverware in the cabinet drawers—and how the religion had claimed them. During my first tentative forays into the ethnographic field—in the botánicas of Chicago, Boston, and Miami, then in Havana and Guantánamo—I made a point of posing the same question to Lucumí practitioners: "Why did you get initiated?" I expected my interlocutors to describe their commitment to the orishas almost romantically, perhaps as a means of recruiting me to their service. Again and again, the answers I received made it clear that they did not get initiated out of desire. In fact, the elders recounted their resistance to initiation in extravagant terms, emphasizing their initial hostility toward the tradition rather than their espousal of its gods. The initiatory wedding was portrayed not as the sacralization of a love match but as an arranged marriage, or ritualized bride abduction. Priests said they surrendered to the orishas because they faced incapacitating infirmity or adversity, and ordination stood the only chance of saving them. No one spoke of initiation as a decision, made with pleasure or at the behest of reason. It was instead discussed as an unchosen choice.[4]

do they have agency or not?

Ouch and Boing Similar to Sati in Devi

While initiation and other rites of passage have animated a number of pioneering studies, the scholarship on Lucumí has yet to grapple with a fundamental irony: the vast majority of practitioners have been initiated as adults and could be categorized as converts, but those consulted in academic studies almost invariably say that they made ocha without wanting to do so. In elders' published narratives, as in my own research, illness and injury have been the main catalysts for initiation. Rather than sing the praises of the tradition in recounting their ordinations, priests have professed themselves alarmed by the financial burden imposed by them, suspicious of mentors' ulterior motives, and wary of Lucumí's reputation as a witchcraft cult for the destitute and credulous. Their resistance is invariably recalled as futile—even dangerous to their health.[5] In *El monte*, Cabrera was the first to record multiple accounts of rebellion against the orishas' wishes for practitioners to become initiated, but she was certainly not the last.[6] The ethnographic literature on Afro-Cuban religions is replete with such stories, particularly in texts reliant on oral histories as a means of ascertaining practitioners' points of entry into Lucumí.

Social actors tend to appropriate the speech patterns of those whose beliefs and practices align with their own.[7] This observation seems particularly germane to religious specialists and virtuosi. In the writing on prophets and shamans, for instance, they often profess to have resisted the pull of their vocations until brought to a crisis.[8] While Lucumí priests' stories bear a family resemblance to those of healers in other cultures, certain features are specific to their experiences within Afro-Cuban religions. Their oral narratives are rife with aversion to initiation itself and to discharging the functions of priesthood, such as performing divinations and officiating during initiations for protégés. In the mid-1980s, for instance, one of Brown's informants told him that, when approached to act as a ritual sponsor for ocha, he was liable to respond,

> "I don't want any more godchildren! I'm tired of this shit, I told you I never wanted to [get initiated], and every time I don't want to [officiate another ocha], everybody tricks me into making it. The Saints and everybody are always blackmailing me into doing something, I'm sick of it. I don't go to nobody's house, I don't do readings. . . ." And as you can see, every one of [these initiations] has been a trick. I just look at him [my patron orisha] and I say, "Boy, you really know how to screw me don't you." And everything that comes to my house is this way. I don't go out looking for it. I don't read [the cowrie shell oracle], I do nothing, it's brought by other people.[9]

I would contend that only the vehemence and profanity of this diatribe are unusual.

In the scholarship on Afro-Cuban traditions, the spirits most frequently accused of extortionary behavior—and indicted in tirades peppered with obscenities—are the ritually enslaved spirits of Palo Monte, called *nfumbi*. The elder in Brown's account appears to put himself in the role of his orisha's nfumbi, a manipulated, objectified slave, performing alienated labor for his deified masters.[10] Lucumí initiates have characteristically depicted their relationships with the orishas in terms more heavily reliant on idioms of familial intimacy and mutual nurturance. Nevertheless, Ashabi instructed her godchildren, "Don't recommend me to nobody."[11] Quoting Bing Crosby's character in *White Christmas* (1954), she told visitors that initiation "costs somewhere 'between ouch and boing.'"[12] This was an onomatopoetic way of conveying the painful surprises involved in supplying the herbs, vessels, cloth, sacrificial animals, travel expenses of visiting priests, ritual fees (*achedís*), food, and myriad other objects needed for ordination and the neophyte's post-ceremonial seclusion. As the sociologist Mary Cuthrell Curry stated, "If a person decides to *make ocha* (some people resist this decision for years, some perhaps indefinitely) then they have an expensive proposition ahead of them."[13]

The financial burden of ordination has been deemed onerous for priests-to-be as well as for their ritual sponsors. Its cost has often gone beyond what godchildren are able to pay, and godparents have marshaled their own financial resources to acquire the necessary materiel and personnel.[14] It has been commonplace for elders to subsidize ceremonies performed for their communities by charging more for services rendered to clients intent on resolving immediate problems, but not in becoming godchildren.[15] Such services have included conducting divinations, administering cleansings, and making "works," or *trabajos*, sometimes with nfumbi, intended to produce quick results.[16] Considering the expense of initiation alone, it is not surprising that godparents have bemoaned the growth of their families, or that those drawn to the religion have wished to postpone initiation or dispense with it altogether. My uninitiated interlocutors agonized over whether they could ever learn enough to become upstanding priests. They worried about the lifelong sartorial, gastronomic, and behavioral taboos that would be unveiled in their itá. They dreaded the inevitable loosening of social and professional ties due to the restrictions placed on them during their iyawo years.[17]

But the orishas have been perceived as formidable and unremitting to the point that they have not scrupled to, as Brown writes, "'fight with,' and 'flog,' people who resist serving them, bringing on misfortunes, sicknesses, and insanity. In Lucumí religion, [the seemingly malevolent spirit] Echú has not disappeared, *eguns* bring death, loss, sickness, etc., and the *orichas* are not above 'blackmailing' people into serving them and punishing them with sickness if they don't."[18] In the ilé, everyone seemed to have an anecdote about someone being driven out of his home, mind, or skin as a result of disobedience to the orishas.[19] Practitioners told cautionary tales about derelict initiates reduced to penury, dementia, or worse by their refusal to abide by moral-ethical precepts, feed the orishas properly, or comply with the spirits' directives. They featured individuals enjoined to get initiated by diviners or possessed mounts, then consumed by the ravages of disease or misfortune after shunning their counsel. Elders shared similar stories about themselves, and the near-death experiences that brought them, through so many shortcuts that turned into detours, to the room in which I sat across from them, listening. I did not have to schedule interviews to hear their accounts; they came to me in Ashabi's kitchen and others'. Priests regularly inquired into each other's religious trajectories and freely shared their own with newcomers, in confidential settings as well as in large groups.

Most of the elders I met through and within Ilé Laroye in the early 2000s maintained that they had struggled with initiation. One of the first to tell me this was Billal. His account is a typical, if uncharacteristically dramatic, example of the way that practitioners related their initial opposition to ocha. In the kitchen of a fellow elder's house, Billal told me he had not believed in the orishas at the time of his initiation.[20] In fact, he said he got ordained solely to appease his mother, one of Ashabi's godchildren, after a string of misfortunes left him open to contemplating courses of action that once seemed inconceivable. His marriage had just ended, prompting him to switch jobs and move house. Living in Manhattan, and dedicated—as he put it—to the twin religions of capitalism and materialism, he was "going through changes": experiencing trouble and endless dilemmas. As the saying goes, his changes were going through changes. Then his godfather Theo called Billal out of the blue one morning and offered to pay for his initiation. Having dreamed the previous night of a figure in scarlet and ebony standing at a crossroads—the very image of Eleggua, identified as his "father" in Lucumí—Billal accepted. He thought he would be able to repay Theo almost at once, due to the financial rewards of his new position: he had just been hired by a major corporation, with an exceedingly impressive starting salary.

Billal had attended few Lucumí rituals and, at his mother's insistence, sat through a handful of divinations, including the one in which Eleggua was determined to be his patron. Before meeting Ashabi, his mother had been a missionary for the Pan-African Orthodox Christian Church, and while she was often traveling during his childhood, his father was entirely absent. Billal had gone from spraying graffiti and rapping on the streets of Detroit in his teens to occupying a respectable perch in corporate America. Achieving professional success had required sacrifices. With memories of grade-school teachers unable or unwilling to pronounce his name properly fresh in his mind, he shortened it from Billal to "Bill" for his white colleagues. Every morning, to render himself as nonthreatening as possible, he meticulously groomed his tidy "bathroom dreads," "worn by folks who can't really give up the comb but who do want the hip, 'antisocial' effect of [dreadlocks]."[21] Despite his efforts, he had grown accustomed to clients closing deals with him over the telephone, then terminating their accounts after meeting him and seeing, for the first time, the color of his face. Although he had lost his wife, his high-school sweetheart, Billal told me he was "living the Black American dream." The gist was clear: it had been as good for him as it got, for any dark-skinned man of African descent in America.

He told himself that life would resume as normal, if perhaps marginally better, after making ocha. Billal's unforeseen head shaving in the initiation chamber was his first indication that life would never be the same again. Then during his itá, Billal was told by the officiating diviner never to return to his office in Manhattan, even to retrieve his personal effects, or bid farewell to friends and associates. In fact, he should never set foot in any part of the Empire State again. Billal's immediate reaction was outrage. He was incensed that he would be ordered to leave his hard-won position. Although Billal planned on returning to the Northeast immediately, his mother begged him to stay in Chicago until at least that November and after the completion of another ceremony. He grudgingly agreed. Then one morning in September, Ashabi's husband, 'Tunde, called, and told him to turn on the television. Billal was initiated in July 2001; his office had been on the nineteenth floor of the World Trade Center. Although employees on higher floors survived, Billal maintained that he would not have. He said that in those days, "getting paid" was his only creed, and if he had been ordered to remain where he was rather than attempt an uncertain descent down the stairs, his mind would have been so occupied by the thought of lucrative projects that he would have stayed not only in his office, but firmly ensconced in his swivel chair.

Some aspects of Billal's narrative are particular to Billal alone, and are tied to his own existential concerns. For him, head shaving was metonymic of initiation, a startling disruption of his everyday life that initially felt oppressive. Yet the cutting of his hair furnished Billal with an opportunity to leave behind the corporate, abbreviated version of himself he had come to disdain. The intransigence exhibited by the orishas in divination stood as a reproach to the compromises he had made in exchange for wealth and status; Billal said that the orishas' nonnegotiable directives allowed him to abandon a consumption-driven lifestyle increasingly at odds with his politicized religious views. His ordination brought him into closer contact with his mother, and he adopted Elegguá as a father precisely at the moment that he found himself wrestling with the emotionally devastating repercussions of divorcing the mother of his only child. Elegguá provided him with a deified image of the paternal confidant he had missed as a young man.

These issues relate specifically to Billal, and it would be easy to conclude that these were the underlying psychosocial "reasons" for his initiation, thus simultaneously explaining an inexplicable course of action—ocha in the absence of religious commitment—and offering the basis for a generalizable model to account for Lucumí conversion as a cultural phenomenon. Yet this would be to ignore the circumstances surrounding Billal's disclosures to me. As textual elements fixed into a sequence, the incidents and impressions rendered above did not exist prior to his ordination. Disparate strands of his experience came together in the shape of a story only afterwards, through his sustained exposure to other priests versed in the same patterns of everyday talk governed by identifiable linguistic structures and rhetorical codes. Billal's recollections must be understood according to the stylistic conventions of the initiation story as well as his likely "speech plan."[22] The speech plan of narrators such as Billal has been not to enumerate objectively the factors that led to ocha; it has been to convey, through the elaboration of so many details, that initiation was thrust upon the narrator.

## Initiation Talk as Speech Genre

Once the *orixá* calls, there is no other path to take.
—Mãe Menininha de Gantois[23]

The stylistic and linguistic conventions of the initiation story are so widely observed that they can be said to form their own category of verbal composition, or "speech genre." A speech genre is a type of utterance that shares both the thematic contents and situational context for the performance of similar communicative events.[24] The stability of speech genres over time derives, in part, from the frequency of their recurrence within groups or among members of particular social strata. In his early study of speech genres, the philosopher and literary theorist Mikhail Bakhtin gave the example of the military command and oral business contract; to these may be added the courtroom jury summation, Roman Catholic confession, individual therapy session, and the self-help meetings mandated in drug addiction programs.[25] Those competent in a speech genre may not realize that they are replicating a well-worn pattern, yet the relatively predictable structure of a given utterance helps to produce its meaning. Novelty may be introduced spontaneously into its sequential organization, content, rhetorical form, or physical circumstances. Despite constraints, speech genres expand and contract according to the needs of individuals and the institutions they inhabit.

Billal's assertion that the orishas literally kept him alive was a crucial aspect of the initiation story. It is a speech genre analogous to "being saved," although salvation for priests has entailed a reprieve from an impending death sentence, whether imposed by illness or calamity, rather than redemption from sin.[26] This is the case even when narrators depict themselves as oblivious to the necessity of ocha at the time of their ordinations. Billal recalled his awareness of its power as deriving from events external to the religion. Some elders, such as Yomí Yomí, cited oracular speech as proving decisive in comprehending ocha as a ritual death and rebirth that staves off physical mortality. In one typical exchange, she referred to both the divinatory sign, or odu, cast for her in her itá, and the pronouncement of a local Spiritist:

> ELIZABETH: You said to me before . . . that you feel like the religion saved your life.
>
> YOMÍ YOMÍ: It did. My [priestly] name, Yomí Yomí, means "salvation." And my odu, and my odu in . . . ocha is, "The debt is paid." I know Yemayá saved my life. Well, my health is [still] an issue, but I was one time at [a Spiritist medium's home], and this other babaláwo who was a *palero* too, he was sitting there in the basement. . . . All of a

sudden it was like [the medium's] *muerto* [or possessing spirit] just
came down on him—we were just sitting there chitchatting—and he
said, "If you didn't make ocha, you'd be dead." See, I get those confirmation messages, and you may get them six years down the line—
that's when mine was given to me—but they'll come.[27]

This statement strongly resembles other initiates' recollections, particularly in its characterization of initiation as the life-prolonging settlement
of a balance with the orishas.

Kristina Silke Wirtz lists four motives for ocha identified by her main
informant in Cuba: "family tradition," "irresolvable problems," "serious
illness," and "affinity for the religion."[28] Yet in the course of my research
among African American, Latino/a, and Anglo practitioners, a lone interlocutor told me that she was "crowned" out of "love" for the tradition. Even those whose families were involved in Lucumí did not say
they wanted to get initiated; in fact, these were the cases in which ocha
initially had been opposed with the greatest tenacity. Tomás Fernández
Robaina asserts that in colonial and early Republican Cuba, "one only
initiated a person as a *santero*, *babaláwo*, or *palero* who really needed
to enter the religion for reasons of health, or in the search for material
or spiritual improvement."[29] With one exception, initiates in Ilé Laroye
said that they made ocha in the pursuit of release from affliction. They
credited their very existence to the intervention of the orishas.[30] Oral
performances tended to progress from the onset of unexplainable and
ineradicable symptoms, frustrated appeals to medical authorities, and
struggle against the suggestion of initiation, to eventual acquiescence.

In the kitchen, initiates vividly described the symptoms of corporeal
affliction, signs from the spirits that they had been determined to ignore or did not yet know how to decipher. My interlocutors told of disease and injury, of sudden diminishments of vigor, lingering infections,
temporary paralysis, nausea, unpredictable lapses of consciousness, and
heart-stopping medical diagnoses.[31] Such stories find corroboration
among practitioners consulted by scholars throughout the twentieth
century. Rodolpho Martin, a Cuban priest interviewed by John Mason,
told him with reference to the prerevolutionary period, "Look, in those
days everybody cooperated. You never had to give anyone a tip [for assisting in an ocha]. No, no, they'd tell you when you offered. The major-

ity of them were poor and made their initiations to avoid that which cripples you (sicknesses)."[32] It is difficult to gauge the veracity of Martin's claim, as much a critique of contemporary mores as a comment on the relationship between health and ocha. Yet it would be even harder to transcribe an oral history from an initiate without some version of the following statement: "One makes saint for two reasons: for health or because one is born with that [oracular] sign, with the odu to walk down that path, whether we like it or not."[33] In fact, even this is to isolate phenomena that have been apt to coincide in practitioners' narratives, where illness has prompted the divination that in turn mandates initiation, and forces a reevaluation of the religion.[34]

Despite its ubiquity in houses of orisha worship, the initiation story has yet to excite substantial interest due to several factors. The first of these is the overwhelming emphasis that has been placed on accounting for the continued survival, if not the globalization, of Lucumí in revolutionary Cuba and the United States.[35] Particularly after the Mariel boatlift of 1980, the literature on orisha worship sought to quantify the amount of syncretism operative in Afro-Diasporic initiatory traditions and situate their growth within economic and sociocultural macrotrends.[36] The latter include the politicization of Black religious identity, greater geographical mobility and improved communication technologies among practitioners, and the expanded transnational market for African-inspired cultural production.[37] Such research created a historical record of inestimable value by ceding precedence to the viewpoints of interlocutors, but it tended to replicate their discourses of "autolegitimation" by framing orisha worship in terms of resistance.[38] These studies joined converts themselves in presenting initiation as an indictment of their material privations and political oppression.

The most common iteration of the initiation story, with its claim that ocha transpired against the will of the practitioner, may have also hampered analysis. In the early scholarship on Lucumí, researchers collected ethnographic data almost exclusively from authoritative senior Cuban and Puerto Rican practitioners steeped in lifelong experiences of the traditions they came to embrace.[39] In the interest of representing the tradition in a manner that would refute patently racist, sensationalistic accounts and to corroborate practitioners' claims to a foundational African past that would ennoble them in the present, scholars moved to cast Lucumí in the mold of familiar monotheisms. They stressed the beliefs ostensibly to be deduced from practices and bowdlerized references to those that seemed irrational or superstitious according to the hegemonic "litmus test of legitimacy."[40] To the extent that an informant was portrayed as wrestling with her religious vocation, the story was cast as a comedy: a series of blunders that ended in a marriage, only in this case, those joined together in holy matrimony were a divine husband and human wife.

Moreover, the tendency of scholars themselves to "get hitched" to the spirits—for to be a bride of the orishas is often to be their "horse" in possession—has fostered inattention to the typical initiation story. While seldom discussed as a research phenomenon, it has been customary for scholars to become ordained while gathering data on Black Atlantic religions, and to concede as much in print.[41] They have been forthcoming about their "double-consciousness" as both practitioners and academics, to the point of operationalizing religious dreams, sensations, and encounters in their analyses.[42] Yet the anomalous circumstances surrounding their ordinations seem to have colored their depictions of ocha as desirable. The authors of academic monographs have tended to say that they sought to be initiated out of an affinity with the traditions under examination, combined with an aspiration to obtain ritual information.[43] This situation is decidedly at odds with that of most initiates, for they overwhelmingly profess to have become priests not because they wanted to, but because the spirits wanted them.

Finally, the initiation story has not occasioned more inquiry due to its very banality. Its recitation is as easy to take for granted in a house of orisha worship as wallpaper, and its prosaic design may be just as monotonous.[44] Palmié has divided the writing on Afro-Cuban religions into "three equally distinct genres: the academic monograph, the 'eyewitness account,' and the *manual de santería*"; while all three have furnished invaluable documentary and theological material for the study of Afro-Cuban religions, in only the rare monograph has the question of initiation stories as rhetorical constructs, sites of ritual performance, or analytical problematics arisen.[45] An ordinary, around-the-kitchen-table form of Lucumí discourse, the initiation story has no place in the compendia of "secrets" that dominate the popular scholarship and trade publications. Since Lucumí practitioners do not proselytize, the "micropractices of persuasion" that have gradually convinced them of the spirits' power, the elders' authority, and their need for ordination seem to have blended into the woodwork.[46]

## Histories of Everyday Talk

I want to suggest that *conversational micropractices are performed memory*, and responsible for reproducing the infrastructures of sociocultural formations. Memory is neither a general nor an abstract idea. A master, for example, is a subject surrendered to experience, someone whose experience produces micropractices demonstrating principles of economy. Experienced micropractices obtain maximum effect from minimum effort. A master makes it look easy. . . . It is the micropractical body that knows, and the experience of such embodied knowledge takes place in time.[47]

The aforementioned Alaafi was one among many interlocutors to tell me that he had long pushed away the thought of getting initiated. He procrastinated until he became ill. Throughout his life, he had suffered from "a lot of head trauma," including an accident during a demolition job in which he was injured while using a sledgehammer. Six months prior to his ordination, he had been hit by a car as a pedestrian, and complications arising from the accident threatened to paralyze his legs and resulted in "issues upon issues, which led up to me getting myself together [for ocha]," although it would still be necessary after initiation to engage in physical rehabilitation.[48] He was supposed to have been ordained in childhood; then, when he had the means to do so during his senior year of high school, he put it off:

> I postponed it, just for personal reasons, not really looking at the big picture, so it ended up being a life-and-death situation. So you know, I didn't really have a choice to get initiated or not to. . . . It was, so to speak, "put upon me" to get it done in order to save my life. And the entire ilé family came together on my behalf, pretty much, in order to get myself together.[49]

Initiation dramatized not only his need for the orishas, but also the indispensability of the community he had previously failed to appreciate.

He told me this story for the first time late one night while I was bead-
ing at Ashabi's kitchen table. Shortly before my conversation with Alaafi,
another elder had said, "The orishas saved my life more than once." As
we stood at the kitchen sink, she explained that she had needed to go to
the hospital during her iyawo year, and came close to dying before the
spirits intervened on her behalf. As the site of taxing labor, alimentation,
and consumption, the kitchen tended to elicit these revelations more
often than other places. "A space of blood and guts, plucked chickens and
cooked tongue, rancid and sweet butter, rising bread and fermenting beers,
and other items only semiformed on their way to the site of ingestion,"
the kitchen facilitated the transgression of social and corporeal boundaries.[50] Perhaps for this reason, practitioners readily disclosed transgressions
against their own bodily integrity there, whether in the form of violence,
illness, or accidents. When they presented initiation as the ultimate rem-
edy, the kitchen became a matrix of micropractices that taught participants
who the orishas are, what it is to live, and how to be saved from death.

Lucumí and Palo Monte are far from the only initiatory traditions in
which refusing to serve spirits leads to suffering, less as a form of pun-
ishment than as evidence for their reality and the urgency of their call.[51]
In Black Atlantic religions, such stories have been legion, in which practitioners have reflected on their resistance and asserted, "It's the only
way [the spirits] can really prove to me that they exist—they have to
do something bad to me, not because they hate me . . . but [because]
they love me."[52] In Brazil, it is said that practitioners of Umbanda enter
this tradition through the door of suffering (*porta do sofrimento*).[53]
One strategy employed to avoid the unwanted attention of the spirits—
whether those in question are lwas, orixás, or mpungus, among others—
has been conversion to Christianity, thereby relinquishing their claims
on one's person.[54] While conversion has sometimes involved a redefini-
tion of the deities as demons requiring constant vigilance against their
machinations, it has reaffirmed their actuality. This type of conversion
does not challenge initiatory traditions at the level of episteme, leaving
untouched the configuration of knowledge that conditions any relationship with their gods.[55] Communal ritual performances are more easily
abandoned than spirit idioms and related narrative forms.

As has been documented for other Black Atlantic religions, in Lucumí
"affliction is potentially a boon, not merely a present pain, for it is the

royal road to ritual eminence in a cult."[56] In practitioners' accounts of their "journeys" to initiation, they have repeatedly incorporated the image of the road as a site of transition. When Billal related his initiation story to me, he remembered Elegguá saying in his dream, "Hey! . . . I cleared the road for you. *Are you ready to walk?*" This choice of words was not coincidental. The depiction of a choice as a path is both a linguistic trope and an emplotment device.[57] It is a chronotope, a spatiotemporal figuration that has historically organized the perception and representation of reality for servants of the orishas.[58] The chronotope of the path in the Lucumí tradition fuses the ideas of egress, progress, itinerary, circuit, milestone (or "turning point"), and way, in the sense of both thoroughfare and modus vivendi.

Multivalent iconographic, mythological, and ritual condensations of these concepts have been generated in this chronotopic matrix, as epitomized by the figure of Elegguá. He is the orisha with no fewer than twenty-one "paths"; "owner" of human feet, and by extension, all perambulation; and master of intersections and thresholds, prime sites for life-altering "meeting, separation, collision, [and] escape."[59] Elegguá both removes impediments from practitioners' paths and overlooks them, depending on whether he has received the proper offering. While Bakhtin focuses on the road as the vehicle of fate or chance, in Lucumí narratives the path embodies the divinatory paradox of destiny as both multi-determined and preordained. Paths run through the proverbs of the sixteen-cowries divination system, and its verses are said to "walk the earth" the instant the shells are thrown.[60] It might seem natural, then, for practitioners to cite the road as a place where time momentarily stops, and its recommencement propels narrators in unsuspected directions. The road symbolizes the possibility of becoming disoriented and getting lost as well as advancing.

For Bakhtin, the road, as a chronotopic motif, pertains to "the adventure novel of everyday life," composed according to the theme of metamorphosis: "Metamorphosis or transformation is a mythological sheath for the idea of development—but one that unfolds not so much in a straight line as spasmodically, a line with 'knots' in it, one that therefore constitutes a distinctive type of *temporal sequence*."[61] So it has been in accounts of initiation, where the path to ocha has been constructed as bumpy, narrow, and tortuous. In verbally retracing their steps, practitioners have paused to recollect past blunders—discounting advice from mentors, refusing to recognize the interconnectedness of their misfortunes—and the gradual diminishment of their options until there was only one alternative left. The choice was not between going one way or another; rather, it was between following the orishas or coming to a complete standstill, that is, death.

This narrative of "unchosen choice" has drawn on a range of preexisting utterance types, four of which are important to mention here.[62] The first is the Christian conversion story. Despite the widespread notion that Saul's epiphany on the road to Damascus set the template for such narratives, historians of Christianity have shown that it did not emerge as a salient speech genre until the early modern period. The idea of conversion as a bolt-of-lightning moment, "a dramatic peripety," is a quite recent phenomenon.[63] The gradual interpellation by the Gospel or "delayed reaction" to it—best exemplified by Augustine of Hippo's *Confessions*—is congruent with, rather than a deviation from, earlier Christian understandings of conversion. Yet by the time Black Atlantic traditions crystallized in the Caribbean and South America, both Roman Catholic and Protestant conversion narratives had become widely disseminated. They often featured the miraculous physical healing of an injured or ailing penitent. Afro-Cuban religious practitioners were exposed to such narratives through devotional texts such as hagiographies, saints' *vitae*, apologia, herbal lore, and adages; religious practices (such as pilgrimage); and oral traditions associated with holy sites.[64]

Other possible precedents for the Lucumí initiation story are older Afro-Cuban modes of religious self-narration, including rhetorical forms that originated within Bantu "cults of affliction," called *ngoma*. In contemporary African ngoma and for centuries before, the motive for participation has been cited as infirmity, identified by a diviner as a call to service from the spirits, "both the cause and the cure" of the sufferer's malady.[65] As the anthropologist John Janzen writes,

> The [presenting] complaints [later] become stories, personal testimonials, that are repeated through song-dances within the ngoma cell composed of the sufferer-novice's therapist-teacher and all of his or her novices. . . . In repeated ngoma sessions the individual develops a song-story that interprets and culturally legitimates his understanding of the world.[66]

Most enslaved people brought to Cuba between the sixteenth and the late eighteenth centuries were Central African. The influx of ethnic groups soon thereafter to be called Yorùbá arrived in the nineteenth century. Kongo-inspired variants of Palo Monte crystallized long before Yorùbá-based Lucumí in Cuba, and it is quite possible that, as multiple initiatory commitments among practitioners became normative, Lucumí incorporated and operationalized aspects of the ngoma songstory. Scholars have speculated that one iteration of ngoma, the Lemba healing society, may have traveled with enslaved peoples and spread throughout the New World.[67] Although the relation of Lucumí initiates' stories has not been accompanied by music or formally ritualized otherwise, their narrative contents and stylistic features—including the chronotopic invocation of paths and the emplotment of autobiography as metamorphosis—would reward comparison with those gathered from ngoma practitioners.[68]

The most obvious point of convergence between such drums and Afro-Cuban traditions is their galvanization of the afflicted in ceremonial action that "re-stories" suffering as a godsend. Many if not most Lucumí priests are initiated into Palo Monte before making ocha, and these traditions cooperate to instill in practitioners a sense of indebtedness to their contrapuntally structured ritual complexes. Those initiated into either, or both, as a result of infirmity have presented almost identical symptoms in oral histories, and cast themselves in the mold of the "wounded surgeon."[69] The folklorist and ethnologist Eoghan Ballard writes,

> Every year more people come to Palo [Monte] for reasons of health than probably for any other reason. . . . This . . . form of calling to religious life is a direct mirror of the Bantu Ngoma. . . . [T]ime after time people would note that the reason they had undergone rayamiento, or initiation into Palo, was for health reasons. "Me rallo por salud" is the phrase that I not only heard over and over in response to my questions, but significantly, was often offered without any inquiry on my part as to their motivations.[70]

In narratives of conversion, elders say that they have paid their dues—in blood, sweat, tears, and other effluvia—to bolster their "professional qualification[s]" as healers, and equally, as a means of grappling with illness as the "most unbeautiful" of aesthetic objects.[71]

Lucumí practitioners have not only incorporated idioms carried from Central Africa to eastern Cuba, they have altered them to reflect their more proximate historico-political contexts. The stigma attached to Black Atlantic religions shaped both their discursive and institutional norms. Since the late nineteenth century, to state a desire for Lucumí initiation has been tantamount to rejecting God as well as science. Both the popular press and academic scholarship have placed the onus on practitioners to differentiate their practices from those of *brujería*, or witchcraft. In what was perhaps the first public defense of Lucumí, in July 1913—exactly one year after the massacre of over three thousand Afro-Cubans in a "race war"—a certain Fernando Guerra circulated a manifesto addressed to the president of Cuba and Havana's mayor, among other government officials, and "to the general public." On behalf of practitioners, Guerra conceded the existence of brujería but distanced Lucumí from it, exhorting journalists to aid the authorities in distinguishing between the two. Asserting that practitioners had not abandoned Catholicism, he nevertheless inveighed against infringements on their constitutional rights, declaring, "Despite the fact that our ancestors are African, we do not practice *brujería*, nor do we use the objects required for its rituals, and if we practice the Lucumí religion, it is to console our suffering on this earth."[72] The source of Afro-Cubans' suffering was left up to readers to infer.

Guerra was far from a lone voice in the wilderness. He was secretary, and later became president, of the Cabildo Africano Lucumí/Sociedad de Santa Bárbara, "the twentieth-century reincarnation of the great Changó Tedún, the most widely remembered and important Lucumí cabildo in Cuba's history," with a vast "institutional reach and diverse membership."[73] Guerra was a liaison between his cabildo and other mutual aid societies and represented them both to the general public. Guerra corresponded with Fernando Ortiz, as well as with other members of the Cuban intelligentsia and literati. As a small group of Cuban- and African-born initiates strove to consolidate authority, standardize protocols for rituals, and ascertain the issues on which distinct lineages could agree to disagree in the early twentieth century, they collaborated on what—pardon the anachronism—closely resembles a public relations strategy. A witch-hunting craze had begun in 1904 after a white toddler was abducted and murdered just outside Havana. A "witch doctor" and his so-called accomplices, who had become acquainted through a local cabildo, were accused of extracting her heart and blood to restore an ex-slave's health.[74] Seven were eventually convicted, with two sentenced to death, and the rest to harsh prison sentences. Similar cases followed over the next two decades, inciting angry mobs to try, and occasionally succeed in, lynching alleged *brujos*. No initiate—whether Lucumí, Palo, or Abakuá—was above suspicion.

Touted as Cuba's foremost expert on brujería, Ortiz had advocated in 1906 for its elimination as a contagious disease or parasite enervating the body of the fledgling nation, and Guerra was responsible for courting him in hopes of modifying his diagnosis.[75] Guerra appealed to his ambition by sending him exclusive, as-yet-unpublished information on Lucumí practices—such as bàtá drumming—and to his vanity by granting him privileged access to the Sociedad de Santa Bárbara, even offering him an honorary presidency in 1911.[76] Guerra and his counterparts in other cabildos recognized the threats posed to the religion by new forms of media spectacle, technical improvements in state surveillance mechanisms, and the advent of a scientific criminological discourse that marshaled "life-history documents," such as autobiographical accounts, in the study and prosecution of populations branded mentally defective or morally delinquent.[77] In boldly worded broadsides, Guerra waged his rhetorical campaign by admitting that his readers had grounds for opprobrium, then ingeniously shifting its targets. Attuned to the prevalence of epidemiological metaphors in the political discourse of his day, Guerra denounced the notion that Lucumí initiates harmed others for physical cures and identified "the microbes infecting [Cuba's] social body" as corruption, ignorance, and prejudice.[78]

Initiation stories and other modes of self-narration among the founders of modern-day Lucumí await further research. Yet it stands to reason that Guerra and his peers endeavored to portray their religious commitment as a response to their own suffering in terms reminiscent of Christian apologetics, at least when acting as criminal-cum-ethnographic informants. Moreover, it appears that their efforts contributed to the adoption of the "unchosen choice" as a rhetorical convention among successive generations of priests, whether at the behest of immediate elders, as a deliberate act of emulative self-fashioning, or due to the attainment of competence in this conversational register through everyday

familiarity with its performance. Lest such an intimate relationship between practitioners and texts sound far-fetched, initiates have creatively
appropriated the classic midcentury ethnographies of William Bascom
and Lydia Cabrera, revising their own discursive practices—particularly
in ritual registers such as divination and praise-singing—in light of their
engagement with these "canonical" volumes.[79] The leap from the page to
the tongue has proven to be a short one for adepts, especially when the
eminent personages quoted appear in their ancestral prayers.

## Getting a Witness

There is one more utterance type that has been a resource for Black
Lucumí initiates: "testifying," or witnessing to salvation through the
action of unmerited grace. Testifying has traditionally occurred in the
liturgical assemblies of the free church or storefront tradition, popular
in Chicago since the early twentieth century, as part of an "altar call"
beckoning participants to share their experiences of divine intervention.
This speech genre has figured in everyday interactions among African
Americans raised in a variety of Protestant denominations as well as
converts to Roman Catholicism, creating a ritualized space in the midst
of mundane routines for the affirmation of faith and informal communication of religious concepts, such as the doctrine of redemption.[80] In
testifying, narrators have named their problems, then vouched for God-
(or gods-) given resolutions to them: the proverbial "way out of no way."
    The research on testifying—and "testifyin'" as a regular feature of
Black talk—in African American literary criticism and religious history has illuminated the interconnections between sacred and secular
linguistic practices and representative forms of historical consciousness.[81] Reading Lucumí stories through the lens of testifying may assist
in reckoning these linkages. As I have argued elsewhere with reference
to the singing of spirituals and other African American church songs
in misas blancas, Black practitioners have introduced innovations into
ritual contexts as a means of transforming their personal and corporate religious identities.[82] An analogous appropriation of speech genres
has taken place as well, dependent on the internalization of preexisting
Afro-Cuban idioms, the performance of memory work, and the corresponding generation of new "structures of feeling."[83]

We must be wary of seeing the effect of the African American confessional tradition on Lucumí narrative through what Robin Horton has
called "Judeo-Christian spectacles."[84] Practitioners seldom framed their
initiations as rescuing them from the wages of moral turpitude, and
never from eternal damnation. Even when someone explicitly equated
the Lucumí iyawo year with being "born again"—as did a member of
Ilé Laroye whose son had made ocha, and who hoped to get initiated
someday—the comparison turned on the similarity between the death of
the "old man" in disposition and behavior, not on a complementary vision
of the afterlife. The Lucumí formulation of "ethicized" reincarnation has
militated against belief in the resurrection of the elect after the Second
Coming.[85] In fact, perhaps the point of greatest conflict between African
American Christianity and Afro-Cuban religions has been the conception
of the self in their respective theological anthropologies. Palo Monte, Espiritismo, and Lucumí have envisioned the self as surpassing conventional
physical and sensory boundaries to encompass various categories of agentive beings. The ritual implications of this approach to personhood may
be suggested by the fact that some practitioners have sought initiation to
improve the imperiled health of close family members.

It is nevertheless worthwhile to raise the subject of testifying in order
to shift the discussion of initiation stories from the meanings they contain
to the actions they perform. Accounts of corporeal affliction prior to ocha
have been cited as straightforwardly locating the causes of religious change
for individual narrators, analyzed "in terms of whether or not it is an accurate *portrayal of* real activity, rather than an internal *component within*
it, an objectifying moment within a larger process."[86] But such utterances
achieve effects in the world even as they participate in its representation.
In relating initiation stories, elders have created countless dialogic situations composed of no fewer than three parts, "an utterance, a reply, and
a relation between the two."[87] Lucumí initiates, along with congregants
testifying in Black churches, have required witnesses to be present, and
far from being passive recipients of information, they have actively collaborated with narrators to realize verbal encounters.[88] They have done
so not by simply replying to statements, but by influencing their initial
formulation through nonverbal cues. Initiates' oral performances have
both instructed listeners in interpreting experiences analogous to those
recalled, and shaped the recollections themselves.

It may seem counterintuitive to ascribe such prominence to listeners, since in initiation stories transcribed from interviews, they are nowhere to be found.[89] Yet their invisibility is an optical illusion, generated by the scrutiny aimed at the autobiographical contents of these narratives. My research indicates that they have been condensed into concise, first-person monologues from far more expansive colloquies detailing narrators' attempts to unravel oracular speech, find reliable sources of religious authority, and cope with recurrent problems. And for the most part, the listeners in these communicative events have been edited out. Their absence from the scholarly literature has been misleading, for it is the rare listener who remains completely silent, especially when call-and-response linguistic interaction has been a cultural norm for the interlocutors.[90] Moreover, while salient in dialogue, the vocal-auditory channel of communication must be evaluated alongside the visual, the tactile, and other sensory channels. Listeners speak in a dialogue, with their bodies if not with their voices. Even when they have punctuated narrators' statements only with facial expressions, variations in posture, and minimal articulatory gestures, they have been coproducers of exchanges replete with the potential to modify narrators' oral performances and other participants' reception of them.[91]

Of course, not all hearers hearken, and listeners seldom have been unanimous in their reactions. Even when nonspeaking interlocutors have played roles in ritualized speech acts such as testifying and the narration of initiation stories, they have not been a homogeneous group. To begin with—borrowing the terminology developed by the sociologist Erving Goffman—hearers of talk are either "ratified" or "non-ratified." The latter are unintentional overhearers of conversations, as well as deliberate eavesdroppers.[92] Ratified hearers, conversely, are those permitted to listen in on a given conversation and participate by taking turns at talk, with the tacit understanding that a ratified speaker "has the floor" for the duration of the social interaction. They are obligated to exhibit attentive behavior. Yet whether ratified or non-ratified, addressed or unaddressed—depending on whether speakers have directed remarks to them—hearers have negotiated their places within communicative events in pursuit of their own agendas.[93] Their objectives may be separated into three main categories: domain or "task" goals, related to the immediate purpose of their conversations; procedural goals (to communicate expeditiously and adroitly, or at any rate, felicitously, in keeping with their desired outcomes); and interpersonal goals (to cement social ties, establish a rapport, or project a certain image of themselves).

Both the main speakers and listeners in conversations are induced to cooperate in the production of communicative events by such goals. Interlocutors' attainment of them is contingent on numerous factors— among them, whether conversations meet others' expectations. Social interactions, for all of their fluidity and dynamism, tend to be judged by participants according to the precedents set by previous encounters of the same type. Storytellers are aided in achieving their objectives by correctly assessing listeners' varying levels of investment in their verbal performances. They must strategically follow, as well as depart from, genre conventions. Some speakers elicit positive reactions from listeners with greater regularity than others; the more impressive their eloquence and delivery, the better their likelihood of "awaken[ing] an attitude of collaborative expectancy" in their listeners.[94] Subject matter alone is not sufficient to ensure their engrossment. The command of listeners' attention rests partly on oratorical skill, and partly on the ease with which speakers have invoked key linguistic and paralinguistic devices to frame their talk as a display of verbal artistry.[95]

Whether offering testimony about the Holy Spirit's saving grace or the orishas' healing power, religious subjects have turned what might have looked like idle chitchat into opportunities for the consolidation and renewal of religious community.[96] As the historian Carla Kaplan writes, among Black Christians, "Testifying and 'call and response' . . . dramatize the constitutive force of a reception context and they enact the conferral and confirmation of both individual and collective identity."[97] Initiation stories have historically done the same for Lucumí practitioners. It is also possible to go further, and assert that the telling of these stories has been as important for the making of casa-templos as cooking is for the orishas. In the midst of ostensibly casual conversations, elders have recounted and modeled the gradual acquisition of a hermeneutical apparatus that renders incidents and sensations intelligible as messages from the spirits. They have shown suffering and uncontrollable events to be freighted with significance. They have partaken in listeners' religious transformations by recapitulating their own.

It is in this sense that narratives of initiation have seasoned practitioners' subjectivity. Rather than just inviting listeners into the world of the orishas, elders' stories have been actual entrées into it, conjuring its dimensions, logics, and objects. In ritual theater, the anthropologist Michael Taussig writes, "imagined worlds become not only theatricalized but factualized as religious axiom and social custom"; initiation stories may be viewed similarly, as instantiating or substantiating the existence of a realm of experience through its representation.[98] They have owed their impact to more than narrators' verbal talent. "The constitutive force of [the] reception context" cannot be overestimated, particularly the hierarchical power relations that set the circumstances for the stories' telling. In published accounts and in my own research, listeners have tended to be uninitiated or, if initiated, younger in ritual age than narrators. In an ilé, senior members have usually participated in their juniors' ochas, and become acquainted with their paths to initiation experientially, rendering narration of their journeys redundant, at least in their estimation. The higher status of narrators, coupled with their reputation for sagacity and healing power, has lent credence to their utterances, authorized their evaluations, and enhanced the plausibility of their descriptions.

I alluded in previous chapters to prostrations and other gestures of respect that have assisted in the social construction of initiates' seniority. Listening may be viewed as a "practice of deference" that has been a central feature of Lucumí communities, bearing in mind that—as the historian Michael McNally notes with reference to the Ojibwe—"Deference . . . has been no mere matter of etiquette but a set of practices that has ceremonialized elders' privilege as teachers."[99] I believe that the recognition of Lucumí priests as educators, mentors, and ritual specialists has turned the relation of their autobiographical narratives into pedagogical occasions for both aleyos and other initiates. Even anecdotes casually ventured from positions of authority have had the potential to become lessons, promoting some behaviors and discouraging others. When elders have admitted to a pre-initiatory tug-of-war between the will of the orishas and their own capacity for procrastination or self-deception, their reputations have not suffered. The moral of their stories has not been that they were at fault, although they said as much. The message has been that they exacerbated their troubles by misunderstanding the courses of action that they had to take, an unhappy state of affairs that their listeners can obviate by learning from their example.

The persuasive rhetorical devices employed to dramatize narrators' struggles contributed to their conversion of communicative events into theaters of transformation. Van de Port writes that among Candomblé practitioners, inexplicable events—including experiences of illness resistant to diagnosis according to conventional etiologies of disease—have been cited in narratives to authenticate belief in the spirits, or at least in the efficacy of ritual interventions. Among Lucumí practitioners, it has also been the case that

> [although] initiation stories are often success stories of coming to understand the causes of inexplicable afflictions through explanation, the inexplicable as such was always underlined. . . . The logic at work in these narratives seems to be that the more poignant the inexplicability of the occurrence . . . the more powerful the really real of the explanation that brought about healing.[100]

The trope of ineffability has underscored the spirits' superiority, in contrast to human beings' corporeal and cognitive limitations. It has been marshaled in an argument for the inadequacy of explanatory models, and indeed of scientific rationality itself. Accordingly, initiates' stories have corroborated the impossibility of gaining mastery over affliction by trying to comprehend it outside the interpretive apparatus provided by the Lucumí religious system.

This points to another essential element in the staging of initiation stories: the metalinguistic, affective component of their verbal performances. When priests have replayed scenes of their affliction, listeners have been moved to "feel them" or "feel their pain," as these idioms have it—to allow their sentiments to be touched by others' predicaments.[101] Initiates' stories have had an emotional impact not because "Don't let this happen to you" invariably has been their subtext, but because their afflictions *did* happen to listeners, momentarily, imaginatively, as they put themselves in narrators' positions.[102] In empathizing with speakers, listeners have made themselves vulnerable to an extension of their sympathies. Thus, by virtue of mimesis, elders' reenactment of their irreducibly subjective, physical pain has had the power to wound those listeners "vicariously reexperiencing" their suffering.[103] Narrators have relived the moment of crisis in their stories to "catch the conscience" of listeners and trigger their own revelations of the orishas' presence.[104]

Belief in the orishas has not been required for listeners to become fellow travelers on narrators' verbal journeys; only a "willing suspension of disbelief" has been necessary to transport them briefly, yet deeply, into narrators' worlds.[105] Bearing in mind the semantic roots of the term *to implicate*—"to convey (a truth) bound up in a fable"—I would argue that participating in narrators' verbal performances has succeeded in implicating listeners in the ontological reconstructions that have been foundational for Lucumí practice.[106] In other words, listeners have become part of the story.[107] For those engaged in serving the spirits, initiation stories themselves have functioned as confirmations. They have come when practitioners were "just sitting there chitchatting," interrupting the everyday with impromptu disclosures that submitted evidence for the reality of the spirits, for those disposed to admit it as such.[108] Narrators' recollections of their calls to ocha have been interpellations, hailing religious subjects into being; accounts of their refusal to get initiated have been improvised enactments of ideological becoming.[109] Of course, not all listeners have answered the testifier's query, "Can I get a witness?" in the affirmative. Some hearers have been insensible to entreaties, and assumed that when their interlocutors said, "When you get initiated, you'll know," the impersonal pronoun was purely generic. For others, however, that knowledge has been undeniable.

The recital of testimony about affliction has transmuted personal straits into shared pain. Practitioners have felt free to say what cannot be said in other contexts, for fear of negative repercussions. They told me stories of abortion, abuse, addiction, assault, and stigmatizing victimization. The hoarseness in their throats came not from speech, but from being silenced. The initiation story furnished them with the language to voice their experiences, while contributing to the creation of a dialogic situation in which listeners acknowledged their suffering as such, and recognized them as occupying the privileged position of elders. Repurposing suffering into a foundation for social connection has been especially important for practitioners in the throes of physical illness and emotional upheaval, yet bereft of adequate social supports.

With reference to the testifying tradition, the sociologist Cheryl Townsend Gilkes observes, "Testimony transforms the collection of worshippers into a community. Oppression and suffering make testimony important for psychological survival. Testimony does not resolve black problems but does transform them from private troubles of distressed individuals into public issues of a covenant community."[110] While Afro-Diasporic religions continue to grow more racially and culturally heterogeneous—with white and light-skinned participants retaining the same degree of privilege they hold outside their communities—[the testimonial component of initiation stories has undoubtedly bound "distressed individuals" into groups with common interpretive frames of reference, as well as ritual performances, reciprocal obligations, and relationships based on sentiments of affinity. It is by attaining proficiency in this spirit idiom that many practitioners have arrived at the visceral feeling of affliction as an urgent summons to the priesthood. I would propose that the cultivation of this sentiment through conversational micropractices has been a critical site for the dissemination of Black Atlantic traditions. Given their historical development in the absence of creedal declarations, official organizational blueprints, or centralized authority figures, the telling of these stories may well have played a considerable role in promoting religious cohesion.]

There are as many types of religious change as there are traditions, with individuals telling stories that accent human agency to a greater or lesser degree.[111] In most cases, narratives of transformation recapitulate religious ideology or a tradition's internal logic. They express configurations of personhood, institutional values, and descriptions of the arc of divine involvement in practitioners' lives.[112] The elders of Ilé Laroye occasionally encouraged the uninitiated to "get made" by enumerating the benefits of ordination, but more often, they endorsed it by asserting its ineluctability with reference to their own experience. They saw priesthood as a fait accompli for their uninitiated interlocutors and effectively redescribed them as initiates-to-be.[113] By thus implicating listeners in the web of the spirits' intentionality, storytelling has been a ritual performance as vital to the reproduction of Black Atlantic religions in their current form as any other.[114] Their initiates have taught listeners how to speak, and therefore how to think, about the spirits' relationship to their bodies. The next chapter delves more deeply into practitioners' everyday talk about how rituals work, and what happens when they do not.

# 6

## Walking the Talk

I said hello to everyone then went in the kitchen, where
Oshunleye was resting with her face in her hands. Imani was
making a necklace: one yellow bead, one orange bead, one
gold bead, one red. I asked what orisha she was making it for,
waking Oshunleye up from the nap she had been trying to
take. She said Ideú. Berta was there and asked "Who?" Oshunleye said that Ideú is Ochún's child, born after she gave
birth to the divine twins and gave them away to Yemayá to
care for them. She said Ochún's life "went downhill" after
that, and Ideú was "her child of luck." She said that the doll
fashioned to accompany Ideú's other sacred objects is a boy
dressed in girls' clothes, because Ochún was told to hide him.

Diahann said the first time she visited Ashabi's house with
her friend Samantha, she felt a connection to the tradition,
but also that it wasn't for her. Her attitude was, I know there
are orishas, and I'm glad there are people who do the work
to worship them, but that isn't going to be me. She thought
of herself as having a complicated life where she would be
sacrificing and plucking chickens all the time. Instead, she
says, since she received her elekes last year, her life has been
"Simplified. It's simple. Real simple." She says that as soon as
she got her elekes she was ready to go further, and when she
found out about receiving Ideú ceremonially she was excited
right away for that too.
—Fieldnotes, October 14, 2005[1]

As we have seen so far, kitchen work in Ilé Laroye gave rise to a host
of conversational micropractices. In mentoring the uninitiated, elders
unburdened themselves, knit together ritual utterances, and condensed
extensive mythologies into bite-sized pieces that left listeners hungry for

more. Ashabi's godchildren deliberated over what the orishas wanted and what they expected to happen after the proper execution of rituals. Priests debated the felicity of ceremonies and disagreed regarding the oracular pronouncements delivered by diviners and possessed mounts.[2] Such "kitchen-table talk" made the ritual calendar coherent as a system, rather than an arbitrary succession of activities.[3] Even more importantly, through casual interactions practitioners discursively formed the objects of Afro-Cuban religious knowledge, including the agency of the spirits.[4] As the anthropologist Martin Holbraad has argued, Lucumí operates through a redescription of reality through "inventive definitions" that are "an indispensable constituent of the logic of worship."[5] The same may be said for other Black Atlantic religions.

The initiation stories treated in the last chapter play a special role in habituating practitioners into the interpretive frames of reference used by their elders. These narratives have helped to enlarge the Lucumí tradition by persuading interlocutors of the reality of the orishas. Their plots have consistently placed orishas in telling relationship to practitioners' bodies—much as an eyewitness account might place a suspect at a crime scene—to dramatize the manner and magnitude of the deities' implication in the mundane world.[6] In relating anecdotes about their affliction, elders have celebrated the orishas' ownership of human bodies and capacity to override any conceivable opposition to their divine will. The subtext of these recollections has been that Lucumí's ritual system creates a uniquely potent channel for the gods' sacred energy, as harnessed by their authoritative representatives. It behooves us to acknowledge that speech genres spring partly from existing sources, yet initiates' stories do not simply remix prepackaged narrative formulae about religious transformation. They are themselves ideologically transformative.

Of course, as historical actors situated in particular places and times, religious subjects bring their own culturally specific metaphors to their adoption of spirit idioms. Arlene once declared, "Everyone says they want to learn how to take out ashés until they get the chicken open!"[7] The selection of a chicken to drive home her point was not coincidental. Chicken has played a vital symbolic role in African American culture since the antebellum period, when the breeding of poultry provided a source of income and mobility to enslaved as well as free Black populations. In the nineteenth century, chicken—once the most expensive of common domestic foods—became central to racist caricatures concerning African American behavior and consumption practices. Long after the Great Migration, middle-class Black folk aspiring to region- and color-based standards of respectability often declined to serve chicken during polite social functions to signal their rejection of both the potentially harrowing labor involved in preparing it and any stereotypes associated with the enjoyment of it. Arlene mobilized the connotations of making chicken as "community cultural work" in her critique.[8] Aiming at those who think they are too good to butcher poultry, she struck out at a politics of respectability at odds with the survival of Lucumí itself.

In what follows, I take up the offhand remarks and seemingly random digressions of practitioners about their ritual experiences. Their comments occasionally articulate pain, discomfort, and doubt, to the extent that their expression could be dismissed as the ventilation of grievances about Lucumí. What unites these statements is that they represent pivotal moments in the adoption of a spirit idiom. They draw attention to aspects of religious subjectivity seldom included in studies of Afro-Cuban traditions. As in the case of the initiation stories, they are echoed by utterances captured in oral histories of other Black Atlantic religions. If the genealogist's duty is to spot "the accidents, the minute deviations—or conversely, the complete reversals—the errors, the false appraisals, and the faulty calculations that gave birth to those things that continue to exist and have value for us," what I want to do here is present a genealogy of "macropractices" in a Lucumí house, from a first divination to the first year of initiation.[9] By testifying to the efficacy of rites of passage, this everyday talk organized practitioners' consciousness of themselves as Lucumí religious subjects.[10]

## Divination and Sacred Necklaces

For a long time Sandra was searching for a community but when she finally found one she says she knew it was the real thing. She said she got really emotional the first time she prostrated to Yemayá. She has her elekes and Warriors and head marked as a child of Elegguá. Her first divination, she said, was like having her midsection unzipped, her entrails

laid out on a table and examined, and then stuffed back in, "but they didn't fit anymore." She said everything foretold in the reading happened within about four days.
—Fieldnotes, April 15, 2005

For would-be practitioners, there were two main points of access to Ilé Laroye. The first was kitchen work. The second was the desire for a sixteen-cowries divination (*diloggún*), or "reading," by Ashabi.[11] Clients were often to be found sitting on the couch with her husband watching news programs, waiting for her to arrive from the office Monday through Thursday nights. Most had heard of her through word of mouth. Although I was not permitted to sit in on most divinations, on one occasion I served as a scribe for a friend. During this session, Ashabi's technique appeared congruent with that of other diviners versed in sixteen-cowries divination. She first sprinkled a libation, then recited the moyubá while rubbing the cowrie shells back and forth against a woven mat. She threw the shells multiple times, and after each casting, counted the number that fell with the natural openings, or "mouths," up; depending on the result, she gave her client a pair of *ibó*, or tools (such as a sea snail shell, a black pebble, a piece of animal vertebra, or button of eggshell powder), to be concealed in the client's hands.

The presentation of one or another at Ashabi's bidding indicated whether her client was in a state of *iré* (blessings) or *osogbo* (misfortune); this act of disclosure also provided "yes" or "no" responses to her questions. Each divinatory sign indicated by the shells was thought to voice the concerns of a particular set of orishas, and betoken certain proverbs, myths, and offerings. A prevalent, if not universal, Lucumí belief has been that individuals select their destinies before birth and forget them in being born. Accordingly, elders framed divination not as a machine for the contrivance of new futures, but as the revelation of what the client has "always already" chosen in heaven.[12] Divination operates as "memory work" undertaken in order to bring the present into alignment with the past.[13] The conversation in this section's epigraph occurred in Ashabi's kitchen, where the imminent removal of ashés provided a ready metaphor for the eviscerating action of divination, constructed as the discovery of an Other lodged within the self. Sandra had felt gutted by the diviner's disclosure of her personal information; she sensed that her self had been enlarged by the knowledge she received, and could not shrink back to its previous size.

Repeated divinations, rogations, and offerings, coupled with the consistent attendance of rituals, built up clients' perception of their relationship with the spirits as familial rather than transactional. Clients like Sandra began to view their dealings with them not as customers conducting business with deified strangers, but as giving gifts to parents or requesting favors from patrons.[14] This change in understanding of the spirits was reflected in a shifting attitude toward the elders as their representatives. Practitioners came to prefix Ashabi and Fadesiye's first names with Iya and Baba—"mother" and "father" in Yorùbá. To cement a relationship of ritual sponsorship, clients sought to receive elekes in a ceremony that prefigures initiation. In the Lucumí tradition, each of the sacred necklaces materializes the presence of one of five major orishas, Elegguá, Obatalá, Shangó, Ochún, and Yemayá; the last four are the complement of orishas received in every initiation, regardless of the patron deity of the priest. In Ilé Laroye, elders consecrated an eleke by exhaling into the knot after the beads were strung onto a cord—thus bestowing their aché to it—and washing it in omiero.[15]

The color patterns of the beads indicated the "paths," or mythologically specific manifestations, of the orishas in question. Ashabi and Fadesiye gave their godchildren necklaces bearing the "paths" of the spirits that they had received at initiation. It was not until their ochas that the godchildren were presented with more elaborate elekes that corresponded to the paths of their own orishas, as determined in their post-initiatory divinations.[16] As in the epigraph above, the elekes create the practitioner's material connection to the orishas through a particular house of worship, and are intended to pave the way for ordination, thus "simplifying" the choices presented by entry into Lucumí. Several of the ritual steps taken in the receipt of elekes recur in ocha. For instance, the rite includes a *rompimiento*, or the destruction of old clothes, a ceremonial bath, and—at least in Ilé Laroye—an overnight stay in the godparents' home.[17] As before initiation, elders change the practitioner's name temporarily to aboku, "the dead one," and rename her iyawo, or "bride." Afterward, she experiences a week of restrictions on dress and social activity that presage those imposed during the first year of priesthood.

sounds literally miser-able...

no wonder no one wants to do it.

Elekes could either be preceded or followed by the ceremonial receipt of the ritual paraphernalia of the Warriors. Elekes mark practitioners' bodies as property of the orishas, and the Warriors do the same for their homes. Although members of the ilé had the option of receiving Elegguá alone if they could not accommodate the other orishas, elders maintained that it was preferable to have the Warriors consecrated all at once, because these orishas act in concert. Ochosi's metal objects, a bow and arrow, are to be found inside the small cauldron housing Ogún's iron implements. It is said that Ogún can kill, but he cannot stalk, whereas his brother Ochosi can hunt, yet not deal a mortal blow. The fourth orisha of the group is Ósun, a small, chalice-shaped staff surrounded by bells, with a rooster perched on top; this object has been described as an altar to the recipient's inner head, and the destiny embedded within it. Reinforcing this association, elders have charged the cup beneath the rooster with some of the same medicines placed on the head in initiation.[18] Ósun is thought to exercise vigilance in the home, and to warn its owner of impending danger by falling over or ringing.[19]

Receipt of the Warriors entails cyclical obligations to these orishas. Ilé elders instructed practitioners to address Elegguá ritually at the beginning of every week, offering him food and beverages, and to clean him occasionally with a combination of red palm oil and honey. Practitioners pledged to render sacrifice to them at least once a year. Some elders considered the Warriors to be addimú, or auxiliary, orishas because they come before initiation, and are consecrated apart from it. But they were not the only such orishas given to the uninitiated. The most common addimú orisha made in Ilé Laroye along with the Warriors was Olokún, usually recommended by elders as a source of health and stability. Other addimú orishas include the divine twins, or Ibeji, and Ideú. But the Warriors and Olokún caused the most significant changes in the daily lives and domestic spatial arrangements of practitioners, since the former needed to be placed near the front door, and the latter had to be put in a secluded area or curio cabinet away from prying eyes. Recipients of both needed to obey sartorial and behavioral taboos whenever in close proximity to the orishas, and their presence could disturb social relationships by altering the expectations for conduct in the affected areas of a home.

In the ilé, elders saw elekes, the Warriors, and Olokún as cementing the foundation for a practitioner's future within the tradition. It is important in this regard to emphasize the parallel construction of body and home as sites for religious training. The donning of elekes was not considered a private affair that affected the wearer alone, but a social act that involved the orishas as agentive beings in her everyday life. It required her to become alert to the new religious power—both to sacralize and to desecrate—of formerly secular or semiotically unmarked acts. Elders prohibited the wearing of elekes in the shower, while sleeping or inebriated, and during acts of sexual intimacy; Ashabi also discouraged godchildren from wearing other necklaces with elekes unless they had been told to do so by the orishas. On one occasion, she upbraided a godchild whose beads had gotten stuck in a string of faux pearls as she attempted to slip it off, seizing on the entanglement as proof of the principle that elekes and mere jewelry do not mix. Bearing in mind the royal status of the orishas, combining their necklaces with trinkets was more than a gesture of disrespect—for Ashabi, it was a violation of their majesty.

In remembering to remove sacred necklaces before bed and bath and other such moments of decision-turned-instinct, the surface of a practitioner's skin became a stage on which an elder's directives and a godchild's routines did battle. The result of this struggle, for aborishas, was the dedication of ever greater corporeal and cognitive-emotional space to the orishas, and the attendant transformation of previously unchallenged choices and dispositions. Since sacred spaces were perceived as either conducing to the orishas' purposes or impeding them, practitioners had to craft physical spaces amenable to ritual practice within the home. They acquired the requisite boundary-staking skills through apprenticeship to their elders. For instance, Ashabi once objected to her godchild's placement of Olokún in a small closet, saying that this orisha did not have "the room to work" in such a tightly enclosed area.[20] Both the body and the home inhabited by the practitioner gradually begin to house the spirits, asserting their desires—through the elders—over those of other social actors.

In this fashion, practitioners converted their bodies and domiciles into extensions of the spirits, so that items embodying or associated with them became fragments of their "distributed personhood."[21] It is also possible to view personified objects such as elekes as the practitioners' own "personhood distributed in the milieu, beyond the body-boundary."[22] Whenever a consecrated object was received in a rite of passage, it came with a combination of temporary and permanent constraints. These could be either explicit prohibitions or mandatory engagement in disciplinary practices aimed at the recipient's transfiguration into a vessel for the orishas. In this way, a practitioner's personhood in religious practice expanded as her agency—defined as the capacity to act with political and moral autonomy—contracted. Ritual macropractices revealed the human self to be "dividual" and dynamic rather than fixed and singular. Ceremonies of consecration—for instance, of Elegguá's concrete image—demonstrated that "inanimate" objects can attain the ontological status of persons, without being credited with consciousness in the commonsense understanding of the word.[23]

Black Atlantic religions are built on, and through, transformative acts that alter the ontological status of phenomena, including human beings. For Lucumí practitioners, no object is entirely inanimate because its aché may be pressed into service during the course of a rite and increased thereby; the desired end of most ceremonial acts is the accumulation of aché for the subject of the ritual intervention and the community as a whole. The most consequential and, indeed, paradigmatic of Afro-Cuban religious transformations occurs in spirit possession, when a spirit appropriates an initiate's body and consciousness for his own purposes, asserting divine right of eminent domain in a temporarily vacated corporeal dwelling. Practitioners of Black Atlantic religions explicitly compare the body to a home in which spirits are invited to reside.[24] Priests are understood to incorporate the spirits' power physically in initiation, within distinct corporeal domains; the rite of passage into Palo Monte involves the placement of patterned scratches on the torso, shoulders, and wrists, while Lucumí ordination "enthrones" the gods in the crown of a practitioner's head. Other ritual competences are added on as duplexes when there appears to be no room left.

John Mason is worth quoting at length on this point:

A woman once told me, "I have to rent an apartment; I need three bedrooms." Why three bedrooms? "One for my son, one for me, and the other for my [orishas]." That indicates the way people think when they are part of this culture. . . . We do not put [the orishas] in a place that we go see everyday. Rather, they are in my house. They will never leave this house. We might have a temple. There will be a space for all of us, but [my altar space] is always upstairs, or at my door, or downstairs, or in my yard, so that my relation to God is always close at hand, and becomes part of my living place. [The spirits] are not outside my space. It's not something outside: it's every space. It's people who wear eleke (beaded necklaces). You wear it around your neck; it takes up space on your body. [Initiates] wear bracelets, etc. It's the clothes you wear. All of this is ritual space. Your body is a temple. To get real technical, your body becomes ritual space that is designed.[25]

Just as a house may be compartmentalized depending on the needs of the moment, so can the practitioner shift to play different roles depending on the social and ritual context, without being regarded as physically or mentally fragmented, much less alienated from her "self." In Black Atlantic traditions, the person is assumed to be "dividual" and the self, rendered coherent through the "norms of intelligibility" enforced by her religious community.[26] The body is not born a temple; it is made into one through regular, ongoing, and disciplined effort, from within and without.[27]

## Initiatory Death and Rebirth

In the kitchen, Fadesiye was doing what he does around infants and youngsters as well as his adult godchildren, when he'll say, "This is *my* baby" or "This is *my* daughter," asserting his motherly qualities as a priest of Yemayá and their ability to trump any claims of biological parentage. Although more slender, graceful, and aquiline than a whippet, he sees (and establishes) himself as the most maternal presence in any room.

Arlene, a priest of the hunter Ochosi with several years in ocha, moved to embrace her son Alaafi—a new initiate now in his early twenties, roughly the same age, at least chronologically, as Fadesiye, and about a foot taller. Fadesiye protested, "No, this is my son!" Arlene exhaled audibly and raised her eyebrows. Fadesiye went on, "No, your son is dead. Now he's mine," referring, presumably, to his becom-

ing aboku before his initiation last autumn. But the arrow-
tongued warrior wasn't ready to give up. "I died first," Arlene
said, and hugged Alaafi tight.
—Fieldnotes, February 18, 2005

Despite practitioners' belief in a limited form of reincarnation, the idea
of death is anathematized in Lucumí. Called *iku* in Yorùbá, it numbers,
along with illness, gossip, and affliction, as one of the misfortunes sent
away in prayers such as the moyubá. In many houses of orisha worship,
flippant mention of death—*la muerte*—is taboo, and the concept itself
is best conveyed by means of euphemism. In myths, the orishas devise
tricks to cheat death or assign it its proper place on earth, but they do
not welcome it. In Ilé Laroye, gestures thought to symbolize death, such
as sweeping someone's feet accidentally when using a broom, were to be
avoided. Members of the house were taught not to court it by ignoring
physical, social, and religious disorders that could be addressed through
ritual practice. And yet there would be no initiation without at least one
human death: the passing away of the initiate-to-be before he or she
crosses the threshold into ordination. In order for a practitioner to be
reborn as a priest, her or his identity must be sacrificed, as literally as
possible without physically injuring the body soon to become a vessel
for the spirits.[28] For the ill and otherwise suffering, healing is thought
to begin with this death and the demise of old ways of feeling, behaving,
and understanding, to be remade radically through the rigors of the first
year of initiation.

After an initiate-to-be ritually presents to her godparents a significant percentage or the full cost of her ocha, as well as a basketful of
clothing and other highly symbolic items to be used in initiation, her
elders strip her of her given names and start to address her as aboku.
The origin and etymology of the term *aboku* is unclear; usually it was
translated as "the dead one."[29] In the ilé, initiates-to-be were referred to
as aboku long before initiation, sometimes for months in advance, even
on paper. For instance, I once served as scribe for a misa dedicated to
the spirit guides of two soon-to-be initiated people, and was instructed
by an elder to write at the top of the first page of my notes "aboku meji":
the two abokus.[30] The significance of this namelessness became more
pronounced on the first afternoon of an initiation, when the initiate-

to-be was not only called aboku, but also treated as if completely bereft of agency. Dressed in old clothes and seated in a stiff chair with her face to the wall, joined at times by her immediate elder in the house (the most junior initiated member of the community), the aboku was not to utter a word, or be accosted except when judged necessary by elders.[31] A towel or other piece of cloth covered her head and she was no longer permitted to see herself in a mirror. At that point, and until after the next stage of initiation, "You aren't human anymore," as Billal put it. "You're just an 'it.'"[32]

Deindividualization does not need to be humiliating to be effective; removing a person's name, even politely, goes a long way toward erasing her identity. Indeed, this renaming is indicative of Lucumí religious ideology regarding the norms and limits of personhood. Elders are actually renamed a total of three times. In the itá, an initiate is given a name based on those of past priests and frequently indicating her tutelary orisha, such as Bamboché for a priest of Shangó, or Eshubí for a priest of Eleggúa. Such names confer social belonging on ordained members of the community, and furnish a sense of continuity within the tradition. During the period of seclusion immediately after ocha and throughout the following year, however, the initiate is most often called iyawo, sometimes modified by the name of her tutelary orisha, as in "iyawo Obatalá." The difference between these names indicates degrees of differentiation among those recognized as persons within the community, with aboku corresponding to the most extreme form of anonymous living-while-dead, and one's priestly name representing the highest degree of honorific possible. It was to be accepted with the understanding that, far from individual, the person in question is highly "dividual," part of a long line of priests.

For those attracted to Lucumí because it seemed to affirm their racial or gender identity and to hold out a path to liberation, becoming aboku has been a rude awakening. The elders of Ilé Laroye wistfully recalled the time before they realized that, as in other Black Atlantic traditions, the spirits wanted not to validate but to reconstruct them. And the surest route to transformation has been through the body. Thus, whenever an iyawo commented that she was freezing cold, hungry, embarrassed, nauseated, sore, or sleepless during her initiation, the answer that could be counted on to come from one or more elders was, "We all were." This

statement was not literally true, since some priests enjoyed their ordination ceremonies, and others insisted that ritual experiences are incommensurable. Yet the elders did maintain that everyone should observe
the same level of discipline.[33] For instance, when one aboku was allowed
to return home to her young children at a crucial point before her ocha
officially commenced, a few priests teased her, saying that nobody had
ever given them the option of doing so.[34] While everyone professed to
be having a lighthearted laugh at her expense, they were also impress-
ing upon her their dismay over this departure from protocol, bearing in
mind the imminent transfer of her allegiance from her biological family
to her ritual family.

A lifetime passes in the transition from aboku to priest.[35] On the first
night of an initiation, under cover of darkness, the aboku is taken to a
river, where—according to the texts that describe this critical juncture—
she is immersed, her old clothes are stripped away, and a stone is re-
trieved for consecration in the forthcoming ocha. Upon returning, the
aboku receives a rogation of the head, and elders perform "the ebó of
entry." This ebó is understood as not only a cleansing but a quite literal disposal of one's existence in the form of symbolic personal effects,
accompanied by offerings to one's patron deity. The ritual progression
from aboku to iyawo has a direct historical referent in the transatlantic
slave trade. In the literature on Lucumí practice, an image emerges of the
aboku as an African captive: nameless and definitively sundered from
family, clan group, and familiar topographical and cosmological frames
of reference, then renamed upon arrival in the New World, sometimes
once again after baptism or sale into a household.

The next day is the matanzas. Its sacrifices consecrate the stones chosen to contain the orishas' aché. David H. Brown and Michael Atwood
Mason have furnished the most detailed accounts to date of the initiatory process that privileges the head as a vessel for the containment
of aché, beginning with the shearing of the aboku's hair with scissors,
shaving of the remaining stubble with a straight razor, and painting of
designs called *fifi okan* in tempera on the scalp.[36] These deeds transform the head into a calabash that, in its roundness and smoothness,
echoes the porcelain and wooden containers in which the ritual sacra of
the orishas will be stored. The regulatory practices imposed on initiates
are underwritten by the principle that they were brought to life by the

orishas, and must abide by their rules in order to prosper, wearing the crown of royalty placed on them.

In her ordination ceremony, the iyawo assumes the status of either a monarch or a warrior, and is dressed as such on the following day, called the Middle Day of initiation. Before lunch on the Middle Day, the iyawo slips out of the white clothes she had been wearing and puts on a colored gingham or burlap outfit. After this meal, the iyawo changes once again, into a costume viewed as the characteristic garb of her patron deity, whose presence the iyawo manifests within the altar to which she is confined.[37] Underneath her crown or hat, the iyawo's head bears the colored patterns of paint daubed on it the previous day, and across her chest, the iyawo carries one mazo for each of the orishas received. Each of the mazos can weigh up to three pounds and carry approximately twelve thousand beads.[38] They symbolize wealth and nobility, as well as the weight of obligation the iyawo has assumed. These gleaming chains tie her to the orishas and the elders, as their terrestrial representatives.

On the afternoon of the Middle Day, amid the "thick smell of good cooking," the iyawo welcomes visitors from outside the religious household.[39] The iyawo becomes the recipient of prostrations for the first time, and is taught to bless those prone at her feet, "raising" them by uttering the words "*A wa wa to, omo/oni* [patron orisha of the person saluting], *a la be o so dide*," and patting them on the shoulder blades. For part of that afternoon, the iyawo is joined by the priest immediately senior to her, resplendent in the garments of her own Middle Day. In Ilé Laroye, the elders explained this practice by saying that the presence of the most junior initiate "lifts" the one to have come before her. Disagreement existed as to whether the company of the older initiate serves a pedagogical purpose, as I learned in October 2005, when I prompted Samantha, enthroned with an iyawo, to elaborate on the concept. Samantha said that the elder being lifted is "teaching [her junior] how to be an iyawo," but on hearing this, Arlene begged to differ. "Actually," she said, while placing cornmeal dumplings around the orishas on the iyawo's throne, "it doesn't have anything to do with teaching." Arlene went on to say that "lifting" has to do with the aché on the head of the younger initiate elevating that of the elder solely by virtue of their proximity.

Through such everyday talk, the elders communicated that their rituals, rightly executed, had accomplished the iyawo's rebirth through the orishas. The magnificence of the iyawo on the Middle Day announced that the transformation claimed to have occurred in the initiation room indeed transpired, and offered evidence that the orishas wield healing powers beyond human comprehension. The glittering garments of those thus enthroned featured the favored hues and iconographic features of their patron deities. The change in appearance from aboku to iyawo could be particularly shocking when someone had undergone ordination while suffering from a protracted sickness, then resurfaced in her Middle Day altar, glowing like a gem at the center of a silk-satin kaleidoscope. Overwhelmed with the majesty of the throne and the splendor of its inhabitants, elders were inspired to tell stories about their own initiations, and aborishas recounted events they saw as confirming the reality and power of the orishas. But in the ilé as elsewhere, when the iyawo's godparents called an end to her audience with the public, she traded her finery for plain white clothes once again, and re-entered the period of strict seclusion that would last several days more.

## Initiatory Healing

In the initiation stories treated in the previous chapter, practitioners itemized the symptoms of illnesses that doctors failed to ameliorate. The impotence of physicians, elsewhere held in esteem as "paragons of learning and virtue," has historically functioned as a rhetorical foil for both the orishas' power and that of Lucumí as a ritual technology and system of signification superior to medical science.[40] Practitioners limned the almost unverbalizable severity of their symptoms in terms that gestured toward somatic and semantic excess, and faulted doctors for a staggering dearth of understanding.[41] They emphasized the puzzling, supernatural nature of their ailments, and that the suffering they endured lay beyond the skill of physicians to assuage.[42] These testimonials dramatized the misrecognition of both the narrators and their doctors, the "men of science" whose diagnostic limitations have symbolized those not only of biomedicine, but also of Enlightenment-derived secular epistemologies more generally.

Almost every Lucumí rite is preceded by a libation that includes a formal request for protection from illness.[43] In communal rituals as well as more private affairs, such as sixteen-cowries divinations and rogations, elders define illness as a disruption in the field of social relations that includes orishas as a privileged category of agentive subjects.[44] In divinations, elders interpret ailments according to their gravity, character, and location. Curative practices involve incantations, stylized movement, and the application of herbal substances according to ethnobotanical conventions, yet the ideas of health and illness are constructed in a more diffuse, informal, ongoing process not confined to ritual contexts. "Anything you do in the religion is quote-unquote 'medicine,'" an elder from Miami once told me.[45]

The stories about illness that practitioners heard and recounted in Ashabi's house contributed to what could be described as Lucumí ethnosymptomatology: an understanding of the body based on the ownership of its constituent parts by different orishas, and predicated on the idea that the orishas may use a practitioner's body to communicate with her.[46] The orishas govern distinct anatomical areas and have the ability to restore them to health, especially in concert with spirits renowned for healing power, such as Olokún. According to Ashabi, one of her first godchildren, a diabetic, almost went blind, but her eyesight was preserved through the intercession of Inle, called "the Divine Doctor."[47] His brother, Osaín, has been regarded as the patron of traditional medicine. Practitioners have depicted him as embodying the somatic disequilibrium caused by suffering: he has a high-pitched voice, one hand, one foot, one eye, one enormous yet deaf ear, and another one that, while tiny, "perceives the sound of the brushing of the wings of a passing butterfly."[48] He was maimed as the result of a quarrel with the patron of Ifá diviners, Orúnmilá, with whom he declined to share either his herbal expertise or his clientele. His physical asymmetry expresses his lopsided priorities, and the perils of exploiting therapeutic power to achieve money and status.[49]

No orisha can heal without the aid of Osaín, "lord of leaves."[50] Numerous myths relate how the orishas came to possess his plants and herbs: "Particular leaves might belong to a certain deity on the basis of mythological associations, ashé (curative and/or magical power), visual appearance (color, shape, and texture), taste, association with a body part or physiological process, or all of these at once."[51] Osaín was often summoned in Ashabi's house, as in praise-songs during the preparation of herbal infusions prior to rituals of consecration. Despite the centrality of Osaín, however, the orisha Babalú Ayé was more frequently cited as a source of healing. During an Elegguá party, for instance, one practitioner volunteered that when he received a consecrated version of Babalú Ayé's ritual implement, a palm-fiber broom, he was beaten lightly on the torso with it. He said that he felt something being pulled out of his body, and since he had been HIV-positive for ten years without any sign of AIDS, the inference was that Babalú Ayé had arrested the disease. Similarly, at the time of my first formal interview with Fadesiye, he described his childhood struggle to straighten his handicapped legs by wearing braces. I was shocked. He had been a professional dancer in a prestigious Chicago troupe and was a sought-after mount whose manifestation of Yemayá, when in possession of his body, was renowned for her vertiginous pirouettes. He explained that in divination, Babalú Ayé had been identified as his father in ocha, and that he owed his ability to walk normally to him and to Yemayá.

The narratives told about Babalú Ayé during his annual cleansing ceremony not only increased attendees' understanding of him, they assisted in reconfiguring practitioners' sense of their own embodiment. Before one of these events in 2005, Ashabi addressed participants, explaining the components of the ritual about to occur downstairs. She told a myth about Babalú Ayé that accounted for the lesions that mar his flesh.[52] Ashabi said that after creation, when Babalú Ayé came to earth from heaven, he was too enamored of worldly—especially carnal—things, and stooped to sexual promiscuity, his mythological descent matching his moral fall. Infected with weeping sores, he was shunned by the other orishas. Olódùmarè, the Supreme Being, was ready to do away with him, until Ochún assumed the form of a vulture and flew to heaven to plead forgiveness for his "sins." Ochún succeeding in saving Babalú Ayé and averting the disaster that would have ensued upon his withdrawal from the world, but he was left with the traces of the venereal diseases that he had contracted. In this myth as in others, the orishas' bodies are not merely iconic of their qualities. They are indexical, pointing to specific circumstances and relationships. They are simultaneously palimpsests and media of signification, as practitioners' bodies are shown to be in divination and other ritual contexts.

In subsequent conversations, I learned that Ashabi did not envision Babalú Ayé as the image of St. Lazarus pictured on countless chromolithographs—propped up on crutches, with feral dogs lapping at his shins—but not because the saint has been depicted as white. Ashabi did not see him having African features either, or any features at all. To her, Babalú Ayé was a mystery, "the hidden mystery of life," since illness can happen at any time, anywhere, to anyone. Although her view of illness was shaped by her own experience of it, it reflected a mindset concerning the ubiquity of illness promoted in oracular speech and prevalent among Lucumí initiates, to the extent that it appears to provide an institutional rationale for the frequency and heterogeneity of ebó. Communal ebó such as the agban counteracted the multiple unseen causes of illness thought to derive from malign forces, while leaving open the possibility that certain symptoms of affliction may be signs of the orishas' favor.

Behind every exhortation to sacrifice was the assumption that some afflictions—as in the stories of Osaín and Babalú Ayé—had rained down as divine chastisement for the flouting of moral-ethical norms, or the order (delivered in oracular speech) to get initiated. Practitioners have understood the orishas to inflict the same fatal illnesses that they heal, and straightforwardly itemized their lethal powers in verbal lists comparable to the one that Cabrera published long ago in *El monte*:

> Thus we see that the saints [the orishas] cause various types of deaths: Babalú Ayé kills through gangrene, smallpox, leprosy; Obatalá blinds and paralyzes; Yewa causes consumption; Inle and Orula madden; Ogún, Oshosi, Eleggua and Aláguna—the cause of solitary deaths—provoke uncontrollable hemorrhaging. . . . "Oshún and Yemayá punish a person through the belly. They kill in fresh or salt water, and they cause consumption due to rain and humidity," says Odedei [the priestly name of Calixta Morales, Cabrera's informant].[53]

With the onset of symptoms interpreted as symbolic of the orishas' ownership, it was said that the only means of restoring health was initiation. Although elders refrained from setting forth the precise mechanics of healing, they maintained that in the initiatory rite, the heads of iyawos were protectively "sealed" by their orishas' aché.[54]

Elders have tended to read even post-initiatory oracular speech through the lens of illness. After one initiation in October 2006, an itá proclaimed that the next uninitiated person to pass through the front door should be ordained.[55] After a little while, Billal walked in followed by Tre, a young African American man whose prendiciónes, as markings for initiation, were the stuff of Ilé legend; he had managed to stumble into rituals and get yoked with a mazo more times than elders could count. Above the televised roar of football in the living room, one could hear the shouts of laughter go up when the aleyo's identity was revealed. That summer, a divination had determined his patron orisha to be Shangó, and Tre had internalized the pronouncement. Tre was often seen wearing red, Shangó's color, with a plastic comb embedded diagonally in his short Afro, the tines pointing outward as if they were the peaks of a slipping crown. One night he could be heard repeating, ad nauseam, the refrain of the Ray Cash song "Sex Appeal," recalling for listeners the myths of Shangó's virility.[56]

Later that evening, Ashabi commented that Tre was not really an aleyo, in the sense of "stranger." Tre had been part of the community for years. Indeed, he had spent much of the evening during the previous matanzas skinning, then quartering, rams after sacrifice, and had already begun gathering the necessary paraphernalia for his initiation. In Ashabi's opinion, the true "next aleyo" was Howard, an African American drummer who had unexpectedly stopped by for a visit shortly after Tre's arrival. Howard belonged to another ilé led by a Cuban woman, yet his plans of traveling to her natal land for ocha had never come to fruition. Howard had recently undergone surgery and was in poor health. In Ashabi's opinion, he was "hung up on" the idea of mentorship by someone with an exotic accent and getting initiated in the birthplace of Lucumí. Ashabi feared that this misbegotten quest for authenticity would cost him not only his livelihood, but also his life. While she would not tell him this, her assessment of the matter was of a piece with elders' interpretation of illness as the preeminent sign of the orishas' possession.[57] Verbalizations of such analyses were rituals in themselves, in which the semiotic links between affliction and ocha were constructed for strangers and family members alike.

## Initiatory Suffering

Initiates readily admitted that ocha did not always heal. In fact, they sometimes claimed that it had inflicted suffering. A young priest named Hasim told me with apparent conviction, "Initiation messes up your head."[58] He said that his jaw, clenched for extended periods of time during the ritual process, had become injured, and was "still sore to this day," almost a year after his ocha.[59] Hasim said that during most of it, he was "in pain, in pain, *in pain*," and at one point thought to himself, "I'm going home and going to bed. . . . As a man, I'm through [with this]. I'm not going to be a bitch today."[60] While I will refrain from speculation on the cause of his distress, his disclosure resonates with scholarly analyses of the ordination ceremony as both infantilizing and effeminizing initiates to turn them into wives for the orishas. The ritual forced him into a subordinate position that he equated with sexual submission and deemed an affront to his masculinity; it messed up his gendered presentation of "face," defined by Erving Goffman as one's "image of self delineated in terms of approved social attributes."[61] In the same conversation, he indicated that the values he once espoused needed to be "messed up" to be put right, and that being destabilized by ocha had been indispensable for his maturation. Yet the freshness of his pain indicated a less-than-thorough reconciliation to the ritual process, and an ongoing adjustment to his new place within the Lucumí community.

Priests' suffering has also been more protracted and severe. During my fieldwork, elders occasionally took others' more disabling illnesses as an opportunity to engage in "reflective discourses" and comment on the effects of ochas made with improper protocols, by those judged to be either incompetent or malicious. Not unlike doctors disputing a case of medical malpractice, they alluded to delicate operations highly susceptible to error, and debated whether a lack of knowledge or of ethics was at fault. In my experience and in published accounts, however, victims of chronic pain and disease have not spoken of their own affliction as the result of botched initiations. In fact, they have been quicker to blame themselves than their godparents, or the orishas, for their continued misfortunes. Yomí Yomí's story may be instructive in this regard. Shortly before traveling for her ocha, she was blindsided on the expressway while on the way to assist in another practitioner's ordination. The accident left her with lasting pain. When I asked her whether the initiation ritual had helped the healing process, Yomí Yomí replied, "It didn't! I have a bad back from it. . . . I was crying during the ceremony, because of the pain in my back. I mean, the tears were coming down my face. I didn't say anything, I just had tears coming, and afterwards . . . the *santeras* came up to me. They said, 'You did good [but] we felt your pain in our back.'"[62] Her physical pain was aggravated by her loneliness and the insurmountable linguistic and cultural barriers separating her, as an Anglophone white American woman, from most priests in attendance.

After initiation, she continued to endure the same intense and unpredictable vaginal hemorrhaging that had preceded her initiation. It continued for a total of five years and impeded her ability to pursue her career. She was consistently misdiagnosed by physicians; her first gynecologist was "a fool." In her conversation with me, Yomí Yomí incorporated themes that run through other initiates' narratives: the obtuseness of doctors and the anxiety provoked by a perplexing sickness that wreaks havoc on professional ambitions as well as social relationships. Finally, she was able to receive three addimú orishas:

> So when I went . . . to receive Inle and Ogún caracoles and Orisha Oko, I said, "I think I want it with four legs." And honest to God, in the middle of the ceremony—I was always bleeding—I stopped bleeding, and never bled again. I never had the problem again. . . . Ogún caracoles stopped me from getting the surgery.[63]

The surgery was to have been a hysterectomy. She fed Ogún with "four legs"—meaning goats—instead of birds, and attributed the consecration ritual's extraordinary potency to that fact. It is fitting that Yomí Yomí described herself as exhibiting shrewd judgment in requesting the sacrifice, evincing the discernment wanting in others. With the aid of the orishas, Yomí Yomí healed herself.

In her story, Yomí Yomí highlighted the contradiction between one of the major organizational rationales of the Lucumí tradition—to heal illness—and individual experience. Her account raises several questions: if conversational micropractices have been a critical site for the dissemination of Black Atlantic traditions, what is the relationship between initiation stories that end in health, and those that do not? Do they also conduce to the formation of religious subjectivity? Or do they represent a counternarrative that ultimately contests, rather than reaffirms, the dominant religious discourse? I would suggest that the answers lie in the narrators' assignment of ultimate responsibility for their plight. Yomí Yomí's account became an argument for the power of the orishas, in the context of the dialogic situation created by its telling. She recoiled from condemning Lucumí as a religious system, and instead conferred legitimacy upon it through her devotion to the orishas.[64] Stories such as these may be among the most pedagogically effective, for their emplotment as tragedies—rather than comedies, with a happy marriage at the denouement—puts an italicized exclamation point on the same message conveyed by other initiation stories.

Yomí Yomí's avowal of persistent affliction signaled the presence of vigorous tensions that can arise between initiates and their communities. The recollection of affliction in everyday talk has insinuated a homology, or isomorphism, between corporeal and social bodies.[65] Physical complaints have taken the shape of sufferers' religious quandaries; the resolution of the latter has brought redress to the former.[66] Yet sometimes bonds with religious communities have been severed or prevented from solidifying due to trauma, incompatible approaches to ritual practice, or incommensurable cultural perspectives. Even seasoned practitioners have experienced discrimination due to their race, class, or gender, and had their trust betrayed. The sadness that has suffused their initiation stories has coincided with their sense of social exclusion. The decision to deprive listeners of a happily-ever-after ending has posed a sharp critique of speakers' inadequate support systems. What has been missing for these narrators is not religious commitment, but a durable vertical bond with elders—or a horizontal bond with peers—that would translate suffering into solidarity.

## The Year of Being a Wife

The iyawo was chatting about his plans, things he has to do and what had gone on that night, when Ashabi suddenly told him, "You know, iyawo, you're turning into a person. You're growing up." He cocked his head to the side, marking exactly one beat, and said, "That's cold-blooded. You saying

I was a machine or something?" She told him that what she
was saying to him is a good thing.
—Fieldnotes, April 29, 2006

She didn't even exist until yesterday.
—Ashabi Mosley, October 28, 2006

It is a far cry from accepting the orishas' existence to becoming initiated and passing through the crucible of iyaworaje. Elders intend for the
first year of priesthood to support the cultivation of diverse virtues, in
the conventional meaning of the term: along with humility, fortitude,
patience, and integrity, the qualities to be fostered include the willing-
ness to assume gender roles associated with the opposite sex in ritual
performance and the capacity for reasoned critique in defense of communal norms. These virtues express values such as obedience to elders
and the valorization of African-inspired forms of association. Initiation also promotes virtue in the archaic sense, as "power," and as those
capacities for ethical action inculcated by corporeal training that the
anthropologist Talal Asad has called "moral potentialities."[67] Elders
frame the endurance of hardship as a character-building exercise and
employ multifarious tactics to force latent capacities into blossom, not
disdaining the manipulation of such ungracious instruments as excru-
ciating boredom. As an iyawo copes with the drastic yet temporary
restrictions shared by most initiates, and lifelong strictures unique to
her, new virtues are supposed to take root.

When the iyawo performs her "ebó of three months"—sometimes
long after three months, due to the financial cost of this ceremony—the
orishas are fed, the iyawo has her hair snipped, and she is ritually presented to a mirror. The prohibition against seeing oneself in any reflective surface for the first three months may be thought of as interrupting
the process of an individual's never-ending self-fashioning in deference
to the community's construction of her personhood through the regulations of iyaworaje and the dictates of her itá.[68] In the words of one
initiate, the iyawo goes from infant to toddler after her three months'
ebó, and some privileges are granted to her: she may wear short sleeves,
comb and cut her hair, and let her head go uncovered for short periods

of time. She no longer must sit on a woven mat to eat, but may pull up a chair and be seated at a table during meals. Significantly, until the three months' ebó, an initiate is unable to raise her orishas from the floor. They rest on it in their vessels as if asleep, and they cannot be aroused for ceremonial purposes or used to initiate others. After the ebó, they are lifted up onto the shelves of cabinets or into an altar display, signaling that they have arisen from their slumber.

For the rest of the year, however, the iyawo is still not allowed to be photographed; eat from china and silverware other than her own special set used in initiation; go out after sunset, unless accompanied by a godparent; imbibe alcohol; spend time in crowded or noisy public places, such as shopping malls or bars; use scented soaps, deodorants, and other toiletries; or have sexual intercourse, unless she is married. The iyawo must sleep on white sheets and pillows and attend to her godparents whenever they call on her. Priests sometimes expound on the origins and theological purpose of these regulatory practices, yet it is indisputably the case that disrupting an initiate's daily routine acts to assert her ritual godparents' kinship, seniority, and rights over her person. Curtailing her movements canalizes her bonds of affiliation, sentiment, and obligation in the direction of the religious community. The iyawo must in effect withdraw herself from circulation, as when she must refuse to be handed anything, and instead request that objects be set down on another surface first. She cannot touch anyone but blood relatives, spouses, and other initiates. This *noli-me-tangere* attitude announces to her social world that the iyawo expects different treatment after initiation, and that her role within it has changed irreversibly. She no longer occupies the positions she once did, nor inhabits the same world.

Iyawos must wear white clothing at all times, from innerwear to outerwear. The religious studies scholar Mary Ann Clark has provided an exhaustive reading of whiteness as a symbol with reference to iyawo-raje as a liminal period.[69] But what wearing white does for and to initiates depends in part on their geographic and social locations. While white clothing usually separates Lucumí practitioners from the rest of their communities, the sartorial conventions of Islam, on the one hand, and hip hop, on the other, allowed those dressed in white on Chicago's

South Side to operate just below the radar of suspicion. For instance, during the period of my research, head coverings such as wraps and skullcaps were widely (mis-)recognized as a badge of Muslim affiliation or Moorish Science Temple membership. Younger initiates managed handily to reconcile the wearing of Lucumí attire with their own sense of style: since white clothes, particularly oversized white tee-shirts, signified gang neutrality, men in their freshly bleached best mostly got no more than a second glance on the street. White baseball caps hovered above white bandannas and durags, hiding the mounds of cocoa butter, coconut, cotton, and eggshell powder placed underneath them during rogations. White high-top sneakers, scrubbed clean with toothbrushes, blended in with friends' fashionable Air Jordans and Adidases. White pants were worn slightly tighter than the baggy ideal, but still big enough to be cool.

Spotless white clothing in urban spaces is a rarity, and may impress the beholder with admiration for the wearer's resources, attracting positive attention.[70] One high school teacher said that after she received her elekes from Ashabi and had to wear white for a week, her students told her, "You a G, you a gangster, Ms. Samantha!" She explained to me that her pupils had equated her ability to pull together a set of entirely white clothing with untold affluence. In that context, "gangster" was merely a synonym for someone rich. But iyawos frequently complained of feeling physically dirty, coated by a layer of grime that began to accumulate moments after their white clothes were pulled over their heads, before they even left their homes. This feeling has been said to intensify in social gatherings that include initiates, since an iyawo must ask everyone she may reasonably suspect is a priest whether she has made ocha, and if so, descend to salute her in prostration. As Ashabi has said, for an iyawo, "that's their whole year, just hitting the floor." Iyawos are instructed to get up and stand after each prostration, rather than scuttle crablike from one elder to the next on all fours. Each one must be shown the proper level of respect, so that she does not have to say—as Ashabi's godfather did—"Don't be crawling to me!"[71]

One priest with more experience wearing white clothes than most was Alaafi. I mentioned the dietary and behavioral restrictions handed to him in his itá in chapter 2. In addition to those, he was told he should never again wear any color but white, except for part of the day, once a month. Alaafi made sense of the need to wear white according to the details of his particular struggle as a young Black man in Chicago. For instance, Alaafi explained that due to his early involvement with gangs and their "color wars," he had forced Ochún's hand, leading her to remove colors from his repertoire of sartorial choices lest he be tempted to endanger himself on the streets of the city: "You don't realize how serious wearing a color is because [of] . . . bullshit issues in Chicago. Colors carry energy, can be too much for a person, or just not right for a person. I just wore out every color [before initiation], because I knew what was coming."

This comment points to the importance of chromatic theory in Lucumí religious ideology, such that material objects and deities are categorized according to the three main color groups that are thought to organize most sensory phenomena. For practitioners, color registers the visual attributes of an item as well as its temperature and temperament. Chromatic (re)cognition simultaneously engages multiple senses: sight, sound, and touch. Internalizing this approach to color has been an important aspect of becoming a Lucumí religious subject. Alaafi said that the color black draws in "weird energy," and that when he wore it, he would feel tired and out of sorts; not coincidentally, wearing black during ritual occasions is usually considered infelicitous, partly since blackness in Lucumí iconography symbolizes "the uncharted region away from the protective wall of civilization and the warmth of the family's hearth."[72]

But the "bullshit issues" that lead one to wear colors cannot be understood only with recourse to Yorùbá or Afro-Cuban precedent. Black has been one of the main colors flashed, along with red and green, to signal affiliation with the "People Nation" gangs of Chicago, including the Black Stone Rangers/Black P. Stone Nation. Items decorated with these colors, such as Chicago Bulls jerseys, have been worn to indicate initiation into these and associated gangs. Flagged in law enforcement "gang awareness" materials, these colors have also been used to justify police harassment of Black and Latino youth—affiliated or not—and the predations of the carceral state.[73] Alaafi was careful not to divulge too much about his past to me, but he was frequently vocal about ocha having saved his life by yanking him out of his social milieu. The phrase "blood in, blood out" denotes the violence that often attends entry into a gang, as well as the trouble with staying away from it, and he was clearly grateful to have been spared the worst.[74]

Alaafi had not always been prepared to play by the rules of his initiation. Months after his ocha, Alaafi chafed against the restrictions imposed on him to the point that his sister Oyeyei would exclaim in exasperation, "He still doesn't know how to be an iyawo!" While iyawos are not expected to understand the reasons for their obedience, Alaafi had been acting as if he possessed knowledge that he did not have. As Alaafi himself said, he had not accepted the fact that ordination had rendered him a child in the eyes of senior priests. Attempts to teach him how to be an iyawo would involve "baby steps," and started with sensorimotor training of the most basic sort before he had even left the altar in which he was confined during his ocha. During his Middle Day, Nancy, the last godchild of Ashabi's to be initiated, sat beside Alaafi in his ilé, and noticed that he failed to sit up straight on the wooden mortar that was meant to serve as his throne. He persisted in slouching and pitching forward from the weight of his mazos. Nancy repeatedly pushed Alaafi's chest up with the flat of her palm so that he would hold his head erect while addressing guests, and thereby project rectitude and grace. Maintaining an august posture was required to show that he had been converted from a denizen of the street to a resident of the palace.[75] Again and again over the next year, elders corrected Alaafi's grooming habits, stance, and demeanor, while he bristled and squirmed.

Then one night at Ashabi's kitchen table, I was privy to an exchange between Alaafi, initiated in the autumn, and an iyawo, the son of a Warrior orisha, initiated the previous summer. I had launched the conversation by touching on their education in service to the spirits. Alaafi offered the opinion that no amount of information acquired on a purely cognitive level could act as a proxy for corporeal experience. I transcribed part of their discussion as follows:

> ALAAFI: It's not about "learning." It's called "the process." You have to go through—from going to the river to—But you know I can't spill too much.
>
> IYAWO: [Unlike you,] I had [to go to] the woods too. . . . Nature was quite cruel.

ALAAFI: The river was still frozen [for my initiation].

IYAWO: You didn't get sick for three days [after your initiation, the way I did].

ALAAFI: You weren't sick. It was all part of your plan.

IYAWO: I couldn't eat! I couldn't stand up!

ALAAFI: [But when you went to the bathroom] *I* had to clean the toilet![76]

Other members of the ilé sometimes tried their luck in games of one-upmanship over the torments of initiation. Yet they were not merely grousing about the hypothermia-inducing conditions of their ochas and the bucket shifts they were compelled to work as iyawos. They were demonstrating their competence in a speech genre as well established in houses of orisha worship as the playing of the dozens in Black communities. The ability to interpret and employ a spirit idiom depends on pragmatic knowledge: the shared "rules of thumb" drawn upon in applying cultural experience obtained in informal, real-world settings.[77] Alaafi's investments in the Lucumí spirit idiom (including conventions surrounding the exposure of ritual secrets) and in the transformative effects of ritual practice were being constructed as he spoke, through and around his speech.

Practitioners sometimes related accounts of their religious insubordination during the iyawo year. Billal once reminisced over his escapades as "the worst iyawo"; he told me that he regularly went out when he should have stayed home, and confided that on the occasion of Ashabi's ocha birthday, he left her home to get high on marijuana with a friend. He arrived at her home long after her bewilderment over his whereabouts had turned to disgust. When he prostrated to her—no doubt with the odor of the herb still clinging to his white clothes—rather than performing the customary blessing and bidding him to rise immediately, she left him on the ground at her feet. Billal estimated that he stayed on the floor for about two minutes, which seemed like an eternity for the man with his forehead and nose pressed against the varnished hardwood floor, his arms at his sides, and his left foot in the air, maintaining the pose deemed appropriate for the child of a Warrior orisha. When Billal pleaded with Ashabi to "raise" him, she said, "This is not Wall

Street. Your money is no good here," simultaneously reminding him that his former life had ended in ordination, and communicating that his actions had no currency in a household governed by the paramountcy of elders. Ashabi thus rendered explicit the symbolism of the ritualized prostration: that to get initiated is to cede control over one's head to the orishas, and pledge devotion to the elders designated to preside over it in their stead.

When elders spun yarns concerning their misbehavior as iyawos, these picaresque stories invariably became cautionary tales. They ended, humorously if bittersweetly, with the novices receiving their comeuppance—white trousers ruined, white mug shattered, special spoon lost forever. As Alaafi said more than once in the course of our discussions, "Respect is respect," meaning that deference to elders was not negotiable. He had started to talk like a priest, speaking of others' initiations as only a matter of time; when a mazo accidentally fell off a wall at my feet, he told me that it was just trying to get itself around my neck. In more subtle ways, he endeavored to collar others into submission to the orishas, and sculpted his life before ocha into a narrative that had the orishas as its main protagonists. In fact, he had reconciled himself to the dictates of his itá to the extent that he saw no conflict between them and his chosen profession: to be a mortician. During the time of his iyaworaje, Alaafi was earning credits in mortuary science at a local college, in hopes of graduating with a degree in forensic science and someday owning his own funeral parlor. While he was staying at Ashabi's house with his girlfriend, Berta, I often saw him poring over anatomy textbooks at the kitchen table, cramming for upcoming exams.

Although his mode of dress prompted stares from fellow students, he would matter-of-factly inform them that he was wearing white for religious reasons, and had no problem envisioning himself donning an ivory suit as a mortician's apprentice or funeral director. Alaafi felt that his lifelong attraction to the funerary arts was partly explained by the path of Ochún he was said to have at his itá: Ibú Kolé, the sorceress whose home is the sewer and whose familiar is the buzzard. Just as, elders say, the buzzard appears to devour carcasses out of gluttony while actually beautifying the world by disposing of its dead, so Alaafi deemed his chosen career a misunderstood yet essential one, best regarded as aesthetic and therapeutic, in its ability to ease suffering by creating a serene environment for mourning. His identification with Ibú Kolé was partly the outcome of Alaafi's effort to align his destiny with Ochún's patronage. In this, he was not exceptional. He was not among the virtuosi—the diviners and artists—often extolled as the heroic custodians of the tradition. Priests like Alaafi nevertheless have been the ones clearing a path for the tradition to take hold in places and people where it has yet to go.

I offer this profile of Alaafi—little more than a silhouette, considering the many angles and textures of his experience left unilluminated—to emphasize that subject formation among practitioners is not consummated at initiation. Although ordination inaugurates the process that authoritatively establishes the personhood of priests, religious subjectivity materializes through repeated linguistic and behavioral citation of the norms that render it culturally intelligible. As in the philosopher Louis Althusser's classic scene of interpellation, Alaafi spun time and again away from the sound of the voices he was hearing. Yet even shrugging off the call was a response to it. Insertion within a "circuit of recognition," not consent, formed the condition of possibility for his religious subjectivity.[78] His transformation crystallized at the nexus of bodily techniques—avoiding sugar, wearing white—and ideological becoming, as he assimilated his elders' words and adopted the spirit idiom in his everyday talk. In speaking casually about their experiences, often in a way that confounded expectations, seasoned practitioners like Alaafi taught their listeners to consider the spirits "participants (albeit unseen and silent ones) in every conversation."[79]

I want to conclude this chapter by noting something that the spirit idiom may share with idiomatic expressions more generally. In everyday talk, figurative idioms are employed to elicit displays of assent from interlocutors, and build common ground between them.[80] Studies have shown that they are most frequently uttered in the transition from one topic to another; in fact, their main function, as an interactional device, is to bring the conversation at hand to an end. Idiomatic expressions are perceived to encapsulate a matter under discussion as a means of enabling interlocutors to leave it behind. As both symbolically robust and impervious to empirical challenge, idiomatic expressions solve the problem of how to change the subject by conjuring the semblance of resolution, the "final say" in a dialogue that, in truth, never has a last word.

Accordingly, among practitioners, the spirit idiom has not explained the inexplicable. The spirit idiom has loosened no knots; it has dealt ineluctable suffering no mythic knife-stroke. What the spirit idiom has done is impose closure—albeit provisional—on the inexhaustible subject of what a life may "mean."[81] In doing so, it has held out the possibility of beginning anew.

# Conclusion

## Microparctices in Macrocosm

*Microparctices in Macrocosm*

Before honey is offered to Ochún, it must be tasted. Lucumí practitioners explained this rule to me by citing an episode in her mythology: someone once tried, unsuccessfully, to poison Ochún, and now anyone petitioning her with honey needs to prove its safety to her by sampling it first. The acts of dipping a finger into a container of honey, putting a drop between one's lips, and pronouncing it good, often in response to an elder's query—*"Is it sweet?" "Yes, it's very sweet!"*—establish Ochún's presence. Even if her supplicant is unable to smell or feel this honey (perhaps as the result of a stuffed nose or burned tongue), sensuous engagement with Ochún's favorite offering brings to the fore her intention to savor and render judgment on the flavors presented to her. When elders refer to honey using the Yorùbá term *oñi*, the African precedents for the Lucumí context rise to the surface of the encounter, calling to mind other myths in which Ochún wields honey as lubricant (to liberate) and adhesive (to arrest). The routine of testing honey through taste also enlists the senses in an awareness of ritual practice as fraught with danger and the potential for transgression. It is taboo to forget.

"History cooks us all," Palmié writes. This book has sketched out the micropractices of cooking and talking that have made Lucumí the tradition it is today: both a cooking religion—characterized by ritually marked spaces of food preparation, tropes of alimentation, and kinship through consumption of shared substance—and one that is cooked by social processes beyond the control of any one set of practitioners or scholars.[1] By beginning with the food that went into the gods' mouths and ending with the words that came out of my interlocutors', I have tried to get at what might be seen as a dialectic: the materiality of the discursive and "discursivity of the material" to be found in the kitchen of Ilé Laroye.[2] Rather than take for granted the beliefs, practices, tropes,

199

materials, and personnel that constitute Lucumí, I have steered a course between its construction in the scholarship on Afro-Cuban religions and its instantiation within one contemporary site actively remade on a day-to-day basis, as both objective institution and subjective experience.[3] While I maintain that hunger is no figure of speech for the gods, cooking has furnished this book with a model for Black Atlantic religious subjectivity that evokes the transformative effects of architectural space, temporality, learning by teaching, the fashioning of a future-directed memory, and innovations that enable taxonomies to be modified and to integrate new categories of information.

The image of religious practice limned above corresponds to data collected in Ilé Laroye over the course of several years, in consultation with a range of interdisciplinary sources amassed to render the most accurate picture possible of its everyday religious transformations. Yet this image still remains quite partial. As a photograph may apprehend an object from unaccustomed angles and in constellations of light that last but a fraction of a second, then go on to represent its existence in the round, so the incompleteness of this record may be concealed sheerly by dint of its materiality. Only time will tell whether the claims set forth here enhance scholarly understanding of religious phenomena within or beyond Black Atlantic traditions. Fixing its glare on the omissions hidden beneath the details, time will turn tattletale soon enough. The incompatibility of my perspective with that of others may not just call into question this book's general approach, but also suggest that any evidence submitted in support of its conclusions is proof of my misunderstanding. Longtime interlocutors may submit contradictory testimony, to which the sole proper response would be gratitude, for abetting this study and aiding in its correction through critique. The responsibility for this premeditated act of scholarship ultimately lies with me alone.

It is my prerogative, though, to anticipate the charges to be brought—or at least the objections—and to hazard a last effort to clarify what I am after. To this end, I want to return to Arlene's observation that to be an iyawo is to be "a tool, a vessel, and a servant" of the spirits. Arlene's statements, and the myriad similar comments made over the years in the ilé, closely mirror the figurations of religious subjectivity conveyed in Black Atlantic spirit idioms. Ceremonies are portrayed as machines that mill human beings into instruments for the gods' use;

personhood derives from ritually inhabiting the psychic and social zone of the abject. The human being prior to priesthood is a wild beast to be domesticated, an African captive to be seasoned; an initiate becomes the spirits' horse and slave, broken, as it were, in order to be made whole.[4] Initiatory rites empty the self to force a vacancy for the spirits, and the "social poetics," if not the erotics, of the resulting human-divine relationship dictates that novices be envisioned as wives and mothers vis-à-vis their tutelary deities.[5] The novice is subordinate not only to the gods, but to the community fed and reproduced through her ritual labor. Among Nigerian Yorùbá devotees of one spirit, Matory writes, "The ritual iconographies . . . are the material signs of the hollow self and the gendered nature of the subjectivity that fills it. . . . Priestly experts replace a received regime of the self with a cooperatively and locally constructed one."[6]

*write about subordination processes*

Butler describes the abject as the "constitutive 'outside'" of the subject, less a position to be occupied than a "zone of uninhabitability" and "site of dreaded identification."[7] The bodies of the abject do not register as real; despite their physicality, they do not materialize—or matter— because their incomprehensibility disqualifies them from subjectivity. In fact, the subject defines herself against the abject, the Other, the "not-me" that must be repudiated.[8] I touch on abjection here because it renders explicit the politics of subject formation in Black Atlantic initiatory traditions. Lucumí initiates must be made into the slaves of the spirits in order to be affirmed as priests. This understanding of ideal religious subjects figures prominently in the Black Atlantic religious imaginary, and supports such phenomena as spirit possession. Rites of passage may thus be viewed as revalorizing the "densely populated" spaces historically condemned as "unlivable," as if asserting squatters' rights to set up house within them.[9] While such repurposing and "taking on of abjection" may trouble hegemonic norms of subjectivity, this volume has been at pains to show that resistance and agency do not lie outside fields of power, but arise within relations of subordination.

*process of Othering*

The central chapters of the book may be read as dissecting the "micropractices of persuasion through which people are made to incline toward one view versus another"—namely, my interlocutors' vision of themselves as the orishas' tools, vessels, and servants.[10] Most accounts of the ordination process indicate that the extraordinary environment of the initiation room does violence to the stability of novices' pre-existing self-representations, the artifacts of their fragile and occasion-ally stalemated negotiations between dominant cultural concepts and ever-shifting, idiosyncratic self-understandings.[11] To all appearances, the first year after initiation goes on to put the majuscular "I" of the iyawo in lowercase. Yet my data strongly confirm that the notion of per-sons as composite or "dividual," rather than individual—and capable of accommodating multiple contending agencies—has been regularly ush-ered into the midst of "the everyday world" prior to initiation, in the in-numerable sensorimotor adjustments made when learning the subtleties of Lucumí cooking and during mundane kitchen-counter conversations with elders.

To the extent that elders expressed the need to fulfill the spirits' de-sires as a problem of agency, they framed it as an issue of cultivating the virtue to put their own "agency in abeyance"; in Lucumí, as in other Black Atlantic religions, this capacity has been conceptualized as the re-quirement for all others to be obtained, even the ability to claim person-hood.[12] To catch practitioners in the contradictions posed by religious subjectivity—that mastery proceeds from surrender—is to confront the larger "paradox of subjectivation" identified by the social theorist and historian of ideas Michel Foucault and operative in many other religions: "The very processes and conditions that secure a subject's subordination are also the means by which she becomes a self-conscious identity and agent."[13] Consecrated objects, including elekes and Warriors, have had a tremendous role to play in instantiating "modes of subjectivation."[14] For practitioners, such person-like things have not only acted as ma-terial indexes of the social relationships and ritual performances that engendered them. They have activated the religious subjectivity of their recipients while simultaneously subjecting them to regulatory norms.[15]

Just as subjectivity requires modes of subjectivation, micropractices are bound to "microphysics of power."[16] There is little sense in pinpoint-ing the former if not to mount an analysis of the latter.[17] The local chains of force relations denoted by the term *power* exist in tension with nested hierarchies most profitably understood from the bottom up. That having been said, my treatment of micropractices may be criticized on several grounds, perhaps the most cogent of which concerns precisely my at-tempt to decipher the power relations that flowed through them. Despite

*[handwritten marginalia: Process of subordination]*

the amount of attention allotted to the micropolitics of legitimation and religious pedagogy—the discursive materialization of elders' authority and practitioners' adoption of rhetorical models that have redounded to the enlargement of Lucumí communities—I could be accused of harboring a reluctance to offer macro-level explanations connecting local structures with the confluence of historical forces that gave rise to Afro-Cuban religions. Moreover, it could be alleged that the questions of autonomy and agency raised by the inhabitation of the spirit idiom remain unanswered. Allow me to address these issues in turn.

I have used the Foucauldian language of micropractices throughout to distinguish routine and small-scale sequences of operations. In the context of the house-temple, micropractices closely approximate tactics, in the historian of religions Michel de Certeau's sense of the term, while larger ceremonies—macropractices—are aligned with the logic of action that he equates with strategy.[18] Within a house of worship, a drum feast may be understood as strategic in demanding a proper place, commandeering resources, and entitling its organizers to control the movements of participants. In its larger sociopolitical context—that of the nation-state and hegemonic religious institutions—the drum feast occupies a marginal space secured solely through tactical gambits and the art of subterfuge.[19] In the literature on Afro-Cuban traditions, the previous point has been minimized in the interest of casting practitioners as unambiguously subversive and oppositional to justify the inclusion of religion in a larger theoretical project that revolves on the axis of the normative liberatory subject.

What has long been at stake in the representation of Black Atlantic traditions—the answer to the "So what?" question for scholars beyond Latin American and Caribbean studies—is the ability of these traditions to provide evidence of systematic ideological resistance to "hegemonic incorporation" among subordinate groups. Consider, for instance, the oft-cited proposition that icons and images of Roman Catholic saints once masked the African identities of Cuban orishas and Haitian lwas. The argument that religious practitioners disguised Black Atlantic spirits with the faces of the saints is meagerly substantiated at best; it has customarily been marshaled to confound the caricature of marginalized groups as mired in the thrall of ideologies that naturalize the ruling classes' supremacy. Along with neo-Marxist thinkers and political scientists, scholars of the Black Atlantic world have reiterated this narrative of iconographic dissimulation to refute the notion that populations of African descent capitulated to the mental and psychological onslaughts of enslavement and colonialism. To the extent that Afro-Diasporic religions have been framed as arming subaltern groups with "weapons of the weak" and "hidden transcripts," they have been rationalized as promoting human autonomy and contributing to the progress of freedom and civilization.[20] Even histories of the Black Church in the United States have tended to silence African American movements not understood as emancipatory, dismissing them as "cults and sects."

While not "intoxicat[ed] with 'agency,'" I am not unsympathetic to the premise that religious action often constitutes political protest. I would readily concede that participation in Black Atlantic religions has been a means for individuals shunted into secondary and tertiary corridors of power to obtain a sense of group identity and a certain degree of sociocultural capital.[21] Commitment to the Lucumí tradition may indeed be of a piece with the "'polytheism' of concealed or disseminated practices" that de Certeau placed in opposition to "the 'monotheism' of the dominant panoptical procedures."[22] This part of the story must be told, yet it is not sufficient to account for the ongoing development of religious subjectivity. Practitioners' portrayal of religious engagement as an act of defiant self-determination needs to be seen as a discursive justification articulated partly to insulate their traditions against a critique they are tired of confronting—namely, that religion is "false consciousness" and complicit in their oppression.[23] I share with the anthropologist Richard Price a reluctance to pinpoint the problems to which religious affiliation acts as a "personal solution"; those commonly enumerated reveal more about the style of biographical reconstruction privileged within the religion of the practitioner's choice than about the factors that led her to choose it.[24]

These issues have dovetailed with others concerning the survival of precolonial West and Central African values and traits in Black Atlantic religions. Their capacity to retain fragments of the past has been applied as a measuring rod for evaluating their authenticity, quite literally in the case of the Herskovitsian "scale of intensity of Africanisms."[25] While current scholarship has moved away from the "verificationist epistemology" problematized by the anthropologist David Scott almost twenty years ago, the tendency to shore up the research paradigm associated with it through appeals to cultural continuity runs deep.[26] The line of inquiry that I have pursued may thus be unsatisfactory, even disquieting, in its refusal to classify modes of subjectivation according to this "calculus of consequence, truth, and proof."[27] The narrative of religious resistance to domination is complicated by an analysis that does not locate ritual performances along a spectrum of greater or lesser liberatory potential, and that sees strategies and tactics as coextensive.[28] Everyday micropractices in a house of orisha worship are both strategic and tactical; another example to hand would be the telling of initiation stories. Narrators' interpretations of their corporeal experience boldly gainsay those imposed by the medical establishment and the dominant cultural milieu. But this speech genre owes its impact largely to the hierarchical status of narrators, and the progressive naturalization of the spirits' desires as those of their representatives.

Participation in Black Atlantic religions has required subordination to religious authorities even as it has opened up possibilities for political resistance. To refrain from casting subject formation in terms of recruitment, indoctrination, or "rational choice" is to leave oneself vulnerable to the complaint lodged against the Foucauldian model of power by the philosopher Charles Taylor, namely, that its positing of "purposefulness without purpose" dissolves into incoherence: "The undesigned systematicity has to be related to the purposeful action of agents in a way that we can understand. . . . It is certainly not the case that all patterns *issue* from conscious action, but all patterns have to be made *intelligible* in relation to conscious action."[29] Although the identity of the "we" in this statement is debatable, I attempted to forestall this critique by using vignettes and fieldnotes to evoke the material relation of agents to their acts, and depict sequences of actions as exhibiting an intelligibility that did not depend on Enlightenment rationality.[30]

The part that "purpose" or intentionality played in my interlocutors' enmeshment in Afro-Cuban traditions is difficult to quantify. The seasoning of individuals into subjects did not result in, but followed from, their mundane conversions of architectural and corporeal spaces into sites for ritual practice. While one could say that innumerable acts culminated in religious transformation, they were not originally performed with that end in mind. Individuals to be called by the spirits were "always-already" subjects of other ideological formations into which they had been interpellated. Concurrent commitments to distinct ideological systems produced ostensible disagreement in word and deed, between what individuals wanted—or said they wanted—and what they did, as when practitioners contested the spirits' onerous demands while dutifully satisfying them.[31] This would at least go some way toward explaining the success of Afro-Cuban religions in the contemporary United States, for while their processes of deindividualization may be adduced as a reproach to the modern "cult of the self," the personalized spirit idiom affirms the uniqueness of every individual in terms of psychic and physical constitution.

## Autonomy and Servitude

What does it mean, then, when we both take the subaltern's views seriously—the subaltern ascribes the agency for their rebellion to some god—and want to confer on the subaltern agency or subjecthood in their own history, a status the subaltern's statement denies?[32]

The question of agency and autonomy reasserts itself here. Practitioners of traditions such as Lucumí have used metaphors of enslavement to conceptualize the actualization of individuals in and through the social, suffused with radically asymmetrical relations of power. They have poached from the verbal tropes and gestural imagery of seasoning in particular to erect a template for the human-divine relationship. These have conveyed particularly well the mutual dependence of priest and god as it manifests in obligation to a community. Ascendancy to eldership lends itself to comparison with servitude; I found that the longer priests remain in the service of the orishas, the greater the chances they will come to narrate the response to their call as a matter of compulsion. This may reflect not only the attainment of proficiency in the speech genre of "unchosen choice," but also the very real increase in their ceremonial duties along with their religious offspring, and the heightened claims on their time made by their own elders. Initiates may even chafe against the bonds of reciprocity that tie them to peers, upon whose fellowship they loyally rely.[33]

Practitioners did not couch their views of agentive action in terms of guarding their autonomy against the encroachment of external powers, but rather, in language that framed the group as the franchise of self-realization. In my interlocutors' statements about their responsibilities to the ilé, they stressed the impossibility of uncoupling the individual from the social. They relinquished sovereignty over the self to the spirits in exchange for membership in a community imagined as overlapping territorially with the state, yet diverging ideologically from it.[34] It is worth noting that in religious traditions throughout the African Diaspora, practitioners refer to distinct orthodoxies as "nations" (Rada, Petwo, Jeje, Quêto/Nagô, Angola, Congo, and so on) in deference to this fact.[35] Accordingly, the house-temple of Lucumí has been portrayed as a government-in-exile. Its heteronomy is not a mere side effect of efforts to put "agency in abeyance"; it is a method, one necessary for the defense and enlargement of the religious commonwealth.[36] Far from impeding citizenship in such a nation, enslavement has been required as the condition of it. Apropos of practitioners' apparent forfeiture of their freedoms, I followed the transcription of Arlene's comments about priestly life as "a tool, a vessel, and a servant" in my fieldnotes with a question: "Why would she want to embrace this religion if her ancestors were slaves?"

I see now that this query was born of an inadequate acquaintance with figurations of slavery in Afro-Cuban religious practice. In the preceding chapters, I mentioned repeatedly the multivalent allusions made to bondage by the members of Ilé Laroye. In similar houses of worship, newcomers have encountered discourses, structures of sentiment, and dispositions narrated as having their roots in the historical experience of unfreedom. Rites of passage throughout the Black Atlantic world recode and revalorize the experience of enslavement as a type of metamorphosis, depicted as proceeding in distinct stages: the subject is caught with rope and cloth, transported to a new world, sold, violently stripped, clothed, renamed, sequestered, assaulted, and eventually transformed into a "sensible" laborer, for whom the master's wish is a command. The ceremonial analogues for these stages recode the seasoning once analyzed as inflicting cultural amnesia on slaves as the basis for their sensorimotor, affective, and cognitive engagement with remembered traditions. Even practitioners' spontaneous displays of resistance within the initiatory process recapitulate aspects of the collective past deemed imperative to relive. Such procedures have disseminated memories of enslavement in ritual performance far beyond practitioners of African descent.

This religious poetics sits ill with definitions of the modern subject as self-governing. The philosopher and intellectual historian Susan Buck-Morss writes, "By the eighteenth century, slavery had become the root metaphor of Western political philosophy, connoting everything that was evil about power relations. Freedom, its conceptual antithesis, was considered by Enlightenment thinkers as the highest and universal political value."[37] The encumbrance of practitioners by their religious commitments may seem to compromise their potential for social action by mystifying relations of power and predisposing them to rehearse, in the secular realm, the deference to authority demonstrated in the religious domain. The idea that both objects and persons stand to be "*humanized* by their very subordination" has been a target of "the iconoclast's hammer" not only in the American pragmatic and European rationalist traditions, but also for intellectuals on every point of the political spectrum.[38] To cite just one example, womanists such as Jacquelyn Grant have indicted Christian "servanthood language" as integral to Black women's oppression by sacralizing their victimization, and urged theologians to revamp their vocabularies in accordance with the ideals of human dignity, equality, and justice.[39]

Such critiques presuppose that tropes of enslavement perpetuate the condition they appear to represent, and that slavery carries the same connotations for the critic as for the practitioner. Both postulates are doubtful. Matory sharply contrasts the symbolism of enslavement in Black Atlantic religions with the "litotic invocation of slavery" as the foil to, and antithesis of, the "normative present-day freedom" that has permeated political discourse in the United States.[40] He points out that the figure of the slave elsewhere in the African Diaspora furnishes "a model of and model for" efficacy in action; while constrained and deprived of most rights—bereft of "a name, or a title, or a position"—the enslaved person does not exhibit any impairment of her faculties and has significant scope for the exercise of her agency, precisely through the competent performance of labor. The slave may occupy an inferior station, yet her moral-ethical superiority to her social betters is undisputed. In houses of worship, slaves of the spirits may be addressed as nonentities one minute, then as coddled babies, cherished brides, or fledgling monarchs the next. In sharp contrast to human slave owners, their masters are deserving of devotion.

In puzzling out the symbolism of enslavement in religious subject formation, we should not discount the ancestral trauma of the Middle Passage and chattel slavery.[41] But we should appreciate the impact of subsequent historical events—comparable to Reconstruction and the Great Migration in the United States—in the Caribbean and Latin America. North American historians sometimes express surprise, even shock, that former slaves would seem to wax nostalgic about their servitude in narratives such as those gathered by the U.S. Federal Writers' Project from 1936 to 1938.[42] Their nostalgia says less about slavery than about the back-breaking hardships that marked freedom. Left after emancipation to eke out a living picking cotton and scrubbing floors, elderly men and women likened themselves to young Black people born free. "Ex-slaves" knew work like kin; they saw sharecropping as slavery with a paycheck, and one that often bounced. They witnessed their children getting robbed, then lynched, and harkened back to the days when labor came with food and shelter, no matter how stale the pork or rickety the shack.

I would argue that the enshrinement of slavery in Black Atlantic religions be interpreted as a critique of the "betrayal of abolition" in republican democracies throughout the African Diaspora, one that has also served to master the inequitable sociopolitical arrangements that are the living legacies of this betrayal.[43] The historian William H. Sewell argues that in analyzing symbols and semiotic systems as "models *for* and models *of*" in his famous definition of religion, Clifford Geertz missed an opportunity to explore the discrepancy between their mirroring and structuring functions. Representations do not automatically replicate, but also can transfigure, reality.[44] I see the iconography of enslavement translated into the spirit idiom as deriving its force from this double movement. It has offered a blueprint for the world and a roadmap to it: "a condensation point for complex truths. Power liberates, power corrupts, power destroys."[45] The sensuous and tactile transposition of slavery's historical excess into the religious realm has triggered a volatile and transformative "mimetic slippage," "whereby reproduction jumps to metamorphosis."[46]

Rather than dispense with hierarchy altogether, practitioners have mimetically appropriated the logic of "vertical encompassment" to mobilize members of their communities in the redress of suffering, and incorporate them into a body politic whose borders are not geographic but corporeal.[47] It may seem that the subject interpellated by the spirit idiom becomes an "animate tool" whose agency and "liberal autonomy" have been amputated. Yet the interpretive apparatus that subsequently mediates between conflicting imperatives, values, and ideological systems also supplements the self, as a sort of prosthetic device.[48] This phrase may be misleading, for the defect lies not in any individual self but in the fragmentary character of subjectivation. Moreover, the practices and discourses that synthesize the subject are artificial only in the sense that they are culturally constructed. In Black Atlantic religions, these are regarded as divulging the nature of interiority in relation to the body, instead of distorting it. I would advance the proposition, then, that traditions with a personalized spirit idiom such as these materialize through the very process of locating the spirits' immanence in the phenomenal world.

It is incumbent upon me here to return briefly to the self—or rather, to the type of self that comes to be known through the micropractices of cooking and talking. In Black Atlantic religions, these "ensembles of procedures" construct knowledge by establishing distinctions between valid and incorrect forms of behavior, along with the authority to adjudicate the difference.[49] They may be seen through a Foucauldian lens as sites for the interplay "of truth and error through which being is historically constituted as experience; that is, as something that can and must be thought."[50] In historicizing the Lucumí subject, the preceding chapters reveal everyday religious interactions as containing points of access to "truths" that enable self-mastery through compliance with disciplinary regimes. For practitioners, the self achieves recognition of its own subjectivity in the course of determining its "ethical substance," the aspects of its being that provide "the prime material of . . . moral conduct."[51] The self to be discovered is one formed through verbalization of the desire not to be a tool, vessel, or servant, and yet converted into them by the spirits nevertheless, in a transformation all the more remarkable for being unchosen.

## Toward a Secret Recipe for Religion

Despite the encyclopedic knowledge about embodied practices that recent work on Black Atlantic religions represents, the analytical emphasis on discourse might lead the casual reader to suppose that they are ultimately all talk, structured by practitioners' speech habits, classificatory schemes, and semiotic ideologies alone, as opposed to the traditions conventionally surveyed in college classes on world religions.[52] The main finding of this book is the secret recipe for the apparent continuity of Lucumí as a religious formation, despite the instabilities inherent within it, as within any social formation: ensembles of micropractices that lend the impression of cohesion to social interaction. Since the micropractices that orchestrate the perception of continuity over time are performed at the behest of those with a vested interest in materializing it, this finding holds out the possibility of more rigorously theorizing subject formation as a didactic process of moral-ethical and ideological becoming.

Although through ordination, Lucumí priests can be said to be "made from scratch," practitioners start to be seasoned as soon as they begin contributing to the everyday conversion of an elder's home into a house of worship. Their cooking continues far beyond the first year of initiation, as they repeatedly taste affliction alongside Ochún's honey. I propose that in Lucumí and other traditions of religious possession characterized by a personalized spirit idiom, subject formation requires (1) sites of social engagement that dramatize the immanence of the spirits; (2) pedagogy devised by social actors motivated to instruct others in the sensorimotor modalities and aptitudes integral to the continued existence of their traditions; (3) discourse as an institutionally supported process of redescription, whereby individuals come to narrate their bodies as belonging to the spirits; and (4) liturgies that bind newcomers to elders in the performance of ritual labor, simultaneously generating fellow feeling and engendering the entities to be served.

These techniques, so to speak, may be most germane to the cooking of Black Atlantic traditions, yet I submit that all religions rely on a secret recipe of micropractices to coalesce and endure. This recipe may be quite an open secret among historians and anthropologists of lived religion, yet it is one frequently obscured by scholars invested in the world religions paradigm, as well as by adherents themselves. In seeking "to speak of things eternal and transcendent with an authority equally transcendent and eternal," elite religious authorities have advertised rites of passage and other rituals with a capital R as the sole "transformative practices" that alter the socio-ontological status of persons and spaces.[53] In the historical study of religion, such truth-claims may appear to be corroborated by the focus on major ceremonies and their virtuosic officiants. But subjectivation inheres in micropractices seldom celebrated within a tradition itself. In fact, they are often not textually elaborated or acknowledged as rituals at all, as opposed to minor routines.

It could be said that the concealment of micropractices is baked into the cake of world religions as an artifact of the post-Enlightenment moment. That was when, to be recognized as religions, social formations had to be accepted as endowed with rationality by bearing a certain family resemblance to Protestant Christianity. Excised from scholarly accounts of many traditions were practices and discourses that went against regnant notions of personhood, agency, somatic experience, semiotic ideology, gender hierarchy, and sexuality. These omissions distorted the historical record and erased groups (such as gay men) whose prominence defied heteronormative and patriarchal conventions. Those traditions that seemed to accentuate ritual risked being ranked as animism or fetishism, or subsumed under any number of other local rubrics. The nineteenth-century evolutionary model popularized by Sir James Frazer, among others—and unwittingly taken up by many a contemporary "new atheist"—postulated that humanity had moved from magic to religion, and could now progress beyond it, to science. This scale of decreasing enchantment was calculated to track with the diminishment of everyday behavior deemed superstitious, while leaving a narrow ideological space free for the occasional liturgy.

This is not to say that rites of passage and capital R rituals are a cynical or content-free diversion, a sort of MacGuffin in the plot of the story world religions tell about themselves. It is, rather, to assert that their citation by dominant factions of practitioners possesses a rhetorical and historiographical dimension.[54] To quote the historian of religions Bruce Lincoln, "Scholarly misrecognitions . . . replicate the misrecognitions and misrepresentations of those the scholars privilege as their informants," whether these are individuals or documents.[55] The solution is not to eschew any definition of religion because the ones privileged thus far have universalized "historically specific" and culturally contingent categories.[56] Religion can be more accurately elucidated with reference to discourse, community, institution, and practice if investigations attend to the formation of subjects within them. This would call for a shift in focus from holy pageantry to the unglamorous micropractices that consolidate and perpetuate those disciplinary regimes accepted as religious traditions.

Micropractices exist in subordinate relationship to the macropractices that dominate religious discourse. As technologies for normalizing power relations, they hide in plain sight. Since micropractices regulate bodies over time, their study cannot be rushed; to understand the significance of micropractices that pass quickly, one must watch, and work slowly.[57] Religious scholarship on embodied and communicative micropractices nevertheless already tackles themes such as the management of hair, jewelry, and apparel; monastic apprenticeship; prayer; scriptural exegesis; the exchange of greetings; musical performance and marketing; burials; seminary education; and menstrual cycles and ritual immersion, to name only a few.[58] As this abridged list indicates, the analysis of religious micropractices lends itself to scrutinizing gender and sexuality as well as processes of racialization, globalization, and indigeneity. This research embraces the challenge of mapping the subtle changes micropractices have wrought on the human sensorium—not simply hearts and minds, but also senses and sensibilities.

Historians of religions stand to profit more than many other scholars from the "turn to affect" that has occurred across the social sciences and humanities. The future lies in synthesizing insights from diverse fields—including linguistics, neurobiology, cognitive science, and cultural studies—that promise to assist in capturing the synaesthetic complexity of religious formations as lived moment to moment. For the student of Black Atlantic religions, there may be no richer ground to cover than the space of cooking, or better point of departure than pathbreaking studies of food in African American traditions.[59] Sacred cuisines have materialized through the micropractices that construct appetite, digestion, and all that lies between them. They lack only for researchers to glance toward the stove—and away from the altar—more often. This move is certain to open up impolite conversations about who cooks, where, and for whom; how; who eats what, when; and why. Everything else is gravy.

# NOTES

## INTRODUCTION

1 See Wirtz, *Ritual, Discourse, and Community*; and Holbraad, *Truth in Motion.*

2 George Lakoff and Mark Johnson, *Philosophy in the Flesh: The Embodied Mind and Its Challenge to Western Thought* (New York: Basic Books, 1999), 6.

3 See the discussion of food preparation in Richman, "They Will Remember Me"; and Richman, *Migration and Vodou.*

4 While this description uses Kantian language, it faithfully represents the attitude of other philosophers. Carolyn Korsmeyer, *Making Sense of Taste: Food and Philosophy* (New York: Cornell University Press, 1999); Lisa Heldke, "The Man of Culture: The Civilized and the Barbarian in Western Philosophy," in *The Center Must Not Hold: White Women Philosophers on the Whiteness of Philosophy*, ed. George Yancy (Lanham, MD: Rowman and Littlefield, 2010), 77–98.

5 L. M. Heldke, "Foodmaking as a Thoughtful Practice," in Curtain and Heldke, *Cooking, Eating, Thinking*, 207.

6 Khan, "Isms and Schisms," 768–70; Masuzawa, *Invention of World Religions.*

7 This is not to imply that food has no place in other religions, merely that it has not been valorized in the intellectual tradition under discussion.

8 Evelyn Brooks Higginbotham, *Righteous Discontent: The Women's Movement in the Black Baptist Church, 1880–1920* (Cambridge: Harvard University Press, 1993).

9 See Andrew Apter, "On African Origins: Creolization and Connaissance in Haitian Vodou," *American Ethnologist* 29 (2002): 233–60; Capone, *Searching for Africa.*

10 Farah Jasmine Griffin, *If You Can't Be Free, Be a Mystery: In Search of Billie Holiday* (New York: Free Press, 2001), 205n47. For extensive discussion of the resulting "ethnographic interface(s)," see Palmié, *Cooking of History.*

11 See Asad, *Genealogies of Religion.*

12 All of these languages are also called by other names, but these are some of the most common.

13 Robert J. Marshak, "A Discourse on Discourse: Redeeming the Meaning of Talk," in *Discourse and Organization*, ed. David Grant, Tom Keenoy and Cliff Oswick (London: Sage, 1998), 15–30; Robert Wuthnow, "Taking Talk Seriously: Religious Discourse as Social Practice," *Journal for the Scientific Study of Religion* 50, no. 1 (2011): 1–21.

14 Elaboration of informal religious speech genres is not only an issue in the study of Afro-Diasporic religions. Of the type of questioning that occurs during mosque lessons, Mahmood writes, "This kind of exchange presents a situation far more complex

than any simple model of 'religious indoctrination' would suggest, and requires an analysis of the micropractices of persuasion through which people are made to incline toward one view versus another." *Politics of Piety*, 106.

15 See Carol Bernadette Duncan, *This Spot of Ground: Spiritual Baptists in Toronto* (Waterloo, Ontario: Wilfrid Laurier, 2008); Carol L. Jenkins, "Ritual and Resource Flow: The Garifuna," in *Blackness in Latin America and the Caribbean: Central America and Northern and Western South America*, ed. Norman Earl Whitten Jr. and Arlene Torres (Bloomington: Indiana University Press, 1998), 149–67; Kean Gibson, *Comfa Religion and Creole Language in a Caribbean Community* (Albany: State University of New York Press, 2001); McDaniel, *Big Drum Ritual of Carriacou*; J. G. Platvoet, *Comparing Religions: A Limitative Approach; An Analysis of Akan, Para-Creole, and IFO-Sananda Rites and Prayers* (The Hague: Mouton, 1983); Maureen Warner Lewis, *Central Africa in the Caribbean: Transcending Time, Transforming Cultures* (Kingston: University of the West Indies Press, 2003); Edwina Ashie-Nikoi, "Beating the Pen on the Drum: A Socio-Cultural History of Carriacou, Grenada, 1750–1920" (PhD diss., New York University, 2007); Sally Price, *Co-Wives and Calabashes* (Ann Arbor: University of Michigan Press, 1984); and Bernice Johnson Reagon, "African Diaspora Women: The Making of Cultural Workers," *Feminist Studies* 12, no. 1 (1986): 77–90. Worth noting is the documentation of Saramaka maroon sacrificial cooking and food offerings, from the perspective of one healer and religious practitioner, in Richard Price, *Travels with Tooy: History, Memory, and the African American Imagination* (Chicago: University of Chicago Press, 2007).

16 Christie, *Kitchenspace*.

17 Beliso-De Jesús, "Religious Cosmopolitanisms."

18 Jenny Mandelbaum, "How to 'Do Things' with Narrative: A Communication Perspective on Narrative Skill," in *Handbook of Communication and Social Interaction Skills*, ed. John O. Greene and Brant R. Burleso (Mahwah, NJ: Erlbaum, 2003), 595–636.

19 J. D. Y. Peel, *Religious Encounter and the Making of the Yoruba* (Bloomington: Indiana University Press, 2000), 93.

20 Regla ocha means "rule of ocha"; ocha is an abbreviation for *kariocha*, the Lucumí initiation ritual.

21 I have changed the names of all of my interlocutors and of the ilé, for reasons of confidentiality. Readers should note that ilés are often named after the orishas' praise names, and there is more than one actual Ilé Laroye in the United States; in fact, one of these is a prominent, long-standing, well-respected house of worship in Miami that officially uses this name. In what follows, however, Ilé Laroye refers only to Ashabi Mosley's casa-templo in Chicago.

22 I generally follow the usage of Todd Ramón Ochoa in speaking in terms of African-inspired religions, in order to accentuate innovation and creativity in the remaking of cultural forms in the New World. See Ochoa, "Aspects of the Dead in Cuban-Kongo Religion," in *Cuba Today: Continuity and Change since the "Periodo Especial*," ed. Mauricio A. Font (New York: Bildner Center for Western Hemisphere Studies, CUNY Graduate Center, 2005), 246.

23 To assist in contextualizing such trajectories, see Capone, *Les Yoruba du Nouveau Monde*, 328.

24 Marilyn Strathern, "Cutting the Network," *Journal of the Royal Anthropological Institute* 2, no. 3 (1996): 517–35.

25 Jennifer Brady, "Cooking as Inquiry: A Method to Stir Up Prevailing Ways of Knowing Food, Body, and Identity," *International Journal of Qualitative Methods* 10, no. 4 (2011): 321–34.

26 Comaroff and Comaroff, *Ethnography*.

27 Curiously, although the term "micropractices" is often attributed to Foucault quite explicitly, a review of the relevant literature in French and English translation failed to uncover a locus classicus. Otherwise scrupulous works of scholarship are somewhat lax in citation of its coinage and subsequent usage.

28 Wirtz, *Ritual, Discourse, and Community*, is instructive in this regard.

29 Márcio Goldman, "How to Learn in an Afro-Brazilian Spirit Possession Religion: Ontology and Multiplicity in Candomblé," in *Learning Religion: Anthropological Approaches*, ed. David Berliner and Ramon Sarró (Oxford: Berghahn, 2007), 103–20.

30 My usage here conforms to that of Machon, *(Syn)aesthetics*. See also Steve Andrews, "Toward a Synaesthetics of Soul: W. E. B. Du Bois and the Teleology of Race," in *Re-Cognizing W. E. B. Du Bois in the Twenty-First Century: Essays on W. E. B. Du Bois*, ed. Mary Keller and Chester Fontenot Jr. (Macon, GA: Mercer University Press, 2007), 142–85.

31 See Ramos, *Adimú*, 1st ed.; John Mason, *Ìdáná Fún Òrìsà*; Aróstegui and González Dias de Villegas, *Afro-Cuban Cuisine*; and Lody, *Santo também come*, among many other publications. Online, see the instructional cooking videos and other information posted on the website Nydia's Sacred Foods, at http://www.adimunetwork.com/index.html, by Iya Nydia Pichardo, spouse of Obá Ernesto Pichardo. (Pichardo is the priest perhaps best known for winning the 1993 U.S. Supreme Court case *Church of the Lukumi Babalu Aye, Inc. v. City of Hialeah*, which upheld the practice of animal sacrifice as a free exercise of religion protected by the First Amendment.) The motto for Nydia's Sacred Foods is "Preservation of our Lukumi Tradition, and Sacred Foods . . . Join Me and Enhance Your Spiritual Connection through the Alchemy of Sacred Foods."

32 Norris, "Examining the Structure and Role of Emotion"; Warnier, *The Pot-King*; Mellor and Shilling, "Body Pedagogics"; and Bourdieu, *Outline of a Theory of Practice*, esp. 93–94.

33 Walter J. Ong, "The Shifting Sensorium," in Howes, *Varieties of Sensory Experience*, 25–30; Charles Hirschkind, *The Ethical Soundscape: Cassette Sermons and Islamic Counterpublics* (New York: Columbia University Press, 2006); and James McHugh, *Sandalwood and Carrion: Smell in Indian Religion and Culture* (New York: Oxford University Press, 2012).

34 For instance, Capone, *Les Yoruba du Nouveau Monde*.

35 See Beliso-De Jesús, "Religious Cosmopolitanisms"; Mattijs van de Port, "Visualizing the Sacred: Video Technology, 'Televisual' Style, and the Religious Imagination in Bahian Candomblé," *American Ethnologist* 33, no. 3 (2006): 444–62; Karen Richman

and Terry Ray, "Congregating by Cassette: Recording and Participation in Transnational Haitian Religious Rituals," *International Journal of Cultural Studies* 12 (2009): 149–66; Bender, *Heaven's Kitchen*; and Luhrmann, *When God Talks Back*.

36 Beliso-De Jesús, "Religious Cosmopolitanisms," 713; Port, "Visualizing the Sacred," 457.

37 Palmié, *Cooking of History*.

38 Rachel E. Harding supplies a provocative rationale for this methodological strategy in "The Lithic Imagination and the Tertia: The Longian Paradigm and Art in the Study of Afro-Atlantic Religion," *Souls* 16, nos. 1–2 (2014): 99–109.

39 See Hughes, "Soul, Black Women, and Food"; and Jualynne E. Dodson and Cheryl Townsend Gilkes, "'There Is Nothing Like Church Food': Food and the US Afro-Christian Tradition: Re-membering Community and Feeding the Embodied S/spirit(s)," *Journal of the American Academy of Religion* 63, no. 3 (1995): 519–38.

40 Meredith Gadsby, *Sucking Salt: Caribbean Women Writers, Migration, and Survival* (Columbia: University of Missouri Press, 2006), 123.

41 Paul Christopher Johnson, "On Leaving and Joining Africanness through Religion: The 'Black Caribs' across Multiple Diasporic Horizons," *Journal of Religion in Africa* 37, no. 2 (2007): 174–211; Tina Campt, "The Crowded Space of Diaspora: Intercultural Address and the Tensions of Diasporic Relation," *Radical History Review* 83 (2002): 97.

42 See also Wirtz, *Ritual, Discourse, and Community*.

43 It was covered by the *Chicago Tribune* on November 6, 2005.

44 See Ana Y. Ramos-Zayas, *National Performances: The Politics of Class, Race, and Space in Puerto Rican Chicago* (Chicago: University of Chicago Press, 2003).

45 Jadele McPherson, "Rethinking African Religions: African Americans, Afro-Latinos, Latinos, and Afro-Cuban Religions in Chicago," *Afro-Hispanic Review* 26, no. 1 (2007): 121–40. One of the most highly regarded priestesses in Chicago is Jamaican.

46 I also attended several drum rituals, or *wemilere*, not sponsored by Ilé Laroye.

47 Margarethe Kusenbach, "Street Phenomenology: The Go-Along as Ethnographic Research Tool," *Ethnography* 4, no. 3 (2003): 455–85.

48 Ibid., 455.

49 Rob Shields, "Meeting or Mis-Meeting? The Dialogical Challenge to Verstehen," *British Journal of Sociology* 47, no. 2 (1996): 275–94. I debated the use of the term "informants" as opposed to "consultants," bearing in mind the law enforcement associations of the former and the corporate connotations of the latter. I settled on "interlocutor" to refer to those who contributed to this project.

50 *King Lear*, act 4, scene 6.

51 See Luke E. Lassiter, *The Chicago Guide to Collaborative Ethnography* (Chicago: University of Chicago Press, 2005); and Stoller, "Sensuous Ethnography."

52 I followed three priests before their initiations and through their first years as priests. In addition to interviews with adults, I conducted a handful with children.

53 Jacob Katz, *The "Shabbes Goy": A Study in Halakhic Flexibility*, trans. Yoel Lerner (Philadelphia: Jewish Publication Society, 1989), 63.

54 See Johnson, "Secret Sits in the Middle," in *Secrets, Gossip, and Gods*, 23–34.

55 Wacquant, *Body and Soul*, 4; Luce Giard, "Part II: Doing-Cooking," in de Certeau, Giard, and Mayol, *Practice of Everyday Life*, vol. 2, 149–256.

56 Personal communication, February 24, 2007.

57 Personal communication, July 14, 2006. See also Robin W. Winks, ed., *The Historian as Detective: Essays on Evidence* (New York: Harper and Row, 1970).

58 Willerslev, *Soul Hunters*, 106.

59 Richard Harvey Brown, "Logics of Discovery as Narratives of Conversion: Rhetorics of Invention in Ethnography, Philosophy, and Astronomy," *Philosophy and Rhetoric* 27, no. 1 (1994): 3.

60 Palmié, *Cooking of History*.

61 Ayana D. Byrd and Lori L. Tharps, *Hair Story: Untangling the Roots of Black Hair in America* (New York: St. Martin's, 2001), 137; Vorris L. Nunnley, *Keepin' It Hushed: The Barbershop and African American Hush Harbor Rhetoric* (Detroit: Wayne State University Press, 2011), 94. See also Kimberly Battle-Waters, *Sheila's Shop: Working-Class African American Women Talk about Life, Love, Race and Hair* (Lanham, MD: Rowman and Littlefield, 2004); Lanita Jacobs-Huey, *From the Kitchen to the Parlor: Language and Becoming in African American Women's Hair Care* (Oxford: Oxford University Press, 2006); and Ginetta E. B. Candelario, *Black behind the Ears: Dominican Racial Identity from Museums to Beauty Shops* (Durham: Duke University Press, 2007).

62 See Michelle Alexander, *The New Jim Crow: Mass Incarceration in the Age of Colorblindness* (New York: New Press, 2010); Vron Ware, *Beyond the Pale: White Women, Racism, and History* (London: Verso, 1992); and Sara Ahmed, *Queer Phenomenology: Orientations, Objects, Others* (Durham: Duke University Press, 2006). From my fieldnotes, December 17, 2005: "For the rest of the night people called me the interpreter and translator. [One of Ashabi's godchildren said,] 'Lisa, you're Cuban? I didn't know you were Cuban. All this time I thought that you were white.'"

63 Cheryl Rodriguez, "Anthropology and Womanist Theory: Claiming the Discourse on Gender, Race, and Culture," *Womanist Theory and Research: A Journal of Womanist and Feminist-of-Color Scholarship and Art* 2, nos. 1–2 (1996–97): 3–11.

64 James Clifford, *The Predicament of Culture: Twentieth-Century Ethnography, Literature, and Art* (Cambridge: Harvard University Press, 1988), 40.

65 Clifford Geertz, "Thick Description: Toward an Interpretive Theory of Culture," in *The Interpretation of Cultures: Selected Essays* (New York: Basic Books, 1973), 3–30. I am alive to the critique that the term "experience" has allowed scholars to signal the existence of a private, subjective realm beyond the empirical or interpretive grasp of the analyst. Robert A. Orsi, "Is the Study of Lived Religion Irrelevant to the World We Live In?," *Journal for the Society for the Scientific Study of Religion* 42, no. 2 (2003): 169–74.

66 David Snow and Richard Machalek, "The Convert as a Social Type," in *Sociological Theory*, ed. Randall Collins (San Francisco: Jossey-Bass, 1983), 259–89.

67 See, for example, Clark, *Santería*.

68 J. Albert Harrill, "Paul and the Slave Self," in *Religion and the Self in Antiquity*, ed. David Brakke, Michael L. Satlow, and Steven Weitzman (Bloomington: Indiana University Press, 2005), 52.

69 The phrases "grammar of racism," "racial grammar," or "grammar of antiblackness" have been used by several scholars, including Eduardo Bonilla-Silva, "The Invisible Weight of Whiteness: The Racial Grammar of Everyday Life in Contemporary America," *Ethnic and Racial Studies* 35, no. 2 (2012): 173–194; and Jane Anna Gordon, "The Gift of Double Consciousness: Some Obstacles to Grasping the Contributions of the Colonized," in *Postcolonialism and Political Theory*, ed. Nalini Persram (Lanham, MD: Lexington Books, 2007), 154.

70 Kristina S. Wirtz shows that these speech registers have been profoundly affected by Cuban *teatro bufo* and other minstrelsy practices in "A 'Brutology' of Bozal: Tracing a Discourse Genealogy from Nineteenth-Century Blackface Theater to Twenty-First-Century Spirit Possession in Cuba," *Comparative Studies in Society and History* 55, no. 4 (2013): 800–833.

71 Melville J. Herskovits, *The Myth of the Negro Past* (Boston: Beacon, 1990 [1941]); Saidiya V. Hartman, *Scenes of Subjection: Terror, Slavery, and Self-Making in Nineteenth-Century America* (New York: Oxford University Press, 1997), 75–76.

72 Harrill, "Paul and the Slave Self," 51.

73 *Inside the Actor's Studio*, season 12, episode 1206, original airdate February 12, 2006.

74 Asif Agha, "The Social Life of Cultural Value," *Language and Communication* 23, nos. 3–4 (2003): 231–73; Agha, "Voice, Footing, Enregisterment," *Journal of Linguistic Anthropology* 15, no. 2 (2005): 38–59.

## CHAPTER 1. SPACE, TIME, AND ACHE

1 My great thanks to Mike Cassidy for this arresting image. Personal communication, January 23, 2005.

2 Upon initiation, at minimum a practitioner receives the orishas Yemayá, Shangó, Ochún, and Obatalá, along with her tutelary deity.

3 Perhaps this is apt, since Elegguá's ribald brand of humor tends to focus on the body's nether regions.

4 A hierarchy of ritual descent relates "godparents," or the senior ritual sponsors of initiates, to their godchildren through a process called "godparentage" (*apadrinación* in Spanish). As noted with the first mention of Ilé Laroye in the introduction, readers should be aware that there is more than one house of worship already officially using this name, including a celebrated casa-templo in Miami.

5 She rose to the level of *hounsi canzo*, the first, most basic grade of initiation, followed by *soupwen* and *asogwe*. Such overlap between Afro-Diasporic traditions is not unheard of; see Karen McCarthy Brown, *Mama Lola*, 399; and Halifu Osumare, "Sacred Dance-Drumming: Reciprocation and Contention within African Belief Systems in the San Francisco-Oakland Bay Area," in *Women and New and Africana Religions*, ed. Lillian Ashcraft-Eason, Darnise C. Martin, and Oyeronke Olademo (Santa Barbara: ABC-CLIO, 2010), 123–44.

6 Raquel Romberg, "Ritual Piracy or Creolization with an Attitude," *New West Indian Guide* 79, nos. 3–4 (2005): 175–218.

7 Personal communication, October 29, 2005.

8 Rush, "Eternal Potential," 66.

9 See Akinwumi Ogundiran and Paula Saunders, *Materialities of Ritual in the Black Atlantic* (Bloomington: Indiana University Press, 2014).

10 Stewart E. Tolnay and E. M. Beck, "Black Flight: Lethal Violence and the Great Migration, 1900–1930," *Social Science History* 14, no. 3 (1990): 347–70. See Farah Jasmine Griffin, *"Who Set You Flowin'?": The African-American Migration Narrative* (New York: Oxford University Press, 1996); Jason David Rivera and DeMond Shondell Miller, "Continually Neglected: Situating Natural Disasters in the African-American Experience," *Journal of Black Studies* 37, no. 4 (2007): 502–22.

11 Christopher Robert Reed, *Black Chicago's First Century*, vol. 1, *1833–1900* (Columbia: University of Missouri Press, 2005), 52; Drake and Cayton, *Black Metropolis*, 8–9.

12 Milton C. Sernett, *Bound for the Promised Land: African American Religion and the Great Migration* (Durham: Duke University Press, 1997), 156.

13 William M. Tuttle Jr., "Contested Neighborhoods and Racial Violence: Prelude to the Chicago Riot of 1919," *Journal of Negro History* 55, no. 4 (1970): 98; James R. Grossman, *Land of Hope: Chicago, Black Southerners, and the Great Migration* (Chicago: University of Chicago Press, 1989), 156.

14 Sernett, *Bound for the Promised Land*, 165–66; Best, *Passionately Human*, 134–35.

15 A. Philip Randolph, quoted in Clarence Taylor, *Black Religious Intellectuals: The Fight for Equality from Jim Crow to the 21st Century* (New York: Routledge, 2002), 30.

16 Don Cusic, *The Sound of Light: A History of Gospel Music* (Bowling Green, OH: Popular Press, 1990), 87.

17 Blair A. Ruble, *Second Metropolis: Pragmatic Pluralism in Gilded Age Chicago, Silver Age Moscow, and Meiji Osaka* (Cambridge: Cambridge University Press, 2001), 258.

18 Susan Nance, "Mystery of the Moorish Science Temple: Southern Blacks and American Alternative Spirituality in 1920s Chicago," *Religion and American Culture* 12, no. 2 (2002): 129.

19 Baldwin, *Chicago's New Negroes*, 166.

20 Wehmeyer, "Indian Spirits on the Rock Island Line."

21 Yvonne P. Chireau, *Black Magic: Religion and the African American Conjuring Tradition* (Berkeley: University of California Press, 2003), 139.

22 Ibid.

23 Eugene V. Gallagher, "'Cults' and 'New Religious Movements,'" *History of Religions* 47, no. 2 (November 2007–February 2008): 205–20.

24 Best, *Passionately Human*, 33–34.

25 They were also young, between the ages of twenty-four and thirty-four. See Carole Marks, *Farewell—We're Good and Gone: The Great Black Migration* (Bloomington: Indiana University Press, 1989).

26 Nance, "Mystery of the Moorish Science Temple," 125.

27 Leonard Norman Primiano, "'Bringing Perfection in These Different Places': Father Divine's Vernacular Architecture of Intention," *Folklore* 115 (2004): 3–26.

28 Higginbotham, *Righteous Discontent*, 15.

29 This definition of "safe space" reflects Griffin's gloss of the term, coined by Patricia Hill Collins, *From Black Power to Hip Hop*, 9. See also Anthea D. Butler, "A Peculiar Synergy: Matriarchy and the Church of God in Christ" (PhD diss., Vanderbilt University, 2001), 2.

30 See Dianteill, *La Samaritaine noire*, 177–78.

31 Wehmeyer, "'Indians at the Door.'"

32 Nicholas Lemann, *The Promised Land: The Great Black Migration and How It Changed America* (New York: Knopf, 1991), 64. One of Noble Drew Ali's disciples was Wallace Dodd Ford, renamed Ford-El, to whom he entrusted the Chicago Temple before his death. Ford-El later relocated to Detroit and organized the Nation of Islam.

33 "As a rule, women participated in all Moorish public events and organizations. In fact, a number of Moorish temple governors were women, as was the editor of the group's newspaper . . . and many of the paper's contributors." Susan Nance, "Respectability and Representation: The Moorish Science Temple, Morocco, and Black Public Culture in 1920s Chicago," *American Quarterly* 54, no. 4 (2002): 653n12.

34 Nashashibi, "Blackstone Legacy."

35 Bryan S. Turner writes, "The components of cosmopolitan virtue are as follows: irony both as a method and as a mentality; distance and reflexivity (coolness); scepticism (towards grand narratives); care for other cultures (arising from an awareness of their precarious condition) and acceptance of hybridization; post-emotionalism; 'presentism' as opposed to nostalgia; and secularity or an ecumenical appreciation of other religions and cultures." "Cosmopolitan Virtue: Loyalty and the City," in *Democracy, Citizenship and the Global City*, ed. Engin F. Isin (London: Routledge, 2000), 143.

36 Charles H. Long, *Significations: Signs, Symbols, and Images in the Interpretation of Religion* (Philadelphia: Fortress, 1986), 7.

37 Hucks, "'Burning with a Flame,'" 90.

38 Among the Nigerian Yorùbá "iya" not only indexes maternity but age-status and can also mean "owner of" or "master of," as in the case of the orishas themselves.

39 Personal communication, September 17, 2005. In "A Fly in Buttermilk," James Baldwin addresses school integration and different segregation practices in the North and South; this may be why the phrase came to mind. *Nobody Knows My Name: More Notes of a Native Son* (New York: Dial, 1961), 95.

40 Personal communication, November 1, 2005. The information given in this paragraph was prompted by a discussion of Rosa Parks's then-recent death; Ashabi had never mentioned it to me before this.

41 Although individual Afro-Cuban religious practitioners have been documented as living in the United States since the 1940s, an initiation that occurred in Manhattan in 1962 has been widely regarded as the first on North American soil. During the same period, the first African American person was initiated into Lucumí in Queens, New York. Capone, *Les Yoruba du Nouveau Monde*, 127.

**42** See Kamari Maxine Clarke, *Mapping Yorùbá Networks: Power and Agency in the Making of Transnational Communities* (Durham: Duke University Press, 2004).

**43** Whether or not Africans would feel the same sense of solidarity is another matter. See Clarke, *Mapping Yorùbá Networks*.

**44** Tanya M. Luhrmann, *Persuasions of the Witches' Craft: Ritual Magic in Contemporary England* (Cambridge: Harvard University Press, 1989), 312–13.

**45** Personal communication, January 7, 2006.

**46** Tim Ingold, "Building, Dwelling, Living: How Animals and People Make Themselves at Home in the World," in *The Perception of the Environment: Essays on Livelihood, Dwelling and Skill* (New York: Routledge, 2000), 186.

**47** See Isidoro Moreno, "Festive Rituals, Religious Associations, and Ethnic Reaffirmation of Black Andalusians: Antecedents of the Black Confraternities and Cabildos in the Americas," in *Representations of Blackness and the Performance of Identities*, ed. Jean Muteba Rahier (Westport, CT: Bergin and Garvey, 1999), 3–17.

**48** David H. Brown, *Santería Enthroned*, 112; his italics.

**49** Ibid., 56. See also David H. Brown, "Thrones of the *Orichas*."

**50** Robin Horton, quoted in Stephan Palmié, "Ethnogenetic Processes and Cultural Transfer in Afro-American Slave Populations," in *Slavery in the Americas*, ed. Wolfgang Binder (Würzburg: Königshausen und Neumann, 1993), 346.

**51** Ramos, "The Empire Beats On," 82. Some of the most famous have been the venerable Havana-based Cabildo Changó Teddún (first located at Jesús Peregrino 49, then at Calle San Nicolás 302); the Cabildo Africano Lucumí; Cabildo San José 80; the two Cabildos Yemayá in Regla; and in Matanzas, the Cabildo Santa Teresa and Cabildo Iyessá Moddú San Juan Bautista.

**52** Thompson, *Face of the Gods*, 146.

**53** David H. Brown, "Altared Spaces: Afro-Cuban Religions and the Urban Landscape in Cuba and the United States," in *Gods of the City: Religion and the American Urban Landscape*, ed. Robert A. Orsi (Bloomington: Indiana University Press, 1999),161.

**54** Initiates usually use the Spanish word *casa* or the Yorùbá term *ilé*.

**55** See Maurice Halbwachs, *On Collective Memory*, trans. Lewis A. Coser (Chicago: University of Chicago Press, 1992).

**56** This offering to the Warriors is not necessarily performed exactly twenty-one days after they are received, but may be made any amount of time after twenty-one days deemed reasonable by the godparent. This also may be the first time an elder visits the home of the godchild in question.

**57** Otero, "Investigating Possession Pasts," 13.

**58** Charles Branham, "Black Chicago: Accommodationist Politics before the Great Migration," in *The Ethnic Frontier: Group Survival in Chicago and the Midwest* (Grand Rapids, MI: Eerdmans, 1977), 211–62.

**59** David H. Brown, "Altared Spaces," 158. Brown distinguishes between "spiritual personages" and "the tenants whose names appear on the lease."

60 Denis Cosgrove and Mona Domosh, "Author and Authority: Writing the New Cultural Geography," in *Place/Culture/Representation*, ed. James S. Duncan and David Ley (London: Routledge, 1993), 281.

61 Van Gennep, *Les rites de passage*.

62 At Ashabi's house, they include Buffalo Soldiers, Romani spirits, nuns, former slaves, and warriors—both Kongo and North American Indian. See Pérez, "Spiritist Mediumship."

63 David H. Brown, "Toward an Ethnoaesthetics of Santería Ritual Arts," 110.

64 Erwan Dianteill and Martha Swearingen, "From Hierography to Ethnography and Back: Lydia Cabrera's Texts and the Written Tradition in Afro-Cuban Religions," *Journal of American Folklore* 116, no. 2 (2003): 273–92.

65 This is a departure from the Cuban Lucumí convention of keeping offerings for the ancestors in the bathroom, under the sink or behind the toilet. Ashabi hypothesized that the bathroom was thought to be a good place to honor the ancestors because the egún are not entirely "in the house" there, since the bathroom is a liminal space where no one goes unless they have to, for a specific purpose. In her account, the marginality of the bathroom mirrors that of the ancestors, and by extension, the dishware they use.

66 While I have characterized Palo as one religious formation, it forms part of a larger complex of traditions in Cuba collectively termed *reglas de congo*.

67 Palmié, *Wizards and Scientists*, 191. The italics are Palmié's. It is emblematic of these traditions' ritual symbolism that initiation into Lucumí is called "seating" and into Palo, "scratching." According to elders, in Santería an initiate is thought to assume the royal throne to which divine parentage entitles her, while in Palo, the initiate is viewed as wrestling an nfumbi into acceptance of an offer that cannot be refused. For insight into the parallel relationship between the Rada and Petwo spirits in Vodou, see Apter, "On African Origins."

68 Personal communication, September 17, 2005.

69 According to Ashabi, altars "create a vibration that opens up things"; she said that in deciding where to place them, "you find yourself creating a space because they're living entities, and they take their personalities with them." Personal communication, September 17, 2005.

70 This ruling was *Church of the Lukumi Babalu Aye, Inc. v. City of Hialeah*, 508 U.S. 520, decided June 11, 1993.

71 Personal communication, October 8, 2005.

72 See Raquel Romberg, *Witchcraft and Welfare: Spiritual Capital and the Business of Magic in Modern Puerto Rico* (Austin: University of Texas Press, 2003), 255ff.

73 de Certeau, *Practice of Everyday Life*, 37.

74 Personal communication, October 8, 2005.

75 This term may acquire additional resonance from its association with the "g-code" holster, whose manufacturers boast that its guard protects handguns from perspiration and snagging on shirttails, thus allowing for the speediest possible draw.

**76** As the Geto Boys rapped in the 2005 song "G Code": "We don't trust in the judicial system—we shoot guns / We rely on the streets; we do battle in the hood / I was born in the G Code, embedded in my blood."

**77** Henri Lefebvre, *The Production of Space*, trans. Donald Nicholson-Smith (Oxford: Blackwell, 1991 [1974]), 143. See also Bourdieu and Wacquant, *Invitation to Reflexive Sociology*, 138.

**78** Bourdieu, *Outline of a Theory of Practice*, 6.

**79** Annual Cuban processions and celebrations in honor of Yemayá have occurred historically on September 7 or 8, depending on the source consulted. Some earlier twentieth-century sources, such as Eduardo Gómez Luaces, *Historia de Nuestra Señora de Regla: Sus fiestas, los cabildos, con datos inéditos y juicios críticos sobre Regla* (Regla, Cuba: El Observador, 1945), 11, give the date as September 8, while more recent research—that of David H. Brown, among others—insists on the date as September 7. Each source is internally consistent.

**80** I have been unable to find consistent dates for annual Yorùbá festivals or cleansings dedicated to Babalú Ayé, a spirit known by many names in West Africa.

**81** See the glossary for a brief explanation of this oracular form.

**82** Another distinction between rituals to be introduced involves their size and purpose.

**83** The notion of expertise as the product of trial and error was perhaps best expressed by Niels Bohr: "An expert is a man who has made all the mistakes which can be made in a very narrow field." Quoted in Andrew D. Oxman, Iain Chalmers, and Alessandro Liberati, "A Field Guide to Experts," *BMJ: British Medical Journal* 329, no. 7480 (2004): 1461.

**84** Taussig, *Nervous System*. Jean-Pierre Warnier explains the relationship between sensorimotor experience and subjectivation in "A Praxeological Approach to Subjectivation."

**85** My use of the term "habitus" here may seem to be at odds with Pierre Bourdieu's use of the term in his early writings, and align more closely with his definition of "hexis." In his later scholarship, however—and in his collaborations with Loïc Wacquant—Bourdieu seems to allow for a change of habitus over the course of subjects' lifetimes as they consciously engage in transformative corporeal training.

**86** Bourdieu, *Practical Reason*, 25.

**87** The performance artist James Kubie, a godchild of Ashabi's, created a month-long installation on this subject in a group show put up with Katrina Chamberlin and Elise Goldstein entitled "Services," at the School of the Art Institute Sullivan Galleries, Chicago, August–September 2009. Kubie made and served Cuban coffee in a small room while discussing the role of this practice in Ilé Laroye, and lined the shelves on the walls with the espresso cups and saucers his guests left behind.

**88** See Stephan Palmié, "How Not to Study 'Afro' 'Cuban' 'Religion'" (Presidential Lecture, Society for the Anthropology of Religion and Society for Psychological Anthropology Joint Biennial Conference, Asilomar, CA, March 28, 2009).

**89** Personal communication, April 14, 2005.

90 Personal communication, January 14, 2006.

91 See Rachel E. Harding, "*É a Senzala*: Slavery, Women and Embodied Knowledge in Afro-Brazilian Candomblé," in *Women and Religion in the African Diaspora*, ed. Barbara Savage and R. Marie Griffith (Baltimore: Johns Hopkins University Press, 2006), 3–18; Yvonne Chireau and Nathaniel Deutsch, eds., *Black Zion: African American Religious Encounters with Judaism* (New York: Oxford University Press, 2000). Riesebrodt has pointed out that the etymology of "liturgy" is "public work" (*leitourgia*), referring to the performance of ceremonies as an obligation to the state. The notion of religious service as unfree labor is thus built into its very history.

92 Personal communication, August 10, 2006.

93 Personal communication, September 24, 2005.

94 Ibid.

95 Rowland Abiodun, "Àxe: Verbalizing and Visualizing Creative Power through Art," *Journal of Religion in Africa* 24, Fasc. 4 (1994): 309–10.

96 Terence S. Turner, "The Social Skin," in *Not Work Alone: A Cross-Cultural View of Activities Superfluous to Survival*, ed. Jeremy Cherfas and Roger Lewin (Beverly Hills: Sage, 1980), 112–40.

97 Personal communication, October 8, 2005. My interlocutors often mentioned this divide.

98 Personal communication, May 11, 2006.

99 Caroline could have heard this word in discussions of socialist organizations such as the Uhuru Solidarity Movement, or seen it in the coverage of African politics in local Black newspapers. The term comes from the Arabic for a freeborn person, used by slave traders. Ali A. Mazrui, "The Semitic Impact on Black Africa: Arab and Jewish Cultural Influences," *Issue: A Journal of Opinion* 13 (1984): 3–8.

## CHAPTER 2. KITCHEN, FOOD, AND FAMILY

1 Personal communication, September 17, 2005.

2 See Aróstegui and González Díaz de Villegas, *Afro-Cuban Cuisine*; Ramos, *Adimú*, 1st ed.; Lele, *Sacrificial Ceremonies*; and Marcelo E. Madan, *Food and Adimu of the Cuban's Santería* (Caracas: Orunmila Edition, 2014).

3 Cabrera, *El monte*, 84–85.

4 By way of comparison, see Aisha Khan, "'Juthaa' in Trinidad: Food, Pollution, and Hierarchy in a Caribbean Diaspora Community," *American Ethnologist* 21, no. 2 (1994): 245–69; Laurel Kendall, "Of Hungry Ghosts and Other Matters of Consumption in the Republic of Korea: The Commodity Becomes a Ritual Prop," *American Ethnologist* 35, 1 (2008): 154–70; Stanley H. Brandes, *Skulls to the Living, Bread to the Dead: The Day of the Dead in Mexico and Beyond* (Malden, MA: Blackwell, 2006); Detienne and Vernant, *Cuisine of Sacrifice*; Nir Avieli, "Feasting with the Living and the Dead: Food and Eating in Ancestor Worship Rituals in Hội An," in *Modernity and Re-enchantment: Religion in Post-Revolutionary Vietnam*, ed. Philip Taylor (Lanham, MD: Lexington Books, 2008), 121–60; Elizabeth den Boer, "Hindu Ritual Food in Suriname: Women as Gatekeepers of Hindu Identity?," in *Caribbean Food Cultures: Culinary Practices*

*and Consumption in the Caribbean and Its Diasporas*, ed. Wiebke Beushausen, Anne Brüske, Ana-Sofia Commichau, Patrick Helber, and Sinah Kloß (Bielefeld: Transcript, 2014), 257–78; Gabeba Baderoon, "Everybody's Mother Was a Good Cook: Meanings of Food in Muslim Cooking," *Agenda: Empowering Women for Gender Equity* 51 (2002): 4–15; and the useful bibliography in Michel Desjardins, "Teaching about Religion with Food," *Teaching Theology and Religion* 7, no. 3 (2004): 153–58.

5 Thompson, *Face of the Gods*, 28. The synaesthetic quality of divine perception and the trickiness of teasing apart the different components of sensory experience may be illuminated by Aïda Kanafani-Zahar, *Aesthetics and Ritual in the United Arab Emirates: The Anthropology of Food and Personal Adornment among Arabian Women* (Beirut: American University of Beirut, 1983).

6 A qualified parallel might be drawn with the Roman Catholic belief in the Eucharist as substantially the body and blood of Christ, a real presence, not a mere representation. Webb Keane, *Christian Moderns: Freedom and Fetish in the Mission Encounter* (Berkeley: University of California Press, 2007), 61.

7 Daniel Miller, *A Theory of Shopping* (Ithaca: Cornell University Press, 1998), 75.

8 For instance, the ritual sacra of Shangó "lives" in a covered wooden container called a batea.

9 Gell, *Art and Agency*, 104.

10 Ibid., 111.

11 Ibid., 114.

12 "The focal elements of Cuban Santería," William Bascom long ago noted, "may not represent a carry-over of the focus of West African religion, but a shift in emphasis which has occurred as a result of culture contact." "The Focus of Cuban Santería," *Southwestern Journal of Anthropology* 6 (1950): 68.

13 The importance of otanes indicates that enslaved people sought to address the collective loss of a place on the African continent within a Cuban space, secretly repossessing bits and pieces of the foreign land on which they labored. Brandon, *Santería*, 155.

14 Ordination itself is called a "crowning"; initiates are envisioned as palace-dwelling "monarchs" and fierce "warriors." David H. Brown has spoken most eloquently of these figurations in *Santería Enthroned*.

15 Karen McCarthy Brown, *Mama Lola*, 253.

16 David H. Brown, "Thrones of the Orichas," 51.

17 *Oxford English Dictionary*.

18 Maya Deren, *Divine Horsemen: Living Gods of Haiti* (Kingston, NY: McPherson and Company, 1983 [1953]), 240.

19 John Egerton, *Southern Food: At Home, on the Road, in History* (Chapel Hill: University of North Carolina Press, 1993 [1987]), 16.

20 Matory, "Sexual Secrets," 167.

21 David H. Brown, *Santería Enthroned*, 264–67.

22 Ibid., 193.

23 Melville J. Herskovits, *Life in a Haitian Valley* (New York: Doubleday Anchor, 1971 [1937]), 269, quoted in Stevens, "Manje in Haitian Culture."

24 Richman, "They Will Remember Me," 241.

25 Matory, *Black Atlantic Religion*, 313n32.

26 Ortiz, *Hampa afro-cubana*, 197; my translation.

27 Ibid.

28 Ortiz does not cite the Brazilian scholar and journalist Gilberto Freyre, but the influence of Freyre's *Casa-grande e senzala* (New York: Knopf, 1964 [1933]) is palpable. *Casa-grande e senzala* blamed Brazil's ills on social rather than biological or environmental factors, refuting with a dizzying array of data every argument against the mingling of races. Freyre also casts dissimilar foods as voluntarily "fraternizing in a single and delicious confection upon the same African bed," indicating that the principle of incorporation through consumption permeates every level of Brazilian life (114).

29 Robin D. Moore, *Nationalizing Blackness: Afrocubanismo and Artistic Revolution in Havana, 1920–1940* (Pittsburgh: University of Pittsburgh Press, 1997), 34.

30 See Alejandro de la Fuente, "Myths of Racial Democracy: Cuba, 1900–1912," *Latin American Research Review* 34, no. 3 (1999): 39–73; and Aline Helg, *Our Rightful Share: The Afro-Cuban Struggle for Equality, 1886–1912* (Chapel Hill: University of North Carolina Press, 1995).

31 Robin Moore, "Representations of Afrocuban Expressive Culture in the Writings of Fernando Ortiz," *Latin American Music Review* 15, no. 1 (1994): 42.

32 Ibid., 41.

33 Vera M. Kutzinski, *Sugar's Secrets: Race and the Erotics of Cuban Nationalism* (Charlottesville: University Press of Virginia, 1993), 43.

34 Alejo Carpentier, *Ese músico que llevo dentro* (Havana: Editorial Letras Cubanas, 1987), 394.

35 Moore, "Representations," 35.

36 Ortiz, *Hampa afro-cubana*, 197.

37 See Palmié, *Cooking of History*.

38 Maria Elisa Christie, "Kitchenspace: Gendered Spaces for Cultural Reproduction, or, Nature in the Everyday Lives of Ordinary Women in Central Mexico" (PhD diss., University of Texas at Austin, 2003), 29, 451.

39 Personal communication, May 7, 2007. See Wacquant, *Body and Soul*, 123.

40 Joan Bliss, Mike Askew, and Sheila Macrae, "Effective Teaching and Learning: Scaffolding Revisited," *Oxford Review of Education* 22, no. 1 (1996): 37–61.

41 In Ilé Laroye, rogations were not usually performed by Ashabi, but by Fadesiye, Oyeyei, Oshunleye, and Billal.

42 Other items may be added as necessary to feed orí: doves or guineas, meat, fish, or fruit. My description relies on Clark, *Santería*; and José Luis Alcaraz, *Santería cubana: Rituales y magia* (Barcelona: Tikal, 2000), 52.

43 Practitioners usually portray Obatalá as male, but in different "roads," or manifestations, Obatalá becomes female. Whether this indeterminacy contributed to his association with healing, especially the "white" parts of the body—nerve tissue, brain matter, and bones, for instance—remains unclear.

44 See one variation in Ralph Alpizar and Damián París, *Santería cubana: Mito y realidad* (Madrid: MR Ediciones, 2004).

45 Elders also repeatedly mapped the recipient's body according to the four cardinal directions.

46 The definitions of "curing" I have in mind here are to prepare (meat, fish, etc.) for preservation by salting, drying, etc.; to promote hardening of (fresh concrete or mortar); to process (rubber, tobacco, etc.) as by fermentation or aging.

47 Michael Atwood Mason, "'I Bow My Head.'"

48 Adapted from fieldnotes written on March 1, 2005.

49 Fieldnotes, February 26, 2005.

50 Wacquant, *Body and Soul*, 69.

51 Personal communication, May 7, 2007.

52 Fieldnotes, May 7, 2005.

53 See Kelly E. Hayes, "Black Magic and the Academy: Macumba and Afro-Brazilian 'Orthodoxies,'" *History of Religions* 46, no. 4 (2007): 283–315.

54 Ibid. See also Holbraad, *Truth in Motion*, 107, for the expression of similar sentiments.

55 Personal communication, May 7, 2007.

56 Personal communication, October 14, 2005.

57 Personal communication, April 15, 2006.

58 Roberto Nodal and Miguel "Willie" Ramos define "an offering of foodstuffs given to the deities or ancestors" as *ebó'shuré*, and count addimú as an act of either thanksgiving or supplication. "Let the Power Flow: *Ebó* as a Healing Mechanism in Lukumí Orisha Worship," in *Fragments of Bone: New-African Religions in a New World*, ed. Patrick Bellegarde-Smith (Urbana: University of Illinois Press, 2005), 173.

59 Adrián de Souza Hernández, *El sacrificio en el culto de los orichas* (Havana: Ediciones Cubanas, 1998), 20–21.

60 Ramos, "The Empire Beats On," 223–24.

61 Ira Berlin, "From Creole to African: Atlantic Creoles and the Origins of African-American Society in Mainland North America," *William and Mary Quarterly* 53 (1994): 251–88.

62 See Pérez, "Crystallizing Subjectivities."

63 Fieldnotes, October 12, 2005.

64 See the discussion of recipes for the orishas' favorite dishes as passed down to religious family members from female elders in Kristine Juncker, *Afro-Cuban Religious Arts: Popular Expressions of Cultural Inheritance in Espiritismo and Santería* (Gainesville: University Press of Florida, 2014), 112–13, 129.

65 David H. Brown, "Thrones of the Orichas," 54. At the drum feasts I have attended, spirits have used foods displayed in plazas to "cleanse" initiates ritually, after which these items are destroyed.

66 Johannes Fabian, *Power and Performance: Ethnographic Explorations through Proverbial Wisdom and Theater in Shaba, Zaire* (Madison: University of Wisconsin Press, 1990), 24.

67 Personal communication, January 7, 2006.

68 In Lucumí, the terms "roads" and "paths" are privileged over the term "avatars." For different manifestations of orishas, the West African Yorùbá use the image of rippling pools in a river, or *ibú*, that are named extensions of the same body of water. See Karin Barber, "*Oríkì*, Women and the Proliferation and Merging of Òrìṣà," *Africa* 60, no. 3 (1990): 313–37.

69 She does so by a logic analogous to that of the South Asian concept of *prasad*. See Andrea Marion Pinkney, "The Sacred Share: Prasada in South Asia" (PhD diss., Columbia University, 2008).

70 See Katherine J. Hagedorn, "Long Day's Journey to Rincón: From Suffering to Resistance in the Procession of San Lázaro/Babalú Ayé," *Ethnomusicology Forum* 11, no. 1 (2002): 43–69.

71 Fieldnotes, November 13, 2004.

72 He is also known as Obaluaiye-Shoponnon, Sagbata, or Aholu in Togo, Benin, and elsewhere in West Africa.

73 His attributes combined to produce an embodied "cognitive category." Morton Marks, "Exploring El Monte: Ethnobotany and the Afro-Cuban Science of the Concrete," in *En torno a Lydia Cabrera*, ed. Isabel Castellanos and Josefina Inclán (Miami: Ediciones Universal, 1987), 229.

74 See the description in Erika Brady, ed., *Healing Logics: Culture and Medicine in Modern Health Systems* (Logan: Utah State University Press, 2001), 69. Woven from henequen, a plant sacred to him, burlap has often been used to transport grain and seeds thought to resemble blisters and other skin disease vectors. In Spanish, the pun is verbal as well as visual; bumps and pimples are referred to as *granos* or *granitos*.

75 Cundiamor is used medicinally throughout the tropics for its anti-inflammatory and antiviral properties. Gabriele Volpato and Daimy Godínez, "Medicinal Foods in Cuba: Promoting Health in the Household," in *Eating and Healing: Traditional Food as Medicine*, ed. Andrea Pieroni and Lisa Leimar Price (Binghamton, NY: Haworth, 2006), 229. See also J. K. Grover and S. P. Yadav, "Pharmacological Actions and Potential Uses of *Momordica charantia*: A Review," *Journal of Ethnopharmacology* 93, no. 1 (2004): 123–32.

76 Parts of this ritual are shown in the context of a visit to Charles Guelperin's house-temple by Kiran Deol, "Soul Food: Santería," *Vice Magazine*, June 1, 2015, https://munchies.vice.com/videos/soul-food-santeria.

77 Nodal and Ramos, "Let the Power Flow," 183. Any money offered during the event would be donated to a local charity. More than once it was Clara's House, a shelter for homeless and battered women and their children.

78 Personal communication, October 15, 2004.

79 Personal communication, December 18, 2005.

80 Katherine J. Hagedorn, "Sacred Secrets: Lessons with Francisco," in *Mementos, Artifacts, and Hallucinations from the Ethnographer's Tent*, ed. Ron Emoff and David Henderson (New York: Routledge, 2002), 40–41.

81 Ibid., 44.

82 See the classic essay by Mary Douglas, "The Abominations of Leviticus," in *Purity and Danger: An Analysis of the Concepts of Pollution and Taboo* (New York: Routledge, 1966), 41–57; and Douglas, "Deciphering a Meal," *Daedalus* 101 (1972): 61–81.

83 Personal communication, October 15, 2004.

84 See Palmié, *Cooking of History*, 238–39.

## CHAPTER 3. ENGENDERING KNOWLEDGE

1 Judith Gleason, *Santería, Bronx* (New York: Atheneum, 1975), 100.

2 Marilyn Strathern, *The Gender of the Gift: Problems with Women and Problems with Society in Melanesia* (Berkeley: University of California Press, 1988), 74. One major exception would be the literature on Jewish kashrut, dietary laws governing the preparation of food according to regulations outlined in the Torah that cover not only the conditions of slaughter but the separation of meat and dairy in cooking and the use of kosher utensils, containers, and surfaces. See Susan Starr Sered, "Food and Holiness: Cooking as a Sacred Act among Middle-Eastern Jewish Women," *Anthropological Quarterly* 61, no. 3 (1988): 129–39. See also Penny Van Esterik, "Feeding Their Faith: Recipe Knowledge among Thai Buddhist Women," *Food and Foodways* 1, no. 1 (1985): 198–215; and Shobha Rani Dash, "Food of Dharma: Rituals at Meals and in the Kitchen, A Case Study of Dongein Imperial Nunnery of Japan," in *Out of the Shadows: Socially Engaged Buddhist Women*, ed. Karma Lekshe Tsomo (Delhi: Sri Satguru, 2006), 123–26.

3 In the case of Lucumí, even recent scholarly volumes dwell at length on mythology and divinatory procedures yet omit the details of butchering, dressing, and roasting meat for the orishas.

4 For an understanding of these tropes from an African American perspective, see Vincent Woodard, Justin A. Joyce, and Dwight McBride, eds., *The Delectable Negro: Human Consumption and Homoeroticism within U.S. Slave Culture* (New York: New York University Press, 2014).

5 For example, see *Caribbean Slaves Working the Sugar Cane*, ca. 1590, by the Flemish engraver Theodor de Bry (1528–98).

6 Marion Halligan, *Eat My Words* (Sydney: Angus and Robertson, 1990), 118–19.

7 Personal communication, October 14, 2005.

8 Lydia Cabrera, "Ritual y símbolos de la iniciación en la sociedad secreta Abakua," *Journal de la Société des Américanistes* 58 (1969): 139–71.

9 The term *hounsi cuisinière* appears in Harold Courlander, *A Treasury of Afro-American Folklore: The Oral Literature, Traditions, Recollections, Legends, Tales, Songs, Religious Beliefs, Customs, Sayings, and Humor of Peoples of African Descent in the Americas* (New York: Smithmark, 1996 [1976]), 29; Milo Rigaud, *La tradition vaudou et le vaudou haïtien* (Paris, Niclaus, 1953), 116–17.

10 Kelly E. Hayes, "Serving the Spirits, Healing the Person: Women in Afro-Brazilian Religions," in *Women and New and Africana Religions*, ed. Lillian Ashcraft-Eason, Darnise Martin, and Oyeronke Olademo (Santa Barbara: ABC-Clio, 2010), 108. *Iya bassê* seems to appear for the first time in print in Carneiro, *Candomblés da Bahia,*

122. See also Bastide, *Les religions africaines*, 301. Different spellings are used contemporaneously with some frequency.

11 In Candomblé communities, this may mean immersion in herbal baths and rinsing one's hands with specially treated water upon entry to the religious compound (*terreiro*).

12 According to Ramos, this should be discouraged because the correct term is *iñalés/inyalés*. Among other substances called *aché* are the contents of the containers that embody the orisha and the herbal mixture placed on the heads of novices during initiation. To understand what type of aché is being cited in a given utterance, one only has recourse to context.

13 Nodal and Ramos, "Let the Power Flow," 173.

14 In my fieldnotes, I continued, "Then I told him I needed to write [that] down; he said that everyone says the same thing about blood." October 14, 2005.

15 An index card reading "Obatalá she-goat/ iyawo Yemayá," for instance, would designate the she-goat given to Obatalá on behalf of the iyawo initiated to Yemayá.

16 Since Shangó and his mother, Yemayá, "eat" together, their animals are combined.

17 In the case of pigeons and guinea hens, the heads are not plucked. Pigeons are almost never dipped, because they are relatively easy to pluck and their thin skin tends to tear when heated.

18 The alashés mandate the containment of bile due to its toxicity.

19 Many thanks to alashé Arlene Stevens for repeated demonstrations of her ashés-removal technique.

20 Ritual infelicities do occur. Badly butchered meat cannot be prepared as intended. There was more than one night during which an unemptied gizzard was placed among otherwise well-prepared ashés, and Arlene was apoplectic at the thought that someone sufficiently well-trained to remove a gizzard would be sloppy enough to neglect to clean it before it became too tough to open and rinse properly.

21 Occasionally the whole doves given to Ochún and her children, the Ibeji, are roasted in the oven.

22 When ashés are served, hominy and banana leaf dumplings, yam-flour balls, and pieces of parboiled corn on the cob accompany them, in the number appropriate to each orisha.

23 They are also covered to allow for steam to assist in the roasting.

24 "White" is the rough translation for the Yorùbá *fúnfún*. The ashés of the palace-dwelling monarch Obatalá may not be exposed to red palm oil. Other fúnfún orishas include Odudúwa and Dadá.

25 Goffman, *Interaction Ritual*, 224–28.

26 For many ilés, the ideal would be for all the orishas to have their own sets of pots and utensils in a religious community, but members seldom have either the resources or the space for this to be a reality.

27 Joelle Bahloul, "Food Practices among Sephardic Immigrants in Contemporary France: Dietary Laws in Urban Society," *Journal of the American Academy of Religion* 63, no. 3 (1995): 492.

28 David H. Brown, "Thrones of the Orichas," 44–59, 85–87.

29 Claude Lévi-Strauss, "The Culinary Triangle," *Partisan Review* 33 (1966): 586–95. See also Paul Shankman, "Le Rôti et le Bouilli: Lévi-Strauss' Theory of Cannibalism," *American Anthropologist* 71, no. 1 (1969): 54–69.

30 Dimitri Tsintjilonis, "Monsters and Caricatures: Spirit Possession in Tana Toraja," *Journal of the Royal Anthropological Institute* 12, no. 3 (2006): 560.

31 Brian K. Smith and Wendy Doniger, "Sacrifice and Substitution: Ritual Mystification and Mythical Demystification," *Numen* 36, no. 2 (1989): 189–224.

32 Sacrifice and possession may also be seen as analogous to the orishas' use of illness as a means of calling their devotees to become initiated; in all three cases, the ownership of bodies is put into the hands of the orishas.

33 Godfrey Lienhardt, *Divinity and Experience: The Religion of the Dinka* (Oxford: Oxford University Press, 1961), 23. Indigenous Yorùbá sacrificial practice may have more in common with the Dinka, since, for instance, "the wife receives the backbone of sacrificial animals." Margaret Thompson Drewal writes, "As [my informant] commented when it was suggested that the backbone has no meat: 'it's not the meat; it's the meaning!'" *Yoruba Ritual: Performers, Play, Agency* (Bloomington: Indiana University Press, 1992), 220n10.

34 Marcel Detienne, "The Violence of Wellborn Ladies: Women in the Thesmophoria," in Detienne and Vernant, *Cuisine of Sacrifice*, 10–11.

35 Fieldnotes, November 6, 2005.

36 Personal communication, November 6, 2005. Although various accounts of possession note that mounts do not experience the ill effects of their activities while possessed—those whose orishas drink massive quantities of alcohol do not emerge drunk from trance, for instance—it is possible for a mount to sustain injuries. It would seem that as long as spirits are acting out aspects of their mythology, as in the case of Shangó eating fire, then the mount remains unharmed, but any deviation from the norm invites mishap. Eating dirty ashés would be one deviation from the norm.

37 In the context of the kitchen, dirt would include the matter that renders "dirty whites" dirty: sweat, excrement, oil, blood, and so forth.

38 See Terry Eagleton, *The Ideology of the Aesthetic* (Oxford: Blackwell, 1990), esp. "The Kantian Imaginary," 70–101.

39 Gell, *Art and Agency*, 6.

40 Deren, *Divine Horsemen*, 246.

41 Compare with Vilson Caetano de Sousa Júnior as quoted in Nadalini, "Comida de santo," 48.

42 Personal communication, April 28, 2007. As the Los Angeles–based priest of Obatalá and *espiritista* Charles Guelperin put it, "Animal sacrifice is only 10% of my religion. 90% is offerings of foods." Kiran Deol, "Soul Food: Santeria," *Vice Magazine*, June 1, 2015, https://munchies.vice.com/videos/soul-food-santeria.

43 Quoted in Lody, *Santo também come*, 17. The translation is mine.

44 Such judgments are based on knowledge of the ritual lineage derived largely from oral tradition.

**45** For instance, one of the elders spent a great deal of time as a child on her grandmother's farm, plucking chickens and being exposed to everyday agricultural routines; she credits this experience with giving her a lack of squeamishness.

**46** Menéndez, "Libreta de Santería." Libretas and other written materials continue to serve as initiates' personalized reference guides and records of religious training. They have also played a part in practitioners' "processes of entextualization to create a seemingly shareable, transmittable culture." Michael Silverstein and Greg Urban, "The Natural History of Discourse," in *Natural Histories of Discourse*, ed. Michael Silverstein and Greg Urban (Chicago: University of Chicago Press, 1996), 2.

**47** Fieldnotes, May 7, 2005.

**48** Compare with A. V. Yannicopoulos, "The Pedagogue in Antiquity," *British Journal of Educational Studies* 33, no. 2 (1985): 173–79; and Norman H. Young, "The Figure of the Paidagogos in Art and Literature," *Biblical Archaeologist* 53, no. 2 (1990): 80–86.

**49** Hollywood, "Performativity, Citationality, Ritualization," 263.

**50** Smith, "Bare Facts of Ritual."

**51** Michael A. Mason, *Living Santería*. I have not found a compelling Lucumí interpretation for the distinction between these two forms of prostration—the male form called *moforibale* or *dobale* (*ìdòbálè* in Yorùbá) and the female form, most often referred to as *ki* (the Yorùbá *ìyíkàá*). Little more was said in Ilé Laroye than that it has to do with the sex of one's orisha.

**52** See Howes, *Sensual Relations*; and Michael Jackson, "Thinking through the Body: An Essay on Understanding Metaphor," *Social Analysis* 14 (1983): 127–48.

**53** Willerslev, *Soul Hunters*, 106.

**54** Personal communication, May 7, 2007.

**55** Ibid. Friedrich Nietzsche, *On the Genealogy of Morals and Ecce Homo* (New York: Vintage, 1969), 61.

**56** As mentioned earlier, the nails were snapped off, but practitioners went to the trouble of pruning the vestigial points from the nail beds.

**57** See the discussion in David H. Brown, *Santería Enthroned*, 264–67.

**58** Charles Malamoud, *Cooking the World: Ritual and Thought in Ancient India*, trans. David White (Delhi: Oxford University Press, 1998), 179.

**59** Rooster is eaten by Elegguá, Ogún, and Shangó, patron of the initiation ritual.

**60** Personal communication, April 28, 2007.

**61** Personal communication, January 7, 2006.

**62** Roland Barthes, *Mythologies*, trans. Annette Lavers (New York: Hill and Wang, 1972 [1957]), 41–42.

**63** The social-psychological research on "costly sacrifice" would seem to bear this out. I am indebted to Philip Deslippe for this insight.

**64** Personal communication, October 15, 2004. Attitudes toward cooking are changing, as evinced by the meteoric rise of celebrity chefs and the success of cookbooks, recipe blogs, and websites dedicated to food consumption and preparation over the last decade. Perhaps most indicative of North Americans' perceptions of cooking is the popularity of the cable channel called the Food Network. However, the success of its programs and related media developments do not represent an elevation of the act of cooking per se, but rather a refinement in ideals of connoisseurship. Viewers of such shows do not cook more than non-viewers, and the practice of home cooking continues to be in decline nationwide. Michael Pollan, "Out of the Kitchen, onto the Couch," *New York Times Magazine*, August 2, 2009, http://www.nytimes.com/2009/08/02/magazine/02cooking-t.html.

65 Personal communication, March 12, 2005.

66 Personal communication, January 7, 2006.

67 Thompson, *Face of the Gods.*

68 Personal communication, May 7, 2005.

69 Personal communication, November 13, 2005; March 12, 2006.

70 Emma Tarlo, *Clothing Matters: Dress and Identity in India* (Chicago: University of Chicago Press, 1996), 165.

71 J. Lowell Lewis, *The Anthropology of Cultural Performance* (New York: Palgrave Macmillan, 2013), 29.

72 My thanks to one of my anonymous reviewers for suggesting this phrase.

73 As the epigraph above suggests, I was not confident in my ability to understand elders' jokes during the period of my fieldwork.

74 Constance Classen, David Howes, and Anthony Synott, *Aroma: The Cultural History of Smell* (London: Routledge, 1994), 97.

75 See, for instance, Martha C. Nussbaum, *Hiding from Humanity: Disgust, Shame, and the Law* (Princeton: Princeton University Press, 2004). My vocabulary in this discussion has been guided in part by David Sander and Klaus R. Scherer, eds., *The Oxford Companion to Emotion and the Affective Sciences* (Oxford: Oxford University Press, 2009).

76 Fieldnotes, March 28, 2004.

77 Susan Buck-Morss, "Aesthetics and Anaesthetics: Walter Benjamin's Artwork Essay Reconsidered," *October* 62 (1992): 6.

78 Personal communication, August 4, 2005.

79 See Bruce Lincoln, *Discourse and the Construction of Society* (New York: Oxford University Press, 1989).

80 Per Hage, "Symbolic Culinary Mediation: A Group Model," *Man*, n.s., 14, no. 1 (1979): 81–92.

81 His italics; quoted in ibid., 82.

82 Lévi-Strauss, *Origin of Table Manners*, 495.

83 See Woodard and McBride, "Sex, Honor, and Human Consumption," in *The Delectable Negro*, 59–94. Seasoning has also been used as a metaphor for socialization through the transculturation process by Lidia Marte, "Afro-Diasporic Seasonings: Food Routes and Dominican Place-Making in New York City," *Food, Culture and Society* 14, no. 2 (2011): 181–204.

84 Bontemps, *The Punished Self*, 103–19.

85 For example, Ester Rebeca Shapiro Rok writes, "I recently described cooking as my most profound spiritual practice, as it is in the kitchen that I enter a creative,

reverential space lovingly dedicated to the soul's sustenance." "Santería as a Healing Practice in Diaspora Communities: My Cuban Jewish Journey with Oshún," in *Healing Cultures: Art and Religion as Curative Practices in the Caribbean and Its Diaspora*, ed. Margarite Fernández Olmos and Lizabeth Paravisini-Gebert (New York: Palgrave, 2001), 86.

**86** For insight into the significance of tying in Vodou that might shed light on the example at hand, see Terry Rey and Karen Richman, "The Somatics of Syncretism: Tying Body and Soul in Haitian Religion," *Studies in Religion/Sciences Religieuses* 39, no. 3 (2010): 379–403.

**87** See David H. Brown, *Santería Enthroned*, 196.

**88** Monica Schuler, "Enslavement, the Slave Voyage, and Astral and Aquatic Journeys in African Diaspora Discourse," in *Africa and the Americas: Interconnections during the Slave Trade*, ed. José C. Curto and Renée Soulodre-La France (Trenton, NJ: Africa World Press, 2005), 191–92.

**89** Taussig, *Mimesis and Alterity*. See also Harding, "*É a Senzala.*"

**90** Quoted in Mattijs van de Port, "Visualizing the Sacred: Video Technology, 'Televisual' Style, and the Religious Imagination in Bahian Candomblé," *American Ethnologist* 33, no. 3 (2006): 450.

**91** Butler, *Bodies That Matter*.

**92** David H. Brown, *Santería Enthroned*, 112; his italics.

## CHAPTER 4. GENDERING THE KITCHEN

**1** My interlocutors were cisgender rather than transgender, meaning that they accepted, or presented in a manner normative to, their gender as assigned at birth. References to men and women in the remainder of this chapter are to "cis" people unless otherwise indicated.

**2** See Cromley, "Transforming the Food Axis"; Abigail Ayres Van Slyck, "Kitchen Technologies and Mealtime Rituals: Interpreting the Food Axis at American Summer Camps, 1890–1950," *Technology and Culture* 43, no. 4 (2002): 668–92; and Molly W. Berger, "The Magic of Fine Dining: Invisible Technology and the Hotel Kitchen," *ICON* 1 (1995): 106–19.

**3** Barbara Smith, "A Press of Our Own Kitchen Table: Women of Color Press," *Frontiers: A Journal of Women Studies* 10, no. 3 (1989): 11–13. The press was established by Smith and a collective of other Black feminists upon the suggestion of the author Audre Lorde, after a meeting of African American and Afro-Caribbean women in 1980.

**4** Here she was referring to me specifically as a woman of Cuban descent.

**5** Personal communication, August 13, 2007. This elder was not a member of Ilé Laroye, but often made herself available to assist in its initiations and other rituals. Men sometimes did participate in plucking and removing the ashés, especially Ashabi's son and her eldest godchild in order of seniority, both initiated to the orisha Yemayá. Uninitiated men were more often to be found dressing the four-legged animals, waiting to be pressed into service, or running errands.

**6** In this old German slogan, widely popularized during the Nazi regime, "Children, kitchen, [and] church" designate with whom, and where, women belong. As a point of comparison with the Lucumí division of labor I have sketched out, see Nilza Menezes, "A divisão do trabalho nos templos das religiões afro-brasileiras em Porto Velho, Rondônia," *Mandrágora* 17, no. 17 (2011): 135–45.

**7** Although women may be initiated as *apetebí*, meaning that they are charged with maintaining the ritual sacra of the diviner-spirit Orúnmilá and assisting babaláwos in their consultations, their exclusion from the sacrifice of "legs" as opposed to "feathers" is absolute. For a review of the rationales for prohibiting women from becoming Ifá diviners and recent controversies, see Carolyn E. Watson, "Witches, Female Priests, and Sacred Manoeuvres: (De)Stabilising Gender and Sexuality in a Cuban Religion of African Origin," *Gender and History* 25, no. 3 (2013): 425–44.

**8** Rather than consult the god Orúnmilá in divination, Ashabi "see[s] what Elegguá has to say" by interpreting the patterns made by sixteen cowries that she casts on a woven mat.

**9** For more on Albear, see Miguel "Willie" Ramos, "La división de la Habana: Territorial Conflict and Cultural Hegemony in the Followers of Oyo Lukumí Religion, 1850s–1920s," *Cuban Studies* 34 (2003): 38–70.

**10** Clark, *Where Men Are Wives*, 115.

**11** See, for instance, Scott Coltrane, "Research on Household Labor: Modeling and Measuring the Social Embeddedness of Routine Family Work," *Journal of Marriage and Family* 62, no. 4 (2000): 1208–33; D. John and B. A. Shelton, "The Production of Gender among Black and White Women and Men: The Case of Household Labor," *Sex Roles: A Journal of Research* 36 (1997): 171–93; Marianne Ekstrom, "Class and Gender in the Kitchen," in *Palatable Words: Sociocultural Food Studies*, ed. Elizabeth L. Furst (Oslo: Solum Forlag, 1991), 145–58; and Radhika Chopra, "Masculinity, Sexuality, and Male Domestic Labor," *Men and Masculinities* 9, no. 2 (2006): 152–67.

**12** Elizabeth Sayre, "Cuban Batá Drumming and Women Musicians: An Open Question," *Center for Black Music Research Digest* 13, no. 1 (2000): 12–15; and Andrea Pryor, "The House of Añá: Women and Batá," *Center for Black Music Research Digest* 12, no. 2 (1999): 6–8.

**13** J. D. Y. Peel, "The Pastor and the Babalawo: The Interaction of Religions in Nineteenth-Century Yorubaland," *Africa* 60 (1990): 343.

**14** See Silvina Testa, "La hiérarchie à l'œuvre: Organisation cultuelle et genre dans les religions afro-cubaines," *Systèmes de Pensée en Afrique Noire* 16 (2004): 175–204.

**15** Clark, *Where Men Are Wives*, 84.

**16** This discussion owes a great deal to the insights of Matory, *Sex and the Empire That Is No More*.

**17** To describe the act of spirit possession, the Yorùbá say that the òrìṣà "mounts" the devotee, called his horse, or *elégùn*; *elégùn* means "the climbed one."

**18** Perhaps the most famous allusion to this analogy is the title of Zora Neale Hurston's account of her fieldwork in Haiti and Jamaica, *Tell My Horse: Voodoo and Life in Haiti and Jamaica* (New York: Harper and Row, 1990 [1938]).

19 See Ramos, "La división de la Habana," 39.

20 Personal communication, October 29, 2005.

21 Ramos, *Adimú*, 1st ed. It has since been revised and expanded in a second edition.

22 The italics are Ramos's. The text is bilingual, and Ramos is more emphatic in Spanish, using exclamation points rather than italics to hammer home his message: "¡los hombres no cocinan!" Ramos, i.

23 See Mirandé, *Hombres y Machos*; and Anton Blok, "Rams and Billy-Goats: A Key to the Mediterranean Code of Honour," *Man* 16, no. 3 (1981): 427–40. For Yorùbá constructions of gender vis-à-vis household labor, see John Mason, *Ìdáná Fún Òrìsà*, 32.

24 Ramos, *Adimú*, 8. Ramos also notes, "A woman must prepare and cook Oba's and Yewá's food," 5. In the case of the latter, however, further qualifications obtain: "To cook for Yewá, the ideal person is a young, virgin woman, or an elderly woman, past menopause. . . . Men may never cook for Yewá," 8.

25 This is simply one of the interpretations that could be drawn from this passage. For example, Randy P. Connor and David Hatfield Sparks write, "Some practitioners of Lucumí or other Yorùbá-based spiritual traditions maintain that Shangó is hostile toward transgender, gay, and bisexual males." *Queering Creole Spiritual Traditions*, 70. Salvador Vidal-Ortiz transcribes a story told by one of his informants concerning Shangó's possession of a female practitioner, and his immediate removal of a tampon his mount was wearing. Vidal-Ortiz writes, "The Changó in this story—mounted in a female body—rejects anything inside his body, anything penetrative." "'Sexuality' and 'Gender' in Santería," 135.

26 Vidal-Ortiz, "'Sexuality' and 'Gender' in Santería," 125.

27 Michael A. Mason, *Living Santería*, 118.

28 Vidal-Ortiz, "'Sexuality' and 'Gender' in Santería," 135.

29 See Omise'eke Natasha Tinsley, "Black Atlantic, Queer Atlantic: Queer Imaginings of the Middle Passage," *GLQ: A Journal of Lesbian and Gay Studies* 14, nos. 2–3 (2008): 191–216.

30 Beliso-De Jesús, "Yemayá's Duck," 45.

31 Along with bàtá drummers, babaláwos have enforced a taboo among their fellow Ifá diviners against being anally penetrated, an act that remains synecdochic for all homosexual activity; they also eschew the spirit possession analogized to it. Any indication of susceptibility to possession compromises initiation into these brotherhoods.

32 The translation from Vidal-Ortiz's transcription is mine. Vidal-Ortiz, "'Maricón,' 'Pájaro,' and 'Loca,'" 912.

33 Shloma Rosenberg, "As Long as They Don't Shove It Down Our Throats—The Relegation of First Class Oloshas to Second Class Status," http://mysticcurio.tripod.com/shove.htm (accessed February 1, 2008). The italics are his. The late Afolabí had ritual ties with several elders from Ilé Laroye.

34 See Lumsden, *Machos, Maricones, and Gays*.

35 In Haitian Vodou, Connor writes, drawing on his correspondence with the filmmaker and anthropologist Anne Lescot, "Although 'roles are not distributed accord-

ing to someone's being "queer" or not," transgender and transsexual male-to-female individuals 'will most likely be assigned a role of cooking alongside the women during Vodou ceremonies.'" *Queering Creole Spiritual Traditions*, 303. See also Bonvini, "Mets afro-brésiliens." Gender in relation to possession has been investigated more thoroughly with reference to Candomblé than to Lucumí; for instance, Brumana, "El sexo de los ángeles"; and Matory, "Homens Montados."

36 Matory, *Sex and the Empire*, 212.

37 Serena Nanda, *Gender Diversity: Crosscultural Variations* (Prospect Heights: Waveland Press, 2000), 45.

38 *Travestis* (male-to-female transgender/transsexual individuals) have been cited among those recognized as *adés/adéfontós*, yet the anthropologist Don Kulick has written that the number of trans people in Candomblé has been greatly exaggerated, due to the presence of queer men who present as effeminate and cross-dress publicly. See Cornwall, "Gender Identities and Gender Ambiguity among Travestis in Salvador, Brazil," in *Dislocating Masculinity: Comparative Ethnographies*, ed. Andrea Cornwall and Nancy Lindisfarne (London: Routledge, 1994), 111–32; Kulick, *Travesti: Sex, Gender, and Culture among Brazilian Transgendered Prostitutes* (Chicago: University of Chicago Press, 1998); and Maria Lina Leão Teixeira, "Lorogun."

39 Classic texts are Landes, *City of Women*; Birman, *Fazendo estilo criando gênero*; and Fry, *Para inglês ver*. See the more recent Rios, "Loce Loce Metá Rê-Lê!"; and Port, "Candomblé in Pink, Green, and Black." It is important to clarify, however, that Brazilian Umbanda and Cuban Palo Monte are two masculine-normative traditions that are often hostile to gay membership.

40 Only a handful of scholars explicitly mention their role in the ritual kitchen: Cornwall, "Gender Identities and Gender Ambiguity," 127; Fry, "Male Homosexuality and Spirit Possession," 146–47; and Jim Wafer, *The Taste of Blood: Spirit Possession in Brazilian Candomblé* (Philadelphia: University of Pennsylvania Press, 1991). Some sources do not mention the affective and sexual orientation of the men cooking, or their gender identities, but it is likely that the men indicated are gay; see Bastide, *O Candomblé da Bahia*, 334; and Nadalini, "Comida de santo." One of Nadalini's male informants told her, "Tem algumas casas que homem não mete a mão em panela"— "there are some houses in which men do not put a hand on a pot [that is, assist in the kitchen]"—but went on to explain the role performed by one male ritual sponsor and functionary (ogã) within his house, 111. Typical in the analytical focus on the adé's role as a possession mount are Birman, "Transas e transes"; and dos Santos, "Sexo, gênero e homossexualidade"; Birman alludes to the domestic sphere and cooking in *Fazendo estilo criando gênero*, 89–90, 136, 144–45, et passim.

Setting aside the cookbooks too numerous to list here, academic works that take cooking firmly into account include Bastide, *A cozinha dos deuses*; Lody, *Santo também come*; Caetano de Sousa Júnior, *O banquete sagrado*; Aguiar, "Os orixás"; Elbein dos Santos, *Os Nagô e a morte*; Cossard, *Awô*; Nadalini, "Comida de santo"; Fábio Lima, *As quartas-feiras de Xangô: Ritual e cotidiano* (João Pessoa: Grafset, 2010); Sérgio Figueiredo Ferretti, "Comida ritual em festas de Tambor de Mina no

Maranhão," *Dossiê: Religião e Cultura*, DOI—10.5752/P.2175-5841.2011v9n21p242; and Lima, *A anatomia do acarajé*.

41 The presence of gay and genderqueer men in the kitchen may have been particularly important in Black Atlantic religious communities that have observed taboos against cooking by menstruating and/or premenopausal women. See Bastide, *A cozinha dos deuses*, 14–16.

42 James N. Green, *Beyond Carnival: Male Homosexuality in Twentieth-Century Brazil* (Chicago: University of Chicago Press, 1999), 86–87; Oscar Lewis, Ruth M. Lewis, and Susan M. Rigdon, "The 'Rehabilitation' of Prostitutes," in *The Cuba Reader: History, Culture, Politics*, ed. Aviva Chomsky, Barry Carr, and Pamela Maria Smorkaloff (Durham: Duke University Press, 2004), 396. The story of Aurora Lamar—Lucumí lineage founder, madam of a Havana brothel, and godmother of several prostitutes—suggests unexplored avenues for research into this issue. David H. Brown, *Santería Enthroned*, 102–3.

43 José Quiroga, *Tropics of Desire: Interventions from Queer Latino America* (New York: New York University Press, 2000), 88.

44 Andrea Stevenson Allen, "'Brides' without Husbands: Lesbians in the Afro-Brazilian Religion Candomblé," *Transforming Anthropology* 20, no. 1 (2012): 17–31.

45 See Amanda Villepastour, "Amelia Pedroso: The Voice of a Cuban Priestess Leading from the Inside," in *Women Singers in Global Contexts: Music, Biography, Identity*, ed. Ruth Hellier (Urbana-Champaign: University of Illinois Press, 2013).

46 Jafari Allen, "One Way or Another: Erotic Subjectivity in Cuba," *American Ethnologist* 39, no. 2 (2012): 333.

47 See Shloma Rosenberg, "The Africa Question: Did They or Didn't They?" http://mysticcurio.tripod.com/afrigay.htm (accessed March 1, 2008).

48 See Pérez, "Nobody's Mammy."

49 It is not always the case that initiations go smoothly. I was present for an Elegguá initiation in July 2005 that appeared to be ruled by his trickster ways, since priests kept losing keys and purses. During a Yemayá initiation in October 2005, it was often remarked that the pace of the ritual was going as slowly as this orisha's favorite food, molasses.

50 Personal communication, October 22, 2006.

51 Rosemary Hennessy, *Profit and Pleasure: Sexual Identities in Late Capitalism* (New York: Routledge, 2000), 194.

52 Butler, *Bodies That Matter*, 10. See Birman, *Fazendo estilo criando gênero* , 89–90.

53 Butler, *Bodies That Matter*, 95.

54 Hollywood, "Performativity, Citationality, Ritualization," 265.

55 Butler, *Bodies That Matter*, 10.

56 Asad, *Genealogies of Religion*, 131.

57 See Matory, "Gendered Agendas."

58 "Oshun," http://mysticcurio.tripod.com/cyclone/oshun.htm (accessed February 20, 2006).

59 David H. Brown, *Santería Enthroned*, 73. Brown also writes that Gaitian was initiated into the Regla-based male sodality called Abakuá. He is part of the lineage Ashabi claims from her Cuban godfather.

60 Ramos, "La división de la Habana," 42. Albear and Obá Tero carried on a legendary feud that escalated into a territorial dispute and resulted in the latter's removal from Havana to Matanzas. David H. Brown writes, "Practitioners agree that religious authority in Matanzas was always centered primarily in the houses of *iyalochas*, the female priests of the *orichas* . . . . [S]ome add that Matanzas was, and continues to be, 'anti-*babalawo*.'" *Santería Enthroned*, 76.

61 David H. Brown, *Santería Enthroned*, 293.

62 Many babaláwos consider their manner of creating Olokún—with, for instance, ritually prepared wooden implements rather than seashells, coral, and metallic objects—to be the only true one, charging that any Olokún not made by a babaláwo is "really just a 'road of Yemayá.'" Ibid., 346n136.

63 Attributing great power to nameless women is not only a feminist strategy attested in Europe since Christine de Pizan's (c. 1365–c. 1430) *Book of the City of Ladies*, but one that has been necessary more recently for Black women to create histories featuring female ancestors as agentive social actors.

64 Jacqueline Bryant, *The Foremother Figure in Early Black Women's Literature: Clothed in My Right Mind* (New York: Garland, 1999), 28.

65 Fieldnotes, October 16, 2004.

66 Personal communication, October 14, 2005.

67 Personal communication, October 9, 2006.

68 Richard Pryor, "Little Feets," *Was It Something I Said?*, BMI CD 7599 27245 2.

69 As Mudbone exclaims, "She was good, too, man!"

70 Personal communication, June 26, 2004. Although recipes for omiero appear in many do-it-yourself guides to Santería practice, initiates insist that either important ingredients or details of the ritual performed to mix omiero are left out. They have also said that learning to create omiero is "Priesthood 101," but prior to ordination, no one should be privy to its secrets.

71 For literary parallels, see Tompkins, *Racial Indigestion*.

72 Personal communication, October 16, 2004.

73 Personal communication, October 29, 2005.

74 John Mason, *Ìdáná Fún Òrìsà*, 56.

75 My reference to the idiomatic expression "the opposite sex" is meant to convey the gist of my interlocutor's response, not to endorse a dualistic approach to gendered categories. See Thomas Laqueur, *Making Sex: Body and Gender from the Greeks to Freud* (Cambridge: Harvard University Press, 1990).

76 This elder warned against analyzing the orishas' food preferences according to their own sex, pointing out that the god Obatalá also eats castrated goat. It may be interesting to note that Obatalá has both male and female "paths" (manifestations).

77 Ochún's beheading of enemies appears in a verse (Ògúndá Ìwòrì) cited by 'Wande Abimbola, "The Bag of Wisdom: Osun and the Origins of the Ifá Divination," in *Osun across the Waters: A Yoruba Goddess in Africa and the Americas*, ed. Joseph Murphy and Mei-Mei Sanford (Bloomington: Indiana University Press, 2001), 151.

78 Isabel Castellanos, "A River of Many Turns: The Polysemy of Ochún in Afro-Cuban Tradition," in Murphy and Sanford, *Osun across the Waters*, 39.

79 Lydia Cabrera, *Yemayá y Ochún (Kariocha, iyalorichas y olorichas)* (Miami: Ediciones Universales, 1980).

80 Claudia Schippert, "Turning on/to Ethics," in *Bodily Citations: Religion and Judith Butler*, ed. Ellen T. Armour and Susan M. St. Ville (New York: Columbia University Press, 2006), 164.

81 See Joan Martin, *More Than Chains and Toil: A Christian Work Ethic of Enslaved Women* (Louisville, KY: Westminster John Knox Press, 2000), 4.

82 Cannon, *Black Womanist Ethics*, 2.

83 Personal communication, May 21, 2006.

84 For other women, the loss of hair in initiation has also severely complicated relationships with colleagues and acquaintances. Personal communication, August 13, 2007.

85 Fieldnotes, June 3, 2005.

86 Ramos, "Afro-Cuban Orisha Worship," 67.

87 Clark, *Santería*, 70.

88 As Tracey E. Hucks has written,

> Many African American women have entered the tradition for four major reasons: (1) They turn to African-derived traditions in search of a direct link to their African ancestry and heritage. (2) Many seek a compatible spiritual counterpart to their nationalist and/or Afrocentric philosophies. (3) Many African American women desire a religious alternative to Christianity or Islam. (4) African-derived traditions such as Yoruba offer a means of exploring new possibilities of black womanhood as such exploration relates to the reverence of female deities.

> Hucks, "'Burning with a Flame,'" 95. While I found that all of the women in Ilé Laroye expressed some combination of these sentiments at one time or another, I would stress them as reasons for moving toward participation in Lucumí, not for initiation.

89 Her recollections of school bore a striking resemblance to those documented in Wendy Luttrell, "'The Teachers, They All Had Their Pets': Concepts of Gender, Knowledge, and Power," *Signs* 18, no. 3 (1993): 505–46.

90 The draping technique Arlene describes echoes twentieth-century Yorùbá fashion trends, especially the men's "Hausa style." Misty L. Bastian, "Female 'Alhajis' and Entrepreneurial Fashions: Flexible Identities in Southeastern Nigerian Clothing Practice," in *Clothing and Difference: Embodied Identities in Colonial and Post-Colonial Africa*, ed. Hildi Hendrickson (Durham: Duke University Press, 1996), 97–132.

91 These words recall those of Malcolm X's 1963 "Message to the Grass Roots":

What you and I need to do is learn to forget our differences. . . . You don't catch hell because you're a Methodist or Baptist, you don't catch hell because you're a Democrat or a Republican, you don't catch hell because you're a Mason or an Elk, and you sure don't catch hell because you're an American; because if you were an American, you wouldn't catch hell. You catch hell because you're a black man. You catch hell, all of us catch hell, for the same reason.

Malcolm X, *Malcolm X Speaks: Selected Speeches and Statements*, ed. George Breitman (New York: Grove, 1965), 4.

**92** See Frantz Fanon, *Black Skin, White Masks*, trans. Richard Philcox (New York: Grove/Atlantic, 2008 [1952]).

**93** Huon Wardle, "A Groundwork for West Indian Cultural Openness," *Journal of the Royal Anthropological Institute* 13, no. 3 (2007): 577.

**94** In many African American circles at the time, relaxing was viewed as a requirement of good hygiene, and in some Black churches, the Afro was condemned from the pulpit as a sign of lax morality and political militancy. See Ayana D. Byrd and Lori L. Tharps, *Hair Story: Untangling the Roots of Black Hair in America* (New York: St. Martin's, 2001), 62–63. For hair straightening as a rite of passage, see bell hooks, "Straightening Our Hair," *Z Magazine*, September 1988, 33–37.

**95** David Brown has spoken most eloquently of these figurations in *Santería Enthroned*.

**96** Gilroy, *Black Atlantic*, 85.

**97** As J. Lorand Matory points out, Black North Americans and the descendants of Africans elsewhere in the Americas conceptualize slavery differently, with the former emphasizing emancipation as a major historical rupture with the slaveholding past, while the latter recognize slavery as existing on a historical continuum of unfreedom. "Free to Be a Slave," 403.

**98** Collins, *From Black Power to Hip Hop*, 111.

**99** Hippocrates, *Epidemics*, bk. 1, sect. 11.

**100** November 4, 2005.

**101** Personal communication, October 9, 2005.

**102** One might add, for starters, Simone de Beauvoir, *The Second Sex* (New York: Knopf, 1952); Germaine Greer, *The Female Eunuch* (London: MacGibbon and Key, 1970); and Kate Millett, *Sexual Politics* (New York: Doubleday, 1970).

**103** See Michele Wallace, *Black Macho and the Myth of the Superwoman* (London: Verso, 1978); Moraga and Anzaldúa, *This Bridge Called My Back*; Gloria Hull, Patricia Bell Scott, and Barbara Smith, *All the Women Are White, All the Blacks Are Men, but Some of Us Are Brave: Black Women's Studies* (Old Westbury, NY: Feminist Press, 1982); Audre Lorde, *Sister Outsider: Essays and Speeches* (Freedom, CA: Crossing Press, 1984); hooks, *Talking Back*.

**104** Brittney Cooper, "Feminism's Ugly Internal Clash: Why Its Future Is Not Up to White Women," *Salon*, September 24, 2014, http://www.salon.com/2014/09/24/feminisms_ugly_internal_clash_why_its_future_is_not_up_to_white_women/.

105 Personal communication, November 14, 2005.

106 Personal communication, July 9, 2005.

107 Personal communication, April 14, 2005.

108 See Carole Pateman, "Equality, Difference, Subordination: The Politics of Motherhood and Women's Citizenship," in *Beyond Equality and Difference: Citizenship, Feminist Politics and Female Subjectivity*, ed. Gisela Bock and Susan James (London: Routledge, 1992), 17–31.

109 Crenshaw, "Mapping the Margins," 1252. See Rose M. Brewer, "Theorizing Race, Class, and Gender: The New Scholarship of Black Feminist Intellectuals and Black Women's Labor," in *Theorizing Black Feminisms: The Visionary Pragmatism of Black Women*, ed. Abena P. A. Busia and Stanlie M. James (New York: Routledge, 1993), 13–30.

110 Moya Bailey, "They Aren't Talking About Me . . . ," http://www.crunkfeminist-collective.com/2010/03/14/they-arent-talking-about-me/ (accessed October 15, 2013). See also Jennifer C. Nash, "Rethinking Intersectionality," *Feminist Review* 89, no. 1 (2008): 1–15.

111 Ashabi has described doing so as "a man's thing." Connor writes, "In my own experience, I have met [only] one lesbian daughter of Eleggua—a middle-aged woman of African-Latino heritage of powerful countenance and wisdom—who has been his priestess in Lucumí/Santería for over twenty-five years and who is able to fashion figures of the deity for practitioners, a task traditionally undertaken by men." *Queering Creole Spiritual Traditions*, 65.

112 Williams, *Sisters in the Wilderness*.

113 JoAnne Marie Terrell, *Power in the Blood? The Cross in the African American Experience* (Maryknoll, NY: Orbis, 1998), 116. See also Monica Coleman, *Making a Way Out of No Way: A Womanist Theology* (Minneapolis: Fortress Press, 2008).

## CHAPTER 5. TASTING AFFLICTION

1 Curry, *Making the Gods in New York*, 91.

2 Jean-François Bayart, *The Illusion of Cultural Identity*, trans. Steven Rendall et al. (Chicago: University of Chicago Press, 1996).

3 "We [are] Black." Personal communication, April 13, 2005. My fieldnotes continue: "Then Berta took my hand, and said, 'You Black [too].' . . . I said, 'I'm learning [about this]!' (this got a big laugh). Keisha said, 'Improvisation is key.' Making do."

4 Paul Ricoeur uses this term in *Figuring the Sacred: Religion, Narrative, and Imagination*, ed. Mark I. Wallace, trans. David Pellauer (Minneapolis: Fortress Press, 1995), 217.

5 This would be an example of a "personal volition disclaimer." Du Bois, "Self-Evidence and Ritual Speech"; John Du Bois, "Meaning without Intention: Lessons from Divination," in *Responsibility and Evidence in Oral Discourse*, ed. Jane H. Hill and Judith T. Irvine (Cambridge: Cambridge University Press, 1993), 48–71.

6 Cabrera, *El monte*. In Lachatañeré, *El sistema religioso de los afrocubanos*, published as articles between 1939 and 1946 and in 1961, the author writes, "Y como la

iniciación no responde siempre a la necesidad obligatoria de ejercer el sacerdocio, sino que ésta es una cualidad vocacional del individuo—los cultos se nutren con 'hijos' de santo que se inician simplemente por su salud" (114).

7 William F. Hanks, "Discourse Genres in a Theory of Practice," *American Ethnologist* 14, no. 4 (1987): 668–92.

8 See, for instance, Michael Taussig, *Shamanism, Colonialism, and the Wild Man: A Study in Terror and Healing* (Chicago: University of Chicago Press, 1987), 142.

9 David H. Brown, "Garden in the Machine," 202.

10 Palmié, *Wizards and Scientists*, 159–200.

11 Personal communication, December 18, 2005; January 7, 2006.

12 Personal communication, January 22, 2006. I am unsure of whether Ashabi consciously chose these words as an invocation of the movie scene or the words came to her unbidden. The cinematic exchange is as follows:

PHIL DAVIS (DANNY KAYE): How much is "wow"?

BOB WALLACE (BING CROSBY): It's right in between, uh, "ouch" and "boing."

PHIL DAVIS (DANNY KAYE): Wow!

13 Curry, *Making the Gods in New York*, 90.

14 At the time of this writing, initiation in the United States ran between $8,000 and $15,000 for most orishas. Being "made" to one of the Warriors or Oyá could cost about $5,000 more.

15 See Brian Brazeal, "Africa, Exú and the Devil: Methodological Perspectives for the Ethnography of Candomblé" (paper presented at the Brazilian Studies Association annual meeting, California State University, Chico, CA, March 29, 2008).

16 See ibid. In the case of godparents living abroad, the godchild who is a foreigner often pays more to offset the costs of performing rituals for local godchildren. See Erika Powell, "The Derecho: An Anthropological Approach to Understanding Money Exchange in Santería" (bachelor's thesis, Haverford College, 2004), 33. This is also the case in Brazilian Candomblé and Vodou in Haiti.

17 Stephen D. Glazier interprets similar rationales among his informants as an issue of belief, rather than the adoption of a speech genre and spirit idiom, in "Demanding Deities and Reluctant Devotees: Belief and Unbelief in the Trinidadian Orisa Movement," *Social Analysis* 52, no. 1 (2008): 19–38.

18 David H. Brown, "Garden in the Machine," 201–2.

19 Practitioners hastened to say that those so punished had destinies that could have been improved with the spirits' help.

20 Here Billal unwittingly echoes John M. Janzen's assertion that the Bantu cult of affliction, ngoma, was "a seventeenth-century 'cure for capitalism,' created by insightful Congo coast people who perceived that the great trade was destroying their society." *Lemba, 1650–1930*, xiii.

21 Tracy Nicholas and Bill Sparrow, *Rastafari: A Way of Life* (Chicago: Frontline Distribution International, 1996), 55.

22 I am using Bakhtin's terminology in order to avoid declaring that a listening participant in an oral performance is always able to grasp the intention of the narrator.

A speech plan may be inferred from the setting of similar communicative events, the identities and roles of the participants in them, and the interpretive orientations of listening subjects.

23 Quoted in Stanley Krippner, "Learning from the Spirits: Candomblé, Umbanda, and Kardecismo in Recife, Brazil," *Anthropology of Consciousness* 19, no. 1 (2008): 9.

24 Bakhtin, "Problem of Speech Genres."

25 See E. Summerson Carr, *Scripting Addiction: The Politics of Therapeutic Talk and American Sobriety* (Princeton: Princeton University Press, 2011).

26 Wirtz, *Ritual, Discourse, and Community*, 89.

27 Personal communication, August 13, 2007. As Martin Holbraad writes, such proofs bring a practitioner "closer to initiation not by 'convincing' him that it may be a good idea, but by implicating him into the world of the [orishas] through successive acts of ontological reconstruction." "Definitive Evidence, from Cuban Gods," S104.

28 Wirtz, *Ritual, Discourse, and Community*, 89. Similarly, in his study of Candomblé, Umbanda, and Kardecist Spiritism in Brazil, Stanley Krippner lists "five pathways that allowed practitioners to receive their call," but in truth, these are entry points into the tradition that do not condition continued involvement. "Learning from the Spirits," 8–9. Kali Argyriadis mentions these narratives briefly in *La religión à La Havane: Actualité des représentations et des pratiques cultuelles havanaises* (Paris: Éditions des Archives Contemporaines, 1999), 144.

29 Robaina, *Hablen paleros y santeros*, 2.

30 Although in some cases, the death forestalled through ocha was a fatal accident or homicide, most often it has been construed by initiates as the outcome of illness.

31 See Richard G. Gelb, "Literacy and Magic: The Role of Oral and Written Texts within a Santería Religious Community" (PhD diss., University of Illinois–Chicago, 1999), 106.

32 John Mason, *Ìdáná Fún Òrìsà*, 3.

33 Robaina, *Hablen paleros y santeros*, 6. In Güerere, *Hablan los santeros*, six of the seven practitioners questioned for his study pointed to illness or detection of sorcery as "confirmations" of the existence of the spirits, and fingered illness as a motivating factor for initiation.

34 See other examples in Theresa Varela, "The Mirror behind the Mask: Experiences of Five People Living with HIV/AIDS Who Practice Santería" (PhD diss., New York University, 2001), 64–65, 77–78; and Richard G. Gelb, "The Magic of Verbal Art: Juanita's *Santería* Initiation," in *Latino Language and Literacy in Ethnolinguistic Chicago*, ed. Marcia Farr (Mahwah, NJ: Erlbaum, 2005), 323–50.

35 See Sixto Gastón Agüero, *El materialismo explica el espiritismo y la santería* (Havana: Orbe, 1961); and Aníbal Argüelles Mederos and Ileana Hodge Limonta, *Los llamados cultos sincréticos y el espiritismo: Estudio monográfico sobre su significación social en la sociedad cubana contemporánea* (Havana: Editorial Academia, 1991).

36 Jesús Guanche, *Procesos etnoculturales de Cuba* (Havana: Editorial Letras, 1983); and Natalia Bolívar Aróstegui and Mario López Cepero, *¿Sincretismo religioso? Santa*

*Bárbara/Changó* (Havana: Pablo de la Torrient, 1990). A significant subset sought to explore Lucumí's potential as an alternative medical system and to explain its popularity for Latinos through an appeal to its therapeutic efficacy. Initiation stories have largely contributed to the interpretation of ocha in these terms, rather than to inquiry into the construction of healing as the domain of the spirits. See Johan Wedel, *Santería Healing: A Journey into the Afro-Cuban World of Divinities, Spirits, and Sorcery* (Gainesville: University Press of Florida, 2004).

37 It is important to underscore that the issue of conversion, as a change in belonging and association, has not been neglected in the scholarship on Lucumí, especially in excellent studies concerning African American practitioners. I am thinking specifically of the fine work of Tracey E. Hucks, Mary Cuthrell Curry, Steven Gregory, and more recently, Stefania Capone, Suzanne Henderson, and Nzinga O. Metzger.

38 In this vein, one should mention Eugene Berhard Filipowicz, "Santería as Revitalization among African-Americans" (master's thesis, Florida State University, 1998); and Carlos F. Cardoza Orlandi, "Drum Beats of Resistance and Liberation: Afro-Caribbean Religions, the Struggle for Life and the Christian Theologian," *Journal of Latino/Hispanic Theology* 3, no. 1 (1995): 50–61.

39 Occasionally this was based on the presupposition "that a body of context-free, prepositional knowledge about spiritual beings, their characteristics and interrelations, lies fully formed inside people's heads." Willerslev, *Soul Hunters*, 156.

40 Khan, "Isms and Schisms," 769.

41 Alluding to this, Palmié says, "I may be one of the few students of 'Afro'-'Cuban' 'religions' of my generation who is not now, and—the gods willing—may perhaps never become an initiate." *Cooking of History*, 221.

42 Du Bois, *Souls of Black Folk*. See Stephan Palmié, "Santería Grand Slam: Afro-Cuban Religious Studies and the Study of Afro-Cuban Religion," *New West Indian Guide* 79, nos. 3–4 (2005): 284–85.

43 Brazeal, "Africa, Exú and the Devil."

44 One could object that it is impossible to confirm whether elders in all houses of ocha tell similar stories, and that my claim only goes further in the politically dubious direction of trying to codify Lucumí as a tradition with characteristic ritual practices seen as authentic. Every single priest may not reproduce the initiation narrative, yet a great number have found it important to relate. The frequent incidence of its recurrence in the publications on the tradition requires some in-depth analysis.

45 Stephan Palmié, "Making Sense of Santería: Three Books on Afro-Cuban Religion," *New West Indian Guide* 70, nos. 3–4 (1996): 291–300. The "eyewitness account" often attempts to explain the development of Lucumí as a tradition, as well as reveal its true nature, as opposed to the distortions of wayward practitioners or the general public. See Miguel A. De La Torre, *Santería: The Beliefs and Rituals of a Growing Religion in America* (Grand Rapids, MI: Eerdmans, 2004).

46 Mahmood, *Politics of Piety*, 106.

47 Hawes, "Becoming Other-Wise," 36. The italics are his.

48 Personal communication, June 4, 2005.

**49** Personal communication, July 2007.

**50** Tompkins, *Racial Indigestion*, 10.

**51** See, for instance, Krishnakali Majumdar, "Healing through the Spirits: Divination and Healing among the Jaunsaris of Uttrakhand, India," in *Divination and Healing: Potent Vision*, ed. Michael Winkelman and Philip M. Peek (Tucson: University of Arizona Press, 2004), 183–206.

**52** Georges René and Marilyn Houlberg, "My Double Mystic Marriages to Two Goddesses of Love: An Interview," in Cosentino, *Sacred Arts of Haitian Vodou*, 287–88.

**53** Diana DeG. Brown, *Umbanda: Religion and Politics in Urban Brazil* (New York: Columbia University Press, 1994), 94.

**54** Converts often "lapse" and consult diviners or engage in propitiatory rituals in cases of illness or persistent misfortunes. See Richman, *Migration and Vodou*; and Birgit Meyer, *Translating the Devil: Religion and Modernity among the Ewe in Ghana* (Trenton, NJ: Africa World Press, 1999).

**55** Michel Foucault, "Truth and Power," in *Power/Knowledge: Selected Interviews and Other Writings, 1972–1977*, ed. C. Gordon (New York: Pantheon, 1980), 196–97.

**56** Turner, *Schism and Continuity*, 303.

**57** White, *Tropics of Discourse*, 83.

**58** Bakhtin, *Dialogic Imagination*, 120–21.

**59** Ibid., 120. The diviner Ócha'ni Lele writes, "In Ifa, it is said that there are 256 paths of Eleggua, one for each odu." *Diloggún*, 593.

**60** Personal communication. Lucumí rites of passage also put their subjects on paths, quite literally. For example, on the last day of an ocha, elders take the new initiate to a market and ask her to deposit offerings for Elegguá at the four corners around it. See David H. Brown, *Santería Enthroned*, 167.

**61** Bakhtin, *The Dialogic Imagination*, 113. The italics are his.

**62** Dervila Layden, "Discovering and Uncovering Genre in Irish Cinema," in *Genre and Cinema: Ireland and Transnationalism*, ed. Brian McIlroy (London: Taylor and Francis, 2007), 23. To my knowledge, the research on speech genres in Yorùbá healing practices has almost exclusively concerned ritual incantation and diagnostic vocabulary. I have found few accounts of how healers assumed their roles. This could be because researchers have not been intent to ask this question, or because a similar speech genre does not exist; it seems that most healers cite the source of their healing powers as apprenticeship to other healers or inheritance from a family member, not a call from the spirits that initially made them ill. See Mary Olufunmilayo Adekson, *The Yorùbá Traditional Healers of Nigeria* (New York: Routledge, 2003); and Barry Hallen, *The Good, the Bad, and the Beautiful: Discourse about Values in Yoruba Culture* (Bloomington: Indiana University Press, 2000).

**63** Karl F. Morrison, *Understanding Conversion* (Charlottesville: University Press of Virginia, 2002), xii. I suspect that the instantaneous conversion may owe much to television and filmic portrayals of the process, with their time-lapse photography encapsulations of human experience. Ibid., xiii.

**64** In many European cultures, special devotion to particular saints is still cast as the result of mysterious illness, either cured or ameliorated through the intercession of a beatified or canonized person.

**65** Kjersti Larsen, *Where Humans and Spirits Meet: The Politics of Rituals and Identified Spirits in Zanzibar* (New York: Berghahn, 2008), 42. See also Tracy Luedke, "Spirit and Matter: The Materiality of Mozambican Prophet Healing," *Journal of Southern African Studies* 33, no. 4 (2007): 715–31.

**66** John M. Janzen, "Self-Presentation and Common Cultural Structures in Ngoma Rituals of Southern Africa," *Journal of Religion in Africa* 25, Fasc. 2 (1995): 146. Although I am wary of positing an unchanging religious genre called "drum of affliction" and related modes of self-narration, the scholarship on which I am drawing stresses the heterogeneity of the religions and time periods in which ngoma has been found, and the adaptation of local variants to historical and economic processes (with an emphasis on mutual constitution of narratives and the social/cultural).

**67** See Todd Ramón Ochoa, *Society of the Dead: Quita Manaquita and Palo Praise in Cuba* (Berkeley: University of California Press, 2010), 9; Betty M. Kuyk, *African Voices in the African American Heritage* (Bloomington: Indiana University Press, 2003), 96–99; Michael Gomez, *Exchanging Our Country Marks: The Transformation of African Identities in the Colonial and Antebellum South* (Chapel Hill: University of North Carolina Press, 1998); Wyatt MacGaffey, "Twins, Simbi Spirits and Lwas in Kongo and Haiti," in *Central Africans and Cultural Transformations in the American Diaspora*, ed. Linda M. Heywood (New York: Cambridge University Press, 2002), 211–26; and Janzen, *Lemba*.

**68** It bears mentioning that just as Lucumí initiates have tended to rely on multiple hierarchized and multiethnic spirits (orishas, mpungus, ancestors, and spirit guides), so too have practitioners of ngoma turned to categories of spirits differentiated by ethnicity and classed accordingly.

**69** Setting aside the Jungian resonances of the term, as elucidated by Laurence J. Kirmayer in "Asklepian Dreams: The Ethos of the Wounded-Healer in the Clinical Encounter," *Transcultural Psychiatry* 40, no. 2 (2003): 248–77, my main referent here is to T. S. Eliot's *Four Quartets*, "The wounded surgeon plies the steel / That questions the distempered part."

**70** Eoghan C. Ballard, "Ndoki Bueno Ndoki Malo: Historic and Contemporary Kongo Religion in the African Diaspora" (PhD diss., University of Pennsylvania, 2005), 100–101.

**71** I. M. Lewis, *Ecstatic Religion: A Study of Shamanism and Spirit Possession* (New York: Penguin, 1971), 172; Thomas Carlyle, *The Works of Thomas Carlyle* (New York: Peter Fenelon Collier, 1897), 489.

**72** Quoted in Bronfman, *Measures of Equality*, 95.

**73** David H. Brown, *Santería Enthroned*, 70.

**74** Aline Helg, *Our Rightful Share: The Afro-Cuban Struggle for Equality, 1886–1912* (Chapel Hill: University of North Carolina Press, 1995).

**75** Ortiz, *Hampa afro-cubana*.

**76** Palmié, *Wizards and Scientists*, 250.

**77** Alfred Lindesmith and Yale Levin, "The Lombrosian Myth in Criminology," *American Journal of Sociology* 42, no. 5 (1937): 653–71.

**78** Cited in Bronfman, *Measures of Equality*, 94.

**79** See Wirtz, "How Diasporic Religious Communities Remember," 116; David H. Brown, "Review of *Africa's Ogun: Old World and New*," *American Ethnologist* 19, no. 2 (1992): 377–78; Erwan Dianteill and Martha Swearingen, "From Hierography to Ethnography and Back: Lydia Cabrera's Texts and the Written Tradition in Afro-Cuban Religions," *Journal of American Folklore* 116, no. 2 (2003): 273–92.

**80** See Moore, "'Testifying' and 'Testimony'"; Elaine J. Lawless, "'The Night I Got the Holy Ghost . . .': Holy Ghost Narratives and the Pentecostal Conversion Process," *Western Folklore* 47, no. 1 (1988): 1–19; and Rosetta E. Ross, *Witnessing and Testifying: Black Women, Religion, and the Civil Rights Movement* (Minneapolis: Fortress Press, 2003).

**81** Smitherman, *Talkin and Testifyin*, 58.

**82** Pérez, "Spiritist Mediumship."

**83** Raymond Williams, *Marxism and Literature* (Oxford: Oxford University Press, 1977), 132.

**84** Robin Horton, "Judeo-Christian Spectacles: Boon or Bane to the Study of African Religions?," *Cahiers d'Etudes Africaines* 24, no. 4 (1984): 391–436.

**85** Gananath Obeyesekere, *Imagining Karma: Ethical Transformation in Amerindian, Buddhist, and Greek Rebirth* (Berkeley: University of California Press, 2002).

**86** Keane, *Signs of Recognition*, 181; his italics.

**87** Michael Holquist, *Dialogism: Bakhtin and His World* (London: Routledge, 1990), 38.

**88** "Testifying as a speech act within black church services has always been preceded by the open invitation, 'Can I get a witness?'" Valerie Lee, *Granny Midwives and Black Women Writers: Double-Dutched Readings* (New York: Routledge, 1996), 79.

**89** Erving Goffman, *Forms of Talk* (Oxford: Basil Blackwell, 1981), 145.

**90** Thomas Hoyt Jr., "Testimony," in *Practicing Our Faith: A Way of Life for a Searching People*, ed. Dorothy C. Bass (San Francisco: Jossey-Bass, 1997), 94.

**91** See Goffman, "Footing."

**92** If acknowledged, non-ratified hearers become bystanders, with access to social encounters yet without an official place within them. This may be the default state of the ethnographic participant-observer.

**93** Herbert H. Clark, *Using Language* (Cambridge: Cambridge University Press, 1996), 34.

**94** Kenneth Burke, *A Rhetoric of Motives* (Berkeley: University of California Press, 1969), 58.

**95** Richard Bauman, "Verbal Art as Performance," in Bauman, *Verbal Art as Performance*, 16.

> Most of the audience are receiving the message as tale, while also receiv-
> ing and judging the variations in style, in voice, in rhetorical *savoir-faire*,
> provided by the performance. The performance, in other words, functions

as metatext to the hearers, and the audience's attention moves, in a form of dialogue, between the tale and the telling. Their judgement is an active one, constantly providing feedback on the demands of variability versus invariability, on the delights of surprise as opposed to the pleasures of the formulaic.

Marie Maclean, *Narrative as Performance: The Baudelairean Experiment* (London: Routledge, 1988), 7–8.

96 In testifying, Christians have also affirmed Jesus's ability to heal physical infirmity.

97 Carla Kaplan, *The Erotics of Talk: Women's Writing and Feminist Paradigms* (New York: Oxford University Press, 1996), 58.

98 Taussig, *Mimesis and Alterity*, 86.

99 Michael D. McNally, "Honoring Elders: Practices of Sagacity and Deference in Ojibwe Christianity," in *Practicing Protestants: Histories of Christian Life in America, 1630–1965*, ed. Laurie F. Maffly-Kipp, Leigh E. Schmidt, and Mark Valeri (Baltimore: Johns Hopkins University Press, 2006), 80.

100 Port, "Circling around the Really Real," 164.

101 During the time of my research, "I feel you" was a common African American Vernacular English expression of sympathy, affirmation, understanding, or assent.

102 Neuroscientific investigations increasingly bear out these insights, as reported in Elizabeth Svoboda, "The Power of Story," *Aeon*, January 12, 2015, http://aeon.co/magazine/psychology/once-upon-a-time-how-stories-change-hearts-and-brains/. See Greg J. Stephens, Lauren J. Silbert, and Uri Hasson, "Speaker-Listener Neural Coupling Underlies Successful Communication," *Proceedings of the National Academy of Science USA* 107, no. 32 (2010): 14425–30; Mary H. Immordino-Yang, "Toward a Microdevelopmental, Interdisciplinary Approach to Social Emotion," *Emotion Review* 2, no. 3 (2010): 217–20; and Mary H. Immordino-Yang, Andrea McColl, Hanna Damasio, and Antonio Damasio, "Neural Correlates of Admiration and Compassion," *Proceedings of the National Academy of Sciences USA* 106, no. 19 (2009): 8021–26.

103 Erving Goffman, *Frame Analysis: An Essay on the Organization of Experience* (Cambridge: Harvard University Press, 1974), 504.

104 *Hamlet*, act 2, scene 2.

105 This is fitting since neither Lucumí nor any other Afro-Cuban tradition trades in creedal declarations. Martin Gaenszle, *Ancestral Voices: Oral Ritual Texts and Their Social Contexts among the Mewahang Rai of East Nepal* (Münster: LIT Verlag, 2002), 129; Samuel Taylor Coleridge, *Biographia Literaria, or Biographical Sketches of My Literary Life and Opinions and Two Lay Sermons* (Boston: Adamant Media, 2004 [1817]), 145.

106 *Middle English Dictionary*, ed. Robert E. Lewis (Ann Arbor: University of Michigan Press, 1968), 107.

107 Michel Foucault's discussion of listening and subjectivation is apt here. *Hermeneutics of the Subject*, 334–42.

108 Russell John Rickford, *Spoken Soul: The Story of Black English* (New York: Wiley, 2000).

109 The concept is Bakhtin's. Judith Butler, *Excitable Speech: A Politics of the Performative* (New York: Routledge, 1997), 28–35.

110 Gilkes, *If It Wasn't for the Women*, 137.

111 James A. Beckford, "Accounting for Conversion," *British Journal of Sociology* 29, no. 2 (1978): 250.

112 Clifford L. Staples and Armand L. Mauss, "Conversion or Commitment? A Reassessment of the Snow and Machalek Approach to the Study of Conversion," *Journal for the Scientific Study of Religion* 26, no. 2 (1987): 144n2.

113 For example, in discussing ocha among non-initiates, elders used the simple future tense ("You'll get initiated someday") and the future real conditional ("When you get initiated, you'll see what I mean"). Initiation was, in conversation, much more often a *when* than an *if* proposition.

114 For mention of recruitment as the attraction of newcomers at the point of entry to the tradition, see George Brandon, "Hierarchy without a Head: Observations on Changes in the Social Organization of Some Afroamerican Religions in the United States, 1959–1999 with Special Reference to Santería," *Archives de Sciences Sociales des Religions* 117 (2002): 151–74.

## CHAPTER 6. WALKING THE TALK

1 See Ysamur Flores-Peña, "'Son dos los Jimagüas' ('The Twins Are Two'): Worship of the Sacred Twins in Lucumí Religious Culture," in *Twins in African and Diaspora Cultures: Double Trouble or Twice Blessed*, ed. Philip M. Peek (Bloomington: Indiana University Press, 2011), 103.

2 As Kristina Silke Wirtz argues, "Santeros' skeptical attitudes turn out to be key features of their religiosity as it is expressed in reflective discourses in which they test possible interpretations of events for their religious implications," and "intracommunity conflict, rather than always and everywhere being antithetical to community-building, might sometimes constitute community." *Ritual, Discourse, and Community*, 103, xv. See also Birman, *Fazendo estilo criando gênero*, 100–101.

3 Riesebrodt, "Religion in Global Perspective," 101. Paule Marshall, quoted in Meredith Gadsby, *Sucking Salt: Caribbean Women Writers, Migration, and Survival* (Columbia: University of Missouri Press, 2006), 6.

4 Michel Foucault, *The Archaeology of Knowledge* (New York: Harper and Row, 1972), 49. The literature on speech acts and performatives that builds on J. L. Austin, *How to Do Things with Words* (Oxford: Oxford University Press, 1962), is too vast to cite here, so I hope this point can be taken at "face value." The classic performative utterance "I now pronounce you man and wife" is particularly apposite in the case of Lucumí initiation, when a practitioner is regarded as marrying her tutelary deity.

5 Holbraad, "Definitive Evidence."

6 Ibid.

7 Personal communication, June 6, 2005.

8 Psyche A. Williams-Forson, *Building Houses out of Chicken Legs: Black Women, Food, and Power* (Chapel Hill: University of North Carolina Press, 2006), 95–96, 108–9.

**9** Michel Foucault, "Nietzsche, Genealogy, History," in *Language, Counter-Memory, Practice*, trans. Donald Bouchard (Ithaca: Cornell University Press, 1977), 146.

**10** *Foucault Live: Interviews, 1966–84*, trans. John Johnston, ed. Sylvère Lotringer (New York: Semiotext[e], 1989), 330.

**11** Rituals regularly performed in casa-templos that use the oracle of Ifá (termed "Ifá-centric" by Brown, *Santería Enthroned*, 19, and elsewhere), such as the "hand of Orula," are not discussed here.

**12** Louis Althusser, *Lenin and Philosophy and Other Essays*, trans. Ben Brewster (New York: Monthly Review Press, 1971), 275–76.

**13** I presume that this is partly what Ashabi meant when she once described practitioners as "converting themselves into becoming themselves." Personal communication, January 7, 2006.

**14** This may fruitfully be compared to what Peter Brown argues in *The Cult of the Saints: Its Rise and Function in Latin Christianity* (Chicago: University of Chicago Press, 1981).

**15** Personal communication, September 29, 2004. Fadesiye said, "We produce our blessing through our body, with breath."

**16** Prior to ocha, a practitioner walks down a trail blazed by her elders, in the sense that physical contact with the consecrated objects and other sacra of the orishas is mediated through them. It is only after ordination that she breaks her own path to the spirits, addressing them directly. In houses that use Ifá divination to discern the will of the orishas, practitioners find out their "paths" prior to initiation.

**17** A similar process is described by Murphy in *Santería*.

**18** David H. Brown, *Santería Enthroned*, 370.

**19** It is placed on its side only at the time of its owner's death.

**20** Other houses differ on this point.

**21** Gell, *Art and Agency*, 104.

**22** Ibid.

**23** Ibid., 123.

**24** The intimate homological relationship between the house and the human subject in Afro-Diasporic religious formations has yet to be explored fully, although it has been documented in other cultural milieus. See, for instance, E. Valentine Daniel, "A House Conceived," in *Fluid Signs: Being a Person the Tamil Way* (Berkeley: University of California Press, 1984), 105–62; Jon L. Berquist, *Controlling Corporeality: The Body and the Household in Ancient Israel* (Piscataway: Rutgers University Press, 2002); and the essays in Janet Carsten and Stephen Hugh-Jones, eds., *About the House: Lévi-Strauss and Beyond* (Cambridge: Cambridge University Press, 1995). The editors credit to Tim Ingold the suggestion that "a homology [exists] between the relations body:house:landscape and organism:dwelling:environment. The former set emphasizes form, the latter function," 4.

**25** Quoted in Zeca Ligièro, "Candomblé Is Religion-Life-Art," in *Divine Inspiration from Benin to Bahia*, ed. Phyllis Galembo (New York: Athelia Henrietta Press, 1993), 105–6.

**26** Marriott, "Hindu Transactions." Traced to Marriott, I use the concept of the "dividual" person as the anthropologist Marilyn Strathern does. This is emphatically not the person according to "the economic construct of individual embodiment and self-possession" that has served as "the hegemonic signifier of social personhood." Palmié, "Thinking with Ngangas," 871. See also Michael Carrithers, Steven Collins, and Steven Lukes, eds., *The Category of the Person: Anthropology, Philosophy, History* (Cambridge: Cambridge University Press, 1985), 123–40.

**27** See Tim Ingold, "Building, Dwelling, Living: How Animals and People Make Themselves at Home in the World," in *The Perception of the Environment: Essays on Livelihood, Dwelling and Skill* (New York: Routledge, 2000), 172–89. Paul Christopher Johnson asserts that Candomblé's temple compounds have served as templates for the human body. See *Secrets, Gossip, and Gods*, 49.

**28** The death of the iyawo may also be viewed through the prism of his impending ascension to royalty as constructed in ritual practices that have been most thoroughly documented to date by David H. Brown. See Ernst H. Kantorowicz, *The King's Two Bodies: A Study in Medieval Political Theology* (Princeton: Princeton University Press, 1957); and Luc de Heusch, "The Sacrificial Body of the King," in *Fragments for a History of the Human Body*, pt. 3, ed. Michel Feher, Ramona Naddaff, and Nadia Tazi (New York: Zone Books, 1989), 387.

**29** In Yorùbá, *abiku* refers to a child who has been stillborn or miscarried, and is thought to exert a malign influence in the life of its would-be mother, yet it is doubtful that any relationship exists between these terms.

**30** Personal communication, June 19, 2005.

**31** See Michael Atwood Mason, *Living Santería*, 76–77.

**32** Personal communication, May 3, 2007.

**33** The term "discipline" (singular) was employed by elders in the community in this context.

**34** Personal communication, September 24/25, 2005.

**35** Even for someone generally familiar with the protocols for ordination, the prospect of confronting them may be enough to induce tremendous anxiety. One initiate-to-be told me that she was planning to use the breathing techniques she learned in preparation for childbirth to get her through the initiatory ordeal.

**36** Sometimes the children of Oyá, Obatalá, and Inle are allowed to keep their hair, although in the case of Obatalá and Oyá's children, even then a fringe of hair will be shaved from the hairline in a sort of reverse-tonsure style. The priest explaining this to me in August 2006 stated that he would prefer to have all of his hair shaved rather than have to deal with this hairdo.

**37** There is one exception: the children of Warrior orishas—Elegguá, Ogún, and Ochosi—do not need to remain in their altar-spaces (also called *ilé*) and may instead wander throughout the home as long as they are dressed as their tutelary deities. When it comes time to change clothes, they must return to their ilés.

**38** David H. Brown, *Santería Enthroned*, 352n39.

**39** Murphy, *Santería*, 84.

**40** John Walton, Paul B. Beeson, and Ronald Bodley Scott, eds., *The Oxford Companion to Medicine* (Oxford: Oxford University Press, 2005), 322.

**41** David B. Morris, "About Suffering: Voice, Genre, and Moral Community," in *Social Suffering*, ed. A. Kleinman, V. Das, and M. M. Lock (Berkeley: University of California Press, 1997), 25–46.

**42** As Wirtz writes, the narrators of such stories are adamant that they adopted commonsense courses of action before pursuing ritual intervention. Wirtz, *Ritual, Discourse, and Community*, 91. See Argelio Frutos, *Panteón Yoruba: Conversación con un santero* (Holguín, Cuba: Ediciones Holguín, 1992); and Juan Manuel Saldívar Arellano, *Nuevas formas de adoración y culto: La construcción social de la santería en Catemaco, Veracruz, México* (Madrid: Editorial Vision Libros, 2009).

**43** The exact formulae for libations differs from house to house, but in one version, the section that begins with *Kosi*, "Let us avert," runs as follows: "*Kosi iku* [Let us avert death]; *Kosi arun* [Let us avert illness]; *Kosi ofo* [Let us avert loss]; *Kosi fitibo* [Let us avert being overwhelmed]; *Kosi idina* [Let us avert obstacles]; *Kosi egba* [Let us avert paralysis]; *Kosi ese* [Let us avert evil]; *Kosi eyo* [Let us avert tragedy]; *Ariku babawa* [Let us not see death, our father]; *Ariku iyawa* [Let us not see death, our mother]."

**44** Jean Comaroff, *Body of Power, Spirit of Resistance: The Culture and History of a South African People* (Chicago: University of Chicago Press, 1985), 219.

**45** Personal communication, August 22, 2006.

**46** I have struggled with the proper term to describe the association of spirits with parts of the body, to which they lay claim through diverse categories of affliction. What is emphasized in ethnosymptomatology, to borrow Luisa Maffi's neologism, is not so much the reading of symptoms to ascertain the underlying causes of a given disease (as in the semeiology taught in medical school), but the construction of symptoms as signs of favor. See Luisa Maffi, "A Linguistic Analysis of Tzeltal Maya Ethnosymptomatology" (PhD diss., University of California–Berkeley, 1994).

**47** David H. Brown, *Santería Enthroned*, 176.

**48** Robert Farris Thompson, "Icons of the Mind: Yoruba Herbalism Arts in Atlantic Perspective," *African Arts* 8, no. 3 (1975): 52–59, 89–90. According to Elizabeth Allo Isichei, among the contemporary Yorùbá, "The herbalist/healer god Osanyin . . . is the paradigm of the wounded healer: he has one eye, one arm, and one leg." *The Religious Traditions of Africa: A History* (Westport, CT: Praeger, 2004), 236.

**49** In historical context, this myth may also be viewed as legitimating the healing practices of Ifá diviners, and their attempts to cast the efforts of non-divining herbalists as inferior to theirs.

**50** Cabrera, *El monte*, 99–100.

**51** Morton Marks, "Exploring El Monte: Ethnobotany and the Afro-Cuban Science of the Concrete," in *En torno a Lydia Cabrera*, ed. Isabel Castellanos and Josefina Inclán (Miami: Ediciones Universal, 1987), 229.

**52** I was pressed into service by Ashabi to translate this message for the benefit of Spanish-speaking participants.

**53** Cabrera, *El monte*, 48.

54 Most academic accounts of initiation have focused on the placement of conse-crated substances on the freshly shaved scalp of the novice, yet according to David H. Brown, the ritual engages the entirety of the body. Brown, *Santería Enthroned*, 193.

55 This was not unusual; Dantine's son Jafari was initiated under similar circum-stances, when he was the first to walk through the door after an itá.

56 See Mary Ann Clark, "You Are (Not) Shango: Jungian Archetypes in Contemporary Santería," *Wadabagei: A Journal of the Caribbean and Its Diaspora* 5, no. 1 (2002): 105–35.

57 She had no intention of interfering in Howard's relationship with his godmother, and critiques of others' godparents, even if unscrupulous, were frowned upon.

58 Personal communication, April 29, 2006.

59 He wondered immediately after his ocha whether he had pulled a muscle, but at the time of our discussion, his doctor was investigating the possibility of a cyst.

60 He said that he could not specify what had happened, and even if he did, I would not be able to understand without becoming initiated myself.

61 Erving Goffman, "On Face-Work: An Analysis of Ritual Elements in Social Inter-action," *Psychiatry: Journal of Interpersonal Relations* 18, no. 3 (1955): 213.

62 Personal communication, August 13, 2007.

63 Ibid.

64 Hermann Strasser and Susan C. Randall, *An Introduction to Theories of Social Change* (London: Routledge and Kegan Paul, 1981), 258. At the time of our discussion, for example, she was about to receive Babalú Ayé to improve the condition of her spine and legs.

65 Anthony Giddens, *Modernity and Self-Identity: Self and Society in the Late Mod-ern Age* (Cambridge: Polity, 1991), 54.

66 This remains a consistent feature both of stories published as oral histories, and of those I heard once I began to become acquainted with Lucumí practitioners.

67 Asad, *Formations of the Secular*, 92.

68 The psychoanalytic theorist Jacques Lacan coined the term "mirror stage" to de-note the moment when a child sees an external image of herself—either in the reflec-tion of a mirror or as revealed by her main caregiver—and learns that she is at once a unified object in the world and separate from it. This scene, Lacan maintained, results in the conceptualization of an "I" that is both identical with the subject and idealized in its apparent solidity. The subject's identity, as she perceives it and offers it up as an image of her self, reflects a continuous process of reinvention, intended to shore up her fragile "I." "The Mirror Stage as Formative of the Function of the I," in *Écrits: A Selec-tion*, trans. B. Fink (New York: Norton, 2002 [1949]), 3–9.

69 Clark, "Asho Orisha," 156, 164–65.

70 Not everyone experiences social difficulties during iyaworaje; some initiates find that the dedication they are seen to demonstrate leads others to perceive them as pious, principled, and modest. Because iyawos are clad in white from head to toe, they have sometimes been told that they resemble angels.

71 At affairs such as drum ceremonies, an iyawo may "drop" many dozens of times in one evening. Sometimes two or more elders will collectively "raise" an iyawo by

tapping their shoulders at the same time, but other priests scoff at this, recalling the incessant "dropping" that their own iyawo years entailed.

72 John Mason, "Yorùbá Beadwork in the Americas," in *Beads, Body, and Soul: Art and Light in the Yorùbá Universe*, ed. Henry John Drewal and John Mason (Los Angeles: Fowler Museum of Cultural History, 1998), 111.

73 See Frank B. Wilderson, *Red, White and Black: Cinema and the Structure of U.S. Antagonisms* (Durham: Duke University Press, 2010).

74 Judith Greene and Kevin Pranis, "Blood In, Blood Out: Why Youth Join Gangs and How They Leave," in *Gang Wars: The Failure of Enforcement Tactics and the Need for Effective Public Safety Strategies* (Washington, DC: Justice Policy Institute, 2007), 45–50.

75 Personal communication, October 17, 2004. As Pierre Bourdieu says of bodily hexis,

> The principles em-bodied in this way are placed beyond the grasp of consciousness, and hence cannot be touched by voluntary, deliberate, transformation, cannot even be made explicit; nothing seems more ineffable, more incommunicable, more inimitable, and therefore, more precious, than the values given body, *made* body by the transubstantiation achieved by the hidden persuasion of an implicit pedagogy, capable of instilling a whole cosmology, an ethic, a metaphysic, a political philosophy, through injunctions as insignificant as "stand up straight" or "don't hold your knife in your left hand."

*Outline of a Theory of Practice*, 94.

76 Personal communication, April 28, 2006. Tales of stomach upset are routine, as are comments about the temperature of the river broached at the commencement of the initiatory process.

77 Roger M. Keesing, "Linguistic Knowledge and Cultural Knowledge: Some Doubts and Speculations," *American Anthropologist* 81, no. 1 (1979): 32.

78 Judith Butler, *Excitable Speech: A Politics of the Performative* (New York: Routledge, 1997), 5.

79 Ibid.

80 Paul Drew and Elizabeth Holt, "Complainable Matters: The Use of Idiomatic Expressions in Making Complaints," *Social Problems* 35 (1988): 398–417.

81 As Paul Drew and Elizabeth Holt write, "Participants themselves orient to these properties and functions of figurative expressions, even in instances where the production of a figurative expression fails to result in topical closure." Paul Drew and Elizabeth Holt, "Figures of Speech: Figurative Expressions and the Management of Topic Transition in Conversation," *Language in Society* 27, no. 4 (1998): 519.

CONCLUSION

1 Palmié, *Cooking of History*, 101.

2 Dana L. Cloud, "The Materiality of Discourse as Oxymoron: A Challenge to Critical Rhetoric," *Western Journal of Communication* 58 (1994): 141–63.

3 In this, I take inspiration from other ethnographic and historical studies on Afro-Cuban traditions. See Diana Espírito Santo, "Spiritist Boundary-Work and the Morality of Materiality in Afro-Cuban Religion," *Journal of Material Culture* 15, no. 1 (2010): 64–82; and Kristina Wirtz, "Hazardous Waste: The Semiotics of Ritual Hygiene in Cuban Popular Religion," *Journal of the Royal Anthropological Institute* 15, no. 3 (2009): 476–501.

4 See Matory, "Free to Be a Slave."

5 See Michael Herzfeld, *Cultural Intimacy: Social Poetics in the Nation-State* (New York: Routledge, 1997).

6 Matory, *Sex and the Empire That Is No More*, 170–71. The reader may wonder whether the coincidence of these interpretations has to do with scholars' influence on practitioners, but Matory was not ubiquitous in practitioners' libraries, although Robert Farris Thompson and William Bascom were. I cite Matory here for his economy of expression. Lucumí protocols for initiation seem to owe a substantial debt to those of the Shangó priesthood among the Yorùbá—as masterfully delineated by David H. Brown—but the citation of the Yorùbá example is not meant to imply that Lucumí protocols are mere copies of a more authoritative "original"; indeed, it is possible that Cuban and Brazilian orisha worship has historically shaped Yorùbá practice. The line of influence does not point only in one direction.

7 "Living under the sign of the 'unlivable' is required to circumscribe the domain of the subject." *Bodies That Matter*, 3.

8 Judith Butler, *Gender Trouble: Feminism and the Subversion of Identity* (New York: Routledge, 1990), 133.

9 Butler, *Bodies That Matter*, 3.

10 Mahmood, *Politics of Piety*, 106.

11 "In the everyday world, the self is experienced as the 'author' of its activities, as the 'originator' of on-going actions, and thus as an 'undivided total self.'" Byron J. Good, *Medicine, Rationality, and Experience: An Anthropological Perspective* (Cambridge: Cambridge University Press, 1994), 124.

12 Hirokazu Miyazaki, *The Method of Hope: Anthropology, Philosophy, and Fijian Knowledge* (Stanford: Stanford University Press, 2004), 106; Vicente L. Rafael, *Contracting Colonialism: Translation and Christian Conversion in Tagalog Society under Early Spanish Rule* (Ithaca: Cornell University Press, 1988), 7.

13 Mahmood, *Politics of Piety*, 17.

14 Simon Coleman, "Continuous Conversion? The Rhetoric, Practice, and Rhetorical Practice of Charismatic Protestant Conversion," in *The Anthropology of Religious Conversion*, ed. Andrew Buckser and Stephen D. Glazier (Lanham, MD: Rowman and Littlefield, 2003), 16.

15 My fieldwork experience and the following analysis are at odds with Matory's claim that "an egalitarian (dare I say republican?) logic underlies even the hierarchical vocabulary and body language of Cuban Ocha." "Free to Be a Slave," 416–17.

16 Foucault, *Discipline and Punish*, 26–28, 160.

17 As the philosopher Hubert L. Dreyfus and the anthropologist Paul Rabinow assert, "To understand power in its materiality, its day-to-day operation, we must go

to the level of the micropractices, the political technologies in which our practices are formed." Hubert L. Dreyfus and Paul Rabinow, *Michel Foucault: Beyond Structuralism and Hermeneutics* (Chicago: University of Chicago Press, 1983), 185.

18 Hawes, "Becoming Other-Wise."

19 Even when legal permits are obtained for these events, or they are held in banquet halls municipally zoned for social gatherings, the understanding is that sacrifice will not be occurring on the premises.

20 See, for instance, James C. Scott, *Weapons of the Weak: Everyday Forms of Peasant Resistance* (New Haven: Yale University Press, 1985); and Rosalind O'Hanlon, "Recovering the Subject: Subaltern Studies and Histories of Resistance in Colonial South Asia," *Modern Asian Studies* 22, no. 1 (1988): 189–224.

21 Quoted in Sindre Bangstad, "Contesting Secularism/s: Secularism and Islam in the Work of Talal Asad," *Anthropological Theory* 9, no. 2 (2009): 197.

22 Michel de Certeau, *Heterologies: Discourse on the Other*, trans. Brian Massumi (Minneapolis: University of Minnesota Press, 1986), 188.

23 Van der Veer, introduction to *Conversion to Modernities*, 15.

24 Richard Price, *Alabi's World* (Baltimore: Johns Hopkins University Press, 1990), 330.

25 See Apter, "Herskovits's Heritage"; and Mintz and Price, *The Birth of African-American Culture*.

26 David Scott, "That Event, This Memory: Notes on the Anthropology of African Diasporas in the New World," *Diasporas* 1, no. 3 (1991): 261–84. See Erik R. Seeman, "Reassessing the 'Sankofa Symbol' in New York's African Burial Ground," *William and Mary Quarterly* 67, no. 1 (2010): 101–22.

27 Robert Hanna, *Rationality and Logic* (Cambridge: Massachusetts Institute of Technology Press, 2006), 35.

28 Michel Foucault, *Society Must Be Defended: Lectures at the Collège de France, 1975–76*, ed. Mauro Bertani and Alessandro Fontana, trans. David Macey (New York: Picador, 2003), 34.

29 Charles Taylor, *Philosophy and the Human Sciences*, vol. 2 of *Philosophical Papers* (Cambridge: Cambridge University Press, 1985), 171; the italics are his. Some of the same misgivings regarding Foucault's "extremely suspect rhetoric of complexity" are shared by Slavoj Žižek. See "Introduction: The Spectre of Ideology," in *Mapping Ideology*, ed. Slavoj Žižek (London: Verso, 1994), 13.

30 As the anthropologist Susan Gal writes, "When Marxist critics want to bring oppressed or neglected groups to the attention of Western audiences, they do so by trying to show that the oppressed are also recognizably like the Western ideal of the political subject, that is, they are dual selves. The critic thus presents the oppressed as self-formed, internally autonomous actors mentally resisting an external domination." "Language and the 'Arts of Resistance,'" *Cultural Anthropology* 10, no. 3 (1995): 414.

31 Slavoj Žižek, *The Sublime Object of Ideology* (London: Verso, 1989), 18.

32 Chakrabarty, *Provincializing Europe*, 103.

33 These dynamics are brilliantly documented among servants of the Afro-Brazilian spirit Pomba Gira in the documentary film *Slaves of the Saints*, by Kelly E. Hayes and Catherine Crouch, included as a DVD with Hayes's *Holy Harlots: Femininity, Sexuality, and Black Magic in Brazil* (Berkeley: University of California Press, 2011).

34 Jennifer W. Nourse, "The Voice of the Winds versus the Masters of Cure: Contested Notions of Spirit Possession among the Laujé of Sulawesi," *Journal of the Royal Anthropological Institute* 2, no. 3 (1996): 437.

35 See J. Lorand Matory, "The Trans-Atlantic Nation: Rethinking Nations and Transnationalism," in *Black Atlantic Religion*, 73–114.

36 Miyazaki, *Method of Hope*, 106.

37 Susan Buck-Morss, "Hegel and Haiti," *Critical Inquiry* 26, no. 4 (2000): 821.

38 Matory, "Free to Be a Slave," 41; his italics. Bruno Latour, *Pandora's Hope: Essays on the Reality of Science Studies* (Cambridge: Harvard University Press, 1999), 273.

39 Jacquelyn Grant, "Servanthood Revisited: Womanist Explorations of Servanthood Theology," in *Black Faith and Public Talk: Critical Essays on James H. Cone's "Black Theology and Black Power,"* ed. Dwight N. Hopkins (Waco, TX: Baylor University Press, 2007), 126–37.

40 Matory, "Free to Be a Slave," 400.

41 Gilroy, *Black Atlantic*.

42 Andrew Goodman said, "I was born in slavery and I think them days was better for the niggers than the days we see now. One thing was, I was never cold and hungry when my old master lived, and I has been plenty hungry and cold a lot of times since he is gone." Quoted in George P. Rawick, ed., *The American Slave: A Composite Autobiography*, vol. 4 (Texas), pt. 2 (Westport, CT: Greenwood, 1972), 75. Andrew Boone asserted that emancipation had failed to alter the basic structure of economic oppression created during slavery: "In slavery time they kept you down an' you had to wurk, now I can't wurk, an' I am still down. Not allowed to work an' still down. It's all hard, slavery and freedom, both bad when you can't eat." *The American Slave: A Composite Autobiography*, vol. 14 (North Carolina), pt. 1 (Westport, CT: Greenwood, 1972), 137. See also ibid., 108, 124, 290, 347, 434; and *The American Slave: A Composite Autobiography*, vol. 4 (Texas), pt. 1 (Westport, CT: Greenwood, 1972), 48, 239.

43 Mia Bay, *To Tell the Truth Freely: The Life of Ida B. Wells* (New York: Hill and Wang, 2009), 145; Paul Stoller, *Embodying Colonial Memories: Spirit Possession, Power, and the Hauka in West Africa* (New York: Routledge, 1995), 195–96.

44 William H. Sewell, *Logics of History: Social Theory and Social Transformation* (Chicago: University of Chicago Press, 2005), 189–94.

45 Karen McCarthy Brown, "Alourdes: A Case Study of Moral Leadership in Haitian Vodou," in *Saints and Virtues*, ed. John Stratton Hawley (Berkeley: University of California Press, 1987), 150.

46 Taussig, *Mimesis and Alterity*, 126.

47 For the development of this idea particularly in the context of the nation-state, see James Ferguson and Akhil Gupta, "Spatializing States: Toward an Ethnography of

Neoliberal Governmentality," in *Anthropologies of Modernity: Foucault, Governmentality, and Life Politics*, ed. Jonathan Xavier Inda (Malden, MA: Blackwell, 2005), 105–34.

**48** This is Aristotle's *empsychon organon*. Albert Harrill, "Paul and the Slave Self," in *Religion and the Self in Antiquity*, ed. David Brakke, Michael L. Satlow, and Steven Weitzman (Bloomington: Indiana University Press, 2005), 53; Sigmund Freud, "Civilization and Its Discontents," in *The Freud Reader*, ed. Peter Gay (New York: Norton, 1989), 722–72.

**49** See J. D. Gauthier, "The Ethics of the Care of the Self as a Practice of Freedom: An Interview," trans. J. D. Gauthier, in *The Final Foucault*, ed. James William Bernauer and David M. Rasmussen (Cambridge: Massachusetts Institute of Technology Press, 1988), 1–20.

**50** Foucault, *History of Sexuality*, vol. 2, 6–7.

**51** Ibid., 26.

**52** Some religious histories may be more freshly cooked than others, yet there is no such animal as a social formation or object of knowledge in the raw.

**53** Lincoln, "Theses on Method," 225; Sidney W. Mintz and Michel-Rolph Trouillot, "The Social History of Haitian Vodou," in Cosentino, *Sacred Arts of Haitian Vodou*, 129; and Brian K. Smith, "Ritual, Knowledge, and Being: Initiation and Veda Study in Ancient India," *Numen* 33, Fasc. 1 (1986): 65.

**54** Urban, "Torment of Secrecy."

**55** Lincoln, "Theses on Method."

**56** Talal Asad, quoted in Lincoln, *Holy Terrors*, 2.

**57** Rabinow and Marcus et al., *Designs for an Anthropology of the Contemporary*, 95–96.

**58** See Kimberly A. Arkin, *Rhinestones, Religion, and the Republic: Fashioning Jewishness in France* (Stanford: Stanford University Press, 2014); Rebecca J. Lester, *Jesus in Our Wombs: Embodying Modernity in a Mexican Convent* (Berkeley: University of California Press, 2005); Jeanette S. Jouili, "Negotiating Secular Boundaries: Pious Micro-Practices of Muslim Women in French and German Public Spheres," *Social Anthropology* 17, no. 4 (2009): 455–70; Christina Zanfagna, "Kingdom Business: Holy Hip Hop's Evangelical Hustle," *Journal of Popular Music Studies* 24, no. 2 (2012): 196–216; Tova Hartman and Naomi Marmon, "Lived Regulations, Systemic Attributions: Menstrual Separation and Ritual Immersion in the Experience of Orthodox Jewish Women," *Gender and Society* 18, no. 3 (2004): 389–408; Terry Grey, "Identity-Forming Theological Education: The Practice of Confession in the Formation of Salvation Army Officers," *Religious Education* 109, no. 2 (2014): 126–41.

**59** I have in mind the work of Black female scholars including Josephine Beoku-Betts, Jualynne Dodson, Marvalene Hughes, Cheryl Townsend Gilkes, Psyche Williams-Forson, and Carolyn Rouse.

# GLOSSARY

All terms are derived from the Yorùbá language and refer to the Lucumí tradition unless otherwise noted (Sp. = Spanish). Spellings are approximate and differ in other accounts of the tradition; variations are given only in cases where they might aid further investigation.

ABAKUÁ: Cuban all-male initiatory tradition of West African Cross-River region (Carabalí) origin.

ABOKU: Individual in a liminal state about to undergo a rite of passage, especially an initiate-to-be before he or she has been ceremonially reborn (literally, "the dead one").

ABORISHA: Servant of the orishas, especially an uninitiated practitioner.

ACHÉ/ASHÉ: Vital, primordial energy embodied by the orishas and their consecrated substances but latent in the entirety of the phenomenal world; the power to make things happen.

ADDIMÚ: Food given in offering to the orishas.

ADDIMÚ ORISHA: Orisha received ceremonially in a context other than the initiation ritual.

ADÉ/ADÉFONTÓ: In Afro-Brazilian religions, "effeminate" gay man presumed to occupy a passive sexual role and suited to service as a "possession mount."

AFRICAN AMERICAN: Person born in the United States and, as commonly employed, descended from enslaved West and Central Africans brought to North America during the transatlantic slave trade; synonymous but not coterminous with Black.

AFRO-CUBAN: Cuban person of African descent; also refers to religious traditions derived and/or inspired by precolonial African practices and discourses.

AGBAN: Ceremonial offering for an orisha, most typically Babalú Ayé or Olokún, that involves presenting several different dishes of food in supplication, cleansing, and/or thanksgiving.

AJIACO: Sp., stew made with garlic, corn, starchy root vegetables, chicken, and pork, among other traditional ingredients; metaphor for the Cuban nation; cooked by Lucumí practitioners as an offering for the ancestors.

AKARÁ: Black-eyed pea fritters.

AKASÁ: Dumplings wrapped in roasted banana leaves and filled with white, cooked grits.

ALASHÉ: Cook for ritual events, especially in the context of matanzas.

ALEYO: Person active in an ilé but uninitiated, and thus not yet a "child" of the house; literally, "stranger," "visitor."

AMALÁ ILÁ: Cornmeal pudding with sauce containing onion, tomato, and okra; associated paradigmatically with Shangó.

AÑÁ/ÀYÀN: Female orisha of music that resides within the sacred bàtá drums.

ARÚN: Sickness.

ASHÉS/ACHÉSES (PL.): Viscera and extremities extracted from sacrificial animals, roasted, and placed in dried gourds as offerings to the orishas; also called iñales/inyales.

BABA: "Father"; title used to address a male priest, especially one's senior.

BABALÁWO: "Father of secrets," Ifá diviner, priest of Orula/Orúnmilá.

BABALÚ AYÉ: Orisha of illness, especially of epidemics, skin ailments, and venereal disease.

BASURA: Sp., garbage.

BÀTÁ: Three consecrated drums of different sizes, together forming a suite used in the rituals called wemilere.

BATEA: Lidded wooden vessel that houses the consecrated objects of Shangó.

BEMBÉ: Drum feast for the orishas, with either consecrated or unconsecrated drums; synonym for wemilere.

BOTÁNICA: Sp., religious supply store that sells items used in Afro-Diasporic religions.

BRUJA/O: Sp., witch, especially as used among Latino/as with reference to practitioners of African-derived religions.

CABALLO: Sp., priest able to incorporate the orishas in possession; mount; literally, "horse."

CABILDO DE NACIÓN: Sp., in the context of colonial Cuba, a mutual aid society for people of African descent nominally organized along ethnic lines; considered to be one of the sites in which the practice of Lucumí crystallized.

CAJÓN PA' MUERTOS: Sp., drum ritual of Cuban origin in which box drums are played for the ancestral deities and the spirits of Palo Monte.

CALABAZA: Sp., Spanish (kabocha) squash, sacred to Ochún.

CALALÚ: stew made for Shangó with tomato sauce, amaranth leaves, and beef or pork, among other ingredients.

CANASTILLERO: Sp., wardrobe or other type of shelved unit with cabinets and often with glass doors, used historically to hold the soperas of the orishas.

CANDOMBLÉ: Afro-Brazilian religious formation; refers especially, but not exclusively, to worship of the orixás according to protocols developed in Salvador da Bahia (particularly when glossed as Candomblé Ketu/Nagô). In Candomblé Angola (also called Bantu or Batuque), the Kongo-inspired *inquices* are prioritized; in Candomblé Jejé, spirits of Dahomeyan origin called *voduns* are privileged.

CASA-TEMPLO: Sp., house-temple; the primary physical site of orisha worship for communities that adhere to ritual protocols of Cuban origin; sometimes refers to a house of worship as a family unit.

COCINERA/O: Sp., cook.

CUNDIAMOR: Vine of the bitter melon plant, one of the herbs belonging to Babalú Ayé.

DADÁ: Orisha of unborn children and newborn babies, sister of Shangó.

DERECHO: Sp., fee for ritual services; also called achedí.

DILOGGÚN: Contraction of "merindínlógún," meaning "sixteen"; divination method conducted by both men and women using sixteen cowrie shells cast on a mat in private consultations. The 256 resulting patterns are each associated with oracular verses called odu, explained by diviners with reference to their clients' everyday lives.

DULCE DE COCO: Sp., coconut candy made with shredded coconut, butter, brown sugar, and vanilla in the shape of balls, especially for Yemayá.

EBÓ: Transformative cleansing sacrifice, prescribed in divination sessions or through the oracular speech of possessed mounts. They often take the form of offerings, of food, animals, or ritual activity (most typically drum feasts).

EBÓ EYÉ OR EBÓ WONÍ: Blood sacrifice.

EFÚN: White chalk made from eggshell powder, used for demarcating spaces, cooling objects, and pacifying spirits.

EGÚN: Spirit of the ancestral dead from either one's biological family or one's religious lineage; Sp., muerto.

EKEDI: Ritual assistant to possession mount in Brazilian Candomblé.

ELDER: Initiate; synonymous with "priest" and "priestess."

ELEGGUÁ: Orisha of crossroads and thresholds, destiny and choice.

ELEKE: Consecrated beaded necklace that indicates the identity of a particular orisha through its colors and repeating numerical patterns; receiving five of these necklaces ceremonially initiates the formal relationship between godparent and godchild and membership in a religious community.

ESPIRITISMO: Sp., Spiritism as practiced in the Caribbean and elsewhere to venerate spirit guides and ancestors, heavily influenced by the nineteenth-century French author Allan Kardec.

ESPIRITISTA: Sp., spirit medium in the Kardecist tradition.

EWO: Taboo or prohibition received in divination.

EYÓ: Tragedy.

FIFI OKAN: Color-coded designs painted in tempera on the shaved heads of novices during the initiation ceremony.

FUNDAMENTOS: Stones where the orishas reside after their consecration during the initiation of novices.

GODFATHER/GODMOTHER/GODPARENT: Senior ritual sponsors of initiates, with protégés called "godchildren."

GOFIO: Sp., roasted and ground whole wheat or maize, especially as rolled into balls with honey or molasses for the orishas.

GÜIRO: Sp., drum ritual, so named after the percussion instrument often used in ceremonies with unconsecrated drums.

HOUNSI CUISINIÈRE: Ritual cook in Vodou temples, especially in the context of sacrificial rites.

IBEJI: Divine twins, the son and daughter of Ochún.

IBÓ: "Tools" used in sixteen-cowries (diloggún) divination, including a sea snail shell, black pebble, piece of animal vertebra, or button of eggshell powder, to be placed randomly in the client's right or left hand in response to a diviner's query.

IDEÚ: Child of Ochún after she lost the twins, born of an alliance to Elegguá.

IFÁ: Divination method conducted normatively by men (babaláwos) in the Americas using sixteen palm kernels affixed to a chain and cast on a ritually prepared wooden tray; can also refer to the priesthood of these diviners.

IGBODÚN: Sacred grove; shrine room or the sacred space where initiatory rituals take place.

IKU: Death.

ILÉ: House; religious family.

IÑALES/INYALES: Viscera and extremities extracted from sacrificial animals, roasted, and placed in dried gourds as offerings to the orishas; also called ashés/ashéses.

INLE: Orisha of medicine and healing; a fisherman and herbalist.

IRÉ: Luck or the state of having good fortune (as determined through divination).

ITÁ: Major divination performed as part of the ordination process that outlines future proscriptions and prescriptions; term also used for divination after rites of passage such as the "three months' ebó" and pinaldo.

IYA: Mother; title used to address a female priest, especially one's senior; term used for the biggest of the three bàtá drums.

IYA BASSÊ/IABASSÉ/AYABASÈ: Ritual cook in houses of Brazilian Candomblé.

IYALOSHA/IYALOCHA: "Mother of the orishas"; title used to address a female priest, especially the leader of a house-temple.

IYÁN: Fight/struggle (in the sense of penury).

IYAWO: New initiate; among the Yorùbá, bride, especially wife younger than the speaker.

IYAWORAJE: First year of initiation, the state of "wifehood."

JA: Decorated broom for Babalú Ayé.

JICARA: Sp., dried gourd used as bowl for ceremonial purposes.

LIBRETA: Sp., handwritten manual produced by initiates containing autobiographical and ritual information.

LUCUMÍ/LUKUMÍ: Yorùbá-inspired Afro-Cuban cultural and religious formation; refers to worship of the orishas according to protocols developed in Cuba; also the liturgical language of the tradition, a form of Yorùbá as passed down through oral tradition, without its three distinctive tones.

MALANGA: Sp., cocoyam.

MATANZA: Sp., act of animal sacrifice, "killing"; pl., matanzas, refers to the sacrifices conducted to consecrate ritual objects, especially those of a new initiate.

MAZOS: Heavy, many-stranded beaded necklaces used as part of the ceremonial prendición and at other key moments in the ritual lives of practitioners.

MISA BLANCA/MISA ESPIRITUAL: Sp., white mass or spiritual mass held in private homes in honor of spirit guides and family ancestors.

MOUNT: Priest able to incorporate Black Atlantic deities in possession.

MOYUBÁ: Ancestral prayer said aloud prior to ritual practices; contains recitation of religious lineage and appeals to the orishas.

MPUNGU: Cuban-Kongo spirit of the Palo Monte pantheon.

MUERTOS: Sp., spirits of the ancestral dead from either one's biological family or one's religious lineage.

NFUMBI: Spirit of a dead person as mobilized in Palo Monte to animate a ritual object called a prenda or nganga.

NGANGA: Central object of veneration in Palo Monte and other Kongo-inspired traditions, a cauldron filled with consecrated matter; also called prenda.

NGOMA: Bantu-derived "cult" or "drum" of affliction.

NKANDEMBO: Office of ritual cook in Abakuá.

ÑAME: Sp., white yam.

OBATALÁ: Cool, elderly creator orisha; owner of heads, heights, and white substances.

OBBA: Orisha of the cemetery grounds; Shangó's faithful wife.

OBI: Kola nut; refers to coconut as used in divination when cut into four pieces; the patterns made when they fall (either on their white tops or brown undersides) indicate answers to "yes"/"no" questions.

OCHA: Contraction of "kariocha," the initiation ceremony into the Lucumí priesthood, and therefore its main ritual of ordination; used as a synonym for the religion, as in "regla ocha."

OCHOSI: One of the Warrior orishas; orisha of the hunt and a consummate tracker.

OCHÚN: Goddess of sweet water, sensual and romantic love, prosperity, and pleasure.

ODU: Divinatory "letter" or "sign" determined by sixteen-cowries or Ifá divination, and the verses, myths, names, and proverbs associated with it.

OGÚN: One of the Warrior orishas; orisha of iron—and by extension, all metals—a blacksmith and tireless worker.

OLÓDÙMARÈ: Supreme Being, the ultimate source of existence and aché.

OLOKÚN: Orisha of the ocean's depths.

OLORISHA: Lucumí priest, male or female.

OMIERO: Ritually prepared herbal infusion.

OMO: Child, especially of the spirits; serves a synonym for initiate.

ORDINATION: Ritual of initiation into the Lucumí priesthood.

ORÍ: The physical head as the seat of the body's capacities and potentialities, governing not only discrete actions and movements, but also such components of personal style as gestures and comportment.

ORIATÉ: Master of ceremonies for initiation ritual and the person entrusted with determining the patron deities of religious practitioners in houses of worship that regard diloggún as the normative form of divination.

ORISHA/ORIXÁ: Deity of Yorùbá origin. Orishas personify concepts, sentiments, and natural occurrences, although the qualities that devotees in the Americas have assigned to them sometimes have varied from those identified in West Africa.

ORISHA OKO: Orisha of agriculture and fertility within families.

ORÚNMILÁ: Orisha of Ifá divination, husband of Ochún.

OSAÍN: Herbalist orisha and traditional plant-based medicine; forest-dwelling and allied with the Warriors.

OSHÍNSHÍN: Dish made for Ochún containing spinach or watercress and freshwater shrimp (dried or fresh) scrambled into five eggs.

OSOGBO/OSOBO: Misfortune.

ÓSUN: One of the Warrior orishas. His primary manifestation is a small chalice-shaped staff ringed with bells and with a rooster perched on top, an object that has been described as an altar to the recipient's inner head (orí), and the destiny embedded within it; not to be confused with Ochún.

OTANES: Stones that embody the orisha installed in them ceremonially through the initiation ritual.

OYÁ: Orisha of the cemetery gates, masquerade, the marketplace, and the hurricane.

PALANGANA: Sp., plastic or aluminum tub used for ritual purposes.

PALO MONTE: Afro-Cuban religious formation, one of the reglas de congo (Kongo-inspired religious orthodoxies) practiced alongside Lucumí in many house-temples.

PATAKÍ: Mythological story or legend embedded in the verses of the sixteen-cowries divination system.

PILÓN: Sp., large mortar sacred to Shangó, used as a seat for the novice in the initiation ritual.

PINALDO: Rite of passage in which an initiate becomes invested with the authority to sacrifice four-legged animals, in houses of worship that regard diloggún as the normative form of divination; commonly referred to as "the knife."

PLÁTANO: Sp., plantain.

PRENDICIÓN: Sp., abduction; the lassoing with a mazo that occurs immediately prior to the initiation ceremony or after someone has unwittingly or deliberately violated certain ritual protocols.

PRIEST: Initiate, used for both male and female elders.

PRIESTESS: Initiate, sometimes used for female elders.

ROGATION: Sp., prayer or petition; ritual cleansing and blessing of the physical head.

ROMPIMIENTO: Sp., breaking; destruction of old clothes as part of entry into liminal stage of Lucumí rite of passage.

SANTERÍA: Sp., way of the saints; widely synonymous with Lucumí but now considered pejorative by many practitioners due to its negative connotations (e.g., that Lucumí is a degraded mix of Catholicism and African witchcraft).

SANTERO/A: Practitioner of Lucumí religion, used to refer to both initiated and uninitiated devotees.

SANTO: Sp., saint; term used, especially by Latino/a practitioners, for an orisha.

SHANGÓ: Orisha of thunder, justice, law, male virility, the initiation ritual, and bàtá drums.

SOPERA: Sp., soup tureen, as used for the purpose of housing an orisha's ritual sacra.

SPIRIT GUIDE: In the tradition of Espiritismo, ethnically differentiated disincarnated entities who act as protectors of human beings.

TAMBOR: Sp., drum; celebration dedicated to deities using either bàtá or unconsecrated drums.

THRONE: Elaborate altar for the orishas.

TRABAJOS: Sp., magical "works" or transformative acts intended to have speedy and specific results, especially as performed for clients.

VODOU: Haitian religious formation with both West and Central African historical precedents; refers to worship of the Vodou spirits, called lwa, according to protocols developed in Haiti.

WEMILERE: Drum celebration using bàtá drums.

YEMAYÁ: Orisha of the oceans, domesticity, and maternal love.

YEWÁ: Virginal female orisha who lives in the grave and assists in the decomposition of the dead.

YORÙBÁ: Influential West African ethnic group historically composed of linguistically related semi-autonomous groups whose members arrived in Cuba, Brazil, and elsewhere throughout the Americas during the transatlantic slave trade, especially in the nineteenth century.

Aguiar, Janaina Couvo Teixeira Maia de. "Os orixás, o imaginário e a comida no Candomblé." *Revista Fórum Identidades* 6, no. 11 (2012): 160–70.

Ahmed, Sara. *The Promise of Happiness*. Durham: Duke University Press, 2010.

Alexander, M. Jacqui. *Pedagogies of Crossing: Meditations on Feminism, Sexual Politics, Memory, and the Sacred*. Durham: Duke University Press, 2005.

Apter, Andrew. "Herskovits's Heritage: Rethinking Syncretism in the African Diaspora." *Diaspora* 1, no. 3 (1991): 235–60.

Apter, Andrew, and Lauren H. Derby, eds. *Activating the Past: History and Memory in the Black Atlantic World*. Newcastle: Cambridge Scholars, 2010.

Argyriadis, Kali. *La religión à La Havane: Actualité des représentations et des pratiques cultuelles havanaises*. Paris: Éditions des Archives Contemporaines, 1999.

Aróstegui, Natalia Bolívar, and Carmen González Díaz de Villegas. *Afro-Cuban Cuisine: Its Myths and Legends*. Havana: Editorial José Martí, 1998.

Asad, Talal. *Formations of the Secular: Christianity, Islam, Modernity*. Stanford: Stanford University Press, 2003.

——. *Genealogies of Religion: Discipline and Reasons of Power in Christianity and Islam*. Baltimore: Johns Hopkins University Press, 1993.

Bakhtin, Mikhail. *The Dialogic Imagination: Four Essays*. Edited by Michael Holquist. Translated by C. Emerson and Michael Holquist. Austin: University of Texas Press, 1981.

——. "The Problem of Speech Genres." In *Speech Genres and Other Late Essays*, edited by V. W. McGee, C. Emerson, and M. Holquist, 60–102. Austin: University of Texas Press, 1986.

Baldwin, Davarian. *Chicago's New Negroes: Modernity, the Great Migration and Black Urban Life*. Chapel Hill: University of North Carolina Press, 2007.

Bastide, Roger. *O Candomblé da Bahia*. São Paulo: Companhia das Letras, 2001 [1958].

——. *A cozinha dos deuses: Alimentação e Candomblé*. Rio de Janeiro: SAPS, 1952.

——. *Les religions africaines au Brésil: Vers une sociologie des interpénétrations de civilisations*. Paris: Presses Universitaires de France, 1960.

Battaglia, Deborah, ed. *Rhetorics of Self-Making*. Berkeley: University of California Press, 1995.

Bauman, Richard, ed. *Verbal Art as Performance*. Prospect Heights, IL: Waveland, 1977.

Beliso-De Jesús, Aisha M. "Religious Cosmopolitanisms: Media, Transnational Santería, and Travel between the United States and Cuba." *American Ethnologist* 40, no. 4 (2013): 704–20.

———. "Yemayá's Duck: Irony, Ambivalence, and the Effeminate Male Subject in Cuban Santería." In *Yemoja: Gender, Sexuality, and Creativity in the Latina/o and Afro-Atlantic Diasporas*, edited by Solimar Otero and Toyin Falola, 43–84. Albany: State University of New York Press, 2013.

Bender, Courtney. *Heaven's Kitchen: Living Religion at God's Love We Deliver*. Chicago: University of Chicago Press, 2003.

Best, Wallace Denino. *Passionately Human, No Less Divine: Religion and Culture in Black Chicago, 1915–1952*. Princeton: Princeton University Press, 2005.

Birman, Patrícia. *Fazendo estilo criando gênero*. Rio de Janeiro: Relume-Dumará, 1995.

———. "Transas e transes: Sexo e gênero nos cultos afro-brasileiros, um sobrevôo." *Estudos Feministas* 13, no. 2 (2005): 403–14.

Bontemps, Alex. *The Punished Self: Surviving Slavery in the Colonial South*. Ithaca: Cornell University Press, 2001.

Bonvini, E. "Mets afro-brésiliens, cuisine des hommes, nourriture des dieux: Nourritures, goûts et symbolism." *Journal des Africanistes* 66, nos. 1–2 (1996): 137–65.

Bourdieu, Pierre. *Outline of a Theory of Practice*. Translated by Richard Nice. Cambridge: Cambridge University Press, 1977.

———. *Practical Reason: On the Theory of Action*. Translated by Richard Nice. Stanford: Stanford University Press, 1998.

Bourdieu, Pierre, and Loïc J. D. Wacquant. *An Invitation to Reflexive Sociology*. Chicago: University of Chicago Press, 1992.

Brandon, George. *Santeria from Africa to the New World: The Dead Sell Memories*. Bloomington: Indiana University Press, 1993.

Bronfman, Alejandra M. "'En Plena Libertad y Democracia': Negros Brujos and the Social Question, 1904–1919." *Hispanic American Historical Review* 82, no. 3 (2002): 549–88.

———. *Measures of Equality: Social Science, Citizenship, and Race in Cuba, 1902–1940*. Chapel Hill: University of North Carolina Press, 2004.

Brown, David H. "Garden in the Machine: Afro-Cuban Sacred Art and Performance in Urban New Jersey and New York." PhD diss., Yale University, 1989.

———. *Santería Enthroned: Art, Ritual, and Innovation in an Afro-Cuban Religion*. Chicago: University of Chicago Press, 2003.

———. "Thrones of the *Orichas*: Afro-Cuban Altars in New Jersey, New York, and Havana." *African Arts* 26, no. 4 (1993): 44–59.

———. "Toward an Ethnoaesthetics of Santería Ritual Arts: The Practice of Altar Making and Gift Exchange." In *Santería Aesthetics in Contemporary Latin American Art*, edited by Arturo Lindsay, 77–148. Washington, DC: Smithsonian Institution Press, 1996.

Brown, Karen McCarthy. *Mama Lola: A Vodou Priestess in Brooklyn*. Berkeley: University of California Press, 1991.

Brumana, F. Giobellina. "El sexo de los ángeles: La sexualidad en la economía religiosa del Candomblé." *Antropología* 1 (1991): 27–41.

Butler, Judith. *Bodies That Matter: On the Discursive Limits of "Sex."* New York: Routledge, 1993.

Cabrera, Lydia. *La medicina popular en Cuba: Médicos de antaño, curanderos, santeros y paleros de hogaño.* Miami: Ultra Graphics, 1984.

———. *El monte: Igbo finda, ewe orisha, vititi nfinda.* Miami: Colección del Chichereku, 1983 [1954].

Caetano de Sousa Júnior, Vilson. *O Banquete Sagrado: Notas sobre os "de comer" em terreiros de Candomblé.* Salvador: Atalhos, 2009.

Cannon, Katie G. *Black Womanist Ethics.* Atlanta: Scholars Press, 1988.

Capone, Stefania. *Searching for Africa in Brazil: Power and Tradition in Candomblé.* Durham: Duke University Press, 2010.

———. *Les Yoruba du Nouveau Monde: Religion, ethnicité et nationalisme noir aux États-Unis.* Paris: Karthala, 2005.

Carneiro, Edison. *Candomblés da Bahia.* Publicações do Museu do Estado, no. 8. Bahia: Secretaria de Educação e Saúde, 1948.

Cave, David, and Rebecca Sachs Norris, eds. *Religion and the Body: Modern Science and the Construction of Religious Meaning.* Leiden: Brill, 2012.

Chakrabarty, Dipesh. *Provincializing Europe: Postcolonial Thought and Historical Difference.* Princeton: Princeton University Press, 2000.

Christie, Marie Elisa. *Kitchenspace: Women, Fiestas, and Everyday Life in Central Mexico.* Austin: University of Texas Press, 2008.

Clark, Mary Ann. "Asho Orisha (Clothing of the Orisha): Material Culture as Religious Expression in Santería." PhD diss., Rice University, 1999.

———. *Santería: Correcting the Myths and Uncovering the Realities of a Growing Religion.* Westport, CT: Praeger, 2007.

———. *Where Men Are Wives and Mothers Rule: Santería Ritual Practices and Their Gender Implications.* Gainesville: University Press of Florida, 2005.

Collins, Patricia Hill. *From Black Power to Hip Hop: Racism, Nationalism, and Feminism.* Philadelphia: Temple University Press, 2006.

Comaroff, John L., and Jean Comaroff. *Ethnography and the Historical Imagination.* Boulder: Westview, 1992.

Connor, Randy P., and David Hatfield Sparks. *Queering Creole Spiritual Traditions: Lesbian, Gay, Bisexual, and Transgender Participation in African-Inspired Traditions in the Americas.* Binghamton, NY: Harrington Park Press, 2004.

Cosentino, Donald, ed. *Sacred Arts of Haitian Vodou.* Los Angeles: UCLA Fowler Museum of Cultural History, 1995.

Cossard, Gisèle O. *Awô: O mistério dos orixás.* Rio de Janeiro: Pallas, 2006.

Crenshaw, Kimberlé. "Mapping the Margins: Intersectionality, Identity Politics, and Violence against Women of Color." *Stanford Law Review* 43, no. 6 (1991): 1241–99.

Cromley, Elizabeth C. "Transforming the Food Axis: Houses, Tools, Modes of Analysis." *Material History Review* 44 (1996): 8–22.

Curry, Mary Cuthrell. *Making the Gods in New York: The Yoruba Religion in the African-American Community*. New York: Garland, 1997.

Curtain, Deane W., and Lisa M. Heldke, eds. *Cooking, Eating, Thinking: Transformative Philosophies of Food*. Indianapolis: Indiana University Press, 1992.

Daniel, Yvonne. *Dancing Wisdom: Embodied Knowledge in Haitian Vodou, Cuban Yoruba, and Bahian Candomblé*. Urbana: University of Illinois Press, 2005.

de Certeau, Michel. *The Practice of Everyday Life*. Translated by Steven Rendall. Berkeley: University of California Press, 1984.

de Certeau, Michel, Luce Giard, and Pierre Mayol. *The Practice of Everyday Life*. Vol. 2, *Living and Cooking*. Translated by T. J. Tomasik. Minneapolis: University of Minnesota Press, 1998.

Detienne, Marcel, and Jean-Pierre Vernant, eds. *The Cuisine of Sacrifice among the Greeks*. Chicago: University of Chicago Press, 1989.

Dianteill, Erwan. *La Samaritaine Noire: Les églises spirituelles noires américaines de la Nouvelle-Orléans*. Paris: Éditions de l'EHESS, 2006.

dos Santos, Milton Silva. "Sexo, gênero e homossexualidade: O que diz o povo-de-santo paulista?" *Horizonte* 6, no. 12 (2008): 145–56.

Douglas, Mary. "Deciphering a Meal." *Daedalus* 101 (1972): 61–81.

———. *Purity and Danger: An Analysis of the Concepts of Pollution and Taboo*. New York: Routledge, 1966.

Drake, St. Clair, and Horace R. Cayton. *Black Metropolis: A Study of Negro Life in a Northern City*. Chicago: University of Chicago Press, 1993 [1945].

Du Bois, John. "Self-Evidence and Ritual Speech." In *Evidentiality: The Linguistic Coding of Epistemology*, edited by Wallace Chafe and Johanna Nichols, 313–36. Norwood, NJ: Ablex, 1986.

Du Bois, W. E. B. *The Souls of Black Folk: Essays and Sketches*. London: Longmans, Green, 1965 [1903].

Elbein dos Santos, Juana. *Os Nagô e a morte*. Petrópolis: Vozes, 1976.

Foucault, Michel. *Discipline and Punish: The Birth of the Prison*. Translated by Alan Sheridan. New York: Vintage, 1977.

———. *The Hermeneutics of the Subject: Lectures at the Collège de France, 1981–1982*. Edited by Frédéric Gros, François Ewald, and Alessandro Fontana. Translated by Graham Burchell. New York: Palgrave Macmillan, 2005.

———. *The History of Sexuality*. Vol. 2, *The Use of Pleasure*. Translated by Robert Hurley. New York: Random House, 1985.

Frutos, Argelio. *Panteón Yoruba: Conversación con un santero*. Holguín, Cuba: Ediciones Holguín, 1992.

Fry, Peter. "Male Homosexuality and Spirit Possession in Brazil." *Journal of Homosexuality* 11, nos. 3–4 (1986): 137–53.

———. *Para inglês ver*. Rio de Janeiro: Jorge Zahar, 1982.

Gell, Alfred. *Art and Agency: An Anthropological Theory*. Oxford: Oxford University Press, 1998.

Gilkes, Cheryl Townsend. *If It Wasn't for the Women: Black Women's Experience and Womanist Culture in Church and Community*. Maryknoll, NY: Orbis, 2001.

Gilroy, Paul. *The Black Atlantic: Modernity and Double Consciousness*. Cambridge: Harvard University Press, 1993.

Goffman, Erving. "Footing." In *Forms of Talk*, 124–57. Oxford: Basil Blackwell, 1981.

———. *Interaction Ritual: Essays on Face-to-Face Behavior*. Chicago: Aldine, 1967.

Gregory, Steven. *Santería in New York City: A Study in Cultural Resistance*. New York: Garland, 1999.

Güerere, Tabaré. *Hablan los santeros*. Caracas: Alfadil Ediciones, 1993.

Hagedorn, Katherine. *Divine Utterances: The Performance of Afro-Cuban Santería*. Washington, DC: Smithsonian Institution Press, 2001.

Hawes, Leonard C. "Becoming Other-Wise: Conversational Performance and the Politics of Experience." *Text and Performance Quarterly* 18, no. 4 (1998): 273–99.

Hayes, Kelly E. *Holy Harlots: Femininity, Sexuality, and Black Magic in Brazil*. Berkeley: University of California Press, 2011.

Henderson, Suzanne Marie. "The African-American Experience of Orisha Worship." PhD diss., Temple University, 2007.

Hirsch, Arnold R. *Making the Second Ghetto: Race and Housing in Chicago, 1940–1960*. Chicago: University of Chicago Press, 1998 [1983].

Holbraad, Martin. "Definitive Evidence, from Cuban Gods." *Journal of the Royal Anthropological Institute* 14 (2008): S93–S109.

———. *Truth in Motion: The Recursive Anthropology of Cuban Divination*. Chicago: University of Chicago Press, 2012.

Hollywood, Amy. "Performativity, Citationality, Ritualization." In *Bodily Citations: Religion and Judith Butler*, edited by Ellen T. Armour and Susan M. St. Ville, 252–75. New York: Columbia University Press, 2006.

hooks, bell. *Talking Back: Thinking Feminist, Thinking Black*. Boston: South End, 1989.

Howes, David. *Sensual Relations: Engaging the Senses in Culture and Social Theory*. Ann Arbor: University of Michigan Press, 2003.

———, ed. *The Varieties of Sensory Experience: A Sourcebook in the Anthropology of the Senses*. Toronto: University of Toronto Press, 1991.

Hucks, Tracey E. "Approaching the African God: An Examination of African-American Yoruba History from 1959 to the Present." PhD diss., Harvard University, 1998.

———. "'Burning with a Flame in America': African American Women in African-Derived Traditions." *Journal of Feminist Studies in Religion* 17, no. 2 (2001): 89–106.

———. *Yoruba Traditions and African American Religious Nationalism*. Albuquerque: University of New Mexico Press, 2012.

Hughes, Marvalene H. "Soul, Black Women, and Food." In *Food and Culture: A Reader*, edited by Carole Counihan and Penny Van Esterik, 273–34. New York: Routledge, 1997.

Jacobs-Huey, Lanita. *From the Kitchen to the Parlor: Language and Becoming in African American Women's Hair Care*. Oxford: Oxford University Press, 2006.

Janzen, John M. *Lemba, 1650–1930: A Drum of Affliction in Africa and the New World.* New York: Garland, 1982.

Johnson, Paul Christopher. *Diaspora Conversions: Black Carib Religion and the Recovery of Africa.* Berkeley: University of California Press, 2007.

———. *Secrets, Gossip, and Gods: The Transformation of Brazilian Candomblé.* Oxford: Oxford University Press, 2002.

Keane, Webb. *Signs of Recognition: Powers and Hazards of Representation in an Indonesian Society.* Berkeley: University of California Press, 1997.

Khan, Aisha. "Isms and Schisms: Interpreting Religion in the Americas." *Anthropological Quarterly* 76, no. 4 (2003): 768–70.

Lachatañeré, Rómulo. *El sistema religioso de los afrocubanos.* Havana: Editorial de Ciencias Sociales, 2004.

Landes, Ruth. *The City of Women.* New York: Macmillan, 1947.

Lele, Ócha'ni. *The Diloggún: The Orishas, Proverbs, Sacrifices, and Prohibitions of Cuban Santería.* Rochester, VT: Destiny Books, 2003.

———. *Sacrificial Ceremonies of Santería: A Complete Guide to the Rituals and Practices.* Rochester, VT: Destiny Books, 2012.

Lévi-Strauss, Claude. *The Origin of Table Manners.* Translated by John Weightman and Doreen Weightman. Chicago: University of Chicago Press, 1979.

Lima, Vivaldo da Costa. *A anatomia do acarajé e outros escritos.* Salvador: Corrupio, 2010.

Lincoln, Bruce. *Discourse and the Construction of Society.* New York: Oxford University Press, 1989.

———. *Holy Terrors: Thinking about Religion after September 11.* Chicago: University of Chicago Press, 2003.

———. "Theses on Method." *Method and Theory in the Study of Religion* 8 (1996): 225–27.

Lody, Raul. *Santo também come: Estudo sócio-cultural da alimentação ceremonial em terreiros afro-brasileiros.* Recife: MEC/Instituto Joaquim Nabuco de Pesquisas Sociais, 1979.

Luhrmann, Tanya M. *When God Talks Back: Understanding the American Evangelical Relationship with God.* New York: Knopf, 2012.

Lumsden, Ian. *Machos, Maricones, and Gays: Cuba and Homosexuality.* Philadelphia: Temple University Press, 1996.

Machon, Josephine. *(Syn)aesthetics: Redefining Visceral Performance.* Basingstoke: Palgrave Macmillan, 2009.

Mahmood, Saba. *Politics of Piety: The Islamic Revival and the Feminist Subject.* Princeton: Princeton University Press, 2005.

Malamoud, Charles. *Cooking the World: Ritual and Thought in Ancient India.* Translated by David White. Delhi: Oxford University Press, 1998.

Marriott, McKim. "Hindu Transactions: Diversity without Dualism." In *Transaction and Meaning: Directions in the Anthropology of Exchange and Symbolic Behavior,* edited by Bruce Kapferer, 109–42. Philadelphia: Institute for the Study of Human Issues, 1976.

Marte, Lidia. "Afro-Diasporic Seasonings: Food Routes and Dominican Place-Making in New York City." *Food, Culture and Society* 14, no. 2 (2011): 181–204.

Mason, John. *Ìdáná Fún Òrìsà: Cooking for Selected Heads.* Brooklyn: Yorùbá Theological Archministry, 1999.

Mason, Michael A. "'I Bow My Head to the Ground': The Creation of Bodily Experience in a Cuban American Santería Initiation." *Journal of American Folklore* 107, no. 423 (1994): 23–39.

———. *Living Santería: Rituals and Experiences in an Afro-Cuban Religion.* Washington, DC: Smithsonian Institution Press, 2002.

Masuzawa, Tomoko. *The Invention of World Religions: Or How European Universalism Was Preserved in the Language of Pluralism.* Chicago: University of Chicago Press, 2005.

Matory, J. Lorand. *Black Atlantic Religion: Tradition, Transnationalism, and Matriarchy in the Afro-Brazilian Candomblé.* Princeton: Princeton University Press, 2005.

———. "Free to Be a Slave: Slavery as Metaphor in the Afro-Atlantic Religions." *Journal of Religion in Africa* 37, no. 3 (2007): 398–425.

———. "Gendered Agendas: The Secrets Scholars Keep about Yoruba Atlantic Religion." *Gender and History* 15, no. 3 (2003): 409–39.

———. "Homens montados: Homossexualidade e simbolismo da possessão nas religiões afro-brasileiras." In *Escravidão e invenção da liberdade*, edited by João José Reis, 215–31. São Paulo: Editora Brasiliense, 1988.

———. *Sex and the Empire That Is No More: Gender and the Politics of Metaphor in Òyó Yorùbá Religion.* Minneapolis: University of Minnesota Press, 1994.

———. "Sexual Secrets: Candomblé, Brazil, and the Multiple Intimacies of the African Diaspora." In *Off Stage/On Display: Intimacy and Ethnography in the Age of Public Culture*, edited by Andrew Shryock, 157–90. Stanford: Stanford University Press, 2004.

Mauss, Marcel. "Les techniques du corps." In *Sociologie et anthropologie*, 362–86. Paris: Presses Universitaires de France, 1950.

Mazzoni, Cristina. *The Women in God's Kitchen: Cooking, Eating, and Spiritual Writing.* New York: Continuum, 2005.

McDaniel, Lorna. *The Big Drum Ritual of Carriacou: Praisesongs for Rememory of Flight.* Gainesville: University Press of Florida, 1998.

McDannell, Colleen. *Material Christianity: Religion and Popular Culture in America.* New Haven: Yale University Press, 1995.

Mellor, Philip A., and Chris Shilling. "Body Pedagogics and the Religious Habitus: A New Direction for the Sociological Study of Religion." *Religion* 40, no. 1 (2010): 27–38.

Menéndez, Lázara, ed. "Libreta de Santería de Jesús Torregrosa." In *Estudios Afro-Cubanos*, vol. 3. Havana: Universidad de La Habana, 1998.

Metzger, Nzinga O. "Life in the Banyan Branches: African Americans and Orisa Tradition in Philadelphia." PhD diss., Florida State University, 2008.

Mintz, Sidney, and Richard Price. *The Birth of African-American Culture: An Anthropological Perspective*. Boston: Beacon, 1992 [1976].

Mirandé, Alfredo. *Hombres y Machos: Masculinity and Latino Culture*. Boulder: Westview, 1997.

Moore, Moses N., Jr. "'Testifying' and 'Testimony': Autobiographical Narratives and African American Religions." In *Teaching African American Religions*, edited by Carolyn M. Jones and Theodore Louis, 95–108. New York: Oxford University Press, 2005.

Moraga, Cherríe, and Gloria Anzaldúa, eds. *This Bridge Called My Back: Writings by Radical Women of Color*. New York: Kitchen Table Press, 1981.

Motta, Roberto Mauro Cortez. "Meat and Feast: The Xango Religion of Recife." PhD diss., Columbia University, 1988.

Muñoz, José Esteban. *Cruising Utopia: The Then and There of Queer Futurity*. New York: New York University Press, 2009.

Murphy, Joseph M. *Santería: African Spirits in America*. Boston: Beacon, 1993.

Nadalini, Ana Paula. "Comida de santo na cozinha dos homens: Um estudo da ponte entre alimentação e religião." MA thesis, Universidade Federal do Paraná, 2009.

Nashashibi, Rami. "The Blackstone Legacy, Islam, and the Rise of Ghetto Cosmopolitanism." *Souls: A Critical Journal of Black Politics, Culture, and Society* 9, no. 2 (2007): 123–31.

Norris, Rebecca Sachs. "Examining the Structure and Role of Emotion: Contributions of Neurobiology to the Study of Embodied Religious Experience." *Zygon* 40, no. 1 (2005): 181–99.

O'Connell, Daniel C., and Sabine Kowal. *Dialogical Genres: Empractical and Conversational Listening and Speaking*. New York: Springer, 2012.

Ortiz, Fernando. *Hampa afro-cubana: Los negros brujos; Apuntes para un estudio de etnología criminal*. Madrid: Librería de Fernando Fé, 1906.

Otero, Solimar. *Afro-Cuban Diasporas in the Atlantic World*. Rochester, NY: University of Rochester Press, 2010.

———. "Investigating Possession Pasts: Memory and Afro-Caribbean Religion and Folklore." *Western Folklore* 66, nos. 1–2 (2007): 7–14.

Palmié, Stephan. *The Cooking of History: How Not to Study Afro-Cuban Religion*. Chicago: University of Chicago Press, 2013.

———. "Of Pharisees and Snark-Hunters: Afro-Cuban Religion as an Object of Knowledge." *Culture and Religion* 2, no. 1 (2001): 3–20.

———. "Thinking with Ngangas: Reflections on Embodiment and the Limits of 'Objectively Necessary Appearances.'" *Comparative Study of Society and History* 48, no. 4 (2006): 852–86.

———. *Wizards and Scientists: Explorations in Afro-Cuban Modernity and Tradition*. Durham: Duke University Press, 2003.

Palmié, Stephan, and Elizabeth Pérez. "An All Too Present Absence: Fernando Ortiz's Work on [the Afro-Cuban secret society] Abakuá in Its Sociocultural Context." *New West Indian Guide* 79, nos. 3–4 (2005): 219–28.

Pérez, Elizabeth. "Cooking for the Gods: Sensuous Ethnography, Sensory Knowledge, and the Kitchen in Lucumí Tradition." *Religion* 41, no. 4 (2011): 665–83.

———. "Crystallizing Subjectivities in the African Diaspora: Sugar, Honey, and the Gods of Afro-Cuban Santería." In *Religion, Food, and Eating in North America*, edited by Benjamin Zeller et al., 175–94. New York: Columbia University Press, 2014.

———. "Nobody's Mammy: Yemayá as Fierce Foremother in Afro-Cuban Religions." In *Yemoja: Gender, Sexuality, and Creativity in the Latina/o and Afro-Atlantic Diasporas*, edited by Solimar Otero and Toyin Falola, 1–20. Albany: State University of New York Press, 2013.

———. "Portable Portals: Transnational Rituals for the Head across Globalizing Orisha Traditions." *Nova Religio* 16, no. 4 (2013): 35–62.

———. "Spiritist Mediumship as Historical Mediation: African-American Pasts, Black Ancestral Presence, and Afro-Cuban Religions." *Journal of Religion in Africa* 41, no. 4 (2011): 330–65.

———. "Staging Transformation: Spiritist Liturgies as Theatres of Conversion in Afro-Cuban Religious Practice." *Culture and Religion* 13, no. 3 (2012): 372–400.

———. "The Virgin in the Mirror: Reading Images of a Black Madonna through the Lens of Afro-Cuban Women's Experiences." *Journal of African-American History* 95, no. 2 (2010): 202–28.

———. "Willful Spirits and Weakened Flesh: Historicizing the Initiation Narrative in Afro-Cuban Religions." *Journal of Africana Religions* 1, no. 2 (2013): 151–93.

———. "Working Roots and Conjuring Traditions: Relocating 'Cults and Sects' in African American Religious History." In *Esotericism, Gnosticism, and Mysticism in African American Religious Experience*, edited by Stephen C. Finley and Margarita Guillory, 40–61. Leiden: Brill, 2015.

Port, Mattijs van de. "Candomblé in Pink, Green, and Black: Re-scripting the Afro-Brazilian Religious Heritage in the Public Sphere of Salvador, Bahia." *Social Anthropology* 13 (2005): 3–26.

———. "Circling around the Really Real: Spirit Possession Ceremonies and the Search for Authenticity in Bahian Candomblé." *Ethos* 33, no. 2 (2005): 149–79.

Price, Richard. *Alabi's World.* Baltimore: Johns Hopkins University Press, 1990.

Rabinow, Paul, and George E. Marcus, with James D. Faubion and Tobias Rees. *Designs for an Anthropology of the Contemporary.* Durham: Duke University Press, 2008.

Ramos, Miguel "Willie." *Adimú: Gbogbó Tén'unjé Lukumí.* 1st ed. Miami: Eleda, 2003.

———. *Adimú: Gbogbó Tén'unjé Lukumí.* 2nd ed. Miami: Eleda, 2012.

———. "Afro-Cuban Orisha Worship." In *Santería Aesthetics in Contemporary Latin American Art*, edited by Arturo Lindsay, 51–76. Washington, DC: Smithsonian Institution Press, 1996.

————. "The Empire Beats On: Oyo, Bata Drums and Hegemony in Nineteenth-Century Cuba." MA thesis, Florida International University, 2000.

Richman, Karen E. *Migration and Vodou*. Gainesville: University Press of Florida, 2005.

————. "They Will Remember Me in the House: The Pwen of Haitian Transnational Migration." PhD diss., University of Virginia, 1992.

Riesebrodt, Martin. "Religion in Global Perspective." In *Global Religions: An Introduction*, edited by Mark Juergensmeyer, 95–109. Oxford: Oxford University Press, 2003.

————. "Theses on a Theory of Religion." *International Political Anthropology* 1, no. 1 (2008): 25–41.

Rios, Luís Felipe. "Loce Loce Metá Rê-Lê!: Posições de gênero-erotismo entre homens com práticas homossexuais adeptos do candomblé do Recife." *Revista Polis e Psique* 1 (2011): 276–300.

Robaina, Tomás Fernández. *Hablen paleros y santeros*. Havana: Editorial de Ciencias Sociales, 2001.

Rotman, Andy. *Thus Have I Seen: Visualizing Faith in Early Indian Buddhism*. New York: Oxford University Press, 2008.

Rubenstein, Diane. "Food for Thought: Metonymy in Late Foucault." In *The Final Foucault*, edited by James William Bernauer and David M. Rasmussen, 83–101. Cambridge: MIT Press, 1988.

Rush, Dana. "Eternal Potential: Chromolithographs in Vodunland." *African Arts* 32, no. 4 (1999): 61–75.

Sered, Susan Starr. "Food and Holiness: Cooking as a Sacred Act among Middle-Eastern Jewish Women." *Anthropological Quarterly* 61, no. 3 (1988): 129–39.

Smith, Jonathan Z. "The Bare Facts of Ritual." *History of Religions* 20, nos. 1–2 (1980): 112–37.

Smitherman, Geneva. *Talkin and Testifyin: The Language of Black America*. Boston: Houghton Mifflin, 1977.

Stevens, Alta Mae. "Manje in Haitian Culture: The Symbolic Significance of Manje in Haitian Culture." *Journal of Haitian Studies* 1, no. 1 (1995): 75–88.

Stewart, Dianne. *Three Eyes for the Journey: African Dimensions of the Jamaican Religious Experience*. New York: Oxford University Press, 2005.

Stoller, Paul. "Sensuous Ethnography, African Persuasions, and Social Knowledge." *Qualitative Inquiry* 10, no. 6 (2004): 817–35.

————. *The Taste of Ethnographic Things: The Senses in Anthropology*. Philadelphia: University of Pennsylvania Press, 1989.

Taussig, Michael T. *Mimesis and Alterity: A Particular History of the Senses*. New York: Routledge, 1993.

————. *The Nervous System*. New York: Routledge, 1992.

Taylor, Charles. *The Ethics of Authenticity*. Cambridge: Harvard University Press, 1991.

————. *Philosophy and the Human Sciences*. Philosophical Papers 2. Cambridge: Cambridge University Press, 1985.

Teixeira, Maria Lina Leão. "Lorogun: Identidades sexuais e poder no candomblé." In *Candomblé: Desvendando identidades*, edited by Carlos Eugênio Marcondes de Moura, 33–52. São Paulo: EMW Editores, 1987.

Thompson, Robert Farris. *Face of the Gods: Art and Altars of Africa and the African Americas*. New York: Museum for African Art, 1993.

Tompkins, Kyla Wazana. *Racial Indigestion: Eating Bodies in the 19th Century*. New York: New York University Press, 2012.

Trouillot, Michel-Rolph. *Silencing the Past: Power and the Production of History*. Boston: Beacon, 1995.

Turner, Victor W. *Schism and Continuity in an African Society: A Study in Ndembu Village Life*. Oxford: Berg, 1996 [1957].

Urban, Hugh B. "The Torment of Secrecy: Ethical and Epistemological Problems in the Study of Esoteric Traditions." *History of Religions* 37, no. 3 (1998): 209–48.

van der Veer, Peter, ed. *Conversion to Modernities: The Globalization of Christianity*. New York: Routledge, 1996.

van Gennep, Arnold. *Les rites de passage: Étude systématique des rites*. Paris: A. et J. Picard, 1909.

Vásquez, Manuel A. *More Than Belief: A Materialist Theory of Religion*. New York: Oxford University Press, 2011.

Vidal-Ortiz, Salvador. "'Maricón,' 'Pájaro,' and 'Loca': Cuban and Puerto Rican Linguistic Practices, and Sexual Minority Participation, in U.S. Santería." *Journal of Homosexuality* 58 (2011): 912.

———. "'Sexuality' and 'Gender' in Santería: Towards a Queer of Color Critique in the Study of Religion." PhD diss., City University of New York, 2005.

Wacquant, Loïc. *Body and Soul: Notebooks of an Apprentice Boxer*. Oxford: Oxford University Press, 2004.

Walker, Alice. *In Search of Our Mothers' Gardens: Womanist Prose*. New York: Harcourt, 1983.

Warnier, Jean-Pierre. *The Pot-King: The Body and Technologies of Power*. Leiden: Brill, 2007.

———. "A Praxeological Approach to Subjectivation in a Material World." *Journal of Material Culture* 6, no. 1 (2001): 5–24.

Wehmeyer, Stephen C. "Indian Spirits on the Rock Island Line: Chicago as 'Gate of Tradition' for African American Spiritualism in the Gulf South." Paper delivered at Annual Meeting of American Academy of Religion ("Gateway of the Spirits: African Diaspora Religions in Chicago" panel), 2008.

———. "'Indians at the Door': Power and Placement on New Orleans Spiritual Church Altars." *Western Folklore* 66, nos. 1–2 (2007): 15–74.

White, Hayden. *Tropics of Discourse: Essays in Cultural Criticism*. Baltimore: Johns Hopkins University Press, 1978.

Willerslev, Rane. *Soul Hunters: Hunting, Animism, and Personhood among the Siberian Yukaghirs*. Berkeley: University of California Press, 2007.

Williams, Delores S. *Sisters in the Wilderness: The Challenge of Womanist God-Talk*. Maryknoll, NY: Orbis, 1993.

Wirtz, Kristina S. "How Diasporic Religious Communities Remember: Learning to Speak the 'Tongue of the *Oricha*' in Cuban Santería." *American Ethnologist* 34, no. 1 (2007): 108–26.

———. *Ritual, Discourse, and Community in Cuban Santería: Speaking a Sacred World*. Gainesville: University of Florida Press, 2007.

# INDEX

*The illustrations, which appear as a group following page 140, are referenced by their figure numbers, Figure 1, Figure 2, and so on.*

# ABOUT THE AUTHOR

Elizabeth Pérez is Assistant Professor of Religion at Dartmouth College.

Printed in the USA
CPSIA information can be obtained
at www.ICGtesting.com
JSHW071258100823
46310JS00007B/244